WITHDRAWN
UTSA LIBRARIES

D0819902

Feminist Legal Theory

Feminist Legal Theory

An Anti-Essentialist Reader

EDITED BY

Nancy E. Dowd and Michelle S. Jacobs

New York University Press

NEW YORK AND LONDON

NEW YORK UNIVERSITY PRESS
New York and London

Library of Congress Cataloging-in-Publication Data

Feminist legal theory: an anti-essentialist reader /
edited by Nancy E. Dowd, Michelle S. Jacobs.
p. cm.
Includes bibliographical references and index.
ISBN 0-8147-1912-0 (cloth: acid-free paper)—
ISBN 0-8147-1913-9 (paper: acid-free paper)
1. Feminist jurisprudence. 2. Feminist theory. 3. Women—Legal
status, laws, etc. I. Dowd, Nancy E., 1949–. II. Jacobs, Michelle S.
K349 .F458 2002
346.01'34—dc21   2002011494

New York University Press books are printed on acid-free paper,
and their binding materials are chosen for strength and durability.

Manufactured in the United States of America
10 9 8 7 6 5 4 3 2 1

Dedication

To Irvine F. Dowd

—NANCY E. DOWD

*To all of my female ancestors whose names and stories were erased
by slavery, and to the earliest ones whose stories were recovered:
Anna Bonner, Polly Hatcher, Sarah Booker, Frances Bouser,
Anna Davis, Esther Russell.*

—MICHELLE S. JACOBS

Contents

Feminist Legal Theory

Introduction

Michelle S. Jacobs

What is feminist theory? At its best it is a wonderful way of knowing and expressing the experiences of women. These experiences are woven together and used to create and guide principles and policies that advance not only the rights of women but of all people. At its worst it is a label to describe the thinking and experiences of liberal middle-class white women, to the exclusion of all other women. For women of color, making the decision to identify as a feminist is often difficult. Theoretically, white women would seem to be natural allies and valuable partners in the coalition-building process. We share certain types of oppression brought about solely as a result of our gender. We share experiences, the onset of menstrual cycles, the possibility of pregnancies, and other health concerns. Unfortunately, a number of factors hamper the possibility of coalition. One of the most significant inhibitors is that, historically, white women have been untrustworthy when we have entered coalitions with them. There are far too many past and current examples in which white women have sacrificed the interests of their sisters of color in order to advance their own political and social gain. In addition, women of color must often consider the needs of other parts of themselves that reflect the larger community of color, to determine whether feminist agendas promote or hinder the goals of those parts of their community. For example, in the domestic violence movement, many women advocated for law enforcement to adopt a policy of mandatory arrest. That policy, however, chafes against the desire of communities of color to reduce the level of police intrusion into a community that already feels under siege. Therefore, feminists of color may not be so willing to support the agenda of mainstream feminism in this regard.

It is not an uncommon occurrence when attending a feminist meeting where women of color are present to find them meeting together separately after the main event. Often in these postmeeting gatherings the frustration of women of color wells up. How can it be, they ask, that after ten or more years of discussing essentialism, the issues of women of color are still relegated to afterthoughts among mainstream feminists? How can it be that the critique of essentialism is not anticipated each time? Is it possible that mainstream feminism is unable or unwilling really to embrace a shift in the center of analysis so that more women, including poor and working-class white women as well as women of color, can find them-selves included in the discussion?

Although mainstream feminism accepts the idea that coalition building should happen, in reality it is not at all evident that building bridges between white femi-nists and women of color will be successful. This book is one small attempt to help shore up the process. The voices of the women on these pages vary across the spec-trum of race, class, and ethnicity. The book is not all inclusive, nor does it pretend to be. We selected four areas because they seemed to describe areas of common ex-perience for most women. We included theoretical essays as well as essays that pro-pose and critique alternative working models. The complexities of communities of color demand a high level of creativity and flexibility and an openness to under-standing and accepting alternative realities when searching for remedies. Perhaps, in the struggles of women of color trying to fashion relief for their communities, feminists can learn something valuable about openness. This is the most exciting benefit that true inclusiveness has to offer. If this book does nothing else, it will eliminate the excuse often used by the mainstream: not knowing.

Acknowledgments

This book is inspired by the lives of twenty million Africans who were kidnapped, sold, and dragged from their homes and loved ones. They were transported across the Atlantic, trussed as human cargo in the bowels of slave ships. Included in that cargo were millions of Black women. The ravaged wombs of the African women who survived that journey helped populate North, Central, and South America and the Caribbean. For the next two hundred years, those women and their offspring survived in a society where the law defined them as chattel and denied them even the most basic rights that whites, including white women, enjoyed. Many of these women were too strong to have their spirits crushed, and others were too weak to die. Their progeny survived the upheaval of the Civil War and the ensuing emanci-pation of enslaved Africans and African Americans. Still, even after Emancipation, the law refused to contemplate the possibility that Black women were worthy of being covered by the law's protective umbrella. Those ancient women produced my own great-grandmothers, grandmothers, and mother and instilled in them the strength, courage, and intelligence required to survive in a society that fails and re-fuses to accord even a shred of dignity and respect to women of color. The spirits of all these women have nourished and supported me through this project.

In a more traditional sense, the University of Florida Levin College of Law has generously supported this project through both the provision of research assistants and summer research support. Howard University also provided writing support during the summer of 2000. Special thanks to my research assistant, Andrea Ritchie, who committed herself to the project even though at times there was no fi-nancial compensation. She served as a valuable sounding board and provided on-going encouragement.

I am indebted to Rosemary Howard for her organizational skills and the calmness with which she approached her tasks. She was persistent, thorough, and professional and never offensive. Her exhortations to finish were appreciated as well. She was truly an invaluable part of this project.

To all the Black women in my life, particularly my mother, Phyllis Scott; my sister Sherri; and my daughter Khalisa: I hope this book will make you proud, and that you will hear your voices and see your stories on at least some of the pages.

Introduction

Nancy E. Dowd

Feminist analysis is like friendship: an ongoing process of deepening complexity, interactive, contradictory, insightful, emotional, enlightening, challenging, conflicted. This book originated in a friendship between a Black woman and a white woman amid the challenges of race and gender divides in the academy. Among our common concerns were to develop teaching materials that reflected the realities of intersections of race, class, and gender and that challenged our students to think critically without artificially separating and simplifying issues of gender by presuming all women are alike.

Those concerns reflected critiques of feminist analysis as essentialist: that it demonstrates an understanding of gender based only on the lived experience of middle-class white women. In the late 1980s and early 1990s a series of scholars, predominantly women of color, articulated this critique. The validity of the critique, and of others that followed based on multiple racial, ethnic, and cultural perspectives; lesbian analysis; and international perspectives, did not spell the rejection of feminist analysis. It caused it to be reoriented and reinvigorated. The goal was not simply theoretical change but, more important, a change in substantive outcomes. Those intended outcomes were equality for all, not for just for some; bringing the margins to the center as equally valued objects of analysis and subjects of activist response; and ensuring that feminism would mean that for all women and all subordinated groups the goal is to "lift as we climb."

The anti-essentialist critique has challenged the persistent pattern of racial divide within the feminist movement. The divergent interests of white women and women of color in the United States have been evident since the nation's birth, as white women played a pivotal role in the oppression of enslaved African women, both participating in and condoning the theft of their labor, their physical abuse, their sexual violation, and the destruction of their families. The conflicting interests of white middle-class women and women of color remained glaringly apparent during the post-Emancipation era through middle-class women's continued exploitative employment of Black women and other women of color, as well as working-class women, as domestic workers. White middle-class women also failed to join or support the anti-lynching and anti-violence campaigns that African American women initiated. Finally, racism was explicitly involved in white middle-class women's quest for suffrage, which did not include suffrage for women of color and which juxtaposed white women's lack of political voice with the newly acquired civil rights of Black men. Throughout the twentieth century, middle-class white woman continued to monopolize and drive the feminist agenda.

The early women's movement strongly advocated for birth control programs directed primarily at women of color and low-income white women, whose entitlement to the domesticity and motherhood enjoyed by middle-class white women was not accepted. Demands for state support of mothers focused solely on "deserving" poor women, who for the most part did not include women of color. The struggle for reproductive choices continues to focus almost exclusively on white women's right to choose not to have children and not on economic and state coercion directed at the right to motherhood of women of color. The mainstream feminist movement's ongoing emphasis on the need for child care and other supports for women entering the workforce continues to fail to acknowledge that provision of such services to white middle-class women comes at the expense of women of color and low-income white women and their families.

Overcoming differences among women requires uncomfortable conversations. It requires processes for meaningful learning and collaboration rather than the reproduction of subtle hierarchies and the continued marginalization of women presumed outside the norm. While the essentialist critique has been widely accepted and validated among feminists, we found that actually practicing anti-essentialism was much more difficult.

This reader takes as its core assumption that the anti-essentialist critique requires feminist analysis to include attention to the differences among women and to the intersections of gender with other critical characteristics of subordination and privilege. The readings included here are those we believe best reflect this mode of analysis from a legal standpoint. They also suggest a variety of methodologies to accomplish anti-essentialism. Among them are the familiar feminist techniques of listening for silences, encouraging all voices, and engaging in bottom-up consciousness-raising rather than top-down theorizing. They also include techniques to accomplish meaningful participation, leadership, and valuing of all women both in combination with other women and within challenges to other forms of subordination. This may mean collaboration or it may mean closed caucuses, interest groups, or advocacy groups organized around critical identities or issues.

The reader is organized around four main sections: theories, strategies, and methodologies; work and wealth; women, children, well-being, and the state; and violence. These divisions are arbitrary to some degree, since many of the readings could fall under more than one category. They also could be replaced by other substantive divisions, given the range and profusion of critical scholarship. The choices we have made reflect key areas of ongoing inequality and are emblematic of a wide range of other substantive issues.

The process of constructing the reader has required our own uncomfortable conversations in the course of meaningful collaboration. We remain committed to the process and have been enriched by this project. Our hope is that this work will contribute to the valuing of all women and the achievement of justice in ways large and small. But we firmly believe that this goal will not be accomplished until feminists become conscious of all women and all forms of subordination.

Acknowledgments

For me this reader began with my students in Gender and the Law. Our discussions and their frustrations with existing materials first generated this project. A second group of students who enrolled in my seminars in Advanced Feminist Theory further contributed to the process of thinking about the reader, as well as serving as initial readers for portions of the collection. I always feel that in many ways I learn more from my students than they do from me. This is particularly the case with respect to this reader and the need for these materials, and therefore, to my students in these courses over the past decade, I owe my deepest debt of appreciation.

My second and equally deep debt I owe to my coeditor and friend, Michelle Jacobs. Words are really not adequate to express my gratitude and respect.

Andrea Ritchie of Howard University contributed extensively to this project as a research assistant to me as well as to Professor Jacobs. Her contribution was particularly crucial in synthesizing historical data and materials on policies regarding families, in addition to other work that she contributed to this collection.

The University of Florida Levin College of Law generously supported the proposal for this book as well as the lengthy process of putting the book together. Dean Jon Mills has been strongly supportive of this project. Summer research leaves were especially critical to the process of selection, winnowing, and editing of materials. The College of Law also supported research assistants who worked on this collection. Mary Vallandingham and Michelle Thresher of the University of Florida contributed to this project in valuable ways. The reference librarians of the College of Law were, as always, tireless and magnanimous in the face of the volume of requests we made in our initial search for potential materials. In addition, the reference staff at Northeastern University School of Law and former Dean Roger Abrams of Northeastern were very supportive of this project when some of the work on the final manuscript was done there. The support staff at both Florida and Northeastern were also very helpful in preparing the manuscript.

Niko Pfund nurtured the idea of this collection from its inception. He continued to strongly support this project even after he left New York University Press, and his insights and support have been invaluable.

Rosemary Howard is simply in a class by herself. Her work in bringing the manuscript to completion by her able preparation of the manuscript for the press made all the difference to making the reader finally available for publication.

Finally, my family and friends have continued to provide the love and support that have enabled me to do this work at all. My children continue to inspire me. My sister, Patty, is an incredible role model. My friends are always there to listen and offer support and encouragement. I especially want to acknowledge the support of my father, Irvine F. Dowd, who let me know how proud he was of what I do. He passed away, suddenly but after a long and wonderful life, at age eighty-five in the spring of 2001, as I was working on this book. He instilled in me a strong work ethic, and working on this book will always be intertwined for me with the flood of memories of him, as well as my sense that he would be terribly disappointed if I did not finish what I had started. So Daddy, I got it done, and I think you would be proud.

Part I

Theories, Strategies, and Methodologies

Introduction

Feminist theories offer a rich array of perspectives from which to understand, analyze, and strategize about issues of particular interest to women, as well as legal issues in general. This section of readings presents a range of theoretical and methodological perspectives that proceed from an anti-essentialist feminist perspective.

Feminist theory centers on women as a category of analysis and concern. The vast array of women and their rich differences, as well as the critical interplay of gender with race, class, sexual orientation, culture, language, and religion, among other identifiers, challenge the very category "woman" as well as the ability of theory to capture the nature of subordination and the potential for liberation from traditions of resistance and value. At the same time, feminist theory has never been a remote academic exercise; rather, it has emerged from and responded to pragmatic, grassroots organizing. It is theory driven by practice as well as practice generated by theory.

In the last quarter of the twentieth century, feminist jurisprudence emerged as a challenge to law at the same time that feminists challenged other disciplines. Feminism is part of a critical tradition of jurisprudence that connects to Legal Realist and socialist criticism of law, as well as to an activist legal tradition grounded in the civil rights movement. Feminist theory also has roots in nineteenth-century women's movements. As the women's movement revived in the 1960s and 1970s, inspired by the civil rights movement, several waves of feminist legal theory emerged that loosely can be categorized as liberal theory, dominance theory, cultural theory, socialist theory, and postmodern theory.

A second thread in the development of feminist theory in the late twentieth century connected to the critique of classic civil rights theories by critical race theory. Black feminists brought this critique home to both feminism and civil rights. They identified and exposed the race essentialism in feminist theory, as well as the absence of gender consciousness in classic civil rights analysis. They articulated an understanding of the intersections and multiple consciousness of gender identity. What began as an African American critique of race theory and feminist theory evolved into a broader multiracial analysis that included LatCrit and AsianCrit reformulations of both race and feminist jurisprudence.

A third strand in the evolution of feminist theory involved the emergence of gay and lesbian jurisprudence and civil rights struggle. As with critical race feminist theory, this included a critique of feminist theory for its heterosexual assumptions, as well as a vision of gender without heterosexual limits.

Finally, increasing globalization and the emergence of a strong human rights discourse has challenged the American dominance in feminist theory and colonialist/imperialist thinking that separates First World and Third World feminists and Northern and Southern Hemisphere priorities and strategies.

Each of these threads is part of the weave of current feminist theory that is represented in this reader. Most critically, however, this reader and these selections from current theoretical works take the view that feminist theory cannot be done without attention to the differences among women. Hence theoretical perspectives from earlier, universalist, essentialist perspectives are not included. Because that background is important to an understanding of these pieces, however, we briefly describe the earlier, classic phase and then suggest a working definition of anti-essentialist feminism with which to approach these readings. Of course, condensing these theoretical perspectives into a single definition might itself be critiqued as essentialist, but we suggest this only as a starting point, not as a boundary.

A. Classic Feminism, Presumed Universalism: Liberal Theory, Dominance Theory, Cultural Theory, Socialist Theory, and Postmodern Theory

Classic feminist theory analyzed women's inequality and devalued status in terms of liberal theory, and this remains a powerful argument. Under liberal theory, women were equal persons to men, and therefore the law was gendered and unjust by treating women as different. The goal of liberal theory typically was equal treatment—treating women the same as men. Liberal theory successfully challenged specific differences in the law based on stereotypes about women's mental, emotional, and physical characteristics. This theoretical perspective supported a series of successful constitutional challenges brought by a team of lawyers, including Justice Ruth Bader Ginsburg. These challenges focused on state statutes that expressly treated women differently than men (although many of the cases were brought by male plaintiffs), and they inscribed the concept of equal treatment into equal protection analysis. Equal treatment was critiqued as inadequate, however, from two perspectives. First, the presumption of sameness ignored women's differences, most notably those associated with childbearing. Second, equal treatment commonly was understood under the same standard as that applied to men, but critics argued that the standard was itself gendered, formed by the lens of men's perspectives.

Focusing on women's differences, then, is a second theoretical perspective, commonly referred to as cultural feminism. Cultural feminists argued that noticing and valuing differences associated with women or typical of women's lives were critical to real equality. Characteristics or lifestyles deemed feminine needed to be valued and honored; equal treatment and a focus on sameness ignored this essential point. The work of Carol Gilligan, a psychologist, was especially important to the development of cultural feminism. Gilligan's work focused on cultural and social difference and how these constructed psychological norms of behavior for both women and men. Constructed differences affected gender identity and social roles. The key to equality from this perspective was in valuing and supporting those things associated with women, even those things unique to women, but not limited to physical differences.

The clash between sameness and difference has bedeviled feminist activists and theorists for several generations. According to dominance theorists, both theories have their focus in the wrong place. It's not about difference; it's about dominance. The key to women's inequality is women's lack of power, particularly how that powerlessness is expressed in concepts of sex and sexuality. The most notable theorist of dominance is Catherine MacKinnon: her work revolutionized feminist theory. Translated into action, dominance theory was particularly effective in naming and describing sexual harassment as well as challenging pornography. Paying attention to power relations and devising means of empowerment or redress for the abuse of power were key elements in dominance analysis. Focusing on sexual relationships and the construction of intimacy also suggested the importance of heterosexual norms to the oppression of women.

Two final important threads in classic feminist analysis were socialist feminism and postmodernism. Socialist feminists pointed to economic relationships and class analysis as critical to understanding inequality. Postmodernists challenged the possibility of grand theory and suggested the provisional nature of gender analysis.

One core link between these theories is their acceptance of a universal "woman," or women as a unified group. At the same time, a tradition of pragmatic thinking and use of theory has been part of this tradition as well.

B. Anti-Essentialist Theory

In the late 1980s and early 1990s, classic feminist theory was challenged as being essentialist: as presuming the universality of women and defining them according to a white middle-class heterosexual model. Angela Harris,[1] Kimberlé Crenshaw,[2] and Mari Matsuda[3] were leaders in the critique of classic theory as well as the construction of new theories of pluralism, multiple consciousness, and intersectionality. Kimberlé Crenshaw's critique of anti-discrimination analysis in the employment context pointed out the erasure of Black women by virtue of doctrinal requirements that discrimination be identified as racial *or* sexual. Discrimination unique to Black women and other women of color that reflected the intersection of race and sex went unrecognized. At the same time, Black women were viewed as sufficiently "different" to be considered ineffective representatives of either race or sex claims in class-action claims. Difference was read as disqualifying, a powerful statement of the unstated norm of maleness in race claims and whiteness in gender claims.

Angela Harris's contemporaneous critique of feminist theory similarly exposed the presumed norm of white women, women for whom racial identity conferred privilege and therefore permitted the isolation of gender alone as a category of analysis. Focusing on the feminist analyses of Catherine MacKinnon and Robin West as examples, Harris compared their universal statements of gender relations against the historical and current position and experience of Black women. Using rape law and feminist critique of rape law as an example, Harris identified the unstated assumptions of theory that reflected the experience of white women, of women for whom gender disadvantage could be isolated from skin privilege. Both Crenshaw and Harris argued not only that race mattered and required the rethinking of feminist analysis in a way that was inclusive rather than essentialist but also suggested that race and gender interacted in sophisticated ways that could not be captured by the simplistic notion of adding two kinds of oppression. The intersection of race and gender was complex and interactive.

Mari Matsuda, the last of the early anti-essentialist critics cited here, described the interaction as one of "multiple consciousness." In contrast to the classic assumption that race and sex were separable and additive forms of discrimination, Matsuda and others described a complex interaction of critical identity characteristics that included agency and resistance as well as victimization, and simultaneous exercise of privilege along with victimization. This meant all women had multiple consciousness, but the intersections played out quite differently based on different identity characteristics and the presence or absence of privilege and stigma.

Many others have followed in the footsteps of these groundbreaking theorists. The challenge to classic feminist theory has been friendly but serious. It does not require that classic theory be jettisoned entirely; rather, it is an interactive process, even arguably a more pragmatic process, using the insights of anti-essentialist critique to reform and strengthen multiple strands of feminist analyses.

Thus anti-essentialist feminist theory combines the best of classic feminism and the anti-essentialism generated by race, class, and sexual orientation. Its orientation is pluralistic, contextual, dialogic, anti-hierarchical, conscious, questioning. Its methods always ask the other question; it always looks to see who is present, who is speaking, who benefits, who has set priorities.

C. An Overview of the Readings

The selections in this part epitomize this stage of feminist theory. They suggest the range and richness of pluralistic theory that retains "women" as a category while functioning from multiple, intersecting, interacting identities and cultures, as well as from links to other forms of subordination. The arrangement of the chapters is somewhat arbitrary, as they connect in a wide variety of ways. It may seem logical, after completing the readings, to imagine different configurations.

The initial piece by Pat Cain chronicles the development of feminist jurisprudence and curricula in law schools, as well as practical results of feminist theory in the late twentieth century. As Cain notes, liberal feminists dismantled a broad range of gender-specific barriers based on arguments that women were men's equals and that sex was irrelevant to most legal classifications. Maxine Zinn and Bonnie Dill, two sociologists, suggest a framework of "multiracial feminism" to theorize difference as an essential part of moving beyond this framework. Patricia Smith offers an explicit vision of a next phase of feminism that imagines equality in distributional terms. The excerpt from john powell further develops the multiple, pluralistic perspective of modern theory and relates this to psychoanalysis and Buddhism, emphasizing the multidisciplinary focus as well as the necessary shift in thinking critical to a reoriented jurisprudence that includes and connects rather than artificially simplifies and prioritizes.

The next set of pieces expands the frame toward the most recent additions to critical analysis, including Asian critical analysis, lesbian critical analysis, and the multiple perspectives of LatCrit analysis.

The final set of articles emphasize the methodological implications of a pluralistic, anti-essentialist analysis. Peggy McIntosh's classic essay suggests ways of uncovering privilege and unconscious assumptions. Mari Matsuda describes the challenges and benefits of coalition. The final readings focus on the comparative and global implications of theory. Cultural relativism and cultural ethnocentrism pose particular challenges for American feminists.

Notes

1. Angela Harris, *Race and Essentialism in Feminist Legal Theory*, 42 Stanford Law Review 581 (1990).

2. Kimberlé Crenshaw, *Demarginalizing the Intersection of Race and Sex: A Black Feminist Critique of Antidiscrimination Doctrine, Feminist Theory and Antiracist Politics*, 1989 University of Chicago Legal Forum 139 (1989).

3. Mari J. Matsuda, *When the First Quail Calls: Multiple Consciousness as Jurisprudential Method*, 14 Women's Rights Law Reporter 297 (1992).

1

The Future of Feminist Legal Theory

Patricia A. Cain

I. Introduction

. . .

1. The past is always an important part of the future. Thus, feminist legal theorists of the future should pay attention to feminist legal history.

2. Current disagreement amongst feminist legal scholars is a good thing. Criticism is necessary for progress.

3. We must never forget that good feminist legal theory is rooted in the experience of real women. Thus, we must guard against theory that becomes so abstract that it fails in practice to contribute to positive material change for women.

. . .

II. Feminist Legal Theory: A Short History

Law and law schools have a long history of male domination. If one thinks of the world of law as progressing in Hegelian-like fashion from "thesis" to "antithesis" to "synthesis," then the thesis of "male domination" remained in full control until at least the early 1970s. There were few women law students before 1970 and even fewer women law professors. The decade of the 1970s laid the groundwork for the "antithesis" to male domination, as women increased their numbers in the legal academy and in the practice of law. In 1970, the first National Conference on Women and the Law was held at New York University. In 1971, the Supreme Court began to rule in favor of sex discrimination claims pursued under the [F]ourteenth [A]mendment. One year later, Congress passed the Equal Rights Amendment, and within months at least 20 state legislatures had ratified the amendment. In 1972, Ruth Bader Ginsburg, the lawyer in the 1971 Supreme Court victory, and also a law professor, helped to organize a conference, again at New York University, on The Law School Curriculum and the Legal Rights of Women.

By the mid 1970s most law schools had developed courses in Women and the Law, sometimes taught by real faculty, but often taught by adjuncts or by students themselves under the supervision of a faculty member. These courses focused on criminal law, family law, antidiscrimination law, and reproductive rights. During this period, feminist litigators developed cutting edge theories to help women improve their legal status. For example, feminist lawyers argued that in determining whether a woman killed in self-defense, the defendant's perspective as a woman in a gendered world should be taken into account. They also argued for the first time that sexual harassment was a form of sex discrimination. This focus on harms to women and on the unmasking of the gendered nature of these harms gave rise to a core of feminist scholarship and the introduction of specialty law school courses, in addition to women and the law courses, known as "feminist jurisprudence" or "feminist legal theory."

. . .

Courts and legislatures are more likely than the academy to produce real change in individual people's lives. And if the ultimate goal of feminist work in the academy is to make real changes in women's lives, then feminist legal theory needs to be useful to the practice of law in real cases. No "synthesis" in male-dominated law will ever result from a feminist "antithesis" based on scholarly work alone.

. . .

III. Feminist Legal Theory: Disagreements and Progress

A. Introduction

When asked to think about the future of feminist legal theory, my focus becomes: how is the theory doing in practice? My short answer is that feminist legal theory, in the hands of feminist lawyers, has certainly produced some short-term gains in the lives of real women, but it has not produced a feminist revolution. Nor should it be expected to have done so. Progress occurs in stages and legal change tends to be evolutionary rather than revolutionary. Feminist legal theory must be forever fine-tuning itself to respond to each new stage in the evolutionary process. In terms of the Hegelian dialectic, we might view the short-term gain position of women as a partial "synthesis" which creates a new "thesis" from which the battle begins anew. If feminist legal theory is to continue the battle successfully and accomplish long-term gains, it must be ever ready to shift in response to each new position or "thesis." In other words, feminist legal theory must be prepared to construct an immediate critique of each short-term gain (the antithesis step) and, at practically the same moment, it must be prepared to construct a new thesis (the synthesis step).

This move from new thesis (usually a short-term solution) to critique of that thesis is required in part by the nature of law reform. The law is reluctant to give up old and familiar categories. Thus once a new legal category is created, the law tends to force it into familiar old frameworks. Feminist legal theory needs to anticipate this tendency and be prepared with a critique that will help new categories resist this domesticating tendency.

Feminist legal theory might create change that [is] more revolutionary if it [is] able in the future to move from antithesis to synthesis more quickly than it has done in the past. Certainly the increase in the number of feminists in the legal academy and the various critiques that we offer (often of each other) make it possible for change to occur more rapidly.

B. Some Examples

. . . Martha Chamallas [has] identified three moves typically made by feminist legal theorists. I will use examples of two of these "moves" to demonstrate how feminist legal theory must be positioned to respond to law's tendency to push new categories back into familiar frameworks.

1. Is the Gender Classification Valid?

The first move identified by Chamallas [is] this: when you see a gender classification, ask whether the classification is valid. I associate this move with the first wave of feminism (which, for example, questioned the male-only vote) and with the early days of the second wave (which, for example, questioned gender restrictions in the workplace such as male-only police forces and male-only pilots). Many short-term gains have been earned by practitioners who mounted legal challenges to gender classifications which resulted in the expansion of public benefits (e.g., jobs and education) to previously excluded individual women.

To accomplish these gains, one thesis in need of challenge was that men belonged in the public sphere as worker[s] whereas women belonged in the private sphere of home and family. One critique of this thesis (the antithesis) was that if contributions to the public sphere of work were based on ability and merit, then there was no justification for excluding women who proved to be as able and meritorious as men. In the short run, this "women are as competent as men" argument won and created short-term gains for women who were as competent as men, so long as they were also unburdened by family needs.

In 1964, Congress bought this argument and enacted Title VII, prohibiting sex discrimination in places of employment. . . . The enactment of Title VII might be viewed as a new thesis that resulted from feminist arguments about equality in the workplace. Title VII was not the only victory for feminist equality arguments. In the early 1970s, a variety of anti–sex discrimination laws were passed by Congress. . . . Those laws gave women the right to claim public benefits, but gave no thought to the existential reality of women's lives. Thus, there were no provisions dealing with pregnancy and childcare, issues that were certain to arise once more women moved into the workforce.

It is worth noting that these early legislative victories occurred long before the legal academy had become populated with women. Indeed, they occurred long before anyone had coined the phrase "feminist legal theory." Once "feminist legal theory" did appear on the scene, its role in addressing workforce gender barriers appeared to be one of responding to the problems of pregnancy and childcare after those problems arose. The explanation for this "responsive" stance, as opposed say to a "predictive" stance, was not that early feminists in the academy were incapable of predicting what the problems would be once male-only workforce rules were removed, but rather, that there were so few feminists in the academy and that courts and legislatures seemed to listen only to those feminist arguments they could understand in terms of existing categories.

Sex equality was the new thesis, but the creators of this new law, courts and legislatures, explained the new thesis using old, familiar doctrines. The radical notion that the law should ignore or undo distinctions made on the basis of sex quickly became the doctrine that women who were similarly situated to men should be treated the same as men, and nothing more. Pregnancy was a fact that made women different from men and thus, pregnancy was outside the new doctrine of sex equality. Feminists responded in different ways to this conservative doctrine. Some argued that pregnancy was just another condition of the human body that could easily be analogized to conditions experienced by men. In other words, they argued that men and women were similarly situated and thus the conservative doctrine was available to provide benefits for pregnant women similar to benefits provided for temporarily disabled men. Other feminists argued that pregnancy was a difference that the law ought to address, and that affirmative action was necessary to create sex equality, given the difference of pregnancy. Still other feminists questioned the core notion of sex equality as it was being developed by the courts, arguing that courts were applying pre-existing male norms. Thus, they claimed, an altogether new theory of sex discrimination that questioned pre-existing norms was required.

To answer the question "Is the gender classification valid?" one must have a theory of sex discrimination. Some theories would strike down every explicit classification, arguing either that gender is always irrelevant or that it is unjust to bar all women when there are always exceptions. Other theories prefer to retain flexibility and argue that, unlike race discrimination, sex differences are sometimes relevant. In my opinion, however, the theories that are likely to create lasting change, even revolutionary change, although perhaps at an evolutionary pace, are those theories that attempt to explain what the harm of sex discrimination is. The harm of sex discrimination is something much more complex than legally imposed gender classifications. Legal rules, explicit or implicit, that burden women are but one means of inflicting the harm of sex discrimination. To determine whether to strike those rules, reform them, or create new, compensatory rules, one must identify the harm that needs to be remedied and must understand the context in which the current remedy is being applied.

The second feminist "move" that Martha Chamallas identifie[s is] . . . when you see a neutral rule, look for the hidden gender bias.[1] Countless examples come to mind regarding the workplace. Height and weight restrictions are one obvious example. Requiring workers to work late at an office in an unsafe neighborhood is another, perhaps less obvious, example. One needs the same sort of theory of sex discrimination to deal with these hidden gender biased rules. If the purpose of reform is to eradicate sex discrimination then it matters little whether rules are explicitly sexist.

2. When Proposing Legal Solutions to an Identified Gender Problem, Pay Attention to Women's Real Life Experiences

[The third] . . . feminist move identified by Chamallas is the consideration of women's experiences in formulating legal remedies. One of Catharine MacKinnon's most lasting contributions to feminist legal theory is her dominance theory of sex discrimination. Dominance theory does not focus on whether women are similar to men, rather it focuses on how men use women's difference to dominate them. Another of MacKinnon's great contributions to feminist legal theory is the application of this theory to the real life experience of women who have been sexually harassed in the workplace.

Naming the harm of sexual harassment, making it visible as an employment issue for women, and convincing lawmakers and courts that the harm was covered by Title VII were events of the 1970s and early 1980s. Before there was any published scholarship on the topic, at Women and the Law [c]onferences throughout the mid 1970s panelists discussed cases in litigation and shared their theories about sexual harassment law. The first Supreme Court case to recognize sexual harassment as a form of sex discrimination under Title VII was decided in 1986.

Women's experience helped to name the harm and to show that the harm was sex-based. But feminists had little say about appropriate remedies once the harm was classified as sex discrimination under Title VII. Those remedies had been statutorily set with no attention paid to women's experience. Women who had suffered sexual abuse for years on the job, and who, when they finally resisted, were fired, found themselves with a cause of action that provided only two remedies: reinstatement and back pay. For many women in this position, reinstatement was totally undesirable. In quid pro quo cases, back pay was not available since the only reason she had suffered the abuse was to gain the benefit of better pay. Much of this problem has been remedied by the Civil Rights Act Amendments of 1991, but the existence of the problem for the first 15 years of sexual harassment litigation does demonstrate the difficulty in forcing new feminist causes of action into pre-existing legal categories.

. . .

There has been little disagreement among feminist legal theorists who have called for the reformation of sexual harassment law. We have been outraged by judicial responses that have ignored the radical potential of sexual harassment law. In this arena, we seem agreed that the point of naming the harm and providing a cause of action was to change the nature of the workplace, to rid it of sexual harassment.

. . .

[F]eminist legal theorists must remain prepared to critique successful cases, ever looking for the domesticating tendency of law to force what today may seem radical or progressive into a more conservative framework. Feminist legal theorists must not lose touch with the real life experiences of the women whose lives they hope to improve.

. . .

NOTE

1. In Patricia Cain's article, this paragraph explaining the second move was originally only a footnote.

2

Theorizing Difference from Multiracial Feminism

Maxine Baca Zinn and Bonnie Thornton Dill

Women of color have long challenged the hegemony of feminisms constructed primarily around the lives of white middle-class women. Since the late 1960s, U.S. women of color have taken issue with unitary theories of gender. Our critiques grew out of the widespread concern about the exclusion of women of color from feminist scholarship and the misinterpretation of our experiences, and ultimately "out of the very discourses, denying, permitting, and producing difference."[1] Speaking simultaneously from "within and against" both women's liberation and antiracist movements, we have insisted on the need to challenge systems of domination, not merely as gendered subjects but as women whose lives are affected by our location in multiple hierarchies.

. . . Our analysis draws on a conceptual framework that we refer to as "multiracial feminism." This perspective is an attempt to go beyond a mere recognition of diversity and difference among women to examine structures of domination, specifically the importance of race in understanding the social construction of gender. Despite the varied concerns and multiple intellectual stances which characterize the feminisms of women of color, they share an emphasis on race as a primary force situating genders differently. It is the centrality of race, of institutionalized racism, and of struggles against racial oppression that link the various feminist perspectives within this framework. Together, they demonstrate that racial meanings offer new theoretical directions for feminist thought.

Tensions in Contemporary Difference Feminism

. . .

Despite the much-heralded diversity trend within feminist studies, difference is often reduced to mere pluralism: a "live and let live" approach where principles of relativism generate a long list of diversities which begin with gender, class, and race and continue through a range of social-structural as well as personal characteristics. Another disturbing pattern, which bell hooks refers to as "the commodification of difference," is the representation of diversity as a form of exotica, "a spice, seasoning that livens up the dull dish that is mainstream white culture."[2] The major limitation of these approaches is the failure to attend to the power relations that accompany difference. Moreover, these approaches ignore the inequalities that cause some characteristics to be seen as "normal" while others are seen as "different" and thus, deviant.

Maria C. Lugones expresses irritation at those feminists who see only the problem of difference without recognizing difference. Increasingly, we find that difference is recognized. But this in no way means that difference occupies a "privileged" theoretical status. Instead of using difference to rethink the category of women, difference is often a euphemism for women who differ from the traditional norm. Even in purporting to accept difference, feminist pluralism often creates a social reality that reverts to universalizing women:

> So much feminist scholarship assumes that when we cut through all of the diversity among women created by differences of racial classification, ethnicity, social class, and sexual orientation, a "universal truth" concerning women and gender lies buried underneath. But if we can face the scary possibility that no such certainty exists and that persisting in such a search will always distort or omit someone's experiences, with what do we replace this old way of thinking? Gender differences and gender politics begin to look very different if there is no essential woman at the core.[3]

What Is Multiracial Feminism?

A new set of feminist theories have emerged from the challenges put forth by women of color. Multiracial feminism is an evolving body of theory and practice informed by wide-ranging intellectual traditions. This framework does not offer a singular or unified feminism but a body of knowledge situating women and men in multiple systems of domination. U.S. multiracial feminism encompasses several emergent perspectives developed primarily by women of color: African Americans, Latinas, Asian Americans, and Native Americans, women whose analyses are shaped by their unique perspectives as "outsiders within"—marginal intellectuals whose social locations provide them with a particular perspective on self and society. Although U.S. women of color represent many races and ethnic backgrounds—with different histories and cultures—our feminisms cohere in their treatment of race as a basic social division, a structure of power, a focus of political struggle, and hence a fundamental force in shaping women's and men's lives.

This evolving intellectual and political perspective uses several controversial terms. While we adopt the label "multiracial," other terms have been used to describe this broad framework. For example, Chela Sandoval refers to "U.S. Third World feminisms,"[4] while other scholars refer to "indigenous feminisms." In their theory text-reader, Alison M. Jaggar and Paula S. Rothenberg adopt the label "multicultural feminism."[5]

We use "multiracial" rather than "multicultural" as a way of underscoring race as a power system that interacts with other structured inequalities to shape genders. Within the U.S. context, race, and the system of meanings and ideologies which accompany it, is a fundamental organizing principle of social relationships. Race affects all women and men, although in different ways. Even cultural and group differences among women are produced through interaction within a racially stratified social order. Therefore, although we do not discount the importance of culture, we caution that cultural analytic frameworks that ignore race tend to view women's differences as the product of group-specific values and practices that often result in the marginalization of cultural groups which are then perceived as exotic expressions of a normative center. Our focus on race stresses the social construction of differently situated social groups and their varying degrees of advantage and power. Additionally, this emphasis on race takes on increasing political importance in an era where discourse about race is governed by color-evasive language and a preference for individual rather than group remedies for social inequalities. Our analyses insist upon the primary and pervasive nature of race in contemporary U.S. society while at the same time acknowledging how race both shapes and is shaped by a variety of other social relations.

. . .

We recognize, of course, certain problems inherent in an uncritical use of the multiracial label. First, the perspective can be hampered by a biracial model in which only African Americans and whites are seen as racial categories and all other groups are viewed through the prism of cultural differences. Latinos and Asians have always occupied distinctive places within the racial hierarchy, and current shifts in the composition of the U.S. population are racializing these groups anew.

A second problem lies in treating multiracial feminism as a single analytical framework, and its principal architects, women of color, as an undifferentiated category. . . . The feminisms created by women of color exhibit a plurality of intellectual and political positions. We speak in many voices, with inconsistencies that are born of our different social locations. Multiracial feminism embodies this plurality and richness. Our intent is not to falsely universalize women of color. Nor do we wish to promote a new racial essentialism in place of the old gender essentialism. Instead, we use these concepts to examine the structures and experiences produced by intersecting forms of race and gender.

It is also essential to acknowledge that race is a shifting and contested category whose meanings construct definitions of all aspects of social life. In the United States it helped define citizenship by excluding everyone who was not a white, male property owner. It defined labor as slave or free, coolie or contract, and family as available only to those men whose marriages were recognized or whose wives could immigrate with them. Additionally, racial meanings are contested both within groups and between them.

Although definitions of race are at once historically and geographically specific, they are also transnational, encompassing diasporic groups and crossing traditional geographic boundaries. Thus, while U.S. multiracial feminism calls attention to the fundamental importance of race, it must also locate the meaning of race within specific national traditions.

The Distinguishing Features of Multiracial Feminism

By attending to these problems, multiracial feminism offers a set of analytic premises for thinking about and theorizing gender. The following themes distinguish this branch of feminist inquiry.

First, multiracial feminism asserts that gender is constructed by a range of interlocking inequalities, what Patricia Hill Collins calls a "matrix of domination."[6] The idea of a matrix is that several fundamental systems work with and through each other. People experience race, class, gender, and sexuality differently depending upon their social location in the structures of race, class, gender, and sexuality. For example, people of the same race will experience race differently depending upon their location in the class structure as working class, professional managerial class, or unemployed; in the gender structure as female or male; and in structures of sexuality as heterosexual, homosexual, or bisexual.

Multiracial feminism also examines the simultaneity of systems in shaping women's experience and identity. Race, class, gender, sexuality are not reducible to individual attributes to be measured and assessed for their separate contribution in explaining given social outcomes, an approach that Elizabeth Spelman calls "pop-bead metaphysics," where a woman's identity consists of the sum of parts neatly divisible from one another.[7] The matrix of domination seeks to account for the multiple ways that women experience themselves as gendered, raced, classed, and sexualized.

Second, multiracial feminism emphasizes the intersectional nature of hierarchies at all levels of social life. Class, race, gender, and sexuality are components of both social structure and social interaction. Women and men are differently embedded in locations created by these cross-cutting hierarchies. As a result, women and men through the social order experience different forms of privilege and subordination, depending on their race, class, gender, and sexuality. In other words, intersecting forms of domination produce both oppression and opportunity. At the same time that structures of race, class, and gender create disadvantages for women of color, they provide unacknowledged benefits for those who are at the top of these hierarchies—whites, members of the upper classes, and males. Therefore, multiracial feminism applies not only to racial ethnic women but also to women and men of all races, classes, and genders.

Third, multiracial feminism highlights the relational nature of dominance and subordination. Power is the cornerstone of women's differences. This means that women's differences are connected in systematic ways. Race is a vital element in the pattern of relations among minority and white women. As Linda Gordon argues, the very meanings of being a white woman in the United States have been affected by the existence of subordinated women of color: "They intersect in conflict and in occasional cooperation, but always in mutual influence."[8]

Fourth, multiracial feminism explores the interplay of social structure and women's agency. Within the constraints of race, class, and gender oppression, women create viable lives for themselves, their families, and their communities. Women of color have resisted and often undermined the forces of power that control them. From acts of quiet dignity and steadfast determination to involvement in revolt and rebellion, women struggle to shape their own lives. Racial oppression has been a common focus of the "dynamic of oppositional agency" of women of color. . . .

Fifth, multiracial feminism encompasses wide-ranging methodological approaches, and like other branches of feminist thought, relies on varied theoretical tools as well. Ruth Frankenberg and Lata Mani identify three guiding principles of inclusive feminist inquiry: "building complex analyses, avoiding erasure, specifying location."[9] In the last decade, the opening up of academic feminism has focused attention on social location in the production of knowledge. Most basically, research by and about marginalized women has destabilized what used to be considered as universal categories of gender. Marginalized locations are well suited for grasping social relations that remained obscure from more privileged vantage points. Lived experience, in other words, creates alternative ways of understanding the social world and the experience of different groups of women within it. Racially informed standpoint epistemologies have provided new topics, fresh questions, and new understandings of women and men. Women of color have, as Norma Alarcon argues, asserted ourselves as subjects, using our voices to challenge dominant conceptions of truth.[10]

Sixth, multiracial feminism brings together understandings drawn from the lived experiences of diverse and continuously changing groups of women. Among Asian Americans, Native Americans, Latinas, and Blacks are many different national, cultural, and ethnic groups. Each one is engaged in the process of testing, refining, and reshaping these broader categories in its own image. Such internal differences heighten awareness of and sensitivity to both commonalities and differences, serving as a constant reminder of the importance of comparative study and maintaining a creative tension between diversity and universalization.

Difference and Transformation

. . . [R]ace matters for everyone. White women, too, must be reconceptualized as a category that is multiply defined by race, class, and other differences. As Ruth Frankenberg demonstrates in a study of whiteness among contemporary women, all kinds of social relations, even those that appear neutral, are, in fact, racialized. Frankenberg further complicates the very notion of a unified white identity by introducing issues of Jewish identity.[11] Therefore, the lives of women of color cannot be seen as a *variation* on a more general model of white American womanhood. The model of womanhood that feminist social science once held as "universal" is also a product of race and class.

When we analyze the power relations constituting all social arrangements and shaping women's lives in distinctive ways, we can begin to grapple with core feminist issues about how genders are socially constructed and constructed differently.

Women's difference is built into our study of gender. Yet this perspective is quite far removed from the atheoretical pluralism implied in much contemporary thinking about gender.

Multiracial feminism, in our view, focuses not just on differences but also on the way in which differences and domination intersect and are historically and socially constituted. It challenges feminist scholars to go beyond the mere recognition and inclusion of difference to reshape the basic concepts and theories of our disciplines. By attending to women's social location based on race, class, and gender, multiracial feminism seeks to clarify the structural sources of diversity. Ultimately, multiracial feminism forces us to see privilege and subordination as interrelated and to pose such questions as: How do the existences and experiences of all people—women and men, different racial-ethnic groups, and different classes—shape the experiences of each other? How are those relationships defined and enforced through social institutions that are the primary sites for negotiating power with society? How do these differences contribute to the construction of both individual and group identity? Once we acknowledge that all women are affected by the racial order of society, then it becomes clear that the insights of multiracial feminism provide an analytical framework, not solely for understanding the experiences of women of color but for understanding all women, and men, as well.

NOTES

1. Chela Sandoval, *U.S. Third World Feminism: The Theory and Method of Oppositional Consciousness in the Postmodern World*, Genders (Spring 1991):1–24.

2. bell hooks, Black Looks: Race and Representation (Boston: South End Press, 1992), 21.

3. Patricia Hill Collins, Foreword to Women of Color in U.S. Society, ed. Maxine Baca Zinn and Bonnie Thornton Dill (Philadelphia: Temple University Press, 1994), xv.

4. Chela Sandoval, *U.S. Third World Feminism: The Theory and Method of Oppositional Consciousness in the Postmodern World*, Genders (Spring 1991):1.

5. Alison M. Jaggar and Paula S. Rothenberg, Feminist Frameworks: Alternative Theoretical Accounts of the Relations Between Women and Men, 3d ed. (New York: McGraw-Hill, 1993).

6. Patricia Hill Collins, Black Feminist Thought: Knowledge, Consciousness, and the Politics of Empowerment (Boston: Unwin Hyman, 1990).

7. Elizabeth Spelman, Inessential Women: Problems of Exclusion in Feminist Thought (Boston: Beacon Press, 1988), 136.

8. Linda Gordon, *On Difference*, Genders 10 (Spring 1991):91–111, 106.

9. Ruth Frankenberg and Lata Mani, *Cross Currents, Crosstalk: Race, "Postcoloniality," and the Politics of Location*, Cultural Studies 7 (May 1993):292–310, 306.

10. Norma Alarcon, *The Theoretical Subject(s) of This Bridge Called My Back and Anglo-American Feminism*, in Making Face, Making Soul, Haciendo Caras: Creative and Critical Perspectives by Women of Color, ed. Gloria Anzaldúa (San Francisco: Aunt Lute, 1990), 356.

11. Frankenberg and Mani [*supra*, note 9], 306.

3

Autonomy, Aspiration, and Accomplishment: Some Steps and Barriers to Equality for Women

Patricia Smith

Imagine a world in which half the senators, governors, legislators, and political leaders were women, as well as half the business leaders, scientists, scholars, writers, doctors, lawyers, artists, engineers, and other professional persons. That world would be equal at least in that one respect. This is the world to which feminists generally are and should be committed.

Of course, feminism today is so splintered and fragmented that it is doubtful whether any single goal or vision could be articulated of which it could be said that all are in fact committed. By definition, all feminists are committed to the liberation of women—you simply are not a feminist if not committed to that—but the idea of the liberation of women is susceptible to highly divergent interpretations. . . .

Still, I intend to stick with my vision of an equal world, despite the possible charge that I embrace the much maligned equality of results. I embrace the vision to which I was introduced when I first encountered feminism. I find it inspiring, and I have not yet seen good cause to alter it. So, to anyone who suggests that equality has been accomplished in our time, I point to my vision, and say, "That is what an equal society should look like and so the society we have now cannot be equal because the discrepancies are just too great."

Immediately questions arise: Why should anyone agree that the vision I have suggested is the right vision of an equal society? Even if it is right, why should we suppose we have any hope of achieving it when it never existed before? On the other hand, if it is achievable, why shouldn't we suppose that it will be accomplished more or less automatically or naturally over time? If it will not be achieved automatically, what will it take to get it? . . .

I.

Why should anyone agree that the vision I described above is the right picture or at least a plausible articulation of an equal society, and especially one to which feminists should be committed? . . .

I am absolutely not suggesting that we should impose any sort of quota system or any other particular program to bring about a 50:50 ratio of women to men in all fields of endeavor. The vision I set out above is intended to be just that—a vision, an ideal. If societies treated men and women equally, roughly half the positions of power and accomplishment would be held by women; that seems to me a reasonable presumption.

This picture is, then, a utopian dream, but not in the sense of being an unreachable ideal toward which we can only strive. I see no reason to suppose that a world in which the opportunities and accomplishments of men and women are roughly equal is unachievable in time. This makes it unlike a utopian vision of a just world which is an unreachable ideal toward which we can only strive. It is also unlike supposing that one day prejudice and discrimination may be eradicated. . . . People can live with prejudice. In fact, if it is not too overwhelming it can, like other obstacles, be motivating. Jews, for example, have lived with prejudice for centuries, and for most of that time it did not eliminate their aspirations or accomplishments. The same could be true of women, if the prejudice is not totally engulfing. Thus, the vision I suggest could be actualized whether sexism can be eliminated or not.

Finally, I am not suggesting that men and women are fundamentally alike, nor do I think it necessary to defend such a claim in order to defend my vision of an equal society. I realize that one argument used to explain (or justify or rationalize) the different accomplishments of men and women and their different positions in society, as well as different expectations we should have of them, is that because of their intrinsic differences, men and women have different abilities, aspirations, and interests. . . .

I will make three responses to this view. First, while it may be that men and women have different interests, we have no idea what those would be in the absence of powerful conditioning to make them as they are. Without any possible control group we can have no idea what intrinsic interests might be, or whether it makes any sense to talk about intrinsic interests that would be manifested in the absence of social conditioning. So, people are already manipulated to fit a preconceived pattern. It was just preconceived centuries ago.

Secondly, . . . over the past 30 years when the public sphere has actually opened up for the first time to women in general (and then pretty grudgingly and ambivalently), the enormous influx of women into the academy, the forum, and the market, at the very least, belies any claim that women simply are not interested in participating.

. . . [Third,] in the absence of any proven facts about natural characteristics and the presence of counterexamples to any claims about them, to make presumptions without proof about such matters to provide explanations for the status quo that could disadvantage half the population of the world seems highly questionable. . . .

Any view that cannot be proven, and which conveniently supports the status quo at the expense of an already marginalized group, should be taken as presumptively suspect. This does not show that the view is false, but it does shift the burden of proof to the other side. This should certainly apply to presuming the unequal ability or aspiration of men and women. Thus, if any presumption must be made (if withholding judgment is not an option) then it must be presumed that men and women are equal unless there is proof otherwise.

Given that, I will reiterate and specify my view: since it is not reasonable to presume unequal ability or aspiration among men and women, such a presumption cannot be used to explain or justify the unequal position of men and women in society. What then can explain or justify this inequality? If the explanation is not internal (i.e., due to innate differences in ability or aspiration) then it must be external. What sort of external explanation might there be? It can only be that social structures treat men and women differently. What can justify such differential treatment? Presumably, the justification must be that the classifications of persons being treated differently are in fact materially (i.e., intrinsically or innately) different. But innate differences between men and women are what we just agreed cannot be presumed.

. . .

II.

I have argued that in the absence of proof to the contrary, it is reasonable to presume that the equal treatment of men and women in a society organized to provide equal opportunity would produce among them roughly equal aspirations and accomplishments, and that feminists should be committed to such a world. But should we suppose that any such world is humanly possible? No such society has ever existed in the history of civilization. Why should we think it possible now?

It is my view . . . that we are living through a full blown cultural revolution equivalent in magnitude to the Industrial Revolution that preceded it. The heart of this cultural revolution—at least a major catalyst and driving force behind it—is a revolution in reproductive practice that has already transformed the identity of women, that will restructure personal and family relations in much the way the Industrial Revolution reorganized the marketplace and the nature of work, and that consequently has significant implications for our legal, social, and political institutions. Furthermore, this is the change that makes the equal participation of men and women in the public sphere possible when it never was before.

. . .

Motherhood is now a part-time vocation in much the way fatherhood always has been. That means that women are no longer fated, single purpose functionaries—breeders, to put it bluntly—predetermined by their reproductive destiny. Women are autonomous beings, responsible for themselves and their choices, determining for themselves what course of life to pursue. That transformation, from fated to free, is so profound that it should be recognized as a change of identity. That transition and all of its manifestations make the equal aspiration and participation of men and women in the public sphere possible when it never was before.

III.

If the twentieth century cultural revolution is, as I have suggested, equalizing the sexes, reorganizing long-standing institutions and reordering personal and social relations, why shouldn't we suppose that equal participation in all spheres of endeavor will occur over time, more or less inevitably? Obviously, a transformation of all institutions to include half the population that was previously excluded from it will not take place over night. Perhaps fighting over this process only causes unnecessary upheaval, animosity, anxiety, and even backlash that might be avoided with more patience.

. . .

[I]t is naive to ignore the subtlety and complexity of psychological and institutional devices for securing the status quo, especially as it relates to entrenched power. The status quo stands for sexual inequality today just as it has for 5,000 years; the mechanisms for maintaining this are many and diverse. While providing a crucial service for any society, these cultural anchors also constitute barriers to any reform that entails a challenge to traditional assumptions. The status quo sets the standard for what is normal, natural, reasonable, and authoritative. Thus any deviations from or challenges to the status quo are always subject to interpretations that make them more congenial to accepted thought. This has the effect of dissipating new movements and diffusing new ideas, while reinforcing and replenishing old ones, thus sapping momentum and diverting movements for change. Let me mention a few such mechanisms to maintain the status quo that constitute barriers to equality for women.

1. Sexual harassment and discrimination continue in both overt and subtle forms that constitute barriers to women. . . .

2. Another obstacle to equality for women lies in the standard division of labor in the home. The status quo is that women are solely responsible for "home-making." Caretaking and domestic duties are women's concerns. This divides the responsibilities of women (as well as their sources of guilt and self-esteem) and presents them with a choice not generally confronted by men. For women, home and career are contradictory; each subtracts from the other. And the situation is a "Catch 22" for men as well in the following respect: if a man tries to spend more time on home and family needs, he will be penalized in the work place at least as severely as women are. . . .

3. A further reinforcement of inequality lies in the weight of authority and public opinion. Repeated "authorities," for example, have asserted that women prefer to be in the home, have a greater need to be with their children, and are less committed to the work place. . . . Theories of feminine nature and psychology continuously find new ways to repostulate old stereotypes of femininity as though they were facts of nature, and to portray circumstances of pragmatic necessity or responsibility as though they were innate features of female psychology. . . .

4. Among some powerful groups, commitment to traditional roles—which is interpreted as commitment to traditional values or even family values—is taken to the level of a sacred mission. These ideas have been strongly represented by the religious right and by many political conservatives. . . .

5. The final point . . . I will call the problem of sharing power. Women are treated as extraordinary outsiders in most professions and positions of leadership. . . .

Thus, the reins of power are not relinquished lightly. The reins of power in this country are still held by white, upper middle class men whose resumes look strikingly similar. Christine Littleton called this "the club." Women could not belong to the club, she said, even though we could make our resumes look very similar to those of its members.

. . .

What is worrisome about [the club]—for aspirations of equality for women—is, first, that the club provides us with our image of authority . . . [and second, that] the power of the club . . . tends to reproduce itself. . . .

[T]he effect of all these mechanisms are cumulative and mutually reinforcing. They are all about restricting change. If there are enough of these devices and they are powerful enough to divert change to a direction more like the status quo, then they provide reason to fear that women may never reach circumstances of equality, even if they would have equal aspirations and accomplishments in societies that did provide equal opportunity.

Consequently, the idea that we can sit back and "let nature take its course," secure in our assumption that equal abilities will overcome unequal opportunities in time, is not so justified as it would be if the unequal social organization were not quite so pervasive or the mechanisms for maintaining it not quite so totally engulfing.

IV.

What, then, is to be done? The obvious answer would seem to be that unequal treatment should be eliminated: Unequal social structures should be corrected, restrictive stereotyping ended, and oppressive socialization stopped. Unfortunately, those are unachievable objectives. Goals of that sort cannot be directly addressed at all by anything short of massive brain washing and totalitarian government, like that of the "Brave New World." So perhaps the first point that should be noted is that there is a sense in which the equal treatment of men and women may not be an achievable goal at all, and if it is ultimately achievable, it certainly will not be in the foreseeable future. Perhaps in a hundred years or so (if we are lucky enough, or wise enough, to manage to overcome the barriers noted earlier), men and women will be treated equally, but at best, that will be a slow and painful evolutionary process.

If this is correct, then the best we can do (and the least we can do) is to counter the unequal treatment enough to meet the demands of justice. So long as unequal treatment persists, it should be counterbalanced enough to make the resulting disadvantage possible for a reasonable number of individuals to overcome. That is, it should be recognized that barriers to advancement probably cannot be equalized (certainly not in the short term), but at least they should not be so badly skewed against any group that it is not reasonable to expect some members of that group to be able to succeed in spite of them. This is not so much because any society that does less is unequal, but that it is unjust.

The question is, then, what should be considered proper and justifiable counteractive measures? . . . [T]he objective should be to make it reasonably possible for men and women to be equally autonomous.

Virginia Woolf once said that in order to be a writer a woman needed a room of her own and an income of 500 pounds annually. Accomplishment ordinarily requires a life that allows independent thought—that is, autonomy. What she said applies to any serious endeavor, and perhaps to aspiration itself. Aspiration (as opposed to a pious wish or an idle dream) generally requires independence, and accomplishment typically requires aspiration. Recognition of this corresponds to a strong philosophical tradition that has long recognized the significance of autonomy, a resource insufficiently mined by feminists.

A serious defect of this tradition is that it overlooks the support system supplied for "autonomous" men by subordinated women who tend to the details of daily living that make "autonomous" personal accomplishments (for men) compatible with personal family life. . . .

The big question, once this is recognized, is whether (or under what kinds of conditions) autonomy can in fact be universalized? I would suggest that an equal society is one which organizes its institutions so as to make possible the universalization of autonomy (and the aspiration and accomplishment that follow from it) without the sacrifice of personal or family relations. This is the form of equality feminists should be concerned to promote. . . . Unfortunately, however, autonomy has come to be regarded with suspicion by some feminists and others on a number of grounds.

For one thing, given the influential psychological theories of Nancy Chodorow and Carol Gilligan, some feminists have argued that individualistic presuppositions of the ideal of autonomy presume a notion of the self that conflicts with women's psychological and moral approaches to relations with others. More importantly, this atomistic concept is inconsistent with the intersubjective nature of the self, whether male or female. It has also been argued that the ideal of autonomy is too closely attached to liberal individualism—in particular with the sharp distinction commonly drawn between public and private spheres of endeavor. As a result, autonomy has been historically defined in terms of traditionally masculine values of independence and citizenship, as contrasted with relations of dependence associated with home life, family, and femininity. And some have argued that traditional conceptions of autonomy presuppose an impossible level of self-knowledge and a rigid identity that is incompatible with a Postmodern conception of the self.

While these objections embody important insights that need to be addressed, they do not, in my view, point to fatal flaws in the concept of autonomy itself. The objections do not lead to the conclusion (suggested by some) that the ideal of autonomy must be scrapped as hopelessly incoherent, unrealistic, or "masculinist."

. . .

[T]he idea of autonomy need not be conceived in such individualistic terms as to exclude social relations. There is no reason to suppose that anyone ever meant the idea of autonomy to imply isolation. [Jennifer] Nedelsky has argued that social relationship is a precondition to autonomy, coining the phrase "relational autonomy." . . . Robert Young and John Christman have attempted accounts of autonomy intended to reconcile socialization with free agency. The important point of this work is to recharacterize the highly abstract traditional notion of autonomy in more concrete terms that connect it to plausible conceptions of human nature that include the social side of human psychology.

. . .

I want to suggest that all this has special application to women in at least two respects. The first, and most basic, is the need to counteract oppressive socialization that restricts the aspirations of women in terms of supposedly limited, innate, or natural inclinations or abilities. . . .

Accordingly, I would suggest that the better job we do of educating our young women, not only in a wide variety of subjects but also in the skill of critical thinking itself, the better equip[ped] they will be to evaluate the influences thrust upon them from all directions, and to consider for themselves which forms of life are limiting or fulfilling. Thus, a feminist program to combat sexist socialization should be centered on promoting educational excellence that includes critical thinking to enable all children to evaluate arguments, to identify prejudice, and to value liberty, autonomy, and justice for all. Consequently, one direction of feminist research should be to continue the examination of what it means to be intellectually autonomous, and what conditions are necessary or sufficient for achieving it.

While combating sexist socialization is a crucial component in a feminist program to understand and equalize autonomy, it is not itself sufficient. Having the ability to engage in autonomous decisionmaking does not guarantee that one will be able to implement or act on one's decisions. . . . Traditional social structures essentially require women (but not men) to choose between a career and a family (or to balance one against the other, thus impairing both). . . . Men never had to make such a choice, and it is an unfair choice for anyone to have to make. . . . The more this tradition breaks down, however, the more the conflict between work and family responsibilities will become a problem for men as well as women. Thus, the question of how to restructure our institutions to resolve this conflict is one of the most pressing issues faced in the twenty-first century. This is the second direction of research I suggest for feminist exploration. . . .

All this suggests that the solution to this problem must lie in progressive institutional reform. The problem is that economic and domestic institutions have developed over the past 300 years or so under the assumptions of separate public and private spheres. These assumptions need to be reconsidered. Feminists should be on the cutting edge of research to study the implications of our institutional structures and their potential for revision. Conflict between responsibilities of work and family is one of the most serious challenges facing all industrialized nations in the twenty-first century. Meeting that challenge in a manner that equalizes family burdens between the sexes and provides more autonomy and freedom for all individuals to pursue their own aspirations should be a high priority in the feminist research agenda.

The Multiple Self: Exploring between and beyond Modernity and Postmodernity

john a. powell

> We are all androgynous, not only because we are all born of a woman impregnated by the seed of a man but because each of us, helplessly and forever, contains the other—male in female, female in male, white in black, and black in white. We are a part of each other. . . . [N]one of us can do anything about it.
>
> —James Baldwin[1]

I frequently have difficulty sorting out how to think about a number of issues in my life. The problem is not so much that I do not know what I think and feel. Instead, it is that I think and feel many different and conflicting things and I do not have the capacity to simply sort them out. Sometimes, I let the different voices engage each other in a dialogue and find an intrasubjective solution. Other times I allow the discordance to exist. . . .

The dominant narrative of Western society would find what I have just written problematic, and perhaps unintelligible. This narrative, purporting to be a meta-narrative, denies that we are or can be multiple and fractured and still remain "normal." It makes many claims upon us regarding the nature of the individual. In fact, its individualistic focus is one of the deeply rooted ideologies of Western society. . . .

In this [e]ssay I attempt to highlight some of the ways that the ideals of individualism, the individual, and the self are used to destructively frame the ways we talk about the self and race. . . . By questioning this largely unexamined norm, I invite the reader to look at what has been traditionally excluded.

. . .

II. Voices of Dissent

The development of the ideology of individualism has very negative consequences. As the modern essentialist conception of individuals informed governmental and jurisprudential theory, there was a concurrent need to construct an ideology to justify certain practices, such as slavery and colonialism, which clearly violated norms emanating from an equal and essential self. Yet the very manner in which modernists defined the self justified those practices. By construing the essence of the human self as individual and autonomous, European thinkers deliberately excluded from selfhood members of non-White societies that were organized around non-individualistic norms. Similarly, the adherence of modernists to Christian beliefs also justified the conquest and subjugation of non-Christian (i.e., non-White) "infidels." Other complementary ideologies have been employed as needed to provide scientific (e.g., eugenics and polygenics) and, more recently, cultural (e.g., the "culture of poverty") explanations for the inequalities of Western society.

Given the exclusively defined "essence" of identity, it is not surprising that criticisms of the Western self have arisen mainly from the groups that Western society has marginalized. Writing at the beginning of the twentieth century, W. E. B. Du Bois articulated his anguish as an African American trying to attain a sense of self-unity in a society that defined him in ways that contradicted his own sense of identity:

> [T]he Negro is a sort of seventh son, born with a veil, and gifted with second-sight in this American world,—a world which yields him no true self-consciousness, but only lets him see himself through the revelation of the other world. It is a peculiar sensation, this double-consciousness, this sense of always looking at one's self through the eyes of others. . . . One ever feels his two-ness. . . . The history of the American Negro is the history of this strife,—this longing to attain self-conscious manhood, to merge his double self into a better and truer self.[2]

Du Bois's reflections suggest the postmodern, intersectional self, the self of "others" fragmented by society's dominant discourse. Importantly, Du Bois demonstrates that those people whom society has marginalized and dehumanized do not experience the unitary self as an essence, but as an aspiration; a "longing" for coherence and self-satisfaction.

Zora Neale Hurston's reflections on her sense of self also question the idea of a unitary and static self. Hurston recounts how her experience of possessing a racialized identity was not an essential one, but rather was largely a product of her placement within a societal framework:

> I remember the very day that I became colored. Up to my thirteenth year I lived in the little Negro town of Eatonville, Florida. . . . [Then] I was sent to school in Jacksonville. I left Eatonville, the town of the oleanders, as Zora. When I disembarked from the river-boat at Jacksonville she was no more. . . . I was now a little colored girl.[3]

This reflection demonstrates that Hurston did not experience her self as unitary—she was both "Zora" and a nameless "little colored girl." Nor was Hurston's sense of self static. Experience created her identity, which changed as her context changed. Concerning her sense of a racial identity, Hurston wrote, "I feel most colored when I am thrown up against a sharp white background."

In this White context we can envision both Du Bois and Hurston grappling with the reconciliation of their own senses of self with the foreign subhuman notion of self thrust upon them. Frantz Fanon, writing about colonizer and colonized, articulates this conundrum of identity that the modern self creates for marginalized groups: "Because it is a systematic negation of the other person and a furious determination to deny the other person all attributes of humanity, colonialism forces the people it dominates to ask themselves the question constantly: 'In reality, who am I?'"[4] Hurston's metaphor of the white background also illustrates how it is that White males may not have a similar experience of fragmented identities. Against a white background—within a theoretical framework that defines them as coherent and human—individual whites are free to choose the manner in which they distinguish themselves. Confident that those aspects they find most central to their identity are legitimate, White males are free to cultivate their "arbitrary contingencies" with little fear of loss of humanity. There is no dissonance between Whites' personal experiences of humanity and societal definitions of humanity. Thus, the smooth fit between societal norms of Whiteness and the constructed identity of Whites creates an illusion of coherence and racial invisibility or neutrality—of "normality." By attaining this sense of racial neutrality, White males are thus able to adhere to notions of the essentialized modern self without problematizing their own sense of identity.

The false unity and transparency of Whiteness and maleness leave those who are not White males futilely seeking the sense of unity they perceive in a White male self that is in reality neither unitary nor transparent. . . . Thus the pull to be an individual, especially by Blacks and other "others," is an effort to claim one's humanity by not being marked by race, gender, etc. It is an effort to become, or pass for, the White male. In a subtle way this error of normalizing the unstated marker of the dominant discourse shadows some of the language of intersectionality.
. . .

III. The Leap to Anti-Essentialism

. . .

If we are to benefit from postmodern criticisms of the modern self, we must address the difficult questions relating to agency, and the seemingly integrated nature of the multiple self. It is also important to consider other conceptions of the self that retain some degree of essentialism.
. . .

Recognizing that the self is multiplicitous does not require the conclusion that there is no essence to the self. Given the ramifications of reconceptualizing the self, we must consider whether there is some viable alternative to the modernist conception of the self that does not rest upon social construction. Although this endeavor may ultimately prove fruitless, it is a valuable one nevertheless. To this end, I briefly offer two conceptions of the self that recognizes its multiplicitous and constructed nature, while leaving room for an essentialist understanding of at least part of the process of consciousness: psychoanalysis and Buddhism.

A. The Psychoanalytic Self

. . .

Psychoanalysis focuses on "the individual in his capacity to generate a sense of 'I-ness' (subjectivity)."[5] According to Freud, this sense of unity is a function of the two basic facets of the mind, the conscious and the unconscious. The conscious mind is generally logical and consists of those mental processes which we are aware of, while the unconscious mind consists of processes that escape our awareness but nevertheless shape identity and actions. The unconscious mind tackles the "desires, wishes, and instincts that strive for gratification."[6] Thus, Freud relocates the self from the conscious mind, where modernism places it, to somewhere in the interactions between the conscious and unconscious. Because it consists of the interplay between the conscious and unconscious, the Freudian self is "fundamentally dialectic in nature."[7]

According to Thomas Ogden, this interplay of the conscious and unconscious is a "dialectic of presence and absence."[8] . . . What is absent from the conscious mind's experience is often present in the unconscious mind, and the Freudian mind uses this dialectic to maintain a sense of wholeness and placidity. When there is tension between the (context-dependent) values of the conscious mind and incongruous thoughts or desires, the subject employs "[d]efensive mechanisms such as repression, denial, introjection, projection, reaction formation, sublimation, and reversal [which] resolve the conflicts between the primary and secondary processes by disguising forbidden wishes and making them palatable."[9]

This dialectical process also has an intersubjective aspect: how we define ourselves and how we define others are interdependent functions of our interactions with others. Psychoanalyst Melanie Klein asserts that the self is actually decentered from its exclusive locus within the individual; instead the subject is conceived of as arising in a dialectic (a dialogue) of self and Other. Through the process of "projective identification," the subject is able to resolve internal conflicts by projecting those aspects of the conflict considered negative onto others. . . .

Thus, the psychoanalytic subject is contextual and relational in at least two key respects: (1) the formation of the conscious self and its ethos, and (2) the stability of the subject as internal conflicts are resolved through the defensive mechanism of projection.

The Freudian account of the self is in many respects consistent with postmodernism's assertion that the self is relational and contextual. The conscious self is largely defined by social interactions. Consequently, it experiences incoherency and multiplicity as individuals in any sociohistorical context do. To this extent, psychoanalysis does not assert an a priori self in the manner that modernity does. Furthermore, the dialectical self of psychoanalysis offers an explanation of how the subject seeks to construct wholeness or unity out of multiplicity and how "others" play an integral role in this process. Yet Freudian theorists believe that these processes of the mind, the interplay of the unconscious and conscious involving drives and instinct, exist in everyone.

The Freudian theory of self provides valuable insight into the way that racism and other systems of oppression function in our society. The dialectic of consciousness and unconsciousness helps us to understand the persistence and pervasiveness of "unintentional" racism in our society despite the general disavowal of explicitly racist ideologies. In a society such as ours where racialized meanings are unavoidably pervasive, the ostensibly antiracist individual is consistently confronted with conflicts between its nonracist ethos and internalized racist attitudes. In order to resolve this conflict, the individual resorts to the aforementioned "defensive mechanisms":

> [T]he human mind defends itself against the discomfort of guilt by denying or refusing to recognize those ideas, wishes, and beliefs that conflict with what the individual has learned is good or right. . . . When an individual experiences conflict between racist ideas and the societal ethic that condemns those ideas, the mind excludes his racism from consciousness.[10]

This helps to explain the pervasiveness of actions that contain racist meanings but are not driven by the actor's conscious "intent" to behave in a racist manner. . . .

B. The Buddhist Self

The conditional and the unconditional, the essential and the unessential, are not contradictory for Buddhism but are always present together.

One of the central tenets of Buddhism is that there is no permanent self. Rather, Buddhists assert that the self and all phenomena are constructed and lack permanent inherent existence. This lack of inherent existence is also described as emptiness. Indeed, the emptiness of inherent existence means that the self and all phenomena are constructed and conditional—that is, put together and unessential. This emptiness of inherent existence is often referred to as the unconditional. But emptiness is not the opposite of, or separate from, phenomena; indeed, phenomena are both unconditioned and conditioned. . . .

The self and all phenomena are put together, compounded, and conditional. While this process of constitution or construction occurs very rapidly, there are gaps nonetheless. In this sense, Buddhism supports structuralist, postmodern claims regarding the self by asserting that self-consciousness is largely put together by language. This assertion of the nonessential self is more persuasive coming from Buddhism, because it is based on a wholly separate tradition, rather than the reactive refutation of modernism. . . .

Buddhists' understanding of the nature of the self does not end at the level of social construction and mental artifices. As mentioned earlier, Buddhists believe that there is the unconditioned emptiness that is not put together or constituted. This uncondition is not a concept or a thing. Emptiness is also empty of inherent condition. Emptiness cannot be grasped directly by the language narrative because it is not part of the conceptual world. This does not mean that emptiness is beyond consciousness, but only that it is beyond conceptual consciousness. Emptiness can, however, be experienced directly through the practice of "'mindfulness,' which is the ability to sustain a calm, intense, and steady focus when one intends to do so."[11] Mindfulness involves accessing a state of consciousness that is beyond and ungoverned by experience and context. Thus, much of the Buddhist practice of sitting is directed toward gaining access to the place that is empty of concepts. One may ask whether this place, if we can even call it a place, is essential or unessential. The problem inherent in this question is that as soon as we ask it we are back in the realm of conceptual duality and not in the "unpatterned" space that is free of concepts. Buddhists agree with postmodernists that the world of language and concepts is constructed and unessential. Buddhists believe there is a consciousness that goes beyond concepts. . . .

In asserting that there is an existence before and beyond concepts, Buddhism asserts that the individual, as distinguished from the individual's identity or self, "cannot be reduced to a 'site of competing discourses,' as it often is in feminist and other postmodern descriptions."[12]

. . .

Because Buddhism accepts the self as multiple and at times conflicting or contradictory, it "departs from the urge to master, override, rein in, or otherwise manipulate the self."[13] Thus, it does not seek to construct a unitary, coherent sense of self. As Klein notes, this practice "of being nonjudgmental toward oneself has special significance in a culture where self-hatred is an issue."[14] By being nonjudgmental, Buddhism also moves beyond the psychic tension that psychoanalysis believes is the source of projecting negative traits onto the "other." "When all the voices of the self are fully owned, they are less likely to be projected onto others. In this way, self-acceptance translates into acceptance of the other."[15] Thus, Buddhism requires, in establishing relations with oneself, that the mindful person "[have] models of self-engagement that do not denigrate or otherwise oppress."[16]

IV. Reconstituting the Legal Subject and the Law

. . .

It is not enough to look at how categories intersect to create a sense of self. We must also examine how the categories themselves are created and maintained. . . . They can and should be contested, though—especially when they implicate privilege and subordination. This approach affects how we think about intersectionality in two ways. . . .

B. The Multiple Self and the Law

There are a number of ways that acceptance of a fractured, multiple, and intersectional self would change the way we think about the law. The issue of agency and choice would clearly be altered by moving away from the unitary self.

. . .

The notion of the multiple self and the way we think about agency clearly implicates the validity of the intent standard used to evaluate claims of racial discrimination. This standard is . . . clearly inapposite in the context of racism because it fundamentally mischaracterizes the way that racism functions within the individual and within society. Under current jurisprudence, the claim that someone intended to discriminate on the basis of race is interpreted as the assertion that this person engaged in the conscious thought process, "I dislike or disfavor this person because of their race, and therefore I shall behave adversely towards them."
. . .

This misconception of how the self functions has grave repercussions. It recognizes only a small subset of racist actions—those that can be proved to be a product of the conscious mind—and leaves unaddressed the vast majority of racist conduct. In our current social context, where overtly racist theories are generally discredited, the vast majority of racist actions are inevitably driven by semiconscious, subconscious, or unconscious motivations.

A related criticism of the intent standard follows from the postmodern critique of the self as socially constructed, constituted, and shaped by social context. Given the centrality of racism to the construction of both society and self (both minority and nonminority), any jurisprudential theory that assumes a static, a priori self will fail to recognize the full extent to which racist actions harm individuals and the full extent to which intersubjective discourses and structures contribute to the creation and perpetuation of these harms. . . .

Because the postmodern self is intersubjective, and thus dependent upon others for definition, oppression is a relational function: "you cannot get rid of subordination without eliminating the privilege as well."[17]
. . .

This requires recognizing that there will be strong, often unconscious, resistance to policies and actions that threaten the stability of the dominant self by threatening the stability of racial discourse. It also requires the fundamental recognition that racism pervades and structures our society and is not merely present in the aberrant minds of a few racists. Finally, the law must address the harm that racism causes by its effect upon the development of racialized identities. What this may require in the form of jurisprudence is uncertain, but our current "tort model" analysis of racism is certainly inaccurate and inadequate. We must reject the assumption that dominant groups are "innocently" marked by privilege.
. . .

NOTES

1. James Baldwin, *Here Be Dragons*, in The Price of the Ticket: Collected Nonfiction 1948–85, at 677, 690 (1985).

2. W. E. B. Du Bois, The Souls of Black Folk 8–9 (1995).

3. Zora Neale Hurston, *How It Feels to Be Colored Me*, in I Love Myself When I Am Laughing 152–53 (Alice Walker, ed., 1979).

4. Frantz Fanon, The Wretched of the Earth 250 (1963).

5. Thomas H. Ogden, Subjects of Analysis 14 (1994).

6. Charles R. Lawrence III, *The Id, the Ego and Equal Protection: Reckoning with Unconscious Racism*, 39 Stanford Law Review 317, 331 (1987).

7. Thomas H. Ogden, Subjects of Analysis 7 (1994).

8. *Id.* at 20.

9. *Id.* at 331–32.

10. *Id.* at 322–23.

11. Anne Carolyn Klein, Meeting the Great Bliss Queen: Buddhists, Feminists and the Art of Self 11 (1995).

12. *Id.* at 81.

13. *Id.* at 80.

14. *Id.*

15. *Id.* at 81.

16. *Id.* at 80.

17. Trina Grillo, *Antiessentialism and Intersectionality: Tools to Dismantle the Master's House*, 10 Berkeley Women's Law Journal 16, 18–19 (1995).

5

The Development of Feminist Consciousness among Asian American Women

Esther Ngan-Ling Chow

. . .

Gender Consciousness: Precursor of Feminist Consciousness

. . .

Being female, awareness of gender roles, and identification with other women are the major ingredients in building gender consciousness. However, it is necessary to understand the social contexts in which the gender consciousness of Asian American women has developed. Domination by men is a commonly shared oppression for Asian American women. These women have been socialized to accept their devaluation, restricted roles for women, psychological reinforcement of gender stereotypes, and a subordinate position within Asian communities as well as in the society at large. Within Asian communities, the Asian family (especially the immigrant one) is characterized by a hierarchy of authority based on sex, age, and generation, with young women at the lowest level, subordinate to father-husband-brother-son. The Asian family is also characterized by well-defined family roles, with father as breadwinner and decision-maker and mother as a compliant wife and homemaker. Although they are well protected by the family because of their filial piety and obedience, women are socially alienated from their Asian sisters. Such alienation may limit the development of gender and feminist consciousness and render Asian women politically powerless in achieving effective communication and organization, and in building bonds with other women of color and White feminists.

. . .

Awakening Feminist Consciousness

In the wake of the civil rights movement in the early 1960s and the feminist movement in the mid-1960s, Asian American women, following the leads of Black and Hispanic women, began to organize. Initially, some of the better educated Asian American women formed women's groups to meet personal and family needs and to provide services to their respective organizations and ethnic communities. These groups, few in number and with little institutionalized leadership, were traditional and informal in nature, and usually supported philanthropic concerns. Although there had been a few sporadic efforts to organize Asian American women around specific issues and concerns that did not pertain to women (e.g., the unavailability or high cost of basic food, Angel Island, the World War II internment of Japanese Americans), these attempts generally lacked continuity and support, and the organization of Asian American women was limited as a political force. Nevertheless, these activities, as stepping stones for future political activism, allowed Asian American women to cultivate their gender consciousness, to acquire leadership skills, and to increase their political visibility.

In the late 1960s and early 1970s, many Asian American women activists preferred to join forces with Asian American men in the struggle against racism and classism. Like Black and Hispanic women, some Asian American women felt that the feminist movement was not attacking racial and class problems of central concern to them. They wanted to work with groups that advocated improved conditions for people of their own racial and ethnic background or people of color, rather than groups oriented toward women's issues, even though they may have been aware of their roles and interests and even oppression as women.

As Asian American women became active in their communities, they encountered sexism. Even though many Asian American women realized that they usually occupied subservient positions in the male-dominated organizations within Asian communities, their ethnic pride and loyalty frequently kept them from public revolt. More recently, some Asian American women have recognized that these organizations have not been particularly responsive to their needs and concern[s] as women. They also protested that their intense involvement did not and will not result in equal participation as long as the traditional dominance by men and the gendered division of labor remain. Their protests have sensitized some men and have resulted in changes of attitudes and treatment of women, but other Asians, both women and men, perceived them as moving toward separatism.

Asian American women are criticized for the possible consequences of their protests: weakening of the male ego, dilution of effort and resources in Asian American communities, destruction of working relationships between Asian men and women, setbacks for the Asian American cause, cooptation into the larger society, and eventual loss of ethnic identity for Asian Americans as a whole. In short, affiliation with the feminist movement is perceived as a threat to solidarity within their own community. All of these forces have restricted the development of feminist consciousness among Asian American women and their active participation in the feminist movement.

Other barriers to political activism are the sexist stereotypes and discriminatory treatment Asian American women encounter outside their own communities. The legacy of the Chinese prostitute and the slave girl from the late nineteenth century still lingers. American involvement in Asian wars continues to perpetuate the image of Asian women as cheap whores and exotic sexpots (e.g., images such as "Suzie Wong" for Chinese women, the "geisha girl" in the Japanese teahouse, the bar girls in Vietnam). The "picture bride" image of Asian women is still very much alive, as U.S. soldiers and business men brought back Asian wives from China, Japan, Korea, and Vietnam with the expectation that they would make perfect wives and homemakers. In the last few years, a systematic importation of Asian "mail-order brides" through advertisements in newspapers and magazines has continued to exploit them as commodities, a practice that has been intensively protested by many Asian American communities. Mistreatment, desertion, divorce, and physical abuse of Asian wives or war brides have been major concerns for Asian American women. The National Committee Concerned with Asian Wives of U.S. Servicemen was specifically organized to deal with these problems.

The result of these cross-pressures is an internal dilemma of choice between racial and gender identity at the personal level and between liberation for Asian Americans (in the broader sense for all racial and ethnic minority groups) and for women at the societal level. [G. M.] Lee reported interviews with two Asian American feminists who reflected the mixed feelings of many Asian American women.[1] One woman, Sunni, said:

> We are *Asian* women. Our identity is *Asian*, and this country recognized us as such. We cannot afford the luxury of fighting our Asian counterparts. We ought to struggle for Asian liberation first, and I'm afraid that the feminist virtues will not be effective weapons. There is no sense in having only women's liberation while we continue to suffer oppression as Asians.[2]

Another woman, Aurora, took the opposite view:

> History has told us that women's liberation does not automatically come with political revolutions; Asian liberation will not necessarily bring Asian women's liberation. . . . We ought to devote our energies to feminism because a feminist revolution may well be the only revolution that can bring peace among people.[3]

When Asian American women began to recognize injustice and became aware of their own strengths as women, some developed a feminist consciousness, giving top priority to the fight against sexism and for women's rights. Others sought to establish women's caucuses within existing Asian American organizations (e.g., the Organization of Chinese American Women), while still others attempted to organize separately outside of the male-dominated Asian American organizations (e.g., the Organization of Pan American Women and the National Network of Asian and Pacific Women).
. . .

Racial Cross-Pressures

. . .

Historically, legal restrictions, as one form of racism, have been used to exploit cheap labor, to control demographic growth, and to discourage family formation by Asians in the United States. These restrictions also hindered the development of gender consciousness and political power among Asian American women. Since the mid-1850s, the legal and political receptivity to Asian American men and women has been low. U.S. immigration policies generally have emphasized imported cheap labor and discouraged the formation of family unity. Some laws specifically targeted Asian American women. As early as the 1850s, the first anti-prostitution law was passed in San Francisco, barring traffic of Chinese women and slave girls. The Naturalization Act of 1870 and the Chinese Exclusion Act of 1882 forbade the entry of wives of Chinese laborers. In 1921, a special act directed against Chinese women kept them from marrying American citizens. The Exclusion Act of 1924 did not allow alien-born wives to enter the United States, but did allow their children to come; this act separated many families until the passage of the Magnuson Act in 1943. The Cable Act of 1932 stipulated that American-born Chinese women marrying foreign-born Asians would lose their U.S. citizenship, although they could regain it later through naturalization. The passage of anti-miscegenation laws (e.g., the California Anti-Miscegenation Law in 1906), which were ruled unconstitutional by the U.S. Supreme Court in 1967, barred marriage between Whites and "Mongolians" and laborers of Asian origins, making it impossible for Asians to find mates in this country. As a result, bachelor communities consisting mainly of single Asian men became characteristic of many Asian groups, especially the Chinese.

In spite of political pressures, repressive immigration laws, and restrictive and discouraging economic hardships, a few Asian women did come to the United States. Chinese women came in the 1850s, followed by Japanese women in the late 1890s and Filipino and Korean women in the early part of the twentieth century. These women were "picture brides," merchant wives, domestics, laborers, and prostitutes. In the popular literature, they were generally portrayed as degraded creatures, cheap commodities, and sex objects who took jobs from Whites, spread disease and vice, and corrupted the young. Descriptions of their sexist, racist, and economically deprived living conditions reveal a personal and private resistance marked by passive acceptance, suppression of feelings, silent protest, withdrawal, self-sacrifice, and hard work.

The repressive immigration laws were repealed after World War II, and the number of Asian families immigrating to the United States increased. By 1980, the sex ratio of this racial and ethnic group was balanced for the first time in U.S. history. Women now constitute half of the Asian American population. Although many of the repressive laws that conspired to bar the sociopolitical participation of Asian American men and women have changed, the long-term effects of culture, socioeconomic, and political exploitation and oppression are still deeply felt, and there are new forms of discrimination and deprivation. The passage of the Immigration Reform and Control Act of 1986, setting restricted immigration quotas for family members of Asian Americans and Hispanic Americans, recalls earlier repressive legislation. As long as legal circumstances restrict the immigration of the mothers, daughters, and sisters of the Asian American women in the United States, the full development of their gender and feminist consciousness will be hampered.

. . .

Although some degree of acceptance of Asian American women and of women of color by certain segments of the White feminist movement has occurred, many problems remain. Ideological acceptance does not necessarily lead to full structural receptivity. Conscious and rigorous efforts to recruit Asian American women and other women of color openly, to treat them as core groups in the movement, and to incorporate them in the organizational policy and decision-making levels have not been made by White feminist organizations. Marynick Palmer points out that ethnocentrism is a major reason that feminist organizations treat race and class as secondary and are not fully accepting women of color.[4] Hooks is critical of a feminist movement based on the White women who live at the center and whose perspectives rarely include knowledge and awareness of the lives of women and men who live at the margin.[5] Thornton Dill states, "Political expediency drove white feminists to accept principles that were directly opposed to the survival and well-being of Blacks in order to seek to achieve more limited advances for women."[6] The same is true for Asian American women.

Inconsistencies between attitudes and behavior of White women are highly evident in the "token" membership of minority women in some feminist organizations, which indicates simply a superficial invitation to join. For women of color, the frustrations of not being included in the "White women's system" run parallel to the experiences of White women who try to break into the "old boy's network." Consequently, Asian American women feel more comfortable making allies with other women of color (e.g., the National Institute for Women of Color) than with their White counterparts. Although there are interethnic problems among Asian American women and between them and other women of color, social bonding and group allegiance are much more readily established, and common issues are more easily shared on the basis of race and ethnicity. A separate movement for women of color may be a viable alternative for the personal development of Asian American women and other women of color and for their struggle for liberation and social equality.

Economic Conditions and Class Cleavages

Economic exploitation and class cleavages also account for the limited development of feminist consciousness and political activism among Asian American women. . . .

Asian American women have lived in racially segregated internal colonies such as Chinatown, Little Tokyo, and Little Saigon. They have experienced social isolation, ghettoization, poverty, and limited opportunities for personal growth and emancipation. Limited resources and lack of access to information, transportation, and social services have made them rely on their families for support and protection. They must also work to maintain their families financially. The labor force participation of Asian American women is much higher than that of White and Black women, but many of them have worked in the secondary labor market sector, which is characterized by long working hours, low pay, and low prestige. Although their educational levels are relatively high, 70 percent are concentrated in clerical, service, and blue-collar work, and are facing tremendous underemployment.

Cultural values that emphasize hard work and that place a stigma on idleness prevent Asian American women from not working and going on welfare. Asian American households generally have a greater number of multiple breadwinners per family than the general U.S. population. The financial burdens on many Asian American women pressure them to continue struggling for economic survival for the good of their families, sacrificing their own interests, and suppressing their feelings and frustrations even in the face of gender and racial discrimination. They have little time to examine the implications of their economic situations; they do not fully understand the dynamics of class position; and they are not likely to challenge the existing power structure.

How economic and class conditions hinder feminist consciousness and political activism is evident for Chinese working-class women living in Chinatowns in many cities. Subject to the impact of internal colonization, their work world is an ethnic labor market that offers few good jobs, low pay, long hours, limited job advancement, and relative isolation from the larger society.

. . .

Because race and ethnicity cut across classes and provide a base for political identification, economic barriers are much easier to overcome among Asian American women than between them and White women. Nevertheless, there is still a great need to address issues concerning working-class Asian American women and to mobilize them to join feminist efforts.

Cultural Factors and Barriers

Asiatic and U.S. cultures alike tend to relegate women to subordinate status and to work in a gendered division of labor. Although Asiatic values emphasizing education, achievement, and diligence no doubt have accounted for the high aspirations and achievements of some Asian American women, certain Asiatic values, especially when they are in conflict with American ideas, have discouraged Asian women from actively participating in the feminist movement. Adherence to Asiatic values of obedience, familial interest, fatalism, and self-control may foster submissiveness, passivity, pessimism, timidness, inhibition, and adaptiveness, rather than rebelliousness or political activism. Acceptance of the American values of independence, individualism, mastery of one's environment through change, and self-expression may generate self-interest, aggressiveness, initiative, and expressive spontaneity that tend to encourage political activism; but these values are, to a large extent, incompatible with the upbringing of Asian American women.

Although cultural barriers seem to pose a greater internal problem for Asian American women, lack of knowledge and understanding of the cultural and language problems faced by Asian American women widens the gap between them and White women. Further effort to enhance cultural awareness and understanding is needed in order for women of all kinds to develop a transcendent consciousness, a more inclusive experience of sisterhood.

. . .

NOTES

1. G. M. Lee, *One Sisterhood*, in Asian Women, edited by Editorial Staff, Berkeley, CA: University of California Press.

2. *Id.* at 119.

3. *Id.*

4. P. Marynick Palmer, *White Women/Black Women: The Dualism of Female Identity and Experience in the United States*, 9 Feminist Studies 152 (1983).

5. b. hooks, Feminist Theory: From Margin to Center, Boston: South End Press (1984).

6. B. Thornton Dill, *Race, Class, and Gender: Prospects for an All-Inclusive Sisterhood*, 9 Feminist Studies 131, 131 (1983).

6

At the Intersection of Gender and Sexual Orientation: Toward Lesbian Jurisprudence

Mary Eaton

I. Introduction

. . .

[T]he question whether there is a need or desire for a specifically lesbian jurisprudence has scarcely been posed, let alone answered. Instead, the bulk of extant legal literature regarding lesbians and our/their status under law has not assumed lesbian specificity or, consequently, the necessity or utility of a jurisprudence of and for us/them. . . . Lesbians most often find themselves grouped somewhat indiscriminately with other "others" under legal-theoretical paradigms of various and often discordant sorts. Primarily, lesbians have been regarded as a species of the larger genus "homosexuals" or "sexual minorities," a genus which certainly includes gay men, but sometimes also includes bisexuals, and other sexual miscreants. Sexual orientation, according to this thesis, is the concept that best captures the characteristic which defines the group. Less common is the suggestion that lesbian oppression is more accurately conceptualized as a brand of gender oppression and therefore that gender, rather than sexual orientation, would be the better rubric under which the rights of lesbians should be conceptualized and advanced. The constituency defined by "gender" and for whom guarantees against gender-based discrimination should protect, however, has been a matter of some dispute. There is, of course, a consensus that women constitute part of the gender underclass, but there has been some disagreement as to whether gay males and the discrimination they face should likewise be regarded as "gendered."

It is a question of substantial importance whether any of these theories of lesbian inequality fully captures the character, function, and extent of lesbian oppression. Politically, sorting out the relationships between various systems of domination may suggest the value, necessity, nature, and form of coalition possibilities in strategizing and lobbying for change. As a legal matter, elucidating the interconnections between gender and sexual orientation may determine litigation strategies in the pursuit of equality and other rights. Theoretically, determining which of the three models is best, in what circumstances, and why, may signal a need to reject or adapt existing explanatory accounts of oppression. . . .

Like feminist legal thought, current writing on the legal position of lesbians also tends to make global assumptions about the homogeneity and essentiality of identity. To varying degrees, it exhibits a tendency to presuppose both the existence and transcendental meaningfulness of certain identity categories (like lesbian, gay, heterosexual, homosexual, man, and woman) and uniformity of experience within them. As is the case with feminist jurisprudence, these criticisms concerning identity and difference have yet to be fully integrated into the lesbian, sexual orientation, and gender approaches now being advocated. Hence, while an original and widely shared assumption of the rightful place for a jurisprudence of "women" distinguishes the legal thought of feminists from that of those concerned with lesbians, these two strains of legal thinking do share a certain commonality inasmuch as neither one of them has fully come to grips with the pitfalls of identity-based theorizing and the elision of racial and other differences that often attend it. . . .

[A]ny attempt to lay out a full-blown theory of lesbian jurisprudence is, at least at this stage, not only premature, but also doomed to obfuscate a set of identificatory relations that is very complex and cannot be anticipated in advance. Although I realize it will disappoint some, for this reason I make no effort to say what lesbian jurisprudence "is." Insofar as any general statement concerning lesbian jurisprudence is presently possible, my analysis leads me to the somewhat uncomfortable but not wholly pessimistic conclusion that the answer to the question whether there is, can, or should be a lesbian jurisprudence is, "[I]t depends."

A. Against the Male Flood: The Feminist Account of Lesbian Domination

The idea that lesbians experience subordination in a way that is fundamentally tied to, indeed indistinguishable from, larger patterns of the oppression of women in general has a long pedigree. However, history also testifies to the fact that lesbian attempts to link our/their oppression to theories of gender domination were not always well received by heterosexual feminists. . . .

Typically, arguments advanced in support of including lesbians or lesbianism within feminist theorizing have been of two types, the first of which has a distinctly biologistic drift. Feminism distinguished itself from other theoretical traditions in two important ways. Most obviously, through its specific concern with the status of women, feminism distanced itself from humanism, Marxism, and a whole variety of other philosophical movements within which the position of women was either overtly discounted or subsumed within the broader category of "human beings." In addition, feminism is methodologically distinct insofar as it formulated its substantive conclusions regarding the status of women by listening to and believing the words of women themselves. What makes feminism, in other words, is that it is specifically concerned with and derived from female reality. Lesbians are, of course, female, and presumptively there is no basis for not heeding, much less for excluding, their accounts of their own lives. What is more, were feminists to remain true to feminism's much touted methodology of building theory out of women's—all women's—lived experience, they would not make the error of conceiving of lesbians as a group for whom sexual orientation, rather than gender, defined their experience and the meaning they attached to it. By definition, then, if feminist theory fails to attend to lesbian reality, that theory is incomplete and perhaps not even feminist.

Not every attempt to articulate feminism's theoretical responsibility to lesbians had the distinctly biologistic thrust inherent in the claim that lesbians had been neglected as a result of feminism's failure to remain loyal to its own methodological claims. Pat Cain, for example, attempts to link the normative status of heterosexuality with the subordination of women. Since heterosexuality is a core element of "male-centered reality," lesbianism is ontologically opposed to male domination. To the extent that feminist legal theory understands the critique of male hegemony to be an essential part of its enterprise, feminism ought not and cannot, if it is at all to succeed in that endeavor, afford to ignore the experience of lesbians. In a similar vein, Diana Majury maintains that lesbian discrimination is sex discrimination because lesbians challenge "dominant understandings and meanings of gender."

Both the first, biologisitic, and this second, more social constructionist, claim exclude gay men from the gender underclass, and therefore from the constituency to which they argue feminism must be held accountable. . . .

B. Homosexuals Are Women Too: Sexual Orientation Discrimination as Sex Discrimination

For many years now, the dominant strain in legal scholarship concerning the equality rights of lesbians and gays has focused on the project of securing for them protection against sexual orientation discrimination. . . . [I]n these appeals for the statutory recognition of the rights of homosexuals little or no attention has been directed to the series of theoretical moves necessary to sustain them. That is to say, implied in such claims is the notion that a class called "homosexuals" exists, that they are defined as such by virtue of their "sexual orientation," and it is this characteristic that forms the basis of their oppression. Reference to gender and other differences among "homosexuals" is rare.

. . .

[B]ecause sexual orientation has attracted so little statutory recognition, attempts have been made to ground lesbian and gay anti-discrimination rights in the guarantees of sex equality. Originally the argument advanced took a simple "but for" form and was quite literalist in its thrust. If heterosexual women were legally permitted to couple or engage in sexual relations with men, but homosexual men were not, only the biological sex of the partner could account for the difference in treatment between the two groups.

The fact that this line of reasoning never once succeeded in the courts perhaps accounts for the development of a more sophisticated elaboration of the relationship between discrimination against lesbians and gays and sex discrimination.

Presently, the argument takes the following form. The courts have recognized that the regulation of female gender role conformity constitutes sex discrimination against heterosexual women. It is illegal, for instance, to fire or fail to promote a woman because she appears "too macho" or insufficiently feminine. If cast in more general terms, the guarantee against sex discrimination could be taken to mean that no one can be legally sanctioned for failing or refusing to abide by gender role norms. Given that discrimination against lesbians and gays is rooted in the notion that they reject or are incapable of respecting gender expectations, like heterosexual women, homosexuals should also be protected under guarantees of sex equality.

Interestingly, the argument linking the oppression of lesbians and gays to the transgression of gender role norms bears a striking resemblance to the lesbian feminist claim that lesbian oppression is intimately connected with the subordination of women under conditions of male supremacy. Under the system of heterosexism, the two genders, "male" and "female," are constructed as polar opposites that complement one another. . . . The products of this system of gender differentiation do not enjoy equal social, political or legal status. Rather, "woman" and her femininity and "man" and his masculinity are arranged in relation to one another such that maleness occupies a superior and dominant position. What distinguishes the gay sex role thesis from the lesbian one is its claim that under the gender system gay men are, in effect, "women" too. That gay men are feminized through the stereotype of the "sissy" is the most obvious evidence of the interconnection between sexual identity and gender. More generally, however, the regime of gender differentiation and hierarchization requires the normalization of heterosexuality to sustain itself. Because the naturalization of the attraction between men and women is integral to the gender system and its devaluation of females and the feminine, discrimination against homosexuals (male and female alike) is thus inextricably bound with the subordination of women.

C. At the Intersection of Gender and Sexual Orientation: Lesbian Oppression as Its Own Thing

The idea that lesbians have their own set of unique interests and concerns, distinct from both those of heterosexual women and gay men, has a certain intuitive appeal and in fact has long been a part of lesbian political culture. Through the pioneering effort of Ruthann Robson, a lesbian-centered approach to law has at last made its way into the legal literature.

. . .

Whereas the essential exercise and goal of feminism is comparing women to men and achieving equality with them on their terms, the method and aim of lesbian jurisprudence is otherwise: "If lesbians are women-identified women, then measurements are not relative to men; men's measurements are in some sense irrelevant."[1] Because legal writing on gay rights tends to marginalize lesbians and lesbianism in a similar way, lesbian jurisprudence is not coextensive with it either.

Lesbian jurisprudence thus implicates "the intersection between realities of gender and sexual orientation, between ideologies of feminism and gay rights."[2]

To the extent that Robson has elaborated on lesbian jurisprudence more affirmatively, it would appear that its basic purpose is to locate lesbians at the center of its analysis. Lesbian legal theory is thus a way of examining laws affecting lesbians from both individualistic and communitarian lesbian perspectives. It respects the variety in lesbian tradition, and it will not discount the claims of lesbian sadomasochists any more than it will refuse to credit lesbian separatism. Such a jurisprudence appreciates lesbian connection in all its manifestations, healthful or harmful. Lesbian legal theory will not emphasize elements of lesbian identity or consciousness over others. It is cognizant of the inevitability of law's influence, but will not be knowingly complicit in the manufacture of law's empire. Lesbian jurisprudence will not accept lesbian invisibility.

. . .

II. Trouble Within: The Seeming Limits of Grand Theory

Each of the above three theories of lesbian inequality has a certain appeal. . . . The fact that each account has its attractions in itself would tend to suggest that none of them standing alone can adequately account for lesbian inequality in all its dimensions. Despite this, each of these theories tends to slide into reductiveness by attempting to install itself as a complete explanation and a full account. . . . [T]he claim to comprehensiveness is not borne out; even within the borders of each, theories of gender, of sexual orientation, and indeed of lesbian specificity fail to realize their own aspirations and undercut their own theoretical ambitions by making sweeping claims that simply do not survive critical examination. To put matters somewhat bluntly, they are internally inconsistent on their own terms. . . .

III. Toward Lesbian Jurisprudence: Plotting the Intersection of Gender and Sexual Orientation

. . .

[T]he point of failure of all three seems to reside in their assumption of community of interest among various constituencies defined as such in identity terms. This suggests that the categories used in this discourse (women, lesbians, gays, men, gender, sexual orientation) are so thoroughly bereft of any transcendent social meaning that they cannot usefully serve as the basis for good theory and that the difficulties with the notion of identity more generally should simply be admitted. Perhaps, as has been feared, no single theoretical paradigm can or should attempt to explain the multifarious and complex fashion in which lesbian or other sorts of identity-based oppressions are manifested, and, to the extent "grand theory" receives any endorsement, it can only be a theory of the most general and aparticularized kind.

If so, the better course of action may well be to make the break with identity and begin to forge a new politic and analytic framework premised upon and constructed out of more generalized notions of social power.

. . .

Because much of the commentary and debate about interacting oppressions has focused almost exclusively on the connections between race and gender domination, the concepts which have emerged from this body of work may not transpose well to the sexual orientation context, particularly given the substantive differences in the history, practice, and ideology of racism and heterosexism/homophobia in contemporary America. Indeed, there is a disturbing tendency among lesbian and gay commentators to draw imperfect and troublesome analogies between the oppression of African Americans and lesbians and gays, the point of which appears to be to secure lesbian and gay rights by piggybacking on the presupposed and overrated legal gains made by communities of color. My project is not to analogize from the experience of women of color or to draw equivalences between race- and sexuality-based oppressions. . . . [M]y aim is to explore the promise of the analytic approach pioneered by women of color for theorizing lesbian legal (in)equality and its remedies.

. . . The real promise of the race and gender scholarship . . . does not reside in its now somewhat quotidian insight that single-headed theories typically fall far short of explaining the dynamics of subordination. Its recognition that race sometimes makes an intersectional difference, at other times a compound one, and at other times still perhaps no difference at all, suggests more profoundly that the nature of the interaction between various oppressions is a complex and shifting one. If so, our theoretical options need not be limited to either using or rejecting identity-based analyses in total, but include as well the possibility that we might usefully track and theorize the different ways in which multiple identities come to be configured together.[3] At the beginning of this essay, I indicated that "[I]t depends" is perhaps the best or only answer presently possible to the question of whether there is or ought to be a lesbian jurisprudence. Although I do believe that my analysis compels this conclusion, I should admit that it causes me some discomfort. The notion that lesbians are invisible has come to play a signal role in lesbian theory, and not just because it makes for good political rhetoric or because it has a nice metaphorical ring. In a very real way, lesbians simply do not exist because the idea that women could or would want to love other women is culturally unintelligible. In an equally tangible way, lesbians do not exist because their political interests have been systematically subordinated to those of the relatively more privileged members of the groups with whom they have found a natural allegiance, namely, gay men and heterosexual women. Anyone familiar with these "truths" of lesbian existence, anyone aware that lesbianism is substantially marked by symbolic erasure and political marginalization, would be more than a little uneasy with the suggestion that the important question of whether we need a jurisprudence of and for lesbians would provoke such a tepid and potentially dangerous reply. "It depends" is the kind of answer that is clearly amenable to misuse, and I am aware that by responding this way, I run the risk not only of obfuscating but of perpetuating the problem of lesbian invisibility. . . . As I read them, theorists engaging the interaction of race and gender make the crucial and courageous point that however much our identities are important to us, we must move beyond the notion that they always already mark us as different and begin to probe more searchingly the question of difference and the difference it makes. If there is a lesson in this for lesbians, it is that the desire to make lesbians visible cannot substitute for rigorous analysis of the circumstances in which our lesbianism makes a difference, of what sort, and why. Accordingly, by "it depends" I mean not that the efficacy of lesbian jurisprudence, as a general proposition, is unclear, but that the need for a specifically lesbian jurisprudential prototype may sometimes exist and sometimes not. Sorting out the circumstances in which, and the reasons why, a lesbian-centered account is necessary should, I suggest, be our project. We need to ask, for example, why it is that our lesbianism sometimes differentiates us from heterosexual women and/or gay men, but sometimes suggests a productive alliance with either or both of them. In those circumstances where there does appear to be a lesbian difference, what sort of difference does lesbianism make? Is it intersectional? Additive? Perhaps even negative? Is there a pattern in the sorts of relationships we observe in particular contexts? Could we say, for instance, that sexual identity makes a difference with respect to sexual relations but not, or not in the same way, to economic ones? To answer the question of whether there can or should be a lesbian jurisprudence with "it depends" should not be taken to mean that we cannot or will not decide, but signals instead our determination to embrace and grapple with the reality of our own identificatory contingency.

NOTES

1. Ruthann Robson, *Lesbian Jurisprudence*, 8 Law and Inequality Journal 443, 448 (1990).

2. Ruthann Robson, *Lifting Belly: Privacy, Sexuality and Lesbianism*, 12 Women's Rights Legal Reporter 177, 177 (1990).

3. My approach suffers from one significant limitation. Because the bulk of lesbian legal literature takes as its referent either gender or sexual orientation or both in arguing the similarity or distinctiveness of lesbian inequality, I have chosen to explore the implications for lesbians by the interaction of systemic sexism and heterosexism. In dealing with the unenvisioned complexities of these dual systems, I do not fully engage the interaction of lesbian inequality with other forms of systemic oppression, such as racism, classism, or ableism. Plainly, the experience of lesbians whose lives are also constructed through the force of such other forms of domination must inform lesbian equality theory. Although I have not dealt with them specifically, it is my sense that the method for developing lesbian jurisprudence I am advocating not only does not foreclose inquiry into the difference that differences of race, class, ability, and the like make to lesbian identity, but places such issues at the center of the analysis.

7

The LatIndia and *Mestizajes*:
Of Cultures, Conquests, and LatCritical Feminism

Berta Esperanza Hernández-Truyol

. . .

I. Introduction

. . .

Critical Race Feminism (CRF) is a movement committed to exploring the reality of the lives of women of color in order to end their subordination and to ensure their full citizenship in all geographies. LatCrit is a closely related theoretical movement premised on an anti-subordination agenda and committed to building community among all peoples and to interrogating the politics of identity through the necessarily pan-ethnic lens of Latinas/os.

Combined, a LatCritical Race Feminist (LCRF) project that embraces our hybridity facilitates an interrogation of the present order, its history and varied power locations, and their impact on socio-economic and psycho-social consequences. LCRF is grounded on the richness endemic to the multiplicity, similarities, and disparateness of our histories. It knows our daily existence within our own, unfamiliar, and foreign communities. Thus, LCRF is a safe, though not quiet, anchor from which to deploy the interrogation of the multiple meanings of feminism, human rights, personhood, and identity. Such a project allows a reconstruction of society that is committed to a principle of social justice, developed from and embracing of all aspects of our identities.

Women of color are world travelers who routinely trespass border crossings across *fronteras* of race, sex, class, ethnicity, nationality, color, sexuality, and language. To locate or identify our forebears we must travel this intricate, elaborate, and tangled expanse. In the process, we need *nuevas teorias* that recognize our hybridity/multidimensionality. As an ideology, LCRF offers an appropriate location from which to launch our search for our mothers.

One of LCRF's tools integral to this exploration is its deconstructive function. It provides a methodology to debunk the majority's "liberal" social, political, economic, historic[al], and legal construction of universal truth, singular reality, and

history. The subjective (and narrow) majoritarian fabrications have become embedded as objective truths in the discursive dominance of the "master narrative."
This master narrative predefines and preordains—effectively *constitutes*—norma-
tivity, which becomes the assumed proper content and context of all of our world
traveling.

However, the textbook versions of history and politics, conquest and colonization, discovery and decimation, war and peace, seduction and surrender, male and
female, sexuality and gender, spirituality and religion, domination and inequality,
civilization and savagery are not all of our truths. The reality of women of color,
because of their multidimensionality—their multiple and varied deviations from the
norm—is worlds apart—worlds of sex, race, ethnicity, class, language, sexuality—
from the designated normative reality. In order to become full citizens and engage
in LatCritical race feminist practice, we must discover, reveal, define, and own our
contexts, our stories. We must give birth to, re/member, and preserve our histories,
experiences, passions, fears, and lived realities.

We can successfully dismantle the master narrative and offer constructive alter-
ations only if we learn about and embrace all of our locations—our hybridity. All
women, and in particular women of color, have to understand, peacefully and pro-
ductively negotiate the immense differences, and bridge the substantial gulfs, between and among us—our histories, our cultures, our experiences. The task for
LatCritical race feminists is to build coalitions in which those differences enrich
rather than impoverish our work, unite rather than tear apart our communities. In
this difficult anti-subordination, coalition-building project it is useful to remember
that many of us have shared, though not identical, experiences. We routinely journey through borderlands of color, race, ethnicity, sexuality, class, language, and nationality. Essentialist approaches that deny differences will weaken the undertaking, but strategic coalitions centering on commonalities and open arms willing to
embrace differences will advance the aspiration of knowing our mothers. There is
not one story, not one feminism, that can accurately re/present all of our realities,
all of our conditions, all of the time. The LCRF challenge and promise depends on
weaving narratives of multiple, non-essentialist feminisms.

To be sure, it is now beyond peradventure that the persistent single axis framework that drives *estado unidense* legal analysis is fatally flawed with respect to
women of color. In the context of women of color, this dominant paradigm is simply incoherent. We should strive to create nuevas teorias which, rather than vivisect
and atomize us, present us as we are in everyday travels, recognize our identities as
multidimensional, and acknowledge our multiple classifications as indivisible and
interdependent. These *teorias* would understand, penetrate, define, and elucidate
the context, content, and meaning of our multidimensional identities and develop,
expand, and transform constructs—legal, social, historical, familial—so that they
reflect, incorporate, and realize the world views of all women.

In locating and designing appropriate contexts for sharing our narratives, for articulating our *nuevas teorias*, it is also important that we understand our own complex and multidimensional mappings. All women of color are "others" in some
venue. Even within women-of-color gatherings we identify as *esto o aquello* (this

or that) often according to groupings that are fluid and change composition even within the architecture of a single weekend meeting. Within our women-of-color *comunidad* some of us are linguistic or "foreign-accented" others, non-citizens, differently abled, or sexual minorities—characteristics that may set us apart from the loosely cohered group. Sometimes, this otherness renders us outsiders within our *comunidades*—outsiders who cause tension and discomfort even as we strain and struggle to be inclusive, to build coalitions, to make communities. It is in the process of deconstruction and interrogation of the validity of the existing classifications, categories, and the established methodologies employed to negotiate such orderings that we may find our solid terrains for community building that include rather than exclude. It is in such ground that the seeds of LCRF as a liberation project will enable our human flourishing.

. . .

So what do we do? What can we do to know our mothers? To borrow from Robert Williams, I can get off my LatCritical race feminist *derrière* and engage in critical race feminist practice. LatCritical Race Feminism can play a tremendously energizing, exciting, and transformative role by practicing *mestizaje* in three specific ways.

First, we must recognize that the personal is political. Knowing our personal position and traditions locates us in our various communities. We must understand and embrace our hybridity, all of our interconnected selves, in order to be successful participants in an all-encompassing, anti-subordination project. If we internalize only some of our traditions and histories, and become the *conquistadores/as*, then we will practice subordination, exclusion, and colonization (even of other parts of ourselves) and distort our heritage. Those of us who roam at the margins will continue to marginalize others. If we are *Latina/o* only because of and in the image of Colón, we will continue the nasty part of his work. We will not question or challenge our relationship as Native peoples with Native peoples. We can be *Latinas/os* and *LatIndias/os* and move the world forward with solidarity in our hearts.

Second, we need to ensure that what has been secreted as the private becomes part of our public goals. We must come out as *mestizas/os* and practice *mestizaje*. We must own our hybridity and recognize we are both the colonizers and the colonized. To understand our location we must explore the meanings and consequences of these contradictions. In order to do so, we must understand all our histories. We cannot allow atomization of our selves simply because unconsciously or subconsciously we think it privileges us. Today we are complex and diverse, just like before Colon we were complex and diverse. It is only by fully utilizing the knowledges derived from such a composite that we will be able to locate ourselves "in the scheme of things." As Luz Guerra has eloquently observed: "Before Colon we were many. We were not Americans. We were not hyphenated. 'Hispanic' came with Colon. 'Latino[/a]' came with Colon. Since Colon, one common experience has been trying to 'de-colon,' decolonize, take Colon out."[1] Perhaps, however, in owning our hybridity, taking Colon out is not appropriate. Rather, we should engage in the understanding that we are partly, but only partly, Colon. We are also Native and myriad other parts.

Guerra further charges that we have done an injustice to history because our version, our story, is dependent upon the internalization of the European epistemology. Seriously considering her observation will assist in furthering the liberation project. If we indeed have internalized dominance, then we have become the ethnographers, the majoritarian outsiders through whose lens anthropology textbooks define the Trobriand islanders even to the Natives themselves. We become the foreign observer who purports to define a culture that s/he may well misunderstand and misinterpret. This self-identification with the history of our captors has distorted our lens and we must reclaim it. In order to rectify this distortion and its resultant incoherence, we must deconstruct the mythical history we live and become the architects of a new political narrative that recognizes the historical distortions and reworks the truth of all of our traditions.

Third, recognizing that the local is global and the global is local, we should search for interconnectivities as well as differences between and among our histories and traditions. Such an exploration will help elucidate the mistranslation of the past and will provide invaluable insights for the reconstructive project. There have been traps everywhere that have encouraged, dispersed, and professed the master narrative as neutral history. Peaceful people become savages; cultured people become uncivilized; deeply spiritual beings become heathens. By promoting and practicing *mestizaje*—by getting to know our mothers—the LatCritical race feminism project can expose that the claimed truths are partisan myths.

LCRF can draw upon all the rich resources available, including native histories and cultures as well as international human rights norms, to further and promote the feminist liberation project. LCRF can show through its complex web of knowledges that a single axis atomization approach is not only inappropriate but ineffectual for understanding deliciously complex beings. LCRF can insist that all of our *mestizajes* are entitled to dignity, respect, self-determination, culture, and freedom—that supremacist feelings exist and that they are wrong.

This project of knowing our mothers, of incorporating other histories, cultures, and knowledges, including Native traditions, into our lives is not going to be easy. Even the lens of feminism is one that we must reconsider; for example, many Native practices are gender-based. It may be difficult for Western and Western-trained feminists to embrace such cultural differences in roles. It forces us to question what is feminism, just like I had to question what it means to be *Latina*. However it may also make us think about gender-differentiation as something different from gender-subordination. We must broaden our horizons and move toward a *feminsmo latcritico y sin fronteras*, a LatCritical feminism without borderlands.

Finally, LCRF can reveal the true sources of some of our knowledges, customs, and practices. . . .

LCRF can help the Americas learn, embrace, and re/member these rich ideas and ideals that so well serve the anti-subordination project. Part of this project entails specifically a call for LCRF to engage the particularities of marginal identities and issues as part of its race and gender critiques. For example, it might be appropriate for LCRF to reach out to indigenous groups both within and outside the United States with the purpose of including Native voices and perspectives in critical analysis as well as the reconstruction projects. More universally, it is a call for LCRF to consciously engage itself in the practice of inclusion of polyvocality in all stages of exploration of social, economic, linguistic, legal, historical, and religious norms. Only through such exploration will we truly learn who our mothers are.

The proposal of a borderless critical movement such as LCRF is itself stressful. While it exhorts us to globalize the local and localize the global, we must try not to impose particularized universalisms or universalize particularities. The "global" aspect might invoke and evoke the thoughts of universalism which have been translations of Northern/Western hegemonic supremacy, imperialism, colonialism, and hierarchy. It is necessary to ask at the outset whether there can be a one global project that transcends our varied times, geographies, and spaces. We must design an endeavor, an enterprise, an experiment that takes us toward new feminisms—for example, away from a culture of an essentialist feminism to non-essentialist feminisms of culture. In other words, we must embrace as part of feminism's anti-gender subordination movements some projects where traditions and perhaps even traditional gender roles remain untouched, so long as the traditions are not mere pretexts for subordination.

Therefore, we must not forget to question whether physiological and psycho-social differences and the division of labor upon which traditional gender roles are based are themselves instruments of women's oppression and consequently, are merely excuses for perpetuating heteropatriarchy. If it is true that "[i]t has been shown conclusively that complementary sex roles within an otherwise competitive society means subordination of women,"[2] are gender roles intrinsically contradictory to women's self-determination, autonomy, or self-governance? If "[f]eminism makes claims for a re/balancing between women and men of the social, economic, and political power within a given society, on behalf of both sexes in the name of their common humanity, but with respect for their differences,"[3] we can easily reconcile traditional/cultural practices that attribute gender roles to individuals based on inclination rather than on biological sex. In this regard, gender role differentiation does not have sex-subordinating meanings or consequences.

Significantly, the foundations of LCRF are the interests in improving feminine geographies as part of a broad anti-subordination project. In dealing with all traditions we must ask if there are social costs attached to a continued acceptance of gender roles and expectations, as it is unlikely that, for example, we would agree to a value of continued acceptance of ethnic or racial roles and expectation[s]. However, we must do so with understanding of the meaning within the tradition. Otherwise, there can be distortions and mistranslations. We also have to be ready in all of our cultures to work against traditions that are sex-subordinating.

Critical theories have brought us far. They have created, enriched, and enlivened the discourse about the conditions of women and racial, ethnic, and religious minorities worldwide. Specifically for women, they have shattered the public/private divides by evaluating work and home, religion and government, culture and tradition, class and race. Western feminism, for example, has exposed and revealed the subordination, oppression, and second-class citizenship of women brought about by the devaluation of women's spheres, historically the personal/domestic sphere. The feminist movement has been transformational and transformed, having gone through various and varied phases, in seeking equality of and for women.

Today, we have myriad forms of feminisms, ranging from difference to dominance, from radical to relational, from pragmatic to maternal, from liberal to lesbian, from Marxist to new wave. Without adequate processes for the necessary translations we will be left with incoherence. We must attempt to reconcile all these variations into one overarching, coherent, epistemological stance under the inclusive penumbra of LCRF. These evolutions, revolutions, cohabitations, and explosions of thought have been necessary and useful to transform theory and idealism to practice and praxis—*mestizaje*. These transformations are central to learning who our mother is.

The voices today are broad and far ranging, speaking many languages. Some bring to the table ideas and concepts that others are encountering for the first time. It is possible that some ideas at first blush might appear unpronounceable, let alone translatable—conditions we do not want to engraft upon future conversations by insisting on, or being blind to, the perils of monolingualism.

V. Conclusion

There is a wealth of information to learn in the process of identifying our mothers. At this stage it is necessary to entertain the growth of critical theories that are guided by a series of principles, goals, and ideals of personhood with the dignity of the human spirit as the driving force. These necessarily include autonomy, self-reliance, self-determination, and self-governance. The master narrative that exalts competition over cooperation, the rich over the poor, men over women, and the white over the colored, should be exposed as a fabrication of few that has served to subordinate many.

The benefits of such reconstruction promise to be great. In particular, remembering Native histories and traditions to design the anti-gender subordination project is full of promise. As Professor Paula Gunn Allen has observed,

> The traditional Indians' view can have a significant impact if it is expanded to mean that the sources of social, political, and philosophical thought in the Americas not only should be recognized and honored by Native Americans but should be embraced by American society. If American society judiciously modeled the traditions of the various Native Nations, the place of women in society would become central, the distribution of goods and power would be egalitarian, the elderly would be respected, honored, and protected as a primary social and cultural resource, the ideals of physical beauty would be considerably enlarged. . . . Additionally, the destruction of the biota, the life sphere, and the natural resources of the planet would be curtailed, and the spiritual nature of human and nonhuman life would become a primary organizing

principle of human society. And if the traditional tribal systems that are emulated include pacifist ones, war would cease to be a major method of human problem solving.[4]

One location of indigenous knowledge from which this anti-subordination movement may greatly benefit is the traditional Native acceptance of multiple genders which likely includes an acceptance of many non-traditional gender and sexual expressions. Imagine the possibilities had *Latinas/os* (and others) embraced the Native approach rather than the conqueror's approach. Pursuant to the latter, *Latinas* are to act in the *marianista* model—be self-effacing, self-sacrificing, virginal, and pure. Almost the worst thing the Latina can be is a whore. And I say almost because as the popular saying *"mejor puta que pata"*—better whore than dyke—tells us there is one worse sin: lesbianism. The conqueror's vision condemns, marginalizes, and subordinates sexual minorities. The Native story lies in stark contrast. As Rigoberta Menchú observed,

> Entre nosotros indigenas, no hacemos distincion entre el homosexual o el que no es homosexual, porque eso ya surge cuando uno baja a otros lugares. No hay tanto rechazo por un homosexual como hay entre los ladinos que es algo que no pueden mirar. Lo bueno entre nosotros es que todo lo consideramos parte de la naturaleza.[5]

Imagine the possibilities if instead of viewing women as chattel, weak, and inferior they were considered valuable, strong, and equal. If instead of viewing sexual minorities as sinful, resulting in ostracism from family, friends, and society, they were respected, powerful, and productive members of a clan and their families. Now think of LCRF embracing such principles, and imagine the value of knowing our mothers, and the possibilities of practicing *mestizaje*.

NOTES

1. Luz Guerra, *LaCrit y La Des-Colonizacion Nuestra: Taking Colón Out*, 19 Chicano[/A]-Latino[/A] Law Review 351, 355 (1998).

2. Karen Offen, *Defining Feminism: A Comparative Historical Approach*, 14 Signs 119, 153 (1988) (quoting Renate Bridenthal, Commentary at the Berkshire Conference, "The History of Women," Bryn Mawr College [June 1976]).

3. *Id.* at 151.

4. Paula Gunn Allen, The Sacred Hoop 210–211 (1986).

5. Rigoberta Menchú, Me Llamo Rigoberta Menchú y Así Me Nació La Conciencia 7–8, 12 (Elisabeth Burgos, ed., 1983). Menchú emphasizes:

> among us [N]atives we don't distinguish between the homosexual and the non-homosexual: that happens when we leave our communities. We do not reject the homosexuals as [L]atinos do, which is something they can't bear us to see. The good thing among us [N]atives is that we consider every part of [N]ature.

8

White Privilege and Male Privilege: A Personal Account of Coming To See Correspondences through Work in Women's Studies

Peggy McIntosh

Through work to bring materials and perspectives from Women's Studies into the rest of the curriculum, I have often noticed men's unwillingness to grant that they are overprivileged in the curriculum, even though they may grant that women are disadvantaged. Denials that amount to taboos surround the subject of advantages that men gain from women's disadvantages. These denials protect male privilege from being fully recognized, acknowledged, lessened, or ended.

Thinking through unacknowledged male privilege as a phenomenon with a life of its own, I realized that since hierarchies in our society are interlocking, there was most likely a phenomenon of white privilege that was similarly denied and protected, but alive and real in its effects. As a white person, I realized I had been taught about racism as something that puts others at a disadvantage, but had been taught not to see one of its corollary aspects, white privilege, which puts me at an advantage.

I think whites are carefully taught not to recognize white privilege, as males are taught not to recognize male privilege. So I have begun in an untutored way to ask what it is like to have white privilege. This paper is a partial record of my personal observations and not a scholarly analysis. It is based on my daily experiences within my particular circumstances.

I have come to see white privilege as an invisible package of unearned assets that I can count on cashing in each day, but about which I was "meant" to remain oblivious. White privilege is like an invisible weightless knapsack of special provisions, assurances, tools, maps, guides, codebooks, passports, visas, clothes, compass, emergency gear, and blank checks.

Since I have had trouble facing white privilege, and describing its results in my life, I saw parallels here with men's reluctance to acknowledge male privilege. Only rarely will a man go beyond acknowledging that women are disadvantaged to acknowledging that men have unearned advantage, or that unearned privilege has not been good for men's development as human beings, or for society's development, or that privilege systems might ever be challenged and changed.

I will review here several types or layers of denial that I see at work protecting, and preventing awareness about, entrenched male privilege. Then I will draw parallels, from my own experience, with the denials that veil the facts of white privilege. Finally, I will list forty-six ordinary and daily ways in which I experience having white privilege, by contrast with my African American colleagues in the same building. This list is not intended to be generalizable. Others can make their own lists from within their own life circumstances.

Writing this paper has been difficult, despite warm receptions for the talks on which it is based.[1] For describing white privilege makes one newly accountable. As we in Women's Studies work reveal male privilege and ask men to give up some of their power, so one who writes about having white privilege must ask, "Having described it, what will I do to lessen or end it?"

The denial of men's overprivileged state takes many forms in discussions of curriculum change work. Some claim that men must be central in the curriculum because they have done most of what is important or distinctive in life or in civilization. Some recognize sexism in the curriculum but deny that it makes male students seem unduly important in life. Others agree that certain individual thinkers are male oriented but deny that there is any systemic tendency in disciplinary frameworks or epistemology to overempower men as a group. Those men who do grant that male privilege takes institutionalized and embedded forms are still likely to deny that male hegemony has opened doors for them personally. Virtually all men deny that male overreward alone can explain men's centrality in all the inner sanctums of our most powerful institutions. Moreover, those few who will acknowledge that male privilege systems have overempowered them usually end up doubting that we could dismantle these privilege systems. They may say they will work to improve women's status, in the society or in the university, but they can't or won't support the idea of lessening men's. In curricular terms, this is the point at which they say that they regret they cannot use any of the interesting new scholarship on women because the syllabus is full. When the talk turns to giving men less cultural room, even the most thoughtful and fair-minded of the men I know will tend to reflect, or fall back on, conservative assumptions about the inevitability of present gender relations and distributions of power, calling on precedent or sociobiology and psychobiology to demonstrate that male domination is natural and follows inevitably from evolutionary pressures. Other resort to arguments from "experience" or religion or social responsibility or wishing and dreaming.

After I realized, through faculty development work in Women's Studies, the extent to which men work from a base of unacknowledged privilege, I understood that much of their oppressiveness was unconscious. Then I remembered the frequent charges from women of color that white women whom they encounter are oppressive. I began to understand why we are justly seen as oppressive, even when we don't see ourselves that way. At the very least, obliviousness of one's privileged state can make a person or group irritating to be with. I began to count the ways in which I enjoy unearned skin privilege and have been conditioned into oblivion about its existence, unable to see that it put me "ahead" in any way, or put my people ahead, overrewarding us and yet also paradoxically damaging us, or that it could or should be changed.

My schooling gave me no training in seeing myself as an oppressor, as an unfairly advantaged person, or as a participant in a damaged culture. I was taught to see myself as an individual whose moral state depended on her individual moral will. At school, we were not taught about slavery in any depth; we were not taught to see slaveholders as damaged people. Slaves were seen as the only group at risk of being dehumanized. My schooling followed the pattern which Elizabeth Minnich has pointed out: whites are taught to think of their lives as morally neutral, normative, and average, and also ideal, so that when we work to benefit others, this is seen as work that will allow "them" to be more like "us." I think many of us know how obnoxious this attitude can be in men.

After frustration with men who would not recognize male privilege, I decided to try to work on myself at least by identifying some of the daily effects of white privilege in my life. It is crude work, at this state, but I will give here a list of special circumstances and conditions I experience that I did not earn but that I have been made to feel are mine by birth, by citizenship, and by virtue of being a conscientious law-abiding "normal" person of goodwill. I have chosen those conditions that I think in my case *attach somewhat more to skin-color privilege* than to class, religion, ethnic status, or geographical location, though these other privileging factors are intricately intertwined. As far as I can see, my Afro-American co-workers, friends, and acquaintances with whom I come into daily or frequent contact in this particular time, place, and line of work cannot count on most of these conditions.

1. I can, if I wish, arrange to be in the company of people of my race most of the time.
2. I can avoid spending time with people whom I was trained to mistrust and who have learned to mistrust my kind or me.
3. If I should need to move, I can be pretty sure of renting or purchasing housing in an area which I can afford and in which I would want to live.
4. I can be reasonably sure that my neighbors in such a location will be neutral or pleasant to me.
5. I can go shopping alone most of the time, fairly well assured that I will not be followed or harassed by store detectives.
6. I can turn on the television or open to the front page of the paper and see people of my race widely and positively represented.
7. When I am told about our national heritage or about "civilization," I am shown that people of my color made it what it is.
8. I can be sure that my children will be given curricular materials that testify to the existence of their race.
9. If I want to, I can be pretty sure of finding a publisher for this piece on white privilege.
10. I can be fairly sure of having my voice heard in a group in which I am the only member of my race.

11. I can be casual about whether or not to listen to another woman's voice in a group in which she is the only member of her race.

12. I can go into a book shop and count on finding the writing of my race represented, into a supermarket and find the staple foods that fit with my cultural traditions, into a hairdresser's shop and find someone who can deal with my hair.

13. Whether I use checks, credit cards, or cash, I can count on my skin color not to work against the appearance that I am financially reliable.

14. I could arrange to protect our young children most of the time from people who might not like them.

15. I did not have to educate our children to be aware of systemic racism for their own daily physical protection.

16. I can be pretty sure that my children's teachers and employers will tolerate them if they fit school and workplace norms; my chief worries about them do not concern others' attitudes toward their race.

17. I can talk with my mouth full and not have people put this down to my color.

18. I can swear, or dress in secondhand clothes, or not answer letters, without having people attribute these choices to the bad morals, the poverty, or the illiteracy of my race.

19. I can speak in public to a powerful male group without putting my race on trial.

20. I can do well in a challenging situation without being called a credit to my race.

21. I am never asked to speak for all the people of my racial group.

22. I can remain oblivious to the language and customs of persons of color who constitute the world's majority without feeling in my culture any penalty for such oblivion.

23. I can criticize our government and talk about how much I fear its policies and behavior without being seen as a cultural outsider.

24. I can be reasonably sure that if I ask to talk to "the person in charge," I will be facing a person of my race.

25. If a traffic cop pulls me over or if the IRS audits my tax return, I can be sure I haven't been singled out because of my race.

26. I can easily buy posters, postcards, picture books, greeting cards, dolls, toys, and children's magazines featuring people of my race.

27. I can go home from most meetings of organizations I belong to feeling somewhat tied in, rather than isolated, out of place, out-numbered, unheard, held at a distance, or feared.

28. I can be pretty sure that an argument with a colleague of another race is more likely to jeopardize her chances for advancement than to jeopardize mine.

29. I can be fairly sure that if I argue for the promotion of a person of another race, or a program centering on race, this is not likely to cost me heavily within my present setting, even if my colleagues disagree with me.

30. If I declare there is a racial issue at hand, or there isn't a racial issue at hand, my race will lend me more credibility for either position than a person of color will have.
31. I can choose to ignore developments in minority writing and minority activist programs, or disparage them, or learn from them, but in any case, I can find ways to be more or less protected from negative consequences of any of these choices.
32. My culture gives me little fear about ignoring the perspectives and powers of people of other races.
33. I am not made acutely aware that my shape, bearing, or body odor will be taken as a reflection on my race.
34. I can worry about racism without being seen as self-interested or self-seeking.
35. I can take a job with an affirmative action employer without having my co-workers on the job suspect that I got it because of my race.
36. If my day, week, or year is going badly, I need not ask of each negative episode or situation whether it has racial overtones.
37. I can be pretty sure of finding people who would be willing to talk with me and advise me about my next steps, professionally.
38. I can think over many options, social, political, imaginative, or professional, without asking whether a person of my race would be accepted or allowed to do what I want to do.
39. I can be late to a meeting without having the lateness reflect on my race.
40. I can choose public accommodation without fearing that people of my race cannot get in or will be mistreated in the places I have chosen.
41. I can be sure that if I need legal or medical help, my race will not work against me.
42. I can arrange my activities so that I will never have to experience feelings of rejection owing to my race.
43. If I have low credibility as a leader, I can be sure that my race is not the problem.
44. I can easily find academic courses and institutions that give attention only to people of my race.
45. I can expect figurative language and imagery in all of the arts to testify to experiences of my race.
46. I can choose blemish cover or bandages in "flesh" color and have them more or less match my skin.

I repeatedly forgot each of the realizations on this list until I wrote it down. For me, white privilege has turned out to be an elusive and fugitive subject. The pressure to avoid it is great, for in facing it I must give up the myth of meritocracy. If these things are true, this is not such a free country; one's life is not what one makes it; many doors open for certain people through no virtues of their own. These perceptions mean also that my moral condition is not what I had been led to believe. The appearance of being a good citizen rather than a trouble-maker comes in large part from having all sorts of doors open automatically because of my color.

A further paralysis of nerve comes from literary silence protecting privilege. My clearest memories of finding such analysis are in Lillian Smith's unparalleled *Killers of the Dream* and Margaret Andersen's review of Karen and Mamie Fields' *Lemon Swamp*. Smith, for example, wrote about walking toward Black children on the street and knowing they would step into the gutter; Andersen contrasted the pleasure that she, as a white child, took on summer driving trips to the south with Karen Fields' memories of driving in a closed car stocked with all necessities lest, in stopping, her Black family should suffer "insult, or worse." Adrienne Rich also recognizes and writes about daily experiences of privilege, but in my observation, white women's writing in this area is far more often on systemic racism than on our daily lives as light-skinned women.[2]

In unpacking this invisible knapsack of white privilege, I have listed conditions of daily experience that I once took for granted, as neutral, normal, and universally available to everybody, just as I once thought of a male-focused curriculum as the neutral or accurate account that can speak for all. Nor did I think of any of these perquisites as bad for the holder. I now think that we need a more finely differentiated taxonomy of privilege, for some of these varieties are only what one would want for everyone in a just society, and others give license to be ignorant, oblivious, arrogant, and destructive. Before proposing some more finely tuned categorization, I will make some observations about the general effects of these conditions on my life and expectations.

In this potpourri of examples, some privileges make me feel at home in the world. Others allow me to escape penalties or dangers that others suffer. Through some, I escape fear, anxiety, insult, injury, or a sense of not being welcome, not being real. Some keep me from having to hide, to be in disguise, to feel sick or crazy, to negotiate each transaction from the position of being an outsider or, within my group, a person who is suspected of having too close links with a dominant culture. Most keep me from having to be angry.

I see a pattern running through the matrix of white privilege, a pattern of assumptions that were passed on to me as a white person. There was one main piece of cultural turf; it was my own turf, and I was among those who could control the turf. I could measure up to the cultural standards and take advantage of the many options I saw around me to make what the culture would call a success of my life. *My skin color was an asset for any move I was educated to want to make.* I could think of myself as "belonging" in major ways and of making social systems work for me. I could freely disparage, fear, neglect, or be oblivious to anything outside of the dominant cultural forms. Being of the main culture, I could also criticize it fairly freely. My life was reflected back to me frequently enough so that I felt, with regard to my race, if not to my sex, like one of the real people.

Whether through the curriculum or in the newspaper, the television, the economic system, or the general look of people in the streets, I received daily signals and indications that my people counted and that others *either didn't exist or must be trying, not very successfully, to be like people of my race.* I was given cultural permission not to hear voices of people of other races or a tepid cultural tolerance for hearing or acting on such voices. I was also raised not to suffer seriously from anything that darker-skinned people might say about my group, "protected," though perhaps I should more accurately say *prohibited*, through the habits of my economic class and social group, from living in racially mixed groups or being reflective about interactions between people of differing races.

In proportion as my racial group was being made confident, comfortable, and oblivious, other groups were likely being made unconfident, uncomfortable, and alienated. Whiteness protected me from many kinds of hostility, distress, and violence, which I was being subtly trained to visit in turn upon people of color.

For this reason, the word "privilege" now seems to me misleading. Its connotations are too positive to fit the conditions and behaviors which "privilege systems" produce. We usually think of privilege as being a favored state, whether earned, or conferred by birth or luck. School graduates are reminded they are privileged and urged to use their (enviable) assets well. The word "privilege" carries the connotation of being something everyone must want. Yet some of the conditions I have described here work to systemically overempower certain groups. Such privilege simply *confers dominance*, gives permission to control, because of one's race or sex. The kind of privilege that gives license to some people to be, at best, thoughtless and, at worst, murderous should not continue to be referred to as a desirable attribute. Such "privilege" may be widely desired without being in any way beneficial to the whole society.

Moreover, though "privilege" may confer power, it does not confer moral strength. Those who do not depend on conferred dominance have traits and qualities that may never develop in those who do. Just as Women's Studies courses indicate that women survive their political circumstances to lead lives that hold the human race together, so "underprivileged" people of color who are the world's majority have survived their oppression and lived survivors' lives from which the white global minority can and must learn. In some groups, those dominated have actually become strong through not having all of these unearned advantages, and this gives them a great deal to teach the others. Members of so-called privileged groups can seem foolish, ridiculous, infantile, or dangerous by contrast.

I want, then, to distinguish between earned strength and unearned power conferred systemically. Power from unearned privilege can look like strength when it is, in fact, permission to escape or to dominate. But not all of the privileges on my list are inevitably damaging. Some, like the expectation that neighbors will be decent to you, or that your race will not count against you in court, should be the norm in a just society and should be considered as the entitlement of everyone. Others, like the privilege not to listen to less powerful people, distort the humanity of the holders as well as the ignored groups. Still others, like finding one's staple foods everywhere, may be a function of being a member of a numerical majority in the population. Others have to do with not having to labor under pervasive negative stereotyping and mythology.

We might at least start by distinguishing between positive advantages that we can work to spread, to the point where they are not advantages at all but simply part of the normal civic and social fabric, and negative types of advantage that unless rejected will always reinforce our present hierarchies. For example, the positive "privilege" of belonging, the feeling that one belongs within the human circle, as Native Americans say, fosters development and should not be seen as privilege for a few. It is, let us say, an entitlement that none of us should have to earn; ideally it is an *unearned entitlement*. At present, since only a few have it, it is an *unearned advantage* for them. The negative "privilege" that gave me cultural permission not to take darker-skinned Others seriously can be seen as arbitrarily conferred dominance and should not be desirable for anyone. This paper results from a process of coming to see that some of the power that I originally saw as attendant on being a human being in the United States consisted in *unearned advantage* and *conferred dominance*, as well as other kinds of special circumstance not universally taken for granted.

In writing this paper I have also realized that white identity and status (as well as class identity and status) give me considerable power to choose whether to broach this subject and its trouble. I can pretty well decide whether to disappear and avoid and not listen and escape the dislike I may engender in other people through this essay, or interrupt, answer, interpret, preach, correct, criticize, and control to some extent what goes on in reaction to it. Being white, I am given considerable power to escape many kinds of danger or penalty as well as to choose which risks I want to take.

There is an analogy here, once again, with Women's Studies. Our male colleagues do not have a great deal to lose in supporting Women's Studies, but they do not have a great deal to lose if they oppose it either. They simply have the power to decide whether to commit themselves to more equitable distributions of power. They will probably feel few penalties whatever choice they make; they do not seem, in any obvious short-term sense, the ones at risk, though they and we are all at risk because of the behaviors that have been rewarded in them.

Through Women's Studies work I have met very few men who are truly distressed about systemic, unearned male advantage and conferred dominance. And so one question for me and others like me is whether we will be like them, or whether we will get truly distressed, even outraged, about unearned race advantage and conferred dominance and if so, what we will do to lessen them. In any case, we need to do more work in identifying how they actually affect our daily lives. We need more down-to-earth writing by people about these taboo subjects. We need more understanding of the ways in which white "privilege" damages white people, for these are not the same ways in which it damages the victimized. Skewed white psyches are an inseparable part of the picture, though I do not want to confuse the kinds of damage done to the holders of special assets and to those who suffer the deficits. Many, perhaps most, of our white students in the United States think that racism doesn't affect them because they are not people of color; they do not see "whiteness" as a racial identity. Many men likewise think that Women's Studies does not bear on their own existences because they are not female; they do not see themselves as having gendered identities. Insisting on the universal "effects" of "privilege" systems, then, becomes one of our chief tasks, and being more explicit about the particular effects in particular contexts is another. Men need to join us in this work.

In addition, since race and sex are not the only advantaging systems at work, we need to similarly examine the daily experience of having age advantage, or ethnic advantage, or physical ability, or advantage related to nationality, religion, or sexual orientation. Professor Marnie Evans suggested to me that in many ways the list I made also applies directly to heterosexual privilege. This is a still more taboo subject than race privilege: the daily ways in which heterosexual privilege makes some persons comfortable or powerful, providing supports, assets, approvals, and rewards to those who live or expect to live in heterosexual pairs. Unpacking that content is still more difficult, owing to the deeper imbeddedness of heterosexual advantage and dominance and stricter taboos surrounding these.

But to start such an analysis I would put this observation from my own experience: The fact that I live under the same roof with a man triggers all kinds of societal assumptions about my worth, politics, life, and values and triggers a host of unearned advantages and powers. After recasting many elements from the original list I would add further observations like these:

1. My children do not have to answer questions about why I live with my partner (my husband).
2. I have no difficulty finding neighborhoods where people approve of our household.
3. Our children are given texts and classes that implicitly support our kind of family unit and do not turn them against my choice of domestic partnership.
4. I can travel alone or with my husband without expecting embarrassment or hostility in those who deal with us.
5. Most people I meet will see my marital arrangements as an asset to my life or as a favorable comment on my likability, my competence, or my mental health.
6. I can talk about the social events of a weekend without fearing most listeners' reactions.
7. I will feel welcomed and "normal" in the usual walks of public life, institutional and social.
8. In many contexts, I am seen as "all right" in daily work on women because I do not live chiefly with women.

Difficulties and dangers surrounding the task of finding parallels are many. Since racism, sexism, and heterosexism are not the same, the advantages associated with them should not be seen as the same. In addition, it is hard to isolate aspects of unearned advantage that derive chiefly from social class, economic class, race, religion, region, sex, or ethnic identity. The oppressions are both distinct and interlocking, as the Combahee River Collective Statement of 1977 continues to remind us eloquently.[3]

One factor seems clear about all of the interlocking oppressions. They take both active forms that we can see and embedded forms that members of the dominant group are taught not to see. In my class and place, I did not see myself as racist because I was taught to recognize racism only in individual acts of meanness by members of my group, never in invisible systems conferring racial dominance on my group from birth. Likewise, we are taught to think that sexism or heterosexism is carried on only through intentional, individual acts of discrimination, meanness, or cruelty, rather than in invisible systems conferring unsought dominance on certain groups. Disapproving of the systems won't be enough to change them. I was taught to think that racism could end if white individuals changed their attitudes; many men think sexism can be ended by individual changes in daily behavior toward women. But a man's sex provides advantage for him whether or not he approves of the way in which dominance has been conferred on his group. A "white" skin in the United States opens many doors for whites whether or not we approve of the way dominance has been conferred on us. Individual acts can palliate, but cannot end, these problems. To redesign social systems, we need first to acknowledge their colossal unseen dimensions. The silences and denials surrounding privilege are the key political tool here. They keep the thinking about equality or equity incomplete, protecting unearned advantage and conferred dominance by making these taboo subjects. Most talk by whites about equal opportunity seems to me now to be about equal opportunity to try to get into a position of dominance while denying that systems of dominance exist.

It seems to me that obliviousness about white advantage, like obliviousness about male advantage, is kept strongly inculturated in the United States so as to maintain the myth of meritocracy, the myth that democratic choice is equally available to all. Keeping most people unaware that freedom of confident action is there for just a small number of people props up those in power and serves to keep power in the hands of the same groups that have most of it already. Though systemic change takes many decades, there are pressing questions for me and I imagine for some others like me if we raise our daily consciousness on the perquisites of being light-skinned. What will we do with such knowledge? As we know from watching men, it is an open question whether we will choose to use unearned advantage to weaken invisible privilege systems and whether we will use any of our arbitrarily awarded power to try to reconstruct power systems on a broader base.

NOTES

1. This paper was presented at the Virginia Women's Studies Association conference in Richmond in April, 1986 and the American Educational Research Association conference in Boston in October, 1986 and discussed with two groups of participants in the Dodge Seminars for Secondary School Teachers in New York and Boston in the spring of 1987.

2. Andersen, Margaret, "Race and the Social Science Curriculum: A Teaching and Learning Discussion," *Radical Teacher*, November, 1984 pp. 17–20. Smith, Lillian, *Killers of the Dream*, New York, 1949.

3. "A Black Feminist Statement," The Combahee River Collective, pp. 13–22 in Gloria T. Hull, Patricia Bell Scott, Barbara Smith, eds., *All the Women Are White, All the Blacks Are Men, But Some of Us Are Brave: Black Women's Studies*. The Feminist Press. 1982.

9

Beside My Sister, Facing the Enemy: Legal Theory Out of Coalition

Mari J. Matsuda

. . .

I. Three Women Working

A. Daughter of Pi'ilani

Haunani-Kay Trask is a paradox to those unfamiliar with the world from which she comes. She writes of working in coalition with environmentalists who, in her community of Hawai'i, are often white in-migrants. Expressing bitterness and frustration, Trask recounts the dispossession of Native Hawaiian people—their landlessness, poverty, unemployment, imprisonment, rates of disease, and illiteracy. Trask speaks of the haole (Caucasian) colonizers who removed the Hawaiian government by force, leaving wounds in the native population that have never healed. Expressing outrage at the haole-backed takeover of Hawai'i has earned Trask the reputation of "haole-hater." She speaks out in the press. She writes. She debates. Trask is constantly engaged in dialogue with the haole. She works with whites in coalition on a variety of issues, from nuclear testing in the Pacific, to South African divestment, to degradation of the environment through geothermal development.

I have heard people say of Professor Trask, "She would be much more effective if she weren't so angry," as though they expect a Native Hawaiian feminist to work in coalition without anger. There is a politics of anger: who is allowed to get angry, whose anger goes unseen, and who seems angry when they are not.

Once, when I intended to compliment an African-American woman on a powerful speech she had made, I said: "I admire your ability to express anger." She looked at me coolly and replied, "I was not angry. If I were angry I would not be speaking here." Another African-American friend of mine jumped into the conversation. "I'm disappointed in you," she said. "This is what always happens to us when a Black woman speaks her mind. Someone calls us angry."

I remember this exchange because it was an uncomfortable one for me, and because it was a moment of learning. Talking across differences, my colleague told me that if she were hatefully angry, beyond hope of coalition, she would not talk. In this light, Professor Trask's strong words are acts of engagement, not estrangement.

73

Would Professor Trask be more effective if she were less angry? There is a cost to speaking without anger of the deaths and dislocation that Native Hawaiians suffered in post-contact Hawai'i. On the simple, communicative level, failure to express the pain created by this legacy obscures the depth of one's feeling and discounts the subordination experienced by one's community. More significantly, the use of polite, rational tones when one is feeling violation is a betrayal of the self.

Professor Trask's many white and Asian colleagues who choose to remain in the room when she speaks in tones of outrage about the destruction of Hawaiian lives, land, and culture inevitably find their understanding greatly enriched. The discomfort brings with it an opportunity for learning. As a third-generation Japanese-American, I have felt the discomfort and benefited from the learning when Professor Trask criticizes the role of immigrants in displacing Native Hawaiians. The choice is mine to remain in the conversation, discussing (sometimes with acrimony) the role of colonialism in bringing my peasant ancestors eastward from Asia to work on land that once belonged to indigenous peoples of Hawai'i and North America.

I could shelter myself from conflict by leaving the conversation, but I have come to believe that the comfort we feel when we avoid hard conversations is a dangerous comfort, one that seduces us into ignorance about the experiences of others and about the full meaning of our own lives.

. . .

C. The Multi-Cultural Feminist

. . .

[Some] suggest that coalition has limits of both tolerance and utility.

Why, then, given the frustration of coalition, do . . . women [of color] not retreat into racial separatism? In the quest for a theoretical underpinning for social change movements, women of color have the choice of remaining in coalition or dispersing to do separate work. The emergence of feminist jurisprudence, critical race theory, critical legal studies, and the women of color and the law movement has raised fears of division and parochial separatism in the legal community. If it is so hard to work together, if the gulfs in experience are so wide, if the false universals of the modern age are truly bankrupt, what need binds us? What justifies unity in our quest for self-knowledge?

My answer is that we cannot, at this point in history, engage fruitfully in jurisprudence without engaging in coalition, without coming out of separate places to meet one another across all the positions of privilege and subordination that we hold in relation to one another.

II. Theory Out of Coalition

Through our sometimes painful work in coalition we are beginning to form a theory of subordination; a theory that describes it, explains it, and gives us the tools to end it. As lawyers working in coalition, we are developing a theory of law taking sides, rather than law as value-neutral. We imagine law to uplift and protect the sixteen-year-old single mother on crack rather than law to criminalize her. We imagine law to celebrate and protect women's bodies; law to sanctify love between human beings—whether women to women, men to men, or women to men, as lovers may choose to love; law to respect the bones of our ancestors; law to feed the children; law to shut down the sweatshops; law to save the planet.

This is the revolutionary theory of law that we are developing in coalition, and I submit that it is both a theory of law we can only develop in coalition, and that it is the only theory of law we can develop in coalition.

A. Looking at Subordination from Inside Coalition

When we work in coalition, . . . we compare our struggles and challenge one another's assumptions. We learn of the gaps and absences in our knowledge. We learn a few tentative, starting truths, the building blocks of a theory of subordination.

We learn that while all forms of oppression are not the same, certain predictable patterns emerge:

- All forms of oppression involve taking a trait, X, which often carries with it a cultural meaning, and using X to make some group the "other" and to reduce their entitlements and power.
- All forms of oppression benefit someone, and sometimes both sides of a relationship of domination will have some stake in its maintenance.
- All forms of oppression have both material and ideological dimensions. The articles on health, socioeconomics, and violence in this symposium show how subordination leaves scars on the body. The damage is real. It is material. These articles also speak of ideology. Language, including the language of science, law, rights, necessity, free markets, neutrality, and objectivity can make subordination seem natural and inevitable, justifying material deprivation.
- All forms of oppression implicate a psychology of subordination that involves elements of sexual fear, need to control, hatred of self, and hatred of others.

As we look at these patterns of oppression, we may come to learn, finally and most importantly, that all forms of subordination are interlocking and mutually reinforcing.

B. Ask the Other Question:
The Interconnection of All Forms of Subordination

The way I try to understand the interconnection of all forms of subordination is through a method I call "ask the other question." When I see something that looks racist, I ask, "Where is the patriarchy in this?" When I see something that looks sexist, I ask, "Where is the heterosexism in this?" When I see something that looks homophobic, I ask, "Where are the class interests in this?" Working in coalition forces us to look for both the obvious and non-obvious relationships of domination, helping us to realize that no form of subordination ever stands alone.

If this is true, we've asked each other, then isn't it also true that dismantling any one form of subordination is impossible without dismantling every other? And more and more, particularly in the women of color movement, the answer is that "no person is free until the last and the least of us is free."

In trying to explain this to my own community, I sometimes try to shake people up by suggesting that patriarchy killed Vincent Chin.[1] Most people think racism killed Vincent Chin. When white men with baseball bats, hurling racist hate speech, beat a man to death, it is obvious that racism is a cause. It is only slightly less obvious, however, when you walk down the aisles of Toys R Us, that little boys grow up in this culture with toys that teach dominance and aggression, while little girls grow up with toys that teach about being pretty, baking, and changing a diaper. And the little boy who is interested in learning how to nurture and play house is called a "sissy." When he is a little older he is called a "f–g." He learns that acceptance for men in this society is premised on rejecting the girl culture and taking on the boy culture, and I believe that this, as much as racism, killed Vincent Chin. I have come to see that homophobia is the disciplinary system that teaches men that they had better talk like 2 Live Crew or someone will think they "aren't real men," and I believe that this homophobia is a cause of rape and violence against women. I have come to see how that same homophobia makes women afraid to choose women, sending them instead into the arms of men who beat them. I have come to see how class oppression creates the same effect, cutting off the chance of economic independence that could free women from dependency upon abusive men.

I have come to see all of this from working in coalition: from my lesbian colleagues who have pointed out homophobia in places where I failed to see it; from my Native American colleagues who have said, "But remember that we were here first," when I have worked for the rights of immigrant women; from men of color who have risked my wrath to say, "But racism is what is killing us. Why can't I put that first on my agenda?"

The women of color movement has, of necessity, been a movement about intersecting structures of subordination. This movement suggests that anti-patriarchal struggle is linked to struggle against all forms of subordination. It has challenged communities of color to move beyond race alone in the quest for social justice.

C. Beyond Race Alone

In coalition, we are able to develop an understanding of that which Professor Kimberlé Crenshaw has called "intersectionality." The women of color movement has demanded that the civil rights struggle encompass more than anti-racism. There are several reasons for this demand. First, and most obviously, in unity there is strength. No subordinated group is strong enough to fight the power alone, thus coalitions are formed out of necessity.

Second, some of us have overlapping identities. Separating out and ranking oppression denies and excludes these identities and ignores the valid concerns of many in our constituency. To say that the anti-racist struggle precedes all other struggles denigrates the existence of the multiply oppressed: women of color, gays and lesbians of color, poor people of color, most people of color experience subordination on more than one dimension.

Finally, perhaps the most progressive reason for moving beyond race alone is that racism is best understood and fought with knowledge gained from the broader anti-subordination struggle. Even if one wanted to live as the old prototype "race man," it is simply not possible to struggle against racism alone and ever hope to end racism.

These are threatening suggestions for many of us who have worked primarily in organizations forged in the struggle for racial justice. Our political strength and our cultural self-worth [are] often grounded in racial pride. Our multi-racial coalitions have, in the past, succeeded because of a unifying commitment to end racist attacks on people of color. Moving beyond race to include discussion of other forms of subordination risks breaking coalition. Because I believe that the most progressive elements of any liberation movement are those who see the intersections (and the most regressive are those who insist on only one axis), I am willing to risk breaking coalition by pushing intersectional analysis.

An additional and more serious risk is that intersectional analysis done from on high, that is, from outside rather than inside a structure of subordination, risks misunderstanding the particularity of that structure. Feminists have spent years talking about, experiencing, and building theory around gender. Native Americans have spent years developing an understanding of colonialism and its effect on culture. That kind of situated, ground-up knowledge is irreplaceable. A casual effort to say, "Okay, I'll add gender to my analysis," without immersion in feminist practice, is likely to miss something. Adding on gender must involve active feminists, just as adding on considerations of indigenous peoples must include activists from native communities. Coalition is the way to achieve this inclusion.

It is no accident that women of color, grounded as they are in both feminist and anti-racist struggle, are doing the most exciting theoretical work on race-gender intersections. It is no accident that gay and lesbian scholars are advancing social construction theory and the analysis of sexuality in subordination. In raising this I do not mean that we cannot speak of subordination second-hand. Rather, I wish to encourage us to do this, and to suggest that we can do this most intelligently in coalition, listening with special care to those who are actively involved in knowing and ending the systems of domination that touch their lives.

NOTE

1. Vincent Chin, a Chinese American, was murdered in Detroit by assailants who shouted racial slurs while attacking Chin with a baseball bat. See Detroit's Asian Americans Outraged by Lenient Sentencing of Chinese American Man's Killer, Rafu Shimpo, May 5, 1983 (on file with the Stanford Law Review).

10

Feminist Methods in International Law

Hilary Charlesworth

. . .

I want to describe two feminist methods that can illuminate the study of international law and then consider the questions they might raise in the particular context of accountability for human rights violations in internal armed conflict. . . . A range of feminist theories and methods are necessary to excavate the issues. In this sense, feminist explorations can be likened to an archaeological dig. There are various layers of practices, procedures, symbols, and assumptions to uncover and different tools and techniques may be relevant at each level. An obvious sign of power differentials between women and men is the absence of women in international legal institutions. Beneath this is the vocabulary of international law, which generally makes women invisible. Digging further down, many apparently neutral principles and rules of international law can be seen as operating differently with respect to women and men. Another, deeper, layer of the excavation reveals the gendered and sexed nature of the basic concepts of international law; for example, "states," "security," "order," and "conflict."

Broad theoretical brushes may be required initially to clear the site of the obvious debris of sexist practices, and increasingly refined methods to unpack and examine hidden assumptions. Use of a range of techniques, however, can lead to charges of methodological and theoretical impurity. I think that this impurity is inevitable in the analysis of complex situations. Feminist investigations of international law require "situated judgment" rather than an overarching theory to work out the most appropriate technique at any time.

I. Feminist Methodologies

Searching for Silences

A methodology sometimes employed to question the objectivity of a discipline is that of detecting its silences. All systems of knowledge depend on deeming certain issues as irrelevant or of little significance. In this sense, the silences of international law may be as important as its positive rules and rhetorical structures. Permeating all stages of the excavation of international law is the silence of women. This phenomenon does not emerge as a simple gap or hollow that weakens the edifice of international law and that might be remedied by some rapid construction work. It is rather an integral part of the structure of the international legal order, a critical element of its stability.

Women are not completely absent from the international legal order: for example, a specialized area of women's human rights law has been developed and there is some specific acknowledgment of women in other areas of international law. But, by and large, when women enter into focus at all in international law, they are viewed in a very limited way, often as victims, particularly as mothers, or potential mothers, in need of protection. Even the Platform for Action adopted by the Fourth World Conference on Women held in Beijing in 1995 endorses this circumscribed idea of womanhood. Debate in Beijing about what might constitute "balanced and non-stereotyped" images of women resulted in a paragraph referring to women's experiences as including the "balancing [of] work and family responsibilities, as mothers, as professionals, as managers and as entrepreneurs."[1] Dianne Otto has noted that this list of women's major life experiences "neatly encapsulates the dominant possibilities for women which are approved by the Platform: the traditional role of mother remains central, but is now augmented by the addition of a role in the free market economy."[2] Many aspects of many women's lives are obscured in this account.

One technique for identifying and decoding the silences in international law is paying attention to the way that various dichotomies are used in its structure. International legal discourse rests on a series of distinctions; for example, objective/subjective, legal/political, logic/emotion, order/anarchy, mind/body, culture/nature, action/passivity, public/private, protector/protected, independence/dependence. Feminist scholars have drawn attention to the gendered coding of these binary oppositions—the first term signifying "male" characteristics and the second "female." Like many other systems of knowledge, international law typically values the first terms more greatly than their complements. . . . [T]he symbolic system and culture of international law is permeated with gendered values, which in turn reinforce more general stereotypes of women and men.

The operation of public/private distinctions in international law provides an example of the way that the discipline can factor out the realities of women's lives and build its objectivity on a limited base. . . . Thus, the definition of torture in the Convention against Torture requires the involvement of a public (governmental) official. On this account, sexual violence against women constitutes an abuse of human rights only if it can be connected with the public realm; for example, if a woman is raped by a person holding a public position for some type of public end. The Declaration on the Elimination of Violence against Women, adopted by the General Assembly in 1993, makes violence against women an issue of international concern but refrains from categorizing violence against women as a human rights issue in its operative provisions. The failure to create a nexus between violence against women and human rights was due to a fear that this might dilute the traditional notion of human rights. It was said that the idea of human rights abuses required direct state involvement and that extending the concept to cover private behavior would reduce the status of the human rights canon as a whole.

This type of public/private distinction in international human rights law is not a neutral or objective qualification. Its consequences are gendered because in all societies men dominate the public sphere of politics and government and women are associated with the private sphere of home and family. Its effect is to blot out the experiences of many women and to silence their voices in international law.

World Traveling

A second methodological issue for feminists in international law is how to respond to the many differences among women. International law asserts a generality and universality that can appear strikingly incongruous in an international community made up of almost two hundred different nationalities and many more cultural, religious, linguistic, and ethnic groups. Thus, the abstract commitments of the Convention on the Elimination of All Forms of Discrimination against Women will be translated in greatly varying circumstances, from political systems that do not allow women to vote, to systems of more subtle discrimination. The occasional nod in the direction of diversity among women in international instruments remains at a very general level; for example, the use of classifications such as "Western women" and "Third World women." These monolithic categories carry a lot of baggage: assumptions of wealth, education, work, and progress, on the one hand, and of poverty, oppressive traditions, illiteracy, and overpopulation, on the other.

. . .

Various methods have been proposed for feminist explorations in an international context. For example, Isabelle Gunning has described a technique of "world traveling" that requires "multicultural dialogue and a shared search for areas of overlap, shared concerns and values." Particularly in the discussion of human rights issues in other cultures, Gunning has counseled feminist international lawyers, first, to be clear about their own historical context; second, to understand how the women involved in the human rights situation might see them; and third, to recognize the complexities of the context of the other women. In turn, Rosi Braidotti has argued that feminists should use "multiple literacies" in engaging the global range of feminisms. This technique requires "being able to engage in conversation in a variety of styles, from a variety of disciplinary angles, if possible in different languages." Braidotti has advised feminists in the international arena to "relinquish the dream of a common language" and to accept that we can achieve only "temporary political consensus on specific issues."

Another strategy for feminists working with international issues has been suggested by [Chandra] Mohanty. She has developed the idea of an "imagined community" (first elaborated by Benedict Anderson) in the context of problems of writing about Third World feminisms in a general, but worthwhile, way. For Mohanty, the epithet "imagined" is used in contrast to existing boundaries—of nation, color, sexuality, and so on—to indicate the potential for collaborative endeavor across them; the term "community" refers to the possibility of a "horizontal comradeship" across existing hierarchies. An imagined community of feminist interests does not imply homogeneity, a single set of feminist concerns, but rather a strategic, political alliance. . . .

How can these various responses to diversity among women in the international community be reflected in international legal analysis? I think that they suggest a number of related moves. First, feminist international lawyers must be aware of the limits of their experience, that is, wary of constructing universal principles on the basis of their own lives. Second, the technique of asking questions and challenging assumptions about international law may be more valuable than generating grand theories of women's oppression. Third, international lawyers must recognize the role of racism and economic exploitation in the position of most of the world's women. They should attend to the "multiple, fluid structures of domination which intersect to locate women differently at particular historical conjunctures"[3] rather than invoke "a notion of universal patriarchy operating in a transhistorical way to subordinate all women."[4] This requires an appreciation of the forms and intersections of systems of oppression.

. . .

II. Individual Accountability for Human Rights Abuses in Internal Conflicts

How might a feminist international lawyer approach the specific question of individual accountability for human rights abuses in armed conflict? There is considerable empirical evidence that women are affected by armed conflict in ways that men are not. . . . Rape has been understood as one of the spoils of the victor, serving also to humiliate the vanquished. Globally, women form only 2 percent of regular army personnel, but as civilians they suffer disproportionately from armed conflict. . . .

Whether and how individuals should be held criminally accountable for human rights abuses in internal conflicts has increasingly exercised international lawyers. . . .

International law has traditionally drawn a distinction between the principles of individual conduct that apply in times of armed conflict (international humanitarian law, IHL) and those that operate in peacetime (human rights law). This dichotomy has led to many anomalies and inconsistencies. From a feminist perspective, the distinction has allowed IHL, with its basis in codes of warriors' honor, to factor out issues that do not relate to the warrior caste. . . . The honor of warriors has nothing to say about the oppression of women. Human rights law, while more expansive in its coverage than IHL, has, as indicated above, provided a more limited response to the harms that women generally face compared with those confronting men. International criminal law . . . is an amalgam of IHL and human rights law. In many ways, it has combined the gendered blind spots of both traditions.

. . . What is the nature of international legal knowledge in this context? What knowledge is privileged and what knowledge is silenced and devalued?

Human Rights Abuses

The category of "human rights abuses" is a contested one from a feminist perspective. Analysis of the understanding of human rights in international law generally has shown that the definition of human rights is limited and androcentric. The limitations of human rights law with respect to women are intensified in the context of IHL. Take, for example, the way that it deals with rape and sexual assault. Article 27 of the Fourth Geneva Convention places states under an obligation to protect women in international armed conflict "against any attack on their honour, in particular against rape, enforced prostitution, or any form of indecent assault."[5] The provision assumes that women should be protected from sexual crimes because they implicate a woman's honor, reinforcing the notion of women as men's property, rather than because they constitute violence. This proprietary image is underlined by the use of the language of protection rather than prohibition of the violence. Additional Protocol I replaces the reference to a woman's honor with the notion that women should "be the object of special respect," implying that women's role in childbearing is the source of special status. Significantly, the provisions on rape are not specifically included in the category of grave breaches of international humanitarian law. In the context of noninternational armed conflict, common Article 3 of the Geneva Conventions does not specifically refer to sexual violence, generally prohibiting violence to life and the person, cruel treatment and torture, and humiliating and degrading treatment.

IHL, then, treats rape and sexual assault as an attack on (the warrior's) honor or on the sanctity of motherhood and not explicitly as of the same order as grave breaches such as compelling a prisoner of war to serve in enemy forces. The statutes of the two ad hoc Tribunals and the ICC, by contrast, provide much fuller responses to sexual violence, constructing it, depending on the circumstances, as potentially a crime of genocide, a crime against humanity, and a war crime. This recognition was the result of considerable work and lobbying by women's organizations, but its limitations should be noted. In the statutes of the Yugoslav Tribunal and the ICC at least, all three categories of international crimes are concerned only with acts forming part of a widespread, systematic, or large-scale attack. Thus, the "new" international criminal law engages sexual violence only when it is an aspect of the destruction of a community.

. . .

Another public/private distinction incorporated (albeit unevenly) in international criminal law—via human rights law—is that between the acts of state and nonstate actors. Such a dichotomy has gendered aspects when mapped onto the reality of violence against women. Significantly, the ICC statute defines torture more broadly than the Convention against Torture, omitting any reference to the involvement of public officials. Steven Ratner has suggested, however, that some sort of distinction based on "official" involvement is useful as a criterion to sort out those actions against human dignity that should engender state and individual international criminal responsibility and those (such as common assault) that should not. The problem, from a feminist perspective, is not the drawing of public/private, or regulated/nonregulated, distinctions as such, but rather the reinforcement of gender inequality through the use of such distinctions. We need, then, to pay attention to the actual operation of boundary drawing in international law and whether it ends up affecting women's and men's lives differently. For example, the consequence of defining certain rapes as public in international law is to make private rapes seem somehow less serious. The distinction is made, not by reference to women's experiences, but by the implications for the male-dominated public sphere.

A different type of silence that might be identified in the legal protection of the human rights of women in armed conflict is the almost exclusive focus on sexual violence. Insights generated by the "world traveling" method suggest that this emphasis obscures many other human rights issues in times of armed conflict, particularly the protection of economic, social, and cultural rights of women. Conflict exacerbates the globally unequal position of women and men in many ways. We know, for example, of the distinctive burdens placed on women through food and medical shortages caused by conflict. When food is scarce, more women than men suffer from malnutrition, often because of cultural norms that require men and boys to eat before women and girls. Humanitarian relief for the victims of conflict regularly fails to reach women, as men are typically given responsibility for its distribution. Economic sanctions imposed before, during, or after armed conflict have had particular impact on women and girls, who are disproportionately represented among the poor. Although the effect of these practices falls heavily on women, they are not understood by international law to be human rights abuses that would engage either state or individual responsibility.

. . .

III. Conclusions

. . . [M]y account of feminism asserts the importance of gender as an issue in international law: it argues that ideas about "femininity" and "masculinity" are incorporated into international legal rules and structures, silencing women's voices and reinforcing the globally observed domination of women by men. . . . The situation of over half the world's population is not seen as relevant to attempts to define universally applicable principles.

Another distinction between feminist methods and many . . . other [methods] . . . is in the way they view the idea of objectivity in international law. . . . Feminist methods question the possibility of objectivity in a system that effectively excludes women's voices. They are skeptical about the construction of the neutral and impartial standards, seeing them as synonyms for male perspectives. Skepticism about the hunt for the objective is, of course, shared by many critical thinkers, but they have remained curiously aloof from examining the implications for gender politics, or indeed for the situation of other marginalized groups. . . .

My version of a feminist analysis suggests that international law rules on accountability for human rights abuses in internal conflicts tend to privilege a certain set of experiences and filter out many issues that touch women's lives in particular. Is there any point in changing the law? Some feminist theorists might dismiss reform of the law as a worthwhile strategy, arguing that this may give undue prominence to law as a site of social change. They may point out that some women will gain more from international law than others. In any event, it may be argued, even if we get the principles right, there is no guarantee that the practice will change. Feminists might point to the greater value of political campaigns or media coverage in reducing the oppression of women. These arguments, while powerful, do not acknowledge that international law has a symbolic, as well as a regulative, function. Claims based on international law can carry an emotional and moral legitimacy that can have considerable political force.

. . .

Feminist methods help us understand women's subordination in ways that are much deeper than those offered by the legal concept of discrimination. How can the two goals of feminism, activism and theorizing, come together in the context of accountability for human rights violations in internal armed conflict? Ensuring equal participation of women in the institutions of international criminal law is an important first step. But this alone will not ensure a change of perspective. . . .

International lawyers require a much richer understanding of gender than the definition provided in the ICC statute, which elides the notion of gender and sex. It does not recognize that gender is a constructed and contingent set of assumptions about female and male roles and that many of the defining dichotomies of international criminal law, such as order/disorder, public/private, international/internal, have a gendered dimension. They should appreciate the way that notions of femininity and masculinity are used in conflict and how such constructions validate "normal" roles for women and men. Rape and sexual assault should be analyzed in international law as crimes against women, rather than offenses against their communities. International legal recognition of persecution based on gender as a crime against humanity offers the possibility of challenging the narrow conception of the social order protected by international criminal law. Most fundamentally, international lawyers need to understand the way that our discipline has legitimated the use of violence by accepting it as an inevitable aspect of international relations, and the implications that this has for our daily lives.

Notes

1. Beijing Platform for Action, UN Doc. A/Conf.177/20 and Add.1, Ann. II, para. 245(b) (1995), reprinted in 35 ILM 401, 457 (1996).

2. Dianne Otto, *Holding Up Half the Sky, but for Whose Benefit? A Critical Analysis of the Fourth World Conference on Women*, 6 Australian Feminist Law Journal 7, 21 (1996).

3. Chandra Mohanty, *Introduction: Cartographies of Struggle*, in Third World Women and the Politics of Feminism, 13 (Chandra Talpade Mohanty, Ann Russo, and Lourdes Torress, eds., 1991).

4. M. Jacqui Alexander and Chandra Mohanty, *Genealogies, Legacies, Movements*, in Feminist Genealogies, Colonial Legacies, Democratic Futures, at xiii, xix (M. Jacqui Alexander and Chandra Mohanty, eds., 1997).

5. *Convention Relative to the Protection of Civilian Persons in Time of War*, Aug. 12, 1949, Art. 27, 6 UST 3516, 75 UNTS 287.

11

Turning the Gaze Back on Itself: Comparative Law, Feminist Legal Studies, and the Postcolonial Project

Brenda Cossman

. . .

The danger of looking when the gaze is not returned is indeed a real danger for comparative law. To state the obvious, comparative law invariably involves comparison—something is always being compared to something else. It therefore invariably encounters all the dilemmas of comparison—of unstated norms against which difference is viewed and judged. Within the context of comparative law, the geopolitical location of the author becomes the unstated norm against which the exotic "other" is viewed. It is a project that is perhaps inherently ethnocentric—there is no way to escape or transcend the ethnocentric gaze. If this gaze is inescapable, some might be tempted to abandon it altogether.

. . .

There may be different ways of negotiating the ethnocentric gaze of comparative law without falling into a cultural relativism that would abandon the very project of looking beyond. Such a refusal to look outside of ourselves and our culture would after all undermine one of the most basic objectives of the postcolonial project, that is, of exploring the transnational flows of culture and the ways in which the colonial binaries—of us/them, here/there, west/non-west, colonizer/colonized—have long been mutually constituting.

. . . The challenge of ethnocentrism is a familiar one within the feminist project in recent years. On the one hand, the unstated norms of feminist theory and practice have become the site of intensive contestation from within—women whose lives do not accord with these norms have demanded that the partiality of feminism's vision be recognized and then be radically transformed. On the other hand, feminism has also been a site of contestation from without—from those who endeavor not to expand its embrace, but to radically curtail it. It has been denounced as quintessentially Western and therefore utterly devoid of cultural legitimacy in non-Western contexts.

The feminist project in recent years has become increasingly adept at negotiating this hazardous terrain somewhere in between un-self-critical ethnocentrism and hyper-self-critical cultural relativism. While not always avoiding the pitfalls, feminist theory in general and feminist theorizing about law in particular have become increasingly self-conscious of the dangers of either extreme, and have attempted to create new paths somewhere in between. Feminist theory may thus provide a rich resource from which new approaches to comparative law can draw in their efforts to renegotiate the comparative gaze.

. . . I consider not how the ethnocentric gaze of comparison might be transcended, but rather how it might be differently inhabited. If the danger lies in a gaze that is not returned, then we might try to find ways of returning it. I explore the potential of a strategy of turning the gaze back on itself. I argue that this strategic intervention may help in the project of negotiating the challenge of comparison without falling into the traps of either ethnocentrism on one side or cultural relativism on the other.

. . . I use some of my recent collaborative work [with Ratna Kapur, an Indian feminist lawyer and researcher] . . . to explore the general dilemmas of feminism's encounter with the comparative project. I use my collaborative work *Subversive Sites: Feminist Engagement with Law in India*[1] as a text to explore some of these dilemmas and the way in which this strategic intervention of turning the gaze back on itself may help negotiate those dilemmas. . . . It is part of a larger project on scattering feminist legal studies, that is, on the possibilities of renegotiating the Anglo-American moorings of feminist legal studies, by displacing the unstated norms and center in favor of multiple norms and frames of reference.

. . .

II. Subversive Sites as Comparative Methodology

. . . We argue that law is a site of discursive struggle where competing visions of the world, and women's place therein, are fought out.

[Our book Subversive Sites] focus[es] on the extent to which the legal regulation of women is informed by and serves to reinforce familial ideology. By familial ideology, we refer to a set of norms, values, and assumptions about the way in which family life is and should be organized. It is a set of ideas that has been so naturalized and universalized that it has come to dominate common sense thinking about the family.

. . .

It is a simple observation that familial ideology in the context of Anglo-American feminist legal studies developed in relation to the nuclear family that is said to be the dominant household arrangement in industrialized, capitalist societies. But in India, the nuclear family is not the dominant ideological form. The joint family is the household structure that is commonly believed to be the dominant form. The tragic self might at this simply abandon ship, fearful of applying a concept that is so clearly foreign to Indian culture. But if we cautiously forge ahead and consider whether the concept of familial ideology might nevertheless have some explanatory potential, we begin an interesting and transformative process.

On [the] one hand, if familial ideology is to have any explanatory value at all, it must be reconstructed around this concept of the joint family, and the gendered roles and identities therein. However, further investigation into the nature of the joint family is illuminating. The joint family—the idea that represents the essence of Indian family culture—was a term first coined by Sir Henry Maine in 1863. Maine, the Law Member of the Government of India from 1862 to 1869, believed that he had discovered "a living example of the patriarchal family in ancient times."[2] As a result of his influential position as Law Member, his view of the joint family came to be accepted by the colonial government as an accurate representation of the most common Hindu family form—a form that was then used in [the] government census. The joint family is thus illustrative of how the colonial past is always indelibly present in ostensibly pure Indian cultural forms. The example of the joint family reveals how the assumption by the tragic self of the purity of Indian cultural and legal forms obscures the already ever present West, and its deep influences on the very construction of tradition. As postcolonial theory has insisted, there is no place of pure Indianness, no place that exists in a pure form prior to the moment of colonial intervention. This strategy of historicization begins to reveal the extent to which Indian culture is very much a hybrid cultural form—produced in and through the colonial encounter. It helps refute the idea of cultural authenticity, displacing it with an insistence on cultural hybridity.

Moreover, as Indian sociologists have revealed, while the idea of the joint family dominates popular thinking about the family, the majority of Indians do not live in joint families. The joint family is neither purely Indian nor descriptive of how millions of Indians live in families. Nevertheless, the joint family and its very particularized roles for women as wives, mothers, daughters, and daughters-in-law, continues to operate as a dominant normative ideal of family—a dominant normative ideal that continues to inform judicial discourse. We try to illustrate, throughout the work, the extent to which this dominant ideology about the family operates in law: the way in which this ideology is partially constitutive of women's identities and the way in which this ideology operates to limit efforts to destabilize these identities.

This idea of the joint family is but one of the most obvious ways in which the concept of familial ideology needs to be reframed and recast in the context of the legal regulation of women in India. It is this process of interrogating, reframing, and recasting that is particularly interesting from the point of view of comparative legal feminism. The process is one that begins to transform the concept itself. Familial ideology looks very different in the Indian context than in the Anglo-American context. And this difference can begin to tell us something interesting about the concept itself. This is where the direction of the flow of analysis and comparison can begin to shift. Instead of understanding the flow of the comparative analysis as unidirectional, the hegemonic discourses of the West might begin to be displaced if we insist that the flow of comparative analysis be multidirectional. Recent cultural studies and postcolonialism have emphasized and examined the transnational and multidirectional flow of culture, traveling theory, and the syncretism and hybridity in contemporary mass culture. Borrowing these insights, we might be able to begin to deconstruct the monolithic categories of Anglo-American legal feminism by turning the gaze of comparison back on itself. We can move from the question of what is culturally specific about familial ideology in India (which retains the West as the unstated norm) to the question of what is culturally specific about familial ideology in Anglo-American legal systems—a question within which non-Anglo-American contexts can become a stated norm. We can begin to shift in subtle ways what is being compared to what and begin to displace unstated and monolithic norms in favor of stated and multiple ones.

When we turn the gaze back upon itself, we are not so much escaping the colonial or imperial gaze, as finding different ways to inhabit the space of that gaze. When we turn the gaze back upon the unstated norm, and reveal its own specificity, we might begin to find and inhabit, in the words of Homi Bhabha, "the in-between space" between West and non-West, an in-between space "through which the meanings of cultural and political authority can be negotiated."[3] It is an in-between space that can recognize and nurture cultural hybridity. In turning the gaze back upon itself, the gaze might thus become something other than what it was; it is reconfigured in a way that it might become the "beyond" or the "in-between" that the "post" in the postcolonial signifies. As a comparative methodology, turning the gaze back upon itself can help make explicit the seemingly inescapable risk of ethnocentrism in the comparative project, while at the same time, deploying the comparison to challenge that ethnocentrism. It can assist in what Gunter Frankenberg has described as the challenge of seeing ourselves as exotically as we see the "other."

The risk, and there are always risks, is that in turning the gaze back upon itself, we (the us/here comparativists located in the West) simply end up back where we started—focusing on ourselves. . . . We need . . . to be attentive to the risk of reducing the comparative analysis to an analysis that is "primarily and fundamentally a critique of the West."[4] In turning the comparative gaze back upon itself, it will be important to remain committed to finding the space in between West/non-West, colonizer/colonized, us/them, here/there, and not simply refocusing our attention back onto ourselves. We must, in other words, not simply gaze into a mirror but retain a keen focus on the kaleidoscope that a postcolonial lens of comparison can provide.

Further, it is in this kind of strategic intervention that comparative feminist legal studies can begin to become part of the postcolonial project and assist in what I describe as scattering feminist legal studies, that is, in displacing the Anglo-American center of feminist legal studies. First, turning the gaze back upon itself, alongside other postcolonial strategic interventions, can help defend the feminist emancipatory project against those who would deny its cultural legitimacy and authenticity. In breaking the here/there, us/them cultural binaries and revealing the hybridity of Indian culture, we can begin to disrupt the very assumptions on which claims of feminism's cultural inauthenticity are based. And in its place, we can defend not feminism's authenticity (for that would be to reinvoke the very binaries we have tried to displace), but simply its political legitimacy and relevance in the analysis of contemporary gender relations.

Secondly, turning the gaze back on itself can help multiply the norms, perspectives, and frames of reference in and through which feminist legal studies is constructed. For example, in the context of our work, the analysis of the historically and materially specific context of feminist engagement with law in India can become a stated norm against which the assumptions of Anglo-American feminist legal studies are viewed, judged, and potentially, rethought. Moreover, the strategy can be seen to move beyond the mere call for a recognition of difference. Caren Kaplan writes of the problem of Western feminist theorists simply "calling for inclusion of 'difference' by 'making room' or 'creating space'" rather than paying attention to the politics of "the production and reception of feminist theories in transnational cultural exchanges."[5] As Kaplan argues, this politics of location in the production and reception of theory can turn the terms of inquiry from desiring, inviting, and granting space to others to becoming accountable for one's own investments in cultural metaphors and values. Such accountability can begin to shift the ground of feminist practice from magisterial relativism (as if diversified cultural production simply occurs in a social vacuum) to the complex interpretive practices that acknowledge the historical roles of mediation, betrayal, and alliance in the relationships between women in diverse locations.

The strategy of turning the gaze back on itself can help shift attention to this politics of location in feminist legal studies. Instead of simply calling for an attention to difference within a preordained theoretical framework, the strategic intervention is one in which the theoretical concepts themselves are subject to interrogation and renegotiation and then redeployed against the initial framework. It is an intervention that can help bring the issue of accountability into sharper relief. Not only does it require that the Anglo-American feminist legal scholar recognize the partiality of her perspective, but it also directs her attention to the way in which that partial perspective shapes how the comparative knowledge is received and interpreted. . . .

Turning the gaze back upon itself can assist in bringing a politics of location to feminist legal studies, which as a project can in turn begin to be freed from its Anglo-American moorings. Feminist legal studies can be rendered more complex, more global, more local, more transnational. It is a project in which the unstated norms and frames of reference of Anglo-American feminist legal studies must be stated and revealed on the one hand and challenged as contingent, temporal, and partial on the other. It is a project that refuses the simple binaries of here/there, us/them (alongside a host of other binaries that the postcolonial project refutes: past/present, modern/tradition, global/local) by insisting on the hybridity of culture, on theory's travels, and on the transnational flow of theory/culture. It is a project that attempts to locate feminist legal studies within postcolonial projects in which Western hegemony is displaced by scattered hegemonies and in which feminist legal studies is itself located within the transnational flow of culture.

. . .

[T]he strategic intervention of turning the gaze back on itself can hardly be expected to accomplish the task of scattering feminist legal studies on its own. A host of other postcolonial strategic interventions will have to be deployed to move this project forward. . . . Scattering feminist legal studies will require that a multiplicity of these postcolonial strategic interventions be deployed. Turning the gaze back on itself, although perhaps particularly well suited to the development of new approaches to comparative law, can be but one of the many strategies that will need to be pursued if feminist legal studies is indeed to be relocated within the postcolonial project.

III. Collaboration, Politics, and Other Stories

The collaborative nature of our work has been an important methodological component of the project of scattering feminist legal studies. This process of collaborative work has been one that parallels, in at least some ways, the insights of postcolonial theory that disrupts the here/there, us/them, colonizer/colonized binaries, and insists on the mutual and multidirectional flow of knowledge and analysis; that is, on the "two-way cultural traffic." Our collaboration has very much been one of two-way cultural traffic. It has helped us in displacing the unidirectionality of the perspective and the flow of analysis, as well as in breaking the "us 'n them" framework. The collaborative nature of our work instantiates, with a certain materiality, the postcolonial insight that theories, and theorists, travel. As authors, we travel back and forth, to and from each of our respective worlds in a manner that begins to complicate any simple effort to locate us as here or there. But, more significantly, it is our ideas and our texts that really rack up frequent flyer points. Our ideas travel back and forth, often with a speed that is dizzying, to the point that they no longer belong to either one of us. They are neither here nor there. But, having said this, it is important to add that we make no claims to have actually accomplished the project of inhabiting the postcolonial space in between in our work. Our claim is rather more modest—to contribute to the development of feminist legal studies in India and to do so in a way that we hope begins to displace the Anglo-American moorings.

. . .

NOTES

1. Ratna Kapur and Brenda Cossman, Subversive Sites: Feminist Engagement with Law in India (1996) (exploring ideological assumptions which inform legal regulation of women in India and ways in which law subordinates women).

2. Patricia Uberoi, Family, Kinship and Marriage in India 31 (1993).

3. Homi K. Bhabha, *Introduction: Narrating the Nation*, in Nation and Narration 1, 4 (Homi K. Bhabha, ed., 1990).

4. Ruth Frankenberg and Lata Mani, Crosscurrents, *Crosstalk: Race, "Postcoloniality" and the Politics of Location*, 7 Cultural Studies 292, 301 (1993).

5. Caren Kaplan, *The Politics of Location as Transnational Feminist Critical Practice*, in Scattered Hegemonies: Post Modernity and Transnational Feminist Practices 137, 138–139 (Inderpal Grewal and Caren Kaplan, eds., 1994).

Part II

Women's Work and Wealth

Introduction

Feminist theory has been successful both in developing new theories to better understand and improve women's economic positions and in providing the analytical basis for efforts to expand women's ability to gain access to the protections of existing law. The first generation of feminist theorists succeeded in bringing public attention to and political pressure to bear on three main issues of concern to women: control of reproductive rights, elimination of violence against women, and access to the workplace. As feminist theory continues to develop, increasingly reflecting the voices of more women across racial, ethnic, and class divides, it is clear that work and the corollary issue of wealth accumulation continue to be troublesome areas. Wealth and work, though not quite as visceral as reproductive rights or violence against women, unmask some of the most profound failures in feminist theory to reconcile or at least acknowledge the vastly divergent experiences of women across class, race, and ethnic lines.

Traditionally, feminist theory focused on the desire of women to move into and compete freely with men in the marketplace. Little, if any, attention was initially given to the work issues of women of color and working-class women, who had always participated in the workforce, often involuntarily and frequently locked into low-wage positions. As white women entered the workforce in greater numbers and in higher positions, their need for paid child-care workers and domestics often inhibited their ability to fully analyze the ways in which their participation in the labor market depended on the exploitation of low-wage female workers. Theories of intersectionality have helped bring attention to the deficit, yet feminist legal scholars are still slow to incorporate the needs of poor and working-class women into the fabric of feminist work theory.

This part begins with an article by Joan Williams, in which she identifies several ways in which commodification of women's work leads to race and class conflict. She critiques feminist notions of domesticity and work, which privilege upper- and middle-class women's needs to the disadvantage of women of color. Williams highlights for white feminists some of the racial and class conflicts that can prevent effective coalition building among feminists. In the next essay, Dorothy Roberts examines the tension between white feminists and some women of color over the issue of motherhood, as well as the value placed on the women who provide child-care services to middle- and upper-class white and Black women. Roberts vividly demonstrates the potential for white women's complicity in the ongoing marginality of child-care workers, who are often women of color or poor white women. Then Taunya Banks, who focuses on the nanny tax problems of U.S. attorney general nominee Zoe Baird, furthers this discussion by analyzing how white women's work issues are used to frame legislation that affects all women, often to the detriment of women of color and lower-class women.

The section then turns its attention to three other classes of women who rarely receive the full attention of feminist theorists: garment workers, commercial sex workers, and women who are forced into the market through "workfare" programs brought about by changes in welfare laws. Laura Ho, Catherine Powell, and Leti Volpp detail the difficulties that the advent of transnational corporations has presented for establishing working conditions for garment workers that meet human rights standards. This selection also poignantly identifies the ways in which middle- and upper-class women have been complicit in the suppression of working wages of garment workers, who are themselves mostly women, as well as the ways in which women and women's organizations are particularly well suited to bringing global attention to the issue and proposing workable solutions.

Sylvia Law analyzes the work conditions of another group of women who consistently present theoretical problems for feminists: commercial sex workers. Feminists' ambivalence toward commercial sex work is well known. While numerous scholarly pieces have been written both supporting and opposing commercial sex work, no comprehensive body of work has developed that would help guide the development of legislation to protect sex workers in the marketplace. Law analyzes the disadvantages that commercial sex workers face in the employment context. The law views sex workers as "independent contractors," as opposed to employees. As a result, commercial sex workers have few rights of unionization and enjoy none of the perks of employee status, such as health benefits.

Finally, the enactment of the Personal Responsibility and Work Opportunity Reconciliation Act of 1996 drew attention to a class of women who, prior to the public discussion about welfare reform, were largely invisible to feminists. Even during the extensive discussions of welfare reform, few feminists took an active role in advocating for women on welfare or exposing the racial and class implications in the welfare "debate." Matthew Diller's article explores the work issues for women forced off welfare rolls and into the marketplace. Diller questions moral judgments about poor women that are implicitly and explicitly incorporated in the welfare reform proposals. In addition, he raises challenging questions about programs that force poor women into work environments without ensuring basic employee protections. Diller exposes the reader to a group of women whose existence has never seemed particularly important to mainstream feminist legal theorists but whose current circumstances force us to reflect on the split between skilled and unskilled labor, forced and unforced labor, and low-wage and high-wage labor, which echoes the historical divide between white women's and working-class women of color's work issues.

Part II then goes on to explore feminist analysis of acquisition of wealth. Wealth is believed to be the great equalizer. The argument is often made that if women and other oppressed people can simply acquire enough wealth, they will be able to compete equally in dominant society, without regard to race or gender. Feminist theory has not substantially challenged this assumption. Examination of this topic begins with Edward McCaffrey's work on feminist analyses of tax policies. By comparing the relative positions of male and female wage earners, McCaffrey is able to demonstrate that the acquisition of wealth, as it is regulated by the U.S. tax code, is gendered. He identifies several areas in the tax code where female wage earners are penalized in ways that similarly situated males are not. McCaffrey's work directly challenges the assumption that wealth is not gendered. His essay is followed by Patricia Hill Collins's analysis of how wealth is acquired and measured for whites and African Americans. She compares inheritance of assets, a white method of wealth acquisition, with receipt of salary. Collins demonstrates that how wealth is measured can facilitate the masking of inequality between whites and Blacks. On paper, the two groups may appear to be similarly situated, but the reliance on salary as an indicator of wealth for people of color is a less concrete measure of wealth, given the often precarious nature of the job market. Part II concludes with Celestine Nyamu's critique of feminist approaches to culture as they relate to women's ability to acquire wealth through property in the Third World context, particularly in Africa. Nyamu identifies threads of feminist analysis that, through cultural ignorance and arrogance, induce feminists to advocate for changes that run against the grain of African cultural practices. Nyamu proposes ways of thinking for feminists that will both encourage respect for indigenous culture and allow cultural strengths to be used in conjunction with feminist theory to advance women's economic interests.

12

Implementing Antiessentialism: How Gender Wars Turn into Race and Class Conflict

Joan Williams

. . .

The traditional feminist assumption is that gender binds women together. In fact, gender divides them. Domesticity's organization of market work and family work pits ideal-worker women against women who have made a conscious, often painful, decision to reject the ideal-worker role in favor of a life defined by caregiving.

. . .

A key message of antiessentialism is that gender is different as lived and imagined by different social groups. The full-commodification model translates those differences into gender, race, and class conflict that erodes the potential for effective alliances. [I] explore strategies designed to transform these differences into resources for gender change.

. . .

I. How Domesticity Creates Gender Wars among Women: How the Full-Commodification Model Exacerbates Them

. . .

Domesticity divides women against themselves. Until feminists acknowledge this dynamic and diffuse it, alliances among women will remain fragile and difficult. Gender wars are not limited to conflicts between employed women and homemakers, for American women are not divided into two dichotomous groups. Instead, they are on a continuum. Some are as work-primary as "high-powered" men; others do no market work. But most American women lie somewhere in the middle, or shift between various points on the continuum at different stages of their lives. These infinite gradations are divisive, as each woman judges women more work-centered than herself as insensitive to their children's needs, and those less work-centered as having "dropped out," or "given up."

. . .

Feminism's full-commodification model feeds gender wars in several ways. Its long-standing association with the devaluation of homemaking triggers a conflict between ideal-worker women and women who have framed their lives around caregiving. Its focus on market child care triggers commodification anxiety over the intrusion of the market into family life. Its insistence that women should enter into employment on the terms traditionally available to men feeds the sense that feminists are male-identified women out of touch with the values associated with traditional femininity. Its failure to address the small matter of who will take care of the children when women work feeds the sense that children's welfare is dependent on the continued marginalization of their caregivers.

The full-commodification model also reflects the social location of privileged, white, "essential" women in important ways. As a result, gender wars often turn into class and race conflicts. . . .

II. Why Gender Wars Take on Elements of Class Conflict and How to Avoid It

Perhaps then we need to rethink what we mean by feminism, recognizing how much our image of what it means to be "liberated" is based on access to opportunities which are only available to middle-class women. —Ellen Israel Rosen[1]

Does the full-commodification model embed class privilege? Upon reflection, it does. Its imagery of market work as liberating and of domesticity as drudgery is framed around the kinds of jobs available to women from the professional middle class. Its vision of the market as a benign force that can enhance family life is one most often held by women with enough wealth to gain access to rewarding work and quality child care. It sees men as oppressors rather than as other individuals in need of solidarity. Feminists need to think through the different meanings of gender for different social groups when they formulate their rhetoric and their goals.

. . .

A. Market Work

. . .

[M]arket work offer[s some] substantial salaries and a respected social role in a professional or managerial position. Working-class people often have more mixed feelings about market work. "Take this job and shove it" is a theme common to their descriptions of work life. Working-class kids complaining about their jobs are told, "Of course you don't like it, that's why they pay you."

. . .

That labor is alienating comes as no surprise. Marx placed working men's alienation at the center of his analysis in the latter half of the nineteenth century.[2] [Lillian] Rubin confirmed his analysis more than a century later. For men in working-class jobs, she reported, bitterness, alienation, resignation, and boredom are the defining features of the work experience. . . . "What's there to talk about?"—not really a question but an oft-repeated statement that says work is a requirement of life, hours to be gotten through until you can go home.[3]

The middle-class custom of asking a new acquaintance, "What do you do?" is met with confusion and discomfort in working-class settings. As a Black working-class source told John Gwaltney:

One very important difference between white people and black people is that white people think that you are your work. . . . Now, a black person has more sense than that because he knows that what I am doing doesn't have anything to do with what I want to do or what I do when I am doing for myself. Now, black people think that my work is just what I have to do to get what I want.[4]

Studies of the white working class confirm that "achievement in a specialized vocation is not the measure of a person's worth, not even for a [working-class] man" and certainly not for a woman.[5] Working-class women's identity is "multi-faceted," framed not only around work but around family and other roles as well. This is true in part because some three-fourths of working-class women hold low-status, low-paying, traditionally female jobs.

. . . Gender has always seemed the most important axis of social power for privileged white women because it is the only one that blocks their way, privileged as they are by class and race. This is not to say that the injustice meted out to them is not injustice. It is. But if privileged women want others to join their struggles, they must re-imagine themselves in ways that take into account the perspectives of their proposed allies.

The potential for cross-class coalitions is greater today than thirty years ago because of the dislocations wrought by the post-industrial economy. Feminists' focus on market work seemed alien to many working-class women twenty years ago because they did not see themselves as permanent, committed workers (despite the fact that a majority of them were in the labor force). In sharp contrast, the demise of the family wage means that today's working-class women know they probably will continue in the workforce even after they have children. Rubin notes in her 1994 Families on the Fault Line, "Although the women I interviewed for this book are the class and status counterparts of those I spoke with twenty years ago, they no longer think that women's issues don't have much to do with them. Quite the opposite!"[6]

Feminists, too, have changed in ways that enhance the potential for cross-class coalitions. They have changed Friedan's argument that women want to work to achieve self-development into an argument that women need to work to help support their families. This is a good start, but it does not go far enough. Feminists need to rethink their inheritance from the viewpoint of working-class women to assess how to appeal to women whose relationships with the key gender axes are different than their own. This includes not only market work, but also family work and market child care.

B. Market Child Care and Family Work

. . .

When working-class wives join the workforce, their families face all the pressures faced by middle-class families without the resources to ease the way. Lillian Rubin found that "[f]or most working-class families . . . child care often is patched together in ways that leave parents anxious and children in jeopardy."[7] In one illustrative family, the nine-year-old was a latchkey child, alone at home after school. The babies, under three years old, went to the wife's mother two days a week.

> But she works the rest of the time, so the other days we take them to this woman's house. It's the best we can afford, but it's not great because she keeps too many kids, and I know they don't get good attention. Especially the little one . . . [s]he's so clingy when I bring her home; she can't let go of me, like nobody's paid her any mind all day.[8]

. . .

Not only are working-class families forced to make sharp trade-offs in choosing child care; they cannot so readily turn to market solutions to help with housework. Because they cannot hire outside cleaners, working-class women spend weekends washing floors and toilets. Because they cannot send out laundry and dry cleaning, they find themselves washing and folding clothes late at night. Because they can't afford takeout, they find themselves pressured to prepare dinner just when babies are needy and older children need help with homework. The time famine that has received so much publicity in middle-class life is much worse for working-class families.

. . .

Lack of time for family life is even more of a problem for the large number of working-class families who fulfill the norm of parental care by having the parents split shifts, with one parent caring for the children while the other is at work. One-fifth of the families Rubin interviewed did this, although this number tends to fall as the economy improves.

. . .

Though the split-shift solution creates many difficulties, it is more likely to lead to a more equitable distribution of family work. Rubin found family work split roughly equally in only about 16 percent of her sample, most often because parents worked split shifts. In many of the families Rubin talked with in the Nineties, the allocation of household work was a source of conflict. Working-class women's willingness to engage in struggle around the division of family work is one of the most striking changes Lillian Rubin noted when she compared the situation today with that twenty years ago. The women who once felt indebted to a husband who "helped out" now demand more equal sharing of family work.

. . .

Family work holds a different aura in working-class contexts. Notes Ellen Israel Rosen, "While domestic work is burdensome it also is seen as providing rewards in terms of intimacy, pride and autonomy, things not available in the commodity-oriented, exploitative marketplace."[9] Commentators often note that family work is seen as important political work by African Americans, because it helps sustain a family life that is seen as protection against racism in the outside world. A similar dynamic is at work in white working-class households. Despite the fact that the family places women in a position of subordination, it also "is almost the only institution in capitalist society that bears both an ideology and a reality of love, of sharing, and of generosity."[10] Feminists' imagery of the family as the locus of subordination seems most convincing to women otherwise privileged by class and race; to working-class women, it may seem instead (or as well) a haven against the injuries of class.

Domesticity holds other attractions in the working-class context. Domesticity was invented as a strategy to differentiate the middle from the working class. For well over two centuries, having a wife at home has signaled middle-class status. This may hold little weight with women who feel themselves solidly middle-class and want to pursue careers, but for many working-class families having a mother at home seems a desirable way of "giving the kids a good start in life," or, less subtly, signaling that the family has achieved a certain level of gentility.

Domesticity is linked with middle-class aspirations for another, very practical reason: having a wife at home is the only way to deliver to working-class children the same kind of care received by middle-class children. The hidden assumption behind the proposal to delegate child care to the market is a family income high enough to buy quality care; implicit is an image of the market as a benign deliverer of quality goods. This image holds true only for the affluent. Working-class children can be protected from their parents' disadvantaged market positions only if child care is handled outside of the market. Many working-class families feel they can access high-quality care only by relying on mothers or other relatives. This explains why care by family members is so much more common in the working class than among the more privileged: one study of DuPont workers found that 40 percent of women in manufacturing used relatives for child care as opposed to only 8 percent of professional women.

. . .

Twenty years ago, white working-class women typically praised domesticity and held typical working-class attitudes toward market work. Today, the situation is more complex. Yet feminists need to remember that, if they had a choice, many working-class women would prefer that their men earned higher wages so that they could care for children in the manner of a middle-class family. To avoid class as well as gender wars, feminist proposals need to maintain a tone of respect for domesticity.

. . .

III. How the Full-Commodification Model Turns a Gender Problem into a Race Problem

. . .

In sharp contrast to the dearth of feminist analysis of the ways gender is experienced differently by people of different classes, a deep and rich literature exists on gender and race, documenting how racial hierarchy affects the ways women of color experience gender. Some of these differences stem from the fact that a higher proportion of people of color are poor or working-class: those differences are reflected in the prior discussion of class. The primary focus is on African Americans because that literature is so fully developed; however, some of its analysis applies to other communities of color as well. The literatures on Latinas and Asian Americans are developing so rapidly that we will soon be in a position to examine in detail the similarities and differences among communities of color.

. . .

A. A Heritage of Anger against White Privilege: Women of Color and Market Child Care

. . .

[T]he full-commodification model has often meant that white women hire women of color to do their domestic work in exploitative employment relationships. Evelyn Nakano Glenn concludes, "Domestic service has played a critical role in the distinct oppression of women of color. White middle-class women benefitted from the exploitation of women of color."[11] In this cultural context, a shift away from the full-commodification model to a model whose aim is to give all workers time for family work takes one step toward diffusing the racial anger surrounding domestic work.

. . .

A second step in diffusing the racial anger surrounding the full-commodification model is to recognize that marriage and domesticity have different meanings in different communities. One way of expressing racial hierarchy in the United States has been to cut people of color off both from marriage and from domesticity's gender ideals.

. . .

Blacks' exclusion from gender ideals was compounded by the practical costs of wives' inability to work for their own families.

. . .

Because one of the key expressions of white supremacy, from slavery until today, is the assault on the Black family, African Americans have often seen the preservation of family life as a deeply important political goal. Peggy Davis, relying heavily on the stories from slavery, has argued recently that preservation of family life is so important that it deserves constitutional status.[12]

. . .

In sharp contrast to white feminist imagery of the family as the "gender factory" that represents a key source of women's disempowerment, for Blacks as well as for working-class whites, the family is often seen as a haven in a harsh and unyielding world: "Black women see their unpaid domestic work more as a form of resistance to oppression than as a form of exploitation by men."[13] In this context, the work of mothering can take on a marked political dimension, simultaneously protecting children from the racism they might otherwise meet in market child care and offering mothers the opportunity to train their children to deal with racism. This sense persists up into the present; in Elsa Barkley Brown's memoir, she remembers her college-educated mother's decision to stay home with her children as "an act of resistance."[14]

. . .

While other people of color have not been as rigorously excluded from gender ideals as Blacks, their sense of the importance of family nonetheless reflects attitudes more similar to Blacks' than to whites'. For Latino/as, "the family is by far the single most important unit in life. . . . It is the basic source of emotional gratifications and support."[15] The reluctance of Latinas to delegate child care outside the family (except to fictive kin called comadres) stems from the traditional Latin focus on family life as well as strong traditions that "cast employment as oppositional to mothering." The reluctance to use market care may also reflect the high cost of market care for big families, since some groups of Latino/as have higher than average birth rates. One study of Chicana families found that over 70 percent used relatives to care for children while mothers worked. In addition, more Latinos than other men express disapproval of married women earning money, even after age, education, income, and marital status are taken into account. One study of Chicano/as found strong support for domestic mothers and provider fathers. Perhaps as a consequence, fewer Latina mothers are in the labor force than are either Black or white mothers, although labor force participation differs among different groups of Latinas. Differences among Asian Americans exist as well, although as a group they tend to have fairly high rates of labor force participation.

In both Latina and Asian cultures, male dominance is tied to custom and religion rather than to the provider role. "Within Asian communities, the Asian family (especially the immigrant one) is characterized by a hierarchy of authority based on sex, age, and generation, with young women at the lowest level, subordinate to father-husband-brother-son."[16] Rubin found that Asian and Latino men "generally participate least in the work of the household and are the least likely to believe they have much responsibility beyond bringing home a paycheck."[17] Men who live in ethnic neighborhoods, Rubin notes, "find strong support for clinging to the old ways."[18] Families who assimilate into the larger society are more like other Americans of the same social class. Recent data suggest that men in Latina and Asian families, like other American men, are under increasing pressure to increase their level of contribution to family work. Research among Korean immigrants suggests that the view that wives are responsible for family work persists long after the belief that men lose face if they do "women's work" has been discarded. In an era when only half of all Asian Americans are foreign-born, the old ways retain considerable influence.

C. Racial Anger as a Fact of Feminist Coalition Building

Gender in communities of color is different than gender as lived and imagined among whites. The full-commodification model ignores this in ways that trigger racial divides. First, the strategy of having women perform as ideal-workers while child care is delegated to the market in effect has meant delegating devalued and underpaid work to women of color. Second, because of the distinct significance of domesticity and family work in the Black community, the full-commodification model's devaluation of domesticity and family work often does not resonate among African Americans. This is also true among Latina/os and perhaps many Asian Americans as well.

White feminists need to be attuned to the ways that assumptions that embed class and race privilege can alienate potential allies. A tone of respect for family and for domesticity is important in a social context where gender ideals and the denial of family life have been key elements of a system of class and race oppression.

A shift to new feminist strategies will not completely defuse tensions that stem from racial privilege, which emerge both in the literature on domestic workers and in the literature on feminism. White feminists intent on building interracial coalitions need to be capable of dealing with the racial anger that often emerges in such coalitions. In a country where "[w]hite women did less demanding work at home and secured better jobs in the labor market,"[19] such anger is a fact of life in feminist coalition building. The following suggests some ways to transform anger against racial hierarchy into a force for gender change rather than a force that undercuts it.

. . .

E. Themes of Equality and Anger against Men

. . .

Recent studies have noted the complexity of working-class women's relationship with feminism: what they say about feminism, notes Lillian Rubin, is different from what they do about it. General agreement exists that most working-class women are reluctant to identify themselves as feminists. One study found that 73 percent of white working-class women and 52 percent of Black working-class women did not embrace feminism. A 1998 survey found that "education more than anything else determines whether a woman defines herself as a feminist";[20] again, education tracks class position. The same survey found that 53 percent of college-educated white women living in cities self-identify as feminists while only about 28 percent of all women do.

The temptation is to dismiss this, given that most women support many traditional proposals made by feminists. It would be a mistake to do so. As Roberta Sigel describes, working-class women often mute their demands for equality because "they feel they have too much invested in [their families'] survival to insist on the genuine equality to which they feel entitled."[21] Rosen agrees, arguing that working-class women fear that demands for equality may threaten family stability in a context where divorce can lead to grinding poverty. Lillian Rubin astutely explains the complexity of working-class women's relationships with feminism. She quotes Maria Acosta, a white twenty-eight-year-old secretary: "I'm a firm believer in making your man feel like a king."[22] Yet Acosta rejects the example set by her mother, who "waits on my father all the time," and claims an entitlement to reciprocal "care" from her husband.[23] Rubin notes the pain Acosta feels when acknowledging "the distance between what her life is and what she'd like it to be" and explaining the practical limitations imposed on women who deal with men: "The problem is that men need to feel important, so if you want to live with them. . . ."[24]

Rubin sees working-class women's distancing themselves from feminism as

> their way of making a public statement that they're "real" women—soft, nurturing, caring; their way of trying to reassure themselves about their femininity, about their capacity to be good wives and mothers; and their attempt to appease the hostility of their husbands. And this, too, is their gift to their husbands—a gift to compensate for the men's pain, for the knowledge both husbands and wives carry inside about the fragility of their lives and their families; a gift that seeks to ease the men's anxiety about their manhood by allowing them to believe they retain the power to define what a woman ought to be.[25]

. . .

Middle-class feminists need to recognize that one of the reasons they feel so free to attack "their" men is that the men hold such a powerful social position. To women whose men are walking wounded, open rifts may seem disloyal and unseemly. "[M]any blue-collar wives recognize that their husbands' sense of manhood is contingent on their shared belief that his paycheck is 'supporting the family.'"[26] With the demise of the family wage, working-class women often eschew (open) feminism in favor of trying to help assuage egos bruised by the injuries of class. In this context, feminism's traditional language of anger towards men can trigger a "surround the wagons" response by working-class women of all hues.

Women of color's relationship with feminism is further complicated by the use of gender ideals as instruments of racial oppression. "[T]he call to be 'treated like a man' is based on extending to men of color the full 'rights' of manhood in the United States."[27] From this perspective, the full-commodification model is seen as privileged white women's decision to remedy their own relative deprivation in relation to privileged white men by taking advantage of their position in the racial hierarchy. As a result, many Black women see feminism as a fight between white men and white women that ultimately leaves them out. This is not to discount the rich tradition of African American feminism, from Angela Davis to bell hooks to Alice Walker to Audre Lorde: Black women's relationships to gender and to feminism are complex. But anyone seeking to build a broad feminist coalition needs to be aware of the dominant strains in the Black community.

White women need to remember that Black women often relate to them not so much as women but as whites: "To Black women the issue is not whether white women are more or less racist than white men, but that they are racist."[28] Moreover, when men of color are stripped of the privileges of masculinity, "women of color are caught between the need to assert their equality and the desire to restore the prerogatives of masculinity denied to their men."[29] Notes bell hooks:

Concurrently, they know that many males in their social groups are exploited and oppressed. . . . While they are aware that sexism enables men in their respective groups to have privileges denied them, they are more likely to see exaggerated expressions of male chauvinism among their peers as stemming from the male's sense of himself as powerless and ineffectual in relation to ruling male groups, rather than an expression of an overall privileged social status.[30]

. . .

Black women in particular are well aware that Black men have often been cut off from steady work and that Black men's labor market position has sharply deteriorated since 1970, more so than that of white men. Hispanic and Asian American men have also experienced a long tradition of workplace discrimination. In this cultural context, a call by white women to challenge "men's" privileged access to market work may be read as a call by privileged white women "envious and angry at privileged white men for denying them an equal share in class privilege."[31]

. . . It should not be overlooked that a strong and articulate movement of African American feminists now challenges a tradition where demands for civil rights are often translated into calls for civil rights of Black men. But when feminists of color demand equality, they often articulate those demands somewhat differently than do white feminists, avoiding the language of anger against men. . . .

This analysis holds the promise of a challenge to traditional male privileges without triggering charges of sowing discord within the Black community. White women have often failed to recognize that a coalition based on gender requires delicate interracial negotiations in which minority women may well be wary of criticizing in public, interracial contexts, actions they would not hesitate to challenge in private. This hesitance in part reflects healthy racial solidarity: "Racial solidarity has been a fundamental element of Black women's resistance to domination."[32] In part, however, it reflects pressures from within the Black community to identify what is good for "the race" in terms of what is good for Black men. As bell hooks has pointed out, Black women can remain seriously concerned about the brutal effects of racism on Black men and, at the same time, denounce sexist behavior in Black men. "The need for unity is often misnamed as a need for homogeneity, and a Black feminist vision mistaken for betrayal of our common interests as a people."[33]

Not only African American, but also Latina and Asian-American feminists, regularly get "criticized for weakening male ego and group solidarity."[34] Notes one commentator, "[F]or Chicanas to challenge Chicano male privilege render[s] them susceptible to the charge that they are acting 'like white women'—an act of betrayal to la cultura. . . ."[35] Chicana feminists have been attacked for developing a "divisive ideology."[36] Asian-American women have had similar experiences.

Asian-American women are criticized for the possible consequences of their protests: weakening the male ego, dilution of effort and resources in Asian-American communities, destruction of working relationships between Asian men and women, setbacks for the Asian-American cause, co-optation into the larger society, and eventual loss of ethnic identity for Asian-Americans as a whole. In short, affiliation with the feminist movement is perceived as a threat to solidarity within their own community.

In summary, women of color not only have different relationships with the key gender axes of domesticity; they also have different relationships with feminism. Thus, reconstructive feminism should address the problems associated with traditional feminist rhetoric by avoiding the language of anger against men in building coalitions for gender change.

IV. Conclusion: Implementing Antiessentialism

. . .

When white feminists (typically behind closed doors) protest that antiessentialism has undercut feminism, they miss a central point. The problem is not that antiessentialism eroded coalitions that used to exist, but that certain coalitions white feminists thought existed never did. Both working-class women and women of color have had many hesitations about joining up. If feminists want to build broad gender coalitions, they need to change their strategies to take account of complex interrelationships of gender, race, and class.

A shift away from the full-commodification model to a strategy of reconstructing the relationship of market work and family work can help defuse gender, class, and race conflicts in a number of ways. Most important is that, instead of focusing on gaining access for women to the kind of meaningful work generally available only for the privileged, we strive to democratize access to domesticity. A restructuring of market work will give to working-class women and women of color greater access to the parental care that remains a widespread social ideal.

Feminists need not to decry domesticity but to use it as a weapon, to argue that if we truly value caregiving, we should restructure market work to end the marginalization of caregivers. This strategy should appeal equally to ideal-worker women who feel they need more time for caregiving, and to marginalized caregivers who feel their family work is undervalued. It should also appeal to working-class women. While the full-commodification strategy reflected privileged women's attitudes toward market work, domesticity, market child care, and family work, reconstructive feminism maintains a tone of respect for family and for domesticity, and holds the promise of allowing nonprivileged people as well as privileged ones more flexibility to care for their own children without jeopardizing their position at work. (This is not to say that parents don't still need high-quality, low-cost child care for the time they are at work.)

A shift away from the full-commodification model also may help defuse the heritage of racial anger surrounding work and family issues in the Black community. Helpful in this context are its avoidance of the language of anger against men, its tone of respect for family life and for domesticity, and its proposal to democratize domesticity rather than using white women's racial privilege to solve their gender problems.

Yet it is unrealistic to expect this heritage of anger to disappear. One resource for defusing it is for feminists to use communities of color as a resource for alternative models of masculinity, femininity, and family life. The Black community in particular provides rich lodes of traditions that offer resources for unbending gender. One is its imagery of motherhood. A strong tradition in the Black community sees market work as an integral part of motherhood rather than as inconsistent with it. This tradition is not uncontested: as discussed above, domesticity's imagery of mothers at home also holds considerable sway as an ideal. But Black mothers often have had to operate in non-ideal conditions that generated ideals of community responsibility for childrearing: "African-American mothers can draw upon an Afrocentric tradition where motherhood of varying types, whether bloodmother, othermother, or community othermother, can be invoked as symbols of power."[37] Notions of "kin-scription" and other forms of community responsibility for children contrast with the peculiarly Euro-American insistence that childrearing is a private matter that does not involve community support. The sense that "it takes a community to raise a child" is in sharp contrast to the dominant white tradition in the United States, which takes a more privatized view of childrearing than do most other communities in the world. (This peculiarly American viewpoint is not shared by most Europeans.) Recent books by Marion Wright Edelman and by Cornel West and Sylvia Hewlett (who is European) show that many of the most important voices calling for more community support for childrearing are African American.[38]

Another resource from the Black tradition is the sense that family work is important political work, which stands in sharp contrast with the dominant white tradition, which tends to belittle family work as part of "just a housewife" syndrome. Related to this is the usage that distinguishes between someone's biological father and his "daddy." Being someone's daddy means that a man has played the social role of male childrearer, a tradition that stresses that biological ties do not exhaust men's role in childrearing. In addition, imagery of mothers as strong and capable women ("my mother was much of a woman") contrasts with the dominant imagery of mothers as selfless and self-effacing ("my mother was a saint"). Moreover, African American traditions contain precious imagery of "independent, self-reliant, strong, and autonomous" women who are not so much feminine as womanly.[39] This imagery provides important resources for reconstructing not only motherhood but womanhood more generally: "[a] new definition of femininity for all American women."[40]

The Black community also offers resources for reimagining the middle-class family. Because of the difficulty Black men have experienced in getting jobs, a much smaller disparity exists between the wages of men and women in Black families than in white ones. Whereas in white, middle-class families, the husband typically earns about 70 percent of the family income (while the wife earns only about 30 percent), in Black, middle-class families, the contributions are considerably more equal: the husband earns roughly 60 percent while the wife earns roughly 40 percent. Another, related pattern is that Black, married fathers contribute more to family work than do white, married fathers. In short, despite domesticity's hold on the Black community, it also offers counterhegemonic gender imagery that provides an important cultural resource for unbending gender.

NOTES

1. Ellen Israel Rosen, Bitter Choices: Blue-Collar Women in and out of Work 172 (1987).

2. See generally Karl Marx, Writings of the Young Marx on Philosophy and Society (Lloyd D. Easton and Kurt H. Guddat, eds., 1967).

3. Lillian Rubin, Worlds of Pain: Life in the Working-Class Family 158, 159 (1976).

4. Mary Anna Madison, *I Can Handle Black Men; What I Can't Handle Is This Prejudice*, in Drylongso: A Self-Portrait of Black America 170, 173–74 (John Langston Gwaltney, ed., 1980) (1993).

5. Myra Marx Ferree, *Family and Job for Working-Class Women: Gender and Class Systems Seen from Below*, in Families and Work 289, 291 (Naomi Gerstel and Harriet Engel Gross, eds., 1987).

6. Lillian Rubin, Families on the Fault Line: America's Working Class Speaks about the Family, the Economy and Ethnicity 72 (1994) [hereinafter Rubin, Fault Line].

7. *Id.* at 93.

8. *Id.*

9. Rosen, supra note 1, at 8.

10. Gita Sen, *The Sexual Division of Labor and the Working-Class Family: Towards a Conceptual Synthesis of Class Relations and the Subordination of Women*, 12 Review of Radical Political Economics 80 (1980).

11. Evelyn Nakano Glenn, *Cleaning Up/Kept Down: A Historical Perspective on Racial Inequality in "Women's Work,"* 43 Stanford Law Review, 1333, 1337 (1991).

12. Peggy Cooper Davis, Neglected Stories: The Constitution and Family Values 12, 213–49 (1997).

13. Patricia Hill Collins, Black Feminist Thought: Knowledge, Consciousness, and the Politics of Empowerment 44 (1991).

14. Elsa Barkley Brown, *Hearing Our Mothers' Lives* 11 (1986) (unpublished paper written for Fifteenth Anniversary of African-American and African Studies, Emory University).

15. Laura Marie Padilla, draft of a work in progress 36 (on file with author).

16. Esther Ngan-Ling Chow, *The Development of Feminist Consciousness among Asian American Women*, in The Social Construction of Gender 256 (Susan A. Farrell and Judith Lorber, eds., 1991).

17. Rubin, Fault Line, supra note 6, at 91.

18. *Id.*

19. Glenn, *Cleaning Up/Kept Down*, supra note 11, at 1343.

20. Ginia Bellafante, *Feminism: It's All about Me! Want to Know What Today's Chic Young Feminist Thinkers Care About? Their Bodies! Themselves!* Time, June 29, 1998, at 54, 57.

21. Roberta Sigel, Ambition and Accommodation 191 (1996).

22. Rubin, Fault Line, supra note 6, at 74.

23. *Id.*

24. *Id.* Acosta uses the language of reciprocity traditionally used to defend separate

spheres to formulate demands on her husband: "I don't mind making him feel important; I like it sometimes. But I want him to take care of me and make me feel important, too." *Id.*

25. *Id.* at 77.

26. Rosen, supra note 1, at 104.

27. Keith Mullings, *Images, Ideology and Women of Color*, in Women of Color in U.S. Society 281 (Maxine Baca Zinn and Bonnie Thornton Dill, eds., 1994).

28. bell hooks, Ain't I a Woman? 124 (1981).

29. Mullings, supra note 27, at 281.

30. bell hooks, Feminist Theory: From Margin to Center 18 (1984).

31. *Id.* at 68.

32. Deborah K. King, *Multiple Jeopardy, Multiple Consciousness: The Context of a Black Feminist Ideology*, 14 Signs 42, 57 (1988).

33. Andre Lorde, Sister Outsider 119 (1984).

34. Mullings, supra note 27, at 281.

35. Denise A. Segura, *Chicanas in White Collar Occupations: Work and the Gendered Construction of Race-Ethnicity*, in Color, Class, and Country: Experiences of Gender 36, 39 (Bette J. Dickerson and Gay Young, eds., 1994).

36. Alma M. Garcia, *The Development of Chicana Feminist Discourse, 1970–1980*, in The Social Constructions of Gender 276 (Susan A. Farrell and Judith Lorber, eds., 1991).

37. Patricia Hill Collins, *Shifting the Center: Race, Class, and Feminist Theorizing about Motherhood*, in Mothering: Ideology, Experience, and Agency 55 (Evelyn Nakano Glenn, Grace Chang, and Linda Rennie Forcey, eds., 1994).

38. See Sylvia Ann Hewlett and Cornel West, The War against Parents (1998); Marian Wright Edelman, The Measure of Our Success: A Letter to My Children and Yours (1992).

39. Bonnie Thornton Dill, *The Dialectics of Black Womanhood*, in Black Women in America: Social Science Perspectives 65, 76 (Micheline R. Malson et al., eds., 1990).

40. *Id.* at 77.

13

Spiritual and Menial Housework

Dorothy E. Roberts

. . .

I. Background: How Labor Became Gendered

The dichotomy between women's spiritual and menial housework exists within an ideology that distinguishes between work in the public and private spheres. The separation of women's work in the home from wage labor, associated with men, has helped to devalue women's work and to keep women dependent on their husbands. Housework overlaps both public and private realms because it is performed by women in their own homes and by women who work for wages in the homes of others or in the service sector. Paradoxically, highly valued spiritual housework is largely confined to the home, while devalued menial housework can be purchased on the market. This section explains the gendered dichotomy between home and market as a backdrop to exploring the spiritual/menial fragmentation of housework.

Women have always performed hard work in their homes for the care of their families. . . . Even today, women perform on average approximately fifty hours of household labor per week. As industrialization drew men into the market of paid labor, women's unpaid work in the home became increasingly invisible and devalued. The conception of work was restricted to labor performed for money-wages. Work performed in the home became associated with women and characterized as unproductive, and essential for the social, as distinct from the economic, welfare of the family. Indeed, women's unpaid care for their families was no longer considered work at all. As Jeanne Boydston puts it, what began as "a gender division of labor" emerged as a "gendered definition of labor."[1]

Under separate spheres ideology, which applied only to white families, the husband sustained the family economically and represented the family in the public arena; the wife cared for the private realm of the home. Despite the material benefits that accrued from their household labor, housewives were rendered economically dependent on their husbands. Although the number of wage-earning women has increased dramatically, those who are not tied to a wage-earning man are stigmatized, denied many social benefits, and more likely to live in poverty.

Feminist historians point out that the ideological split between home and work is relatively recent and disregards the long history of women's experience of home as a workspace for both paid and unpaid labor. These scholars show that women have always contributed to the economic support of their families by producing valuable goods and services in their homes. Women's valuable domestic labor often includes tasks that if performed outside the home for a wage would be readily recognized as work. Before hospitalization was common, for example, women provided skilled nursing care to sick family members. Other activities women perform in their homes are more easily identified as work. Many women help in family businesses attached to the living space, such as farms, restaurants, and laundries, without compensation. Keeping boarders was a lucrative source of income for women at the turn of the century. Others engaged in industrial home work, doing paid piecework in their homes, such as sewing garments, typing documents, or rolling cigars. While waged homework used to be relegated to women of lower economic status, the advent of the personal computer and high-tech means of communication have enabled growing numbers of professional women to work from their homes.

. . .

II. The Fragmentation of Domestic Labor

Women's domestic labor is divided into two categories—spiritual and menial housework. This division exists within the context of the public/private split and also facilitates it. The ideological dichotomy between home and work incorporated a belief in women's spiritual nature. In this ideal division of labor, marriage constituted an exchange of the husband's economic sustenance for the wife's spiritual succor. The mother dispensed moral guidance to her family while the husband provided its primary financial support. The separate spheres ideology gave women a place, a role, and importance in the home, while preserving male dominance over women. The "cult of domesticity" legitimized the confinement of women to the private sphere by defining women as suited for motherhood (and unsuited for public life) because of their moral or spiritual nature. Thus, the very idealization of women's spirituality bolstered the opposition between maternal nurturing in the home and masculine work in the cutthroat marketplace.

Household labor, however, is not all spiritual. It involves nasty, tedious physical tasks—standing over a hot stove, cleaning toilets, scrubbing stains off of floors and out of shirts, changing diapers and bedpans. The notion of a purely spiritual domesticity could only be maintained by cleansing housework of its menial parts. The ideological separation of home from market, then, dictated the separation of spiritual and menial housework. Housework's undesirable tasks had to be separated physically and ideologically from the moral aspects of family life.

This dichotomy has two important consequences. First, women may delegate housework's menial tasks to others while retaining their more valuable spiritual duties. Second, this fragmentation fosters a hierarchy among women because the menial aspects of housework are typically delegated by more privileged women to less privileged ones. At the same time, the availability of a class of menial workers, sustained by race and class subordination, makes this division of women's house-work possible. Although women's participation in the market is now widely accepted, the assignment of household work to women and the distinction between spiritual and menial housework both persist.

. . .

An early example of the distinction between spiritual and menial housework is embodied in the relationship between Mammy and her mistress. The image of Mammy was that of a rotund, handkerchiefed house servant who humbly nursed her master's children. Mammy was both the perfect mother and the perfect slave; whites saw her as a "passive nurturer, a mother figure who gave all without expectation of return, who not only acknowledged her inferiority to whites but who loved them."[2] It is important to recognize, however, that Mammy did not reflect any virtue in Black motherhood. The ideology of Mammy placed no value in Black women as the mothers of their own children. Rather, whites claimed Mammy's total devotion to the master's children, without regard to the fate of Mammy's own offspring. Moreover, Mammy, while caring for the master's children, remained under the constant supervision of her white mistress. She had no real authority over either the white children she raised or the Black children she bore. Mammy's domestic labor is the perfect illustration of menial housework; her mistress, on the other hand, performed the spiritual work in the house.

. . .

The modern household worker's job is defined in a way that prevents its interference with the female employer's spiritual prerogatives. Even if a child spends the entire day with her nanny while her mother is at work, the hour of "quality time" mother and child share at bedtime is considered most important. Of course, the mother expects the nanny to develop a warm and caring relationship with the child. She wants the nanny to treat the child as a special person, and not as a chore. But the mother nevertheless desires her own relationship with her child to be superior to—closer, healthier, and more influential than—the relationship the child has with the nanny.

. . .

In [a] study of private child care arrangements, Julia Wrigley discovered that parents were torn between their desire to hire a high-status substitute mother and their preference for a manageable subordinate. . . . Parents often resolve this dilemma by relying on their spiritual supervision of the low-status employees' menial work. For example, one employer commented that "sometimes it was better to accept 'dumb' employees who are under the parents' control rather than deal with cocky ones."[3]

. . .

III. The Racialized Value of Women's Housework

The dichotomy between spiritual and menial housework is inextricably connected to a racial division between domestic laborers, a division that has survived dramatic changes in women's relationship to the market. It is true that housework has always been women's work, but polishing floors, scrubbing clothes, and tending to children for pay has been Black and other minority women's work. Even as aspects of housework have shifted from the home to the market, women of color continue to fill a disproportionate share of the menial jobs.

. . .

The racial division of housework persisted in the face of women's expanded participation in the paid labor force and the increased commodification of household chores. The collapse of rigid color barriers in the labor market after World War II allowed greater numbers of women of color to leave domestic work in white people's homes. The percentage of Black women workers employed as domestics fell from 36.2 percent as recently as 1960 to 5.0 percent by 1980. Yet the remaining ranks of domestics continued to be filled disproportionately by women of color. In 1988, the Department of Labor reported that 22.6 percent of female household workers were Black and 16.3 percent were Hispanic. These statistics do not take into account most undocumented laborers working "off the books," who also tend to be women of color.

The racialized division of household work has also survived the post–World War II transfer of many menial tasks from household to market. A growing number of services that were traditionally performed by women in their homes can be purchased on the market. Just as industrialization almost completely shifted goods production from the home to the market, so the conditions of urban America increasingly commodify domestic tasks. Daycare centers, fast food restaurants, maid services, nursing homes, and recreation facilities offer a reprieve from housework to women who can afford them. The commodification of housework, however, has not altered its gendered nature. Although this work occurs outside the home, it too is performed primarily by women. Black and Latina women hold a disproportionate share of low-level institutional service jobs. The shift to a service economy had a different impact on white and Black women: while many white women "moved up" to jobs formerly occupied exclusively by men, most Black women only "moved over" to the less prestigious jobs traditionally reserved for white women.

The importance of service workers' personal characteristics intensifies this racial stratification. Because social interaction is such a critical part of many service jobs, employees' personal traits shape the very nature of the work. As a result, "race and gender determine not only who is considered desirable or even eligible to fill certain jobs, but also who will want to fill certain jobs and how the job itself is performed."[4] Thus, although white women constitute a majority of service workers, they are preferred for positions requiring physical and social contact with customers, leaving minority women to do the rest. [Evelyn Nakano] Glenn summarizes the way in which the stratification of the market mirrors that in the home:

> Racial-ethnic women are employed to do the heavy, dirty, "back-room" chores of cooking and serving food in restaurants and cafeterias, cleaning rooms in hotels and office buildings, and caring for the elderly and ill in hospitals and nursing homes, including cleaning rooms, making beds, changing bed pans, and preparing food. In

these same settings white women are disproportionately employed as lower-level professionals (e.g., nurses and social workers), technicians, and administrative support workers to carry out the more skilled and supervisory tasks.[5]

. . .

IV. The Denial of Menial Workers' Spirituality

The delegation of menial housework to less privileged women has been supported by the denial of their capacity for spiritual housework. The expectation that poor women, immigrant women, and women of color would work for wages disqualified them from the ideal of domesticity. This disqualification has been compounded by the disparagement of their moral traits. Dominant images have long depicted Black mothers as unfit, uncaring, and immoral—just the opposite of the spiritual mother. Contemporary rhetoric blames single Black mothers on welfare for perpetuating poverty by transmitting a deviant lifestyle to their children. Courts often treat Black childrearing patterns and conditions of poverty as evidence of maternal unfitness. It becomes national news when a poor Black or Latina mother is arrested for raising her children in a rat-and roach-infested house. We hear only about the immorality of the class of mothers who are assigned to menial household tasks.

The spiritual/menial split is therefore racialized not only because women of color hold a disproportionate number of menial jobs, but also because any domestic labor performed by women of color is considered menial rather than spiritual. Mammies, Black domestic servants, and "surrogate" mothers are examples of menial domestic laborers whose spirituality has been devalued.

. . .

In other words, Black women were suitable to perform menial housework in white people's homes but incapable of fulfilling spiritual duties in their own.

B. What Happened to Domestic Servants' Children?

A corollary to the transferal of menial housework to less privileged women was the disregarding of the housework they performed in their own homes. In addition to devaluing their servants' capacity for spiritual domesticity, white employers generally assumed that Black women had a special ability to handle their own menial duties. Domestic servants' home life was simply ignored. An essential quality of a good servant was that her personal life did not interfere with her service to her employer. . . . White mistresses rarely inquired about the childcare arrangements of the domestic help, and this pattern persists in the present day. . . .

In fact, the demands of work within white homes undermined Black women's own roles as mothers and homemakers. Black domestics at the turn of the century were unable to attend to their children during the day. They returned home late at night and had to entrust their children to the care of a neighbor, relative, or older sibling, or leave them alone to take care of themselves. . . .

Other domestic servants coped with their impossible bind by sending their children away to relatives. Today many West Indian immigrants who come to the United States as childcare workers leave their children behind with foster families. Although domestics' working conditions have improved and there are exceptional employers who show concern about their employees' personal affairs, the structure of paid household work typically devalues the importance of workers' home life. Household workers, moreover, often come from a class of women whose maternal fitness continues to be disparaged.

. . .

D. The View from the Other Side

. . . It is important to remember . . . that the spiritual/menial dichotomy is constructed and not natural. We could think about housework in other ways. In fact, from the domestic's point of view, the spiritual/menial dichotomy looks very different. Black women's work in the home has had a unique dimension born of their dual service to whites and to their own families. The meaning of Black women's domestic labor has depended on whether it was performed in white people's homes or in their own. For slave women and paid domestics, work outside their homes was an aspect of racial subordination while the family was a site of solace from white oppression. . . .

Black domestic employees often view their work in white homes as a form of both subservience to their employers and spiritual labor for their own families. . . .

In addition, some domestics transformed the personal meaning of their work, recognizing that it ensured that their daughters would not follow in their footsteps. As a retired domestic servant, Pearl Runner, told Bonnie Thornton Dill,

> I really feel that with all the struggling I went through, I feel happy and proud that I was able to keep helping my children, that they listened and that they all went to high school. So when I look back, I really feel proud, even though at times the work was very hard and I came home very tired. But now, I feel proud about it. They all got their education.[6]

. . .

Just as Black women's work in the market shattered the myth of female domesticity, so their work in the home shattered the divide between spiritual and menial housework.

. . .

V. *Labor, Welfare, and Immigration Policy*

In addition to the ideological forces that distinguish between menial and spiritual domestic workers, government policies also reinforce the racialized division of housework. . . . The spiritual/menial dichotomy reflects the realization that menial tasks are essential to the functioning of a home and therefore to the functioning of the market. In other words, it's a dirty job, but someone's got to do it. American labor and welfare policy have been geared toward ensuring a ready supply of menial houseworkers from the ranks of minority and immigrant women. . . . Today, domestics are also exempted from coverage under basic labor laws, including the National Labor Relations Act, Occupational Safety and Health Act regulations, and workers' compensation protection in most states.

Domestics were also excluded from the New Deal social welfare laws. Northern Democrats struck a deal with their Southern brethren that systematically denied Blacks eligibility for social insurance benefits. Core programs allowed states to define eligibility standards and excluded agricultural workers and domestic servants in a deliberate effort to maintain a Black menial labor caste in the South. Whites feared that Social Security would make both direct recipients and those freed from the burden of supporting dependents less willing to accept low wages to work in white people's homes.

. . .

Even after the welfare rights movement of the 1960s succeeded in adding Black mothers to the welfare rolls, welfare policy continued to encourage them to work for low wages. As AFDC became increasingly associated with Black mothers already stereotyped as lazy, irresponsible, and overly fertile, it became increasingly burdened with behavior modification, work requirements, and reduced effective benefit levels. During the 1967 congressional debate over adding mandatory work provisions to the welfare laws, Senator Russell Long expressed white people's interest in keeping poor Black mothers available for cheap domestic service:

> One thing that somewhat disturbs me is this idea that all these mothers who are drawing welfare money to stay at home have to be provided with a top paid job, that they have to be trained so they can be the top secretary in your office. You know somebody has to do just the ordinary everyday work. Now, if they don't do it, we have to do it. Either I do the housework or Mrs. Long does the housework, or we get somebody to come in and help us, but someone has to do it, and it does seem to me that if we can qualify these people to accept any employment doing something constructive, that is better than simply having them sitting at home drawing welfare money.[7]

Five years later, in 1972, Southern white politicians helped to defeat the Family Assistance Plan, which provided for a guaranteed income, with similar arguments. As one Congressman complained about the Plan, "There's not going to be anybody left to roll these wheelbarrows and press these shirts."[8]

. . .

Private employers often help to exclude household workers from social insurance programs by failing to pay their employees' Social Security, Medicare, and unemployment taxes, as well as other benefits. Even after the Zoe Baird controversy brought "nanny-tax" fraud to national attention, it has been observed that the compliance rate remains very low. The fact that household work is located in private homes has hindered workers' ability to organize, as well as government efforts to enforce employee rights.

. . .

VI. *The Conflict between Spiritual Homemakers and Menial Houseworkers*

Another force sustaining the racialized dichotomy between spiritual and menial housework grows out of the advantage privileged women appear to gain from it. The fragmentation of women's domestic labor complicates feminist approaches to housework and raises problems for women's unity in confronting the devaluation of household labor.

A. Domestics and Their Employers

As I have already discussed, the nature of the household worker's relationship to her employer often creates a tension between the needs of each party. . . . According to Judith Rollins, even contemporary relationships between domestic servants and their female employers are characterized by rituals of deference and maternalism that symbolically reinforce the domestic's inferiority and enhance the employer's ego.[9]

. . .

The possibility of replicating this hierarchy in relationships between daycare center workers and clients raises questions about the promotion of universal day care as panacea for women's economic problems. Universal day care is critical to women's financial well-being. It will help to ensure women's ability to handle childcare responsibilities while holding down a job. Yet feminist efforts to establish universal, government-supported childcare must simultaneously seek to secure the economic well-being and respect for workers in these settings. If these positive conditions are fostered, childcare centers have the potential to be sites for grassroots women's community-building efforts.

B. Employment as Emancipation?

The problems arising from the spiritual/menial split also raise questions about advocacy of women's waged employment as a means of emancipation from male domination. Women's increased participation in the market alone will not eliminate the racial division of women's labor or the distinction between spiritual and menial housework. This racial hierarchy has survived the dramatic transition of women's labor from the home to the office in the second half of this century.

Reva Siegel's account of feminists' first demands concerning household labor reveals that the spiritual/menial dichotomy is quite compatible with the singleminded goal of increased female market participation.[10] Siegel describes how the early women's movement abandoned its claims to joint rights in marital property based on the value of wives' household labor. "In the years after the Civil War," Siegel writes, "feminists began to disparage the household labor they originally sought to emancipate and to argue that women could achieve economic equality with men only by working outside the home for a market wage like men."[11] Instead of advocating a joint property regime that recognized women's work in the home, the movement's leaders placed their hopes in earnings statutes that recognized wives' rights to wages.

Some feminists accompanied the shift in their goals by embracing the split between spiritual and menial housework. Advocating the two-career marriage as a route to women's liberation had to account for wives' menial chores in the home. One solution they promoted was "cooperative housekeeping," a proposal to emancipate women from housework by removing it from the home and organizing it on a collective basis. But these feminists did not intend their scheme to displace the gendered allocation of domestic labor to liberate all women; rather they envisioned that "women would be emancipated from household labor on socially differentiated terms."[12] Women of the upper classes managed domestic servants who were working-class women. As one activist put it, "[T]he true function for educated women is the superintendence and organization of manual labor, not the doing of it themselves."[13] Cooperative housekeeping was seen not only as a means of relieving privileged women from restricting chores, but also as a way of keeping tighter control over household help. Freedom from menial housework became a privilege that women of the upper classes could share with their husbands. It was a sign that they had achieved equality with men—achieved it at the expense of greater inequality between women.

In *The Organization of Household Labor*, the prominent feminist Anna Garlin explicitly adopted the fragmentation of housework that this [a]rticle explores:

> [H]ome-making and housekeeping are not synonymous terms. The one is spiritual, and is successful or unsuccessful according to the individual character. The other is a collection of industrial pursuits which lie nearest the home-life, and are therefore dependent on the home maker's direction; but which are susceptible, like all other industries, of organization into an orderly process of business.[14]

Thus, the dichotomy between spiritual and menial housework became a premise of feminists' efforts to join the male-dominated workplace.

Feminists at the turn of the century also relied on the separation of menial from spiritual housework to argue the equal economic value of women's household labor. The spiritual wife who oversaw an assembly of servants was critical to the process of reproducing a skilled modern labor force, in the same way that the male manager of a company's staff of employees was critical. As Anna Howard Shaw, president of the National American Woman Suffrage Association, explained in 1909: "The woman furnishes her share of work-wealth in the world, and she is of intense economic value, because she utilizes her work to make the home such that the individuals who go out from it are better fitted to do the work of the world intelligently."[15] This contention required elevating the value of the wealthy wife's work of superintendence above that of purchased domestic labor. While feminists like Shaw "offered a sophisticated account of the work of social reproduction a wife performed,"[16] they simultaneously devalued the menial housework performed by working-class women.

Evelyn Nakano Glenn questions whether feminists' more recent campaign for comparable worth will resolve the racial division of women's work. This strategy attempts to eliminate the wage gap between "male" and "female" jobs by demanding equivalent pay for work requiring similar levels of skill. But such analysis might only strengthen the existing racial division of labor on the ground that the menial jobs performed by women of color deserve less remuneration. The concept of comparable worth does not call for a more egalitarian wage structure that reduces the wage differentials between skilled and unskilled women's work. "Thus, comparable work challenges the devaluation of traditionally female jobs," Glenn concludes, "but leaves intact the concept of a hierarchy of jobs."[17] Strategies to achieve gender equality in the workplace must incorporate the goals of racial and economic justice in order to succeed for all women.

C. How the Spiritual/Menial Dichotomy Devalues All Women's Work

While fostering conflicts among women, the spiritual/menial dichotomy ultimately harms all women. . . . [T]his division of women's labor privileges white, affluent women both materially and ideologically, and it perpetuates the devaluation and deprivation of women of color. Affluent white women, however, bear a terrible cost for their support of this hierarchy. Rather than increase the value of white women's domestic labor, the spiritual/menial split works to depress the value of all women's housework. Spiritual housework is by definition unpaid and unsupported. As Robin West writes, "[W]herever intimacy is, there is no compensation."[18] Spiritual housework is the aspect of domestic labor that is most foreign to the marketplace. It cannot be evaluated by the currency of the market economy. It can only be performed by women. Menial housework, on the other hand, can be delegated to others, commodified, and traded on the market. It is performed by women of subordinated classes for the cheapest wages. Moreover, the spiritual/menial split mischaracterizes the housework that all women do. This dichotomy is false. The truth is that housework usually involves both menial and spiritual aspects; women view many of their household and childcare tasks as an inseparable combination of manual labor and social nurturing. Fragmenting this experience robs it of its full meaning to women and value to society.

The spiritual/menial split also has consequences for state support of housework. The women in greatest need of support are those considered most suitable for menial chores and least suitable for spiritual ones. . . . [W]elfare policies are structured to push poor mothers into menial jobs working for wealthier women and to reform their spiritual traits. Because the women who perform menial housework are not considered spiritual, they receive inadequate social benefits or none at all. The increase in women's participation in the wage labor market may only strengthen this hierarchy. Women's tax dollars, as well as men's, go to welfare payments for mothers who are out of work. Women who must work to support their families often resent contributing part of their pay check to women who do not. The result of this dichotomy, then, is the depression of menial houseworkers' wages, the lack of any compensation for spiritual housework, and the inadequate social support for all household labor.

VII. Conclusion

Valuing all mothers' domestic labor involves challenging not only the false dichotomy between the spheres of home and work, but also the racial hierarchy among women fostered by notions of spiritual and menial housework. We are in the midst of an economic crisis for women that rests largely on the devaluation of poor Black women's domestic labor. Current welfare reform laws strip poor mothers of social support, expecting these mothers to replace their benefits with menial housework for wealthier families, if necessary. Will these developments increase the conflict among women in the arena of housework, further depressing the value of women's domestic labor, or will women unite in their demand for just compensation and support? Household chores and childcare are necessities of life, and many working women have little choice but to hire others to perform them. In the past, the mainstream women's movement has tried to resolve the problem of housework on the backs of poor and working-class women of color. Our future struggles for an equitable approach to housework must center on the fight for economic justice and social support for the women who have been labeled fit for menial but not spiritual work.

NOTES

1. Jeanne Boydston, Home and Work: Housework, Wages, and the Ideology of Labor in the Early Republic 55 (1990).

2. bell hooks, Ain't I a Woman: Black Women and Feminism 84–85 (1981).

3. Julia Wrigley, Other People's Children 6 (1995).

4. Cameron Lynne Macdonald and Carmen Sirianni, *The Service Society and the Changing Experience of Work*, in Working in the Service Society 15 (Cameron Lynne Macdonald and Carmen Sirianni, eds., 1996).

5. Evelyn Nakano Glenn, *From Servitude to Service Work: Historical Continuities in the Racial Division of Paid Reproductive Labor*, 18 Signs 1, 20 (1992).

6. Bonnie Thornton Dill, *The Means to Put My Children Through: Child-Rearing Goals and Strategies among Black Female Domestic Servants*, in The Black Woman 113 (La Frances Rodgers-Rose, ed., 1980).

7. Judith Olans Brown et al., *The Mythogenesis of Gender: Judicial Images of Women in Paid and Unpaid Labor*, 6 UCLA Women's Law Journal 457, 487 n.134 (1996) (citing Social Security Amendments of 1967: Hearings on H.R. 12080 before the Senate Finance Committee, 90th Cong. 1127 (1967) [statement of Senator Russell Long]).

8. Jill Quadagno, The Color of Welfare: How Racism Undermined the War on Poverty 130 (1995).

9. Judith Rollins, *Between Women: Domestics and Their Employers* (1985), reprinted in Working in the Service Society (Cameron Lynne Macdonald and Carmen Sirianni, eds., 1996).

10. Reva B. Siegel, *Home as Work: The First Woman's Rights Claims concerning Wives' Household Labor, 1850–1880*, 103 Yale Law Journal 1073 (1994).

11. *Id.* at 1079.

12. *Id.* at 1200.

13. *Id.* at 1195.

14. *Id.* at 1200 n.508.

15. *Id.* at 1207 n.539.

16. *Id.*

17. Evelyn Nakano Glenn, *Cleaning Up/Kept Down: A Historical Perspective on Racial Inequality in "Women's Work,"* 43 Stanford Law Review 1333, 1365 (1991).

18. Robin West, *Jurisprudence and Gender*, 55 University of Chicago Law Review 1, 59 (1988).

Toward a Global Critical Feminist Vision: Domestic Work and the Nanny Tax Debate

Taunya Lovell Banks

Feminism's adoption of the liberalist assumption that Apropertied individualism affords the necessary foundation for . . . freedom and equality led feminists to focus on gender to the exclusion of class and race.[1]

I. Introduction

In the spring of 1990, Lillian Cordero, an undocumented Peruvian woman, applied for a job with a Connecticut couple. The couple, a corporate lawyer and a law professor, advertised for a live-in nanny for their seven-month-old son. The nanny also would do light housekeeping and cook dinners. The couple hired Lillian along with her husband, also an undocumented worker. Lillian worked many weeks for up to seventy hours in exchange for a weekly wage of $250 plus room and board. During those weeks her hourly wage amounted to no more than $3.50, less than the minimum wage. Lillian's employer did not pay Social Security taxes on those wages.

In December 1992, Zoe Baird, Lillian's employer, became the first woman nominated as Attorney General of the United States. Baird subsequently withdrew her nomination following the disclosure that she failed to pay Social Security taxes for her undocumented live-in childcare worker. At the time of Baird's nomination, only 25 percent of households with domestic workers complied with the Social Security requirements. Baird, like a majority of working affluent women, knowingly and unlawfully failed to pay Social Security taxes for her domestic employee.

. . .

Influenced by Zoe Baird's plight, Congress enacted the Social Security Domestic Employment Reform Act of 1994, popularly known as the Nanny Tax law. The new law increases the threshold amount of employee wages required to trigger the tax from $50 quarterly to $1,000 annually and requires annual instead of quarterly payments of the tax to ease the reporting burden on employers like Baird. During the congressional hearings on this legislation, Florida Representative Carrie

Meek, a Black woman, said she spoke for the "nameless, faceless [household] workers" who were not considered during the Zoe Baird controversy.[2] She put a face on these women—her sisters', her mother's, and her own. While Representative Meek spoke of Black women as household workers who needed financial security, other legislators spoke of childcare workers as babysitters and nannies who created problems for their employers. Throughout the legislative debate little attention was paid to the real nanny at the heart of the Nannygate controversy, Lillian Cordero, the undocumented Peruvian woman.

. . .

II. The Under Regulation of Domestic Labor

A. Domestic Work Is Not Real Work

Since housewives traditionally did domestic work for no pay, domestic work has little or no economic value. . . .

The names we call women who labor as resident childcare workers reinforce the noncommercial nature of domestic work. Names like babysitter and nanny, a child's pet name for a caregiver, mask the value of childcare work. Society commonly believes that young children are not capable of any serious learning; thus, childcare workers are not considered education providers and generally are not paid as much as teachers. Calling childcare workers babysitters and nannies makes it easier for employers to justify paying poor women meager wages for their work. Thus, the name Nanny Tax struck a chord with some affluent parents like Meg Reggie, an Atlanta public relations consultant, who thought that paying Social Security taxes and providing health care benefits makes it "feel more like a real job to the nanny."[3] Workers most in need of Social Security benefits, and least likely to have the resources to save for old age, remain uncovered by the Social Security law because the arrangement between employers and household workers is a private matter.

B. Domestic Work Is a Private Matter

In the United States the law draws distinctions between work performed in the public sphere and work performed in the private sphere. Feminists often condemn courts and legislative bodies for their expressed reluctance to intervene in this private sphere. Domestic work, especially residential childcare, not only has low economic value, but also occurs in the private sphere. Feminist legal theory, while "[c]oncern[ed] with the ideological separation between home and work . . . has all but ignored the women who stand at the very nexus of the ideological split between home and work—paid household workers."[4] Thus, paid domestic labor performed in the home goes largely unregulated, or when regulated, laws passed for the benefit of household workers go unenforced.

Laws reflect shared social values and play an important role in shaping societal perceptions of these values. Recently, Yale Law professor Stephen Carter asked whether hiring a nanny should be defined as a privacy issue.[5] Since child-rearing may be considered a fundamental right under *Meyer v. Nebraska*,[6] Carter argues that laws regulating child-rearing, like the Nanny Tax, must be strictly scrutinized because they interfere with a fundamental right. But even Carter believes that a family's privacy interest should be overridden when employers fail to pay Social Security taxes because noncompliance with this law allows employers to exploit or harm their employees, and that concern constitutes a sufficiently compelling governmental interest. Using Carter's rationale, the continued invocation of the public-private distinction to justify the failure to remedy the exploitative labor arrangement between employers and household workers seems insupportable and disingenuous.

C. Domestic Work as Women's Work

A less pejorative view is that the failure of labor laws to effectively protect domestic workers simply reflects the social organization of housework, including childcare. Arguably, the persistent overrepresentation of women as childcare providers could be the result of each individual working woman's failure to renegotiate childcare responsibilities with her husband or partner. Mothering does not have to be women's work.

. . .

The increased numbers of middle-class women working outside the home face "a dilemma: how to excel at their jobs outside of the home while ensuring that their children are attended to. . . . The solution has often been to hire domestic help."[7] They hire other women, and thus, childcare remains solidly within the realm of women's work. Despite advances in the condition and status of women in the United States during the latter part of the twentieth century, household work, including childcare, remains women's work.

Feminists need to resolve the tension many women face between career and motherhood. It may be in the best interest of children and society for a parent to stay home to "mother" young children. If young children benefit from parental "mothering" then feminists need to decide whether women lose something of value by giving up or sharing primary responsibility for child-rearing. Feminists may have to admit that it is impossible to be simultaneously both a good mother and a full-time worker outside the home.

Zoe Baird's dilemma, however, is quite different from the circumstances faced by most working mothers in this country. Finding childcare is always problematic for poor and working-class women because they lack Baird's financial resources. Ironically, the Nanny Tax debate was triggered because Baird and her husband did not comply with laws designed to protect poor working women. Yet the reform measure addressed the preferences of affluent employers of home care workers, protecting the interests of the propertied-class employers who benefit from the public-private distinction. Affluent working women, like Zoe Baird, adopted an unsisterly position by supporting a simplified tax measure that actually decreased rather than increased the financial security of their female household employees. Gender, class, and even race are inextricably intertwined in any discussion of mothering, childcare, and household work.

III. *Legislative Narrative: Framing the Public Policy Debate*

The narratives of members of Congress and witnesses who participated in the hearings juvenilized, gendered as female, and raced as Black in-home or resident childcare workers. Professional women like Baird called childcare workers nannies, powerful male members of Congress called them babysitters, and Black members of Congress called them "Black female domestic workers." Whether nanny, babysitter, or Black female domestic worker, resident childcare workers discussed in the hearings also are presumptively native-born, virtually erasing foreign-born workers like Lillian Cordero from the debates.

A. The Legislative Debates about Employees

. . .

Although Congress, as a whole, agreed that simplification of the taxing scheme was needed for the employer's sake, members disagreed over the amount of annual wages needed to trigger payment of the tax. Those arguing for a higher threshold focused on the needs of employers for a simplified means of reporting that excluded occasional or part-time employees.

Under the new law, workers whose earnings from a single employer fell short of the $1,000 annual threshold had no Social Security coverage. Thus, the law does not cover workers earning less than $4.25 per hour, then the minimum wage, or workers earning as much as $5.00 per hour who only work one day every two weeks, or half-days every week for the same employer. A home care worker employed four hours each, for five or six different households every week at $5.00 per hour, could earn a yearly income between $4,000 and $5,000, but still not be covered under the new legislation. Under the old law, this worker's employers would be legally obligated to pay Social Security and Medicare taxes on the worker's wages.

The loss of Social Security coverage for some domestic workers was foreseen by Congress. Black members of Congress, while supportive of any measure to increase employer compliance with the Social Security law, feared that a higher triggering threshold would remove some currently covered workers from the Social Security system. During the legislative debates, Black members of Congress argued that under the new law, a worker earning $9,000 annually in aggregated wages might receive no Social Security credit if no single employer paid the worker $1,000 per year.

B. The Legislative Debates about Employers

While Representative Meek spoke of native-born minority domestic workers who needed financial security, other legislators spoke of babysitters and nannies who created legal problems for employers. Most members of Congress identified with Zoe Baird and her husband, Paul Gewirtz. Thus, the mainstream legislative and public debate focused on the problems faced by employers—well-to-do women and their husbands—not household workers, and especially not foreign-born resident childcare providers. Either the law or the workers were the cause of the problem, never the employer.

. . .

Another argument advanced during the hearings was that the current law covered women who were not real workers. For many legislators, childcare labor was not real work, it was child's work. Thus, the Social Security law made otherwise law-abiding households tax cheats because they occasionally hired teenagers to babysit their children, yet were liable, under the law, for the Social Security taxes on their wages. Remember now, Lillian Cordero was neither a part-time nor an occasional worker.

Some members of Congress blamed household workers for encouraging their employers to evade minimum wage and Social Security laws by paying wages under the table, a point countered by Diane Williams and Queen E. Sledge, a former household worker. Both women testified that most household workers did not know the law and just assumed that their employers would pay in cash. Ignoring the tremendous power and informational imbalance between employer and worker, legislators persisted in justifying employers' failure to comply with the law by asserting that household workers resent having to pay Social Security taxes and income taxes. According to these legislators the employees, not the employers, were the real tax cheats. Their arguments blindly ignore what drives workers' concerns—low wages for hard labor.

During the debates legislators repeatedly stressed that the Nanny Tax bill was not intended to cover babysitters. The word "babysitter" invokes the image of a teenage girl who works occasionally for short periods of time and receives token compensation. She is a youthful or unskilled casual worker not engaged in a serious occupation. In reality, babysitters often provide full-time childcare for women working outside their homes. In contrast, the word "nanny" invokes the image of a skilled woman who cares for the children of wealthy women, and who often lives in her employer's home. Both words, "nanny" and "babysitter," describe essentially the same work, the care of children in their parents' absence, but these two terms invoke different images—the inexperienced occasional worker and the experienced, full-time professional childcare provider. The mainstream members of Congress characterized childcare providers as babysitters, not nannies, and the difference between these two images had economic consequences for domestic workers.

C. Public Debates: What's in a Name—Racial Markers

The news media labeled the controversy surrounding Baird's nomination Nannygate because Baird called Lillian Cordero a nanny. Job titles are important because they do invoke certain images in the minds of the public, and these images influence public policy. The term "domestic worker" invokes the historic image of a native-born Black woman, the mammy, an "ideological construct of the plantation's faithful household servant and the South's most perfect slave."[8] Even today in the minds of many, the contemporary maid or household worker is an unskilled Black woman.

. . .

Even the names domestic workers call themselves are significant. Labor historian David Roediger writes about the language of labor in the formation of the American white working class. To European immigrants in the nineteenth century "hard, drudging labor" was synonymous with the kind of labor reserved for Black workers—"arduous unskilled jobs or . . . subservient positions."[9] In the northern United States the term "servant" became closely associated with Black labor, whether slave or free. "[D]omestic service bore an indelible badge of racial inferiority. It was stigmatized as 'n[*****]'s work,' a form of voluntary slavery or wage slavery that was incompatible with the values of democracy."[10] For this reason, Irish immigrant women, overrepresented as household workers during this period, resisted the "servant" and "domestic" labels in order to distinguish themselves from Black women. Thus, white workers who performed domestic work advertised for work describing themselves as "help," "helper," and "hand" rather than "servant" and "domestic" to convey a more equalitarian notion of their labor. These labels also served as a means of separating the labor performed by white workers from that performed by Black workers, whether free or slave.

Today the terms "nanny" and "domestic worker" serve similar purposes. The term "nanny" invokes the image of a "foreign" woman, unless you are a Brooklyn-accented television nanny. Many Americans have "vastly sentimentalized notions from old English history books or PBS television series that a typical nanny came to change the diapers and stayed on for the weddings."[11] Literature and mass media construct nannies as cultured, educated, unmarried women—surrogate mothers for upper-class children. Therefore, it is no accident that both the press and Zoe Baird called Lillian Cordero a nanny. The term erases the most negative connotations of in-home childcare—low wage work often performed by non-white women in a potentially exploitative environment. The significance of job titles is apparent in the public and congressional debates surrounding the enactment of the Nanny Tax law. Strangely, strong feminist voices were missing from the public debates.

IV. Competing Gendered Narratives about Domestic Work: Affluent Working Women and Black Feminists

During and following the Nannygate controversy neither affluent working women nor Black feminists questioned the gendered nature of paid domestic labor. In distancing themselves from Zoe Baird, both groups tacitly accepted that domestic work, including in-home or resident childcare, is women's work, but each group operated from different perspectives, influenced by race, and often class. This section compares and contrasts the narratives of affluent working women with Black feminists' writings about and reactions to paid domestic work.

A. Affluent Women: Zoe Baird, Not One of Us?

. . .

[L]egal feminist Joan Williams wrote that women lawyers with children have two alternatives: spend little time with their children, like "the typical workaholic father," or juggle home and career "in ways that interfere with one's ability to perform as an ideal worker—in other words, to join the mommy track."[12] Zoe Baird chose the first alternative, working the hours of a traditional workaholic man. Thus, she needed adequate childcare to pursue her career as a corporate lawyer. Baird's solution was to hire a less privileged woman, Lillian Cordero, to care for her child. Feminists like Williams would argue that Baird's solution preserves and reinforces the gendering of domestic labor as women's work. Williams' concern, however, is the plight of upper-middle-class or affluent women, not the women hired to do domestic labor. With few exceptions, feminist legal theory does not address the plight of paid household workers.

The failure of mainstream feminists to press harder for better childcare arrangements for working women and better wages for the women who work as nannies and house cleaners reflects feminists' "reluctance and ambivalence" about the topic of family and motherhood. The reaction of other affluent women to Nannygate reflects a similar reluctance and ambivalence about work outside the home and parenting, and may explain why some affluent women employers of household workers distanced themselves from Baird, even when they, too, paid no Social Security taxes on their workers' wages.

Sociologist Pierrette Hondagneu-Sotelo surveyed and interviewed affluent women employers of paid household workers in Los Angeles.[13] Hondagneu-Sotelo found that an overwhelming majority of the women employers surveyed did not pay Social Security, Medicare, and federal withholding taxes as required by law. Yet these affluent working women believed Zoe Baird acted inappropriately in not paying Social Security taxes on Lillian Cordero's wages.

Echoing the legislative hearings, the women employers interviewed justified their own failure to comply with the law, stating that non-compliance is normative practice. A few of the women employers surveyed even blamed the federal government or domestic workers for imposing these problems on hard-working families. These women employers distinguished their non-compliance with the law from Baird's, holding Baird to a higher standard than non-lawyers. Some women also applied this higher standard of accountability to "celebrities and people of Baird's socio-economic group."[14] Their responses, however, provide no clear guide to determine when one falls into Baird's socio-economic group.

Hondagneu-Sotelo's study suggests that women employers, usually working women, of paid household workers seldom admit that they are part of the problem. Yet these employers are participants in an informal economy that exploits less privileged working women. "[T]he informal economic sector . . . [consists of] those income-generating activities that occur outside of state regulation, where formal labor contracts, payment of taxes and benefits, and standard hiring are generally absent."[15] Upper-middle-class and affluent working women hire household workers without formal contracts and pay these workers under the table to avoid liability for taxes and benefits—working conditions most working women employers would not tolerate.

B. Black Feminists: Zoe Baird, Not One of Us—Black Women as Domestic Workers, Myth or Reality

A few Black feminists focus on race rather than class aspects of Nannygate. These feminists interpreted Baird's explanation for hiring an undocumented, non-Black woman immigrant as a cover for the intentional displacement of Black women as in-home child caregivers and domestic workers.

. . .

Many Black feminists operate from the presumption that most Black mothers work outside the home, sometimes in the homes of white women. Twila Perry, for example, places primary emphasis on the role of race in driving exploitative domestic employment arrangements. Speaking directly to the Nannygate controversy she writes:

> One of the largely unaddressed issues in the media controversies over the failed nominations of Zoe Baird and Kimba Wood to be Attorney General was the potential exploitation of women who take care of the children of white middle and upper-middle class professional women while they pursue careers outside of the home. These women usually end up employing poor minority women, often at low wages. Frequently, these arrangements are "off the books," which means that the workers do not receive job-related benefits such as social security, health insurance, unemployment compensation, or other protections.[16]

Her assessment of the problem is only partially correct. Professor Perry overlooks the experiences of white European ethnics and non-white immigrants. The racial composition of childcare and other household workers is not constant, but varies based on economic, political, and social circumstances. The racial or ethnic composition of paid domestic workers also depends on the type of domestic work.

Class can mediate race, even for Black women. Although more white than Black women can afford to employ household workers, affluent Black women also participate in exploitative employer-employee domestic worker relationships. Thus, affluent Black women, like their white counterparts, may escape being exploited as domestic workers only to participate in the exploitation of less privileged women, who may or may not be Black. The Black feminist critique often fails to acknowledge how class differences influence the concerns of Black women.

. . .

V. Paid Domestic Workers: Working-Class Women Immigrants

Largely ignored during the Nannygate controversy was Cordero's status as an undocumented worker. Baird raised the issue of Cordero's immigration status only to justify nonpayment of Social Security taxes. In the end, Baird employed an undocumented foreign-born woman as a childcare provider, driven, she claimed, by the fact that she could not obtain satisfactory services from native-born workers.

. . .

Today, approximately 25 percent of foreign-born women in the United States are household workers. [As in] the past, there is a racialized hierarchy among immigrant domestic workers. In New York City, for example, non-English-speaking Haitian women are paid less than women from English-speaking Caribbean countries. Latinas who do not speak English earn more than Black women from Haiti or English-speaking Caribbean countries because some employers consider (presumably light-skinned) Latinas white.

Some migrant women work as in-home childcare providers. These foreign-born household workers with limited job options are especially vulnerable to employer abuse. Although protected by labor laws, undocumented (and documented) foreign-born workers rarely report employers because they fear loss of income and possible deportation. Their stories of abuse are common and horrifying.

. . .

A family relative of an Indian businessman and his Indonesian wife recruited Francesca Ekka, a twenty-three-year-old Indian woman described by a newspaper as "an au pair and housekeeper for an affluent couple with two children."[17] Ms. Ekka entered the United States on a tourist visa and was held in virtual servitude and physically abused by the couple in Miami. The couple was convicted of "conspiring to hold Ms. Ekka in involuntary servitude, inducing her to reside in the United States illegally and harboring her in violation of immigration laws."[18]

The conviction of this couple is unusual. Criminal action against employers is rare, according to news reports, because abuse of domestic workers occurs in the privacy of the home making the abuse difficult to document and expose. Stories like Ms. Ekka's involving abuses by foreign-born employers from Asian or Middle Eastern countries often are widely publicized, which gives the mistaken impression that cultural differences, rather than the exploitative nature of the employee-employer relationship, explain employer abuse of domestic workers, but there is documentation that employer abuse has no cultural limits.

United States immigration laws also facilitate the exploitation of foreign-born household workers by middle-class and affluent employers. Employers hire foreign childcare providers who are either: (1) J-1 visa (exchange visitor visa) candidates; (2) H-2B non-immigrant visa candidates (unskilled workers); or (3) undocumented workers. A brief review of the procedures for the J-1 and H-2B visas illustrates why recruiting undocumented workers, although illegal, is the easiest and most inexpensive route for employers.

A. Au Pairs

Although the exchange visitor visa (au pair program) is the easiest legal way to obtain a foreign-born childcare worker, there are few exchange programs. Since 1986, approximately 60,000 women between the ages of eighteen and twenty-five entered the United States on J-1 visas to work as au pairs. . . .

Although difficult to get, au pairs are a cheap and unregulated source of childcare, making them desirable childcare options for many affluent families. According to one agency, "[A]n au pair 'costs . . . less than day care and gives your family a culturally enriching experience of hosting a well-educated, English-speaking European.'"[19] More importantly, employers are not required to pay Social Security taxes on au pairs' wages, nor file IRS W-2 employment forms. In addition, as mentioned previously, most au pairs are white and come from Western Europe, satisfying those employers who want a live-in employee who looks most like them.

. . .

B. Unskilled Workers

The unskilled worker visa process is a less attractive option for obtaining a foreign-born resident home care worker. The lengthy visa process requires potential employers to prove that they are unable to fill the position with an American worker, and "sponsored" workers only receive temporary visas. In addition, there are few visas available for unskilled workers. Foreign-born workers are permitted to work temporarily in the United States only if their presence will not have a harmful impact on American workers. Although the unskilled worker visa is a less attractive option from an employer's perspective for the reasons previously stated, it is a legal means of obtaining foreign-born domestic help.

Following the Nannygate controversy, pressure to simplify this visa process grew. In February 1993, the Federal Commission on Immigration Reform heard testimony supporting some type of immigration program for household workers. One proposal, modeled after Canada's "Live-in Caregiver Program," would have created a subcategory of H-2B non-immigrant visas for employers who swear that they cannot find a "qualified" U.S. citizen or resident home care worker. Under another proposal, foreign-born workers outside and inside the country could apply directly for H-2B visas once the Department of Labor determines that there is a shortage of household workers and if applicants demonstrate previous work in the "home care" industry, as well as an intention to remain in the industry.

Neither proposal was accepted. In April 1994, the Department of Labor created a job classification for "nannies" with two years of formal training and childcare experience. Quickly reversing itself, a Labor Department official wrote that "the move was 'based on insufficient fact-finding and research.'"[20] Despite these problems, foreign-born women may be lured into live-in domestic situations on unskilled worker visas by the promise of a green card.

To the immigrant, [an employer's promise to sponsor a green card application] seems a worthy gamble—a few years work as a domestic may lead to citizenship. The sponsoring employer needs to prove it's a necessity to have a live-in domestic or that there aren't enough Americans to fill the job . . . [but t]here's no guarantee that sponsorship will lead to a green card and many cases have been denied at the initial stage.[21]

The au pair and H-2B nonresident visa programs work against unskilled native-born women and foreign-born women with families. Pressure to retain both programs and facilitate visas for foreign-born resident home care workers illustrates how affluent working women and powerful men perpetuate a division of labor in the home that is gendered female, undervalued, and consequently underpaid. Mainstream feminism's failure to effectively articulate and actualize policies that value and adequately compensate people who perform traditional household tasks contributes to the continued impoverished circumstances of home care workers.

VI. *Searching for Solutions*

A. Complex Problems Suggest Complex Solutions

. . .

Given the multiple issues connected to paid domestic work, developing an analytical lens through which to process and address all the issues is difficult. A decade ago critical race feminist Kimberlé Crenshaw advanced her intersectionality theory, the notion that some types of subordinating conduct cannot be analyzed using "a single categorical axis."[22] Professor Crenshaw's theory of intersectionality captures an approach to feminism similar to the unified-systems theory adopted by some socialist feminists. Unlike liberal, radical, or cultural feminism, socialist feminism argues "that because male dominance, capitalism, and racism are inextricably intertwined, it is necessary to construct a [feminist] theory that takes account of the multiple bases of oppression[, because] a challenge to any one alone is inadequate."[23] As a result, socialist feminists might view the status of women household workers in the context of how the under regulation and gendering of childcare and other domestic work as women's work reinforces both the public/private and worker/mother dichotomies, and creates a market for migrant women workers, an approach used in this article. Socialist legal feminists, for example, might argue that women who stay home to care for young children should be paid a salary commensurate with school teachers since mothering involves many of the same skills. Mothering must be seen as work that is highly valued in both moral and monetary terms.

Socialist feminism also is a helpful analytical lens because it allows us to consider how globalization contributes to the resurgence of a female, largely non-white servant class in the United States. By looking at domestic workers from a global perspective it is easy to understand how the lack of work in poor countries creates a flow of low paid workers into more developed countries. Adopting a socialist feminist approach to the plight of home care workers, however, might result in a theory without practical application. Socialist feminism requires significant structural changes that are unlikely to occur in a capitalistic country like the United States. Socialist feminism also requires a level of activism and involvement to reach and mobilize working-class women.

. . .

B. Mobilizing Household Workers

Almost a decade ago Suzanne Goldberg wrote about the limitations inherent in relying only on legal regulation to improve the working conditions and wages of household workers.[24] Goldberg advocates developing laws that "enhance 'community' organizing" so that workers might support laws that facilitate a balancing of the often conflicted interests of people who do the same type of work. History suggests, however, that community organizing alone seldom produces significant structural changes. At various points in the twentieth century, household workers organized to improve working conditions. Most of these efforts were either unsuccessful or resulted in small changes.

More recently, social scientist Mary Romero studied Chicana household workers in Denver, documenting the humiliation and degradation of the workers at the hands of their employers.[25] Romero found, however, that the Chicana household workers she studied resisted their subordination, establishing informal strategies to improve their position, negotiating schedule changes, length of work day, and payment by the job rather than the hour. They negotiated with individual employers for their labor. Romero argues that the transformation by the Chicana workers in Denver of their work from hourly into fee-for-service work holds the promise of "eliminat[ing] aspects of hierarchy along the lines of gender, race, and class."[26]

The women in Romero's study may be exceptional, and if not, then the reasons for their success bear closer scrutiny by feminists as we search for solutions. Nevertheless, the household work most likely to be transformed into a fee-for-service occupation is house cleaning and group childcare outside the home, not residential childcare. Residential or in-home childcare, the preferred model for affluent parents, will remain a potentially exploitative and under regulated employment situation. Feminists, some of whom are employers of domestic workers themselves, may find it difficult to encourage their workers to press for better employment conditions because of conflicting interests.

C. Ambivalent and Affluent Mothers

. . .

Affluent feminists who supported the Nanny Tax law constitute a group against patriarchy, yet not for women. The failure of women's groups to strongly support comprehensive government regulation of wage and hour provisions for household workers, which is a rather modest proposal, leaves labor performed in the home undervalued, underpaid, and under regulated. Although Black feminists, using race as a starting point, acknowledge that the gender and class of the employer and the worker influence government labor policies, their critique does not go far enough. There is an international market for household workers and few regulations to protect women like Lillian Cordero from exploitation. Thus, a more global analysis is needed.

VII. Conclusion

. . .

The feminist movement has never adequately addressed this displacement of a woman's "second shift" down the class ladder. To some extent, the feminist carries a double burden. Our society holds her to a higher moral standard—than her husband . . . if she decides to pursue her own professional interests. Advocates for domestic workers hold the feminist accountable for oppressing the woman who takes on "her" domestic role, just as the workers themselves blame the woman, not the male breadwinner, for their poor salaries.

Rather than demonstrate, legislatively, that the work of caring for children is valuable, the Nanny Tax law simply confirms the lack of value society places on the women who perform domestic work, whether paid or unpaid. The failure of all feminists to coalesce around domestic work and press for structural changes, or even effective reforms, leaves labor performed in the home undervalued, underpaid, and under regulated. The narratives surrounding the enactment of the Nanny Tax law illustrate how the venue of work, gender, race, class, and citizenship of employer and worker influenced government labor policies.

. . .

NOTES

1. Marion Crain, *Between Feminism and Unionism: Working Class Women, Sex Equality, and Labor Speech*, 82 Georgetown Law Journal 1903, 1924–25 (1994).

2. 140 Cong. Rec. 9703 (1994) (statement of Rep. Meek).

3. Maureen Downey, *Baird Case Forces Parents to Face the Nanny Issue: Green Cards, Taxes and Insurance*, Atlanta Journal and Constitution, Jan. 23, 1993, at A8.

4. Peggie R. Smith, *Regulating Paid Household Work: Class, Gender, Race, and Agendas of Reform*, 48 American University Law Review 851, 852–54 (1999).

5. Stephen L. Carter, The Confirmation Mess: Cleaning Up the Federal Appointments Process 179 (1994).

6. 262 U.S. 390 (1923).

7. Twila L. Perry, *Alimony: Race, Privilege, and Dependency in the Search for Theory*, 82 Georgetown Law Journal 2481, 2508–9 (1994).

8. Smith, supra note 4, at 864 n.75.

9. David R. Roediger, The Wages of Whiteness: Race and the Making of the American Working Class 144–45 (1991).

10. Smith, supra note 4, at 877.

11. 135 Cong. Rec. 12,692 (1989) (statement of Linda Burton).

12. Joan C. Williams, *Sameness Feminism and the Work/Family Conflict*, 35 New York Law School Law Review 347, 352–53 (1990).

13. Pierrette Hondagneu-Sotelo, *Affluent Players in the Informal Economy: Employers of Paid Domestic Workers*, 17 International Journal of Society and Social Policy 130, 130 (1997).

14. *Id*. at 148.

15. *Id*. at 133.

16. Perry, supra note 7, at 2509.

17. Mireya Navarro, *In Land of the Free, a Modern Slave*, New York Times, Dec. 12, 1996, at A22.

18. *Id*.

19. Alvin A. Snyder, *A Look at . . . Au Pairs: Uncle Sam's Babysitting Service*, Washington Post, Nov. 9, 1997, at C3.

20. Sue Shellenbarger, *Nannygate Reversal Enrages Advocates*, Wall Street Journal, Apr. 27, 1994, at B1.

21. Maria Laurino, *"I'm Nobody's Girl": New York's New Indentured Servants*, Village Voice, Oct. 14, 1986, at 17–18.

22. Kimberlé Crenshaw, *Demarginalizing the Intersection of Race and Sex: A Black Feminist Critique of Antidiscrimination Doctrine, Feminist Theory and Antiracist Politics*, 1989 University of Chicago Legal Forum 139, 140.

23. Crain, supra note 1, at 1931–32.

24. Suzanne Goldberg, *In Pursuit of Workplace Rights: Household Workers and a Conflict of Laws*, 3 Yale Journal of Law and Feminism 63 (1990).

25. Mary Romero, Maid in the U.S.A. (1992).

26. *Id*. at 15.

15

(Dis)Assembling Rights of Women Workers along the Global Assembly Line: Human Rights and the Garment Industry

Laura Ho, Catherine Powell, and Leti Volpp

. . .

Introduction

On August 2, 1995, a multi-agency raid found sixty-seven Thai women and five Thai men kept in slave-like conditions in an apartment complex in a Los Angeles community called El Monte. Under the constant surveillance of armed guards and confined behind a ring of razor wire, they had been held for several years and had been forced to work as garment workers up to eighteen hours per day for far less than the minimum wage. They were refused unmonitored contact with the outside world and threatened with rape or harm to themselves and their families if they tried to escape. On one occasion, a worker who tried to escape was brutally beaten, his photograph taken and shown to the other workers as an example of what might happen to them if they too tried to flee.

. . .

Some observers would like to explain away sweatshops as immigrants exploiting other immigrants, as "cultural," or as the importation of a form of exploitation that normally does not happen here but occurs elsewhere, in the "Third World."

. . .

Sweatshops, like the one in El Monte, are a home-grown problem with peculiarly American roots. Since the inception of the garment industry, U.S. retailers and manufacturers have scoured the United States and the rest of the globe for the cheapest and most malleable labor—predominantly female, low-skilled, and disempowered—in order to squeeze out as much profit as possible for themselves. Along with this globalization, the process of subcontracting, whereby manufacturers contract out cutting and sewing to contractors to avoid being considered the "employer" of the workers, has made it extremely difficult for garment workers in the United States to assert their rights under domestic law.

. . .

I. History and Current Status of the Garment Industry in the United States

. . .

While the garment industry has provided women, particularly women of color and immigrants, access to the manufacturing work force, this result has been accompanied by a downward spiral of wages and consistent exploitation. Wages are especially low in thriving "underground" economies in such cities as Los Angeles and New York, where garment workers usually make much less than $4.25 an hour—the current federal minimum wage—and work ten to twelve hour days without the overtime compensation mandated by federal law.

As predominantly working-class women of color, garment workers face severe structural barriers to exercising their rights. Positioned at the intersection of oppressions based on race, gender, class, and frequently immigrant status, these women workers must also struggle against the power of international capital. Their organizing attempts are often met by a shift to offshore production, where their counterparts—primarily low-wage women workers in developing countries—are paid even less for the same work.

II. The Creation of the Global Sweatshop and the Need for an Alternative Strategic Paradigm

The garment industry is one of the most global industries in the world. The proliferation of industrial garment production follows broader patterns in trade globalization and economic restructuring. . . . Many developing countries have switched from the model of "import substitution"—industrialization through substituting imports with goods produced domestically—to a model of "export promotion"—export-led industrialization. Export promotion typically involves strategies that attract foreign investment through such incentives as tax holidays, the promise of cheap controllable labor for transnational corporations [TNCs], and the establishment of export-processing zones (EPZs) that ease importing/exporting restrictions.

In addition to engaging in direct foreign investment (for example, through their own branch offices), TNCs also arrange arms' length relationships through subcontracting and licensing agreements, which often allow them to limit their liability for labor violations. TNCs benefit from their ability to scour the globe for the cheapest sources of labor in developing countries, as well as in advanced-industrialized countries, where extensive immigration from less-developed countries has created a "Third World within."

. . .

These trends in garment production and trade highlight ways in which the concept of the nation-state is becoming an increasingly ineffective model for designing market-controlling mechanisms. States are often unable to control the activities of TNCs, although strong governments exercise considerable influence through trade policies and development assistance. While the nation-state traditionally has been viewed as the locus for the declaration of rights-based norms (through courts) and their enforcement (through police and army), the state cannot adequately respond to dynamics that arise from markets that cut across borders. . . . The decline of geographic sovereignty and conceptual boundaries such as the traditional public/private, state/market, political/economic, and national/international dichotomies testifies to the fact that simplistic, nationalistic approaches for securing worker rights are no longer viable.

Thus, more sophisticated approaches that are transnational in scope and that explore the interplay of labor rights and free trade must be examined. . . . While the free trade debate addresses the current inexorability of globalization in a way that domestic economic policy conversations do not, the free trade/protectionist dichotomy does not adequately frame a space within which transnational strategies that protect workers can be developed.

An alternative paradigm to the free trade/protectionist paradigm is a post–free trade approach, which posits transnational mechanisms through which to harmonize labor, environmental, and human rights standards. Such mechanisms allow for trade liberalization while offering protections to workers both at home and abroad. They include, among other things, social clauses in trade laws that may be enforced through adjudicatory bodies. While in theory these mechanisms are attractive, in practice they have often failed to live up to their mission because of inadequate resources, investigatory capability, and enforcement powers. Addressing these limitations is essential.

. . .

III. Praxis: Labor Protection via Formal Legal Regimes

TNCs have adopted two effective strategies that allow them to maintain sweatshops on the global assembly line. First, TNCs use the contracting system, whether domestically or abroad, to avoid legal liability for the workers' wages or working conditions. Second, TNCs use their ability to relocate production to virtually any country as a threat to all their current workers: if workers demand higher wages, TNCs can move their production to lower wage sites. Combating these two tactics necessitates coupling U.S. legal strategies with transnational ones, such as deploying the extraterritorial application of U.S. laws, public international law, U.S. trade laws, and multilateral trade agreements. . . .

A. Extraterritorial Application of U.S. Laws

In seeking to assert their rights across national boundaries, garment workers and advocates should be aware of the implications and possibilities of the extraterritorial application of U.S. laws in the secondary boycott prohibition of the National Labor Relations Act (NLRA). While most groups outside of unions arguably fall beyond the NLRA's reach, the more a group looks and acts like a union, the more a court may interpret its activities as proscribed by the NLRA's secondary boycott prohibitions. On the other hand, the extraterritorial application of protective provisions of the NLRA, such as collective bargaining protections, could greatly enhance protections for garment workers laboring for U.S. corporations abroad.

More promising is the extraterritorial application of Title VII, which clearly provides antidiscrimination protection for garment workers in U.S. plants overseas. In 1991, in response to the Supreme Court's refusal to extend Title VII of the Civil Rights Act extraterritorially, Congress specifically amended Title VII to have such reach. For workers employed by U.S. companies in factories outside U.S. borders, the law provides a way to combat the sexual harassment, as well as other forms of discrimination, common in many factories both domestically and abroad.

Garment workers, however, are not always well served by the extraterritorial application of U.S. laws. To the extent U.S. labor law is an amalgamation of corporate and labor interests, specific provisions may be the product of political deal making rather than concern for the protection of workers' rights. Moreover, the extension of U.S. laws to the activities of U.S. companies in other national jurisdictions could be viewed as a form of neocolonialism. As such, more cooperative approaches to developing and enforcing transnational labor standards should be explored.

. . .

C. U.S. Trade Laws

Of all U.S. trade laws available to assert labor rights, worker advocates have used the Generalized System of Preferences (GSP) petition process most frequently. The GSP provides duty-free tariff treatment on certain products for designated "beneficiary developing countries" (BDC) in order to promote economic development in those countries. When the GSP program was renewed in 1984, section 502(b) of the Renewal Act added mandatory worker rights criteria to the statute. Furthermore, section 502(b)(7) of the Renewal Act mandated that "the President shall not designate any country a beneficiary developing country under this section . . . if such country has not taken or is not taking steps to afford internationally recognized worker rights to workers in the country (including any designated zone in that country)."[1] Those internationally recognized worker rights are: (1) freedom of association; (2) the right to organize and bargain collectively; (3) a prohibition on the use of forced or compulsory labor; (4) a minimum wage for the employment of children; and (5) acceptable conditions of work with respect to minimum wages, hours of work, and occupational safety and health.

Following a review of BDCs in 1985–1986, the United States Trade Representative issued regulations that allow "any person," on an annual basis, to "file a request to have the GSP status of any eligible beneficiary developing country reviewed with respect to any of the designation criteria. . . ."[2] Pursuant to these regulations, at least thirty-four petitions were filed challenging BDCs on worker rights grounds as of the beginning of the 1991–1992 review cycle. Eight countries have been suspended or terminated. Because the United States imports garments from many BDCs, the GSP can and has been a useful tool for garment workers.

D. Multilateral Trade Agreements

. . .

2. NAFTA

. . . [T]he North American Free Trade Agreement (NAFTA) contains labor and environmental side agreements and thus affords worker rights greater protection. Article I of the labor side agreement identifies one of its objectives as the promotion, "to the maximum extent possible, [of] the labor principles set out in Annex 1."[3] Annex 1 states that each country should promote the following: (1) protection of the rights to organize, bargain, and strike; (2) prohibition of forced labor, child labor, subminimal wages, and employment discrimination; and (3) promotion of equal pay for equal work, occupational safety and health, and equal treatment for migrant workers.

These standards, however, are merely hortatory. The side agreement provides for enforcement of each country's existing labor laws in only three areas: (1) occupational health and safety, (2) child labor, and (3) minimum wages. Significantly, the right to organize and bargain collectively is listed only in the aspirational Annex I rather than as an enforceable obligation governed by the procedures in the side agreement.

. . .

Worker advocates have put the NAFTA labor rights regime into immediate use and have begun testing its parameters, including pushing it to promote worker organizing. U.S. unions have brought three submissions against Mexico for anti-union discrimination in violation of Mexican law, at Honeywell, General Electric, and Sony factories. Conversely, the Telephone Workers' Union of Mexico brought a submission to its government, asking it to challenge the closing of La Conexion Familiar, a San Francisco–based subsidiary of Sprint, which shut down eight days before a scheduled union vote, leaving 200 women jobless. The NLRB considered a complaint from the Communication Workers of America (CWA), and found that while Sprint had violated labor law in its handling of the union, it had closed La Conexion Familiar primarily for financial reasons. CWA has appealed and is hoping that a hearing stemming from Mexico's complaint will lead to a proposed code of conduct for employers in NAFTA countries as a way to prevent future factory closings in response to union activities.

IV. Less Formal Terrain: Using Nonlegal Strategies to Fight the Might of Garment Transnationals

Notwithstanding the few successes of the application of U.S. laws or the use of international law in protecting workers' rights, the persistent shortcomings of such formal legal mechanisms demand an alternative approach to advocacy on behalf of garment workers. Such advocacy should employ tactics that do not rely solely on the state or formal legal mechanisms, but rather combine them with worker organizing, consumer pressure, and other "nonlegal" strategies.

A. Voluntary Codes of Conduct

. . .

1. Corporate Codes of Conduct

. . .

While some observers call these standards strict, the codes contain significant limitations. First, they usually do not contain mechanisms for enforcement. Further, they generally do not contain any provisions regarding monitoring of business partners. Even when a code requires or recommends such monitoring, the monitoring is almost never conducted by an independent agency. As a result, they are standards without teeth and function primarily as a public relations gesture.

Recently, a campaign run by the National Labor Committee (NLC) compelled the Gap to become the first garment manufacturer/retailer to agree to independent monitoring of all its plants in Central America. The Gap had conducted its own investigation of its plant in El Salvador and found no violations but continued to receive mounting reports of abuses from Salvadoran human rights groups. In November 1995, the company announced that it would no longer source work to the plant, effectively punishing the workers by stripping them of their jobs. Increasing pressure from consumers and shareholders persuaded the Gap to return to the plant, reinstate the fired workers, improve working conditions, and agree to independent monitoring throughout Gap factories in Central America.

. . .

2. Union Codes of Conduct

In the United States, the International Ladies Garment Workers' Union (ILGWU) and the Amalgamated Clothing, Textile Workers Union (ACTWU), and the union formed by their merger, the Union of Needletrades, Industrial and Textile Employees (UNITE), have won union contracts with manufacturers and retailers that contain codes of conduct to be applied to any overseas vendors with which the manufacturers or retailers do business. The ILGWU "Code of Conduct for Overseas Vendors" requires vendors—business partners or contractors—to comply with applicable local laws regarding wages, hours and benefits, child labor, free association, discrimination, and safety in the workplace. Vendors are prohibited from using forced labor, and monitoring is facilitated by the employer's obtaining from each vendor a signed statement indicating its understanding of the code.

The ACTWU 1993 "National Agreement" with the Clothing Manufacturers Association is far stronger, both in the restrictions it places on vendors and in its enforcement mechanisms. Vendors cannot require more than a forty-eight hour work week, engage in discrimination, use child labor, or use forced or compulsory labor. Manufacturers and/or retailers and ACTWU periodically monitor compliance with

these standards and report to each other. If the union chooses, it may take any violations to binding, expedited arbitration; if the union proves its case, the manufacturers and/or retailers shall cease to contract with the vendor in violation, or with all manufacturers in a particular country if the problem is sufficiently widespread.
. . .

B. Worker Organizing

Unions and other worker advocacy groups have begun to respond to global economic restructuring through transnational organizing. For instance, unions are strengthening ties among workers of different countries so that when a plant announces that it is closing in the United States, workers at the relocation site can put concerted and simultaneous pressure on the manufacturer. Likewise, UNITE and other U.S.-based trade unions have begun to create joint movements with independent Mexican unionists to support organizing in maquiladoras. For example, when Leslie Fay threatened to shut its remaining production plant in the United States to move to Central America, UNITE engaged in cross-border organizing, bringing before Congress a twenty-year Honduran worker to testify that she found a forty dollar skirt in a New York store which she was paid forty-three cents to sew.

Both unions and nonunionized workers' associations have begun worker exchanges, which encourage workers to see their commonalities and the potential of their combined strength, rather than allowing protectionist impulses, racism, or xenophobia to convince them that they will be well served by competing with the workers of other countries. Along these lines, in July 1991, the Tennessee Industrial Renewal Network (TIRN) sponsored a group of women from East Tennessee to visit women employed in Mexican maquiladoras. Similarly, the Clean Clothes Campaign organized a tour of Europe in April 1996 for several representatives of garment workers from Asia. California-based Asian Immigrant Women Advocates (AIWA) has engaged in worker exchanges within the United States, with workers from La Mujer Obrera in Texas, the Common Ground Economic Development Corporation of African American Women in Dallas, and the Ramah Weavers Association of Navajo Women in New Mexico.
. . .

E. UN Fourth World Conference on Women:
Beijing as a Site for Mobilizing Women Workers

International women's conferences have also served as a site for the creation of transnational solidarity. The growth of the women's human rights movement as a global phenomenon is apparent in the ability of women to engage the UN and other multilateral organizations, thereby compelling these institutions to hold themselves accountable to the world's working women. Few practical gains in economic justice, however, have been achieved as a result of such conferences, in part because economic and social rights have not received the same degree of attention as civil and political rights in those fora. When reformulated as civil or political rights, economic justice concerns, such as worker rights, have been conceived as the "right" to government enforcement of national labor laws (as is required, for instance, under the NAFTA labor side agreement). Such an approach is imperfect because it requires the complainant to prove not only the original violation of labor rights, but also to prove—by demonstrating, for instance, exhaustion of administrative remedies—that the government failed adequately to respond.

Although the Platform for Action adopted at the 1995 UN Fourth World Conference on Women in Beijing, China provided major breakthroughs in terms of the articulation of standards of economic justice, it is still painfully inadequate. The Platform for Action is not a treaty nor does it have the status of any other legally binding instrument. Moreover, the UN has not designated a lead agency with adequate resources to implement the Beijing Platform.

Despite these shortcomings, many women's human rights advocates view the document as a politically binding contract between governments and the world's women. It represents an interpretative text that informs human rights norms in legally binding instruments. Finally, the Platform and other outcomes of Beijing present an enormous potential for grassroots organizing.

Coinciding with the UN conference was the 1995 Non-Governmental Organization (NGO) Forum—the largest gathering of women in history—held in Huairou, China. The authors, along with other garment worker advocates from the United States, organized the only workshop specifically addressing the garment industry among the 5,000 events and activities organized at the NGO Forum. At the workshop, entitled "The Struggle of Garment Workers on the Global Assemblyline," garment workers and worker advocates from countries including the Philippines, Thailand, Bangladesh, and the United States spoke of conditions they found in their regions and different strategies they had pursued. After the workshop, several informal discussions took place in which advocates learned more about country conditions and discussed ways to collaborate transnationally in assisting workers to assert their rights. A joint statement, titled "The Global Assemblyline," was prepared and distributed to NGO Forum participants to build their awareness as consumers and to increase worker solidarity.

Conclusion

We, as consumers, too often fail to engage in conscious reflection about the hands that sewed our clothes. We thus live with and normalize everyday violations of workplace rights of garment workers. This is facilitated by society's historical and persistent dehumanization of and lack of concern for poor women of color workers.

If we, as advocates, neglect to develop and implement new strategies that reveal and contest the adverse consequences of economic globalization, more sweatshops will undoubtedly proliferate along the global assembly line. Unless we radically redefine the terms of the debate, violations will continue. The widespread abuse of garment workers across the globe will not automatically be eliminated by removing unnecessary fetters on free trade or immigration; for instance, violations of workplace rights would not end by opening national borders. It is not simply the relative immobility of workers and unions in contrast to the increasing mobility of capital that puts workers at a severe disadvantage, nor is the ultimate source of the problem insufficient state-sponsored protectionism in the United States, contrary to xenophobic claims that have permeated political discourse of late.

The endemic and systematic violations of workplace rights of garment workers in the United States and overseas result primarily from the overriding lawlessness of transnational corporations, whose pursuit of profit runs roughshod over the human rights of those whose labor allows them to thrive. Garment worker advocates must attempt transnational strategies to fight such corporations through both formal legal mechanisms and strategies that use the pressure of consumers, workers, and the community. Political lawyers must envision creative strategies that move beyond traditional legal frameworks that dichotomize civil and political from economic and social rights, and U.S. domestic law from international law.

. . .

Notes

1. 19 U.S.C. § 2462(b)(7) (1994).
2. 15 C.F.R. § 2007, 2007.0(b) (1996).
3. *North American Agreement on Labor Cooperation*, Sept. 14, 1993, U.S.-Can.-Mex., art. 1(b), H.R. Doc. No. 160, 103d Cong. 1st Sess. 48, 50, 32 I.L.M. 1502, 1503 (1993).

16

Commercial Sex:
Beyond Decriminalization

Sylvia A. Law

. . .

B. The Application of Traditional Work Law to Commercial Sex

[In this Article, I] . . . explore what it would mean to treat commercial sex "as any other profession" or employment. If commercial sex were decriminalized women might work in an organized context, such as the ranches in Nevada or the brothels in Hawaii during World War II. . . . [F]irst [I] consider sex as work in an organized context and explore the rights and protections that the law provides to employees. I conclude that there are many obstacles to applying employee protection laws to sex workers and that the concrete benefits of these laws are likely to be minimal. Second, [I] explore the rights and protections that sex workers might enjoy as independent professionals.

In the United States, many state and federal laws that protect workers only apply to the employer/employee relationship. The employee status triggers the protection of laws governing minimum wage, workers' compensation, unemployment compensation, protection against sex discrimination, including sexual harassment, and the right to unionize. In addition, benefits, including health insurance and pensions, are often tied to employment.

Laws defining employee rights and benefits distinguish between "employees," who are entitled to the benefits of the law, and "independent contractors," who are not. The distinction between employees and independent contractors is complex and indeterminate. The key factors include "the degree of control over the worker's work, the worker's opportunity for profit or loss, the worker's investment in tools and materials, whether the work requires skill, the duration of the relationship, and whether the service is an integral part of the employer's business."[1]

Many commercial sex workers are inappropriately classified as "independent contractors" rather than "employees." For example, the Nevada ranches characterized workers as "independent contractors," even though the ranch managers exert substantial control over their lives and work. Similarly, erotic dancers are often classified as "independent contractors" even though the establishment managers exercise the forms of control that typically characterize the employment relation. The problem is not unique to sex workers. Internal Revenue Service studies "demonstrate massive fraud on the part of employers in this area."[2] Nonetheless whether commercial sex workers are better off as "employees" or as "independent contractors" requires exploration of the concrete benefits that attach to the status as employees.

Under the federal Fair Labor Standards Act [FLSA] employees are entitled to earn the minimum wage. In several recent cases involving exotic dancers courts have rejected employer claims that the women were independent contractors rather than employees and required compliance with the minimum wage, overtime, and record-keeping provisions of the FLSA. The guarantee of a minimum wage is of little consequence to many commercial sex workers who earn more than that. The women who earn least, street workers, are most difficult to characterize as "employees," rather than independent contractors. Margot Rutman observes that exotic dancers are often better off economically as independent contractors than as employees, even though the employee status triggers other legal protections.[3]

Similarly, state workers' compensation programs, providing payment for workplace related injuries, distinguish between employees and independent contractors. Two recent cases involving workers' compensation claims by exotic dancers reach opposite conclusions, under similar legal standards and facts. In workers' compensation cases, in addition to demonstrating that the injured worker is an employee, the claimant must demonstrate that the injury arose out of the course of employment. The "arising out of" requirement usually demands a showing of a causal connection between the risk of injury and the employment. In *Hanson v. BCB Inc.*,[4] the plaintiff was shot and killed in the parking lot of the bar late at night as she was leaving her work as an exotic dancer. Her husband and son filed for survivors' benefits provided by the state workers' compensation law. The defendant did not contest that the injury was employment related, but only argued, unsuccessfully, that she was not an employee. Given the level of violence associated with sex-related work, it seems fair to conclude that violence is a risk associated with sex work. Other courts have held that sex worker injuries from alcohol-related accidents are compensable under workers' compensation. While workers' compensation protection is an important benefit for people who are injured at work, or for the surviving families of those who are killed, employers have wide latitude to structure work to avoid the employer/employee relationship. Further, for many sex workers the long-term benefit of workers' compensation protection that comes with the employment relationship may be outweighed by greater freedom and earnings of the independent contractor.

The distinction between independent contractors and employees is also key to eligibility for unemployment compensation. While federal law requires that states adopt an unemployment compensation system, the details are left to the states. Exotic dancers who demonstrate that they are full-time employees have qualified for unemployment compensation and required employers to contribute to the compensation fund. However, most states require coverage only for employees who work for an employer who hires more than a minimal number of workers. In addition, all states exclude part-time workers from mandatory coverage for unemployment compensation, and part-time workers are typically defined as those who work less than twenty hours a week. Employers increasingly rely on part-time workers, and almost one-fifth of the entire U.S. workforce now works part-time. While some workers prefer part-time work, the numbers of involuntary part-time workers has grown rapidly. If commercial sex were legal, it is probable that employers could join the growing trend to rely on part-time workers to avoid liability for unemployment compensation.

The employment relationship also triggers the protection of the federal anti-discrimination laws, including the laws against sexual harassment. Even though commercial sex workers offer sex for money, they also sometimes experience unwanted advances, harassment, and violence. Actionable sexual harassment may take two forms: (1) "quid pro quo," where sexual favors are demanded in exchange for a job, a promotion, or other work-related benefit, and (2) "hostile work environment," where the atmosphere or situation at work becomes unbearably uncomfortable or offensive due to jokes, posters, comments, touch, or other behavior. Justice Rehnquist, writing for a unanimous Court in 1986, noted that "hostile work environment" (that is, non–quid pro quo) harassment violates Title VII because employees have "the right to work in an environment free from discriminatory intimidation, ridicule, and insult."[5] The Court further ruled that "[f]or [non–quid pro quo] sexual harassment to be actionable, it must be sufficiently severe or pervasive to alter the conditions of [the victim's] employment and create an abusive working environment."[6] EEOC [Equal Employment Opportunity Commission] guidelines provide that "[a]n employer may be responsible for the acts of non-employees, with respect to sexual harassment of employees in the work-place, where the employer . . . knows or should have known of the conduct and fails to take immediate and appropriate corrective action."[7] Lower courts have applied this principle to hold employers liable for customer harassment that creates a hostile work environment.

How, if at all, do these general principles apply to commercial sex workers? The easiest and earliest cases involve situations in which employers require women workers to dress and behave in sexually provocative ways, while doing work in which sexual titillation is not an obvious or necessary part of the job. For example, when a New York City management company required a female lobby attendant to wear a revealing costume and customers subjected her to repeated sexual harassment, the court found the employer liable. In these, and other cases, the courts found that sexual provocation was not an essential part of the job and invited customer harassment. The harder question is whether legal protection against sexual harassment extends to women whose job it is to offer sexual titillation, or sex itself, for money.

The closest case on point involved a claim by waitresses at a Hooters Restaurant that the employer's requirement that they wear scanty costumes, combined with promotion of burgers with sex appeal, subjected the plaintiffs to unwanted and predictable sexual harassment, for which the employer was responsible. The restaurant settled with the plaintiffs on confidential terms, and thus the case provides little precedential support or guidance for future claims by sex workers who assert employer responsibility for unwanted customer harassment. The case has generated much popular and academic commentary. Some observers argue that women who work at Hooters, or in other contexts in which sexual titillation is a significant part (or all) of the service offered, assume the risk of sexual harassment, and that employers cannot reasonably be held responsible when it occurs. Others assert that even when a woman is hired to offer some forms of sexual observation, conversation, or physical contact, the woman should nonetheless be free to determine what is welcomed, and that employers should be responsible for customer behavior that is unwelcome, beyond the scope of employment and reasonably known to the employer. As the Supreme Court has recognized, "The gravamen of any sexual harassment claim is that the alleged sexual advances were 'unwelcome.' . . . The correct inquiry is whether respondent by her conduct indicated that the alleged sexual advances were unwelcome. . . ."[8] Even if sexual harassment law applies to erotic dancers, nude dancers, and commercial sex workers as a matter of theory and doctrine, women asserting such claims would face formidable practical difficulties of proof, both in showing that customer behavior was unwelcome and that the employer had reasonable opportunity to know and prevent it.

In the United States health insurance and pension benefits are traditionally provided through employment. Commercial sex workers have little access to health insurance, or health care services, through either public or private insurance programs. Employers are not required to offer health insurance or pensions and many do not. Many commercial sex workers are not employees. Even if they are employees, as for example, exotic dancers, employers typically do not provide health coverage or pension benefits to part-time workers.

Lack of health insurance is a problem for over 16 percent of Americans. This is a deep problem in the U.S., and it is only growing worse. It is difficult to imagine a politically realistic scenario in which the U.S. will commit itself to providing health insurance for all its citizens. Because the U.S. has been exceptionally unable to create programs to assure health care, or health insurance, to all people, we have often created focused programs to deal with particular health problems or population groups. COYOTE's work in the 1990s suggests the possibility of creating focused programs to provide health care services to commercial sex workers, motivated by the concern about sexually transmitted disease.

People who argue that criminal penalties against commercial sex workers should be abolished, and who also recognize the vulnerability of those who provide sex for money, sometimes suggest that unionization might provide protection. One of the most effective ways for commercial sex workers to promote decent working conditions and protect themselves from violence, abuse, and health and safety hazards, is to work in a collective context. That seems to be the lesson of Hawaii during World War II, and Australia. Unionization is possible only in a context in which people work as employees.

The unionization experience of exotic dancers and other legal sex workers is not encouraging. Despite the exponential growth of exotic and nude dancing in the United States, only one establishment, the Lusty Lady in San Francisco, has recognized a union. Where women have sought to organize a union, they have been rebuffed by established labor organizations. Only a small minority of all U.S. workers are now unionized. Amongst those whose work is structurally most similar to sex workers, that is, part-time, temporary service work primarily done by women, unionization is rare. The collective bargaining agreement established at the Lusty Lady after months of negotiation provides for one sick-day and one holiday, New Year's Eve, on which workers can receive time and one-tenth pay.

In short, treating commercial sex "like any other profession" is not likely to offer commercial sex workers much assurance of unionization, access to health insurance, or decent working conditions. Rather, commercial sex workers, like other part-time, self-employed, and contingent workers, confront problems of economic and social insecurity that are particularly acute in fields, like commercial sex, where most of the workers are women. It seems more likely that such problems would be addressed through measures applicable to all workers, and extended to commercial sex workers if commercial sex were legal, rather than through special programs for commercial sex workers.

Professionalism may provide an alternative model for the organization of commercial sex work. The classical professions—law and medicine—require long education in a complex subject and deal with matters in which incompetence has serious adverse affects. Commercial sex does not seem to fit this description. But not all professionals have undergone a long education in a complex subject, or provide a service that can cause serious harm if done badly. Barbers and beauticians, practical nurses, massage therapists, social workers, and many others are licensed professionals. The hallmarks of professionalism are control of access to defined forms of work and definitions of standards of excellence. Groups that consider themselves professionals use a variety of ways of communicating safety and excellence to potential customers. For example, private, professionally controlled organizations certify that licensed physicians possess the additional quality of, for example, a member of The American College of Surgeons.

Often professionals seek to enlist the power of the state to create licensing programs that control who is allowed to practice, for example, law or medicine. Professionals licensed by the state enjoy wide latitude while those not licensed are guilty of the crime or offense of unauthorized practice. In many cases licensing results because the professional group seeks it as a form of legitimation and as a tool of self-regulation. Given the long history of state punishment of commercial sex and disrespect for the interests of women who sell sex, commercial sex workers are unlikely to seek state-controlled licensing, even if commercial sex were legal. Further, the experience of Nevada and Australia confirms that licensing is unlikely to serve the needs of the people licensed.

Notes

1. Jennifer Middleton, *Contingent Workers in a Changing Economy: Endure, Adapt, or Organize?* 22 New York University Review of Law and Social Change 557 n.86 (1996).
2. *Id.* at 569.

3. Margot Rutman, *Exotic Dancers' Employment Law Regulations*, 8 Temple Political and Civil Rights Law Review 515, 531 (1999).

4. 754 P.2d 444 (Idaho 1988).

5. *Meritor Savings Bank v. Vinson*, 477 U.S. 57, 65 (1986).

6. *Id.* at 67.

7. 29 C.F.R. § 1604.11(e) (1995).

8. *Meritor*, 477 U.S. at 68.

17

Working without a Job:
The Social Messages of the New Workfare

Matthew Diller

The proposition that welfare recipients should be required to work in exchange for their benefits has achieved such widespread support that arguments to the contrary have been relegated to the political fringes. Although at one time there may have been serious debate about whether poor mothers should be forced into the labor market or permitted to remain at home with their children, for at least ten years even liberal politicians have been unwilling to oppose work requirements. Liberals crossed this Rubicon in 1988 when they voted for the Family Support Act, legislation intended to transform the Aid to Families with Dependent Children (AFDC) program from a means of income support into a vehicle for promoting work.
. . .

Given this consensus in favor of work requirements, the key questions become not whether welfare recipients should be required to work, but what they should be required to do and upon what terms and conditions they should be expected to labor. Answers to these questions are inevitably based on beliefs about the purposes of work requirements. These beliefs in turn are ultimately grounded on assumptions about the causes of poverty and on normative conceptions of the social obligations of single mothers. In contrast to the consensus in favor of work requirements, these issues are hotly contested. Thus, the ambivalence and disagreements in society over poverty and gender roles are now played out in the debate over the content and nature of welfare work requirements.

In this respect, the new Personal Responsibility and Work Opportunity Reconciliation Act of 1996 (PRWORA)[1] reflects a dramatic shift in emphasis from the prior law, the Family Support Act of 1988 (FSA).[2] The FSA reflected the view that poverty stems from a mismatch between the skills of poor mothers and the demands of the job market, as well as barriers to work such as lack of child care. Although filtered through a layer of state discretion, the FSA's work requirements were intended to supply welfare recipients with the skills, training, and experience necessary to facilitate entry into the job market.
. . .

II. The Personal Responsibility and
Work Opportunity Reconciliation Act

The PRWORA adopts an approach to work requirements that is the antithesis of the FSA: it limits the ability of states to place recipients in educational and training assignments and removes all constraints on workfare assignments. The PRWORA replaces the sixty year old AFDC program with a new Temporary Assistance to Needy Families (TANF) block grant program that gives states broad authority to construct their own assistance programs while at the same time freezing the level of federal funding. Thus, states have given up the fiscal security of open-ended federal funding in exchange for policy-making authority.

Two of the principal strings that the PRWORA puts on states are work requirements and a five-year lifetime limit on the receipt of TANF benefits. The work requirements take two forms. First, the PRWORA requires that parents receiving assistance engage in work after receiving benefits for no more than twenty-four months. This requirement, however, has no particular content. For purposes of the two-year work rule, states may define work in any way they wish. Apparently, a state may declare recipients who work or attend courses five hours per week to be working.

Second, the PRWORA has an additional regime of work requirements modeled on the structure of the FSA. The PRWORA requires states to place escalating percentages of the TANF caseload in work activities by specific dates. It also requires that recipients engage in these activities for a minimum number of hours per week to be counted toward the participation requirement. By the year 2002, the PRWORA requires that 50 percent of all TANF households headed by a single parent participate in work activities for no less than thirty hours per week. A separate provision, however, deems twenty hours of work by a parent with a child under the age of six to be sufficient.

To be considered "engaged in work" for purposes of the calculation of the participation requirements, a recipient must be engaged in one of the twelve kinds of work activities listed in the statute. The list includes many of the same activities as the FSA, but there are significant differences, primarily in the area of education. First, although the PRWORA lists a number of training and educational activities, including secondary school education, study toward a GED, job skills training, and "education directly related to employment" for individuals who have not received high school diplomas, participation in these activities does not count toward the first twenty hours per week of work activity. A separate provision permits states to count teen heads of households who attend secondary school as engaged in work activities. There appear to be no circumstances in which post-secondary education may be considered a work activity.

Vocational education is not subject to this restriction, but it is subject to other limitations. Individuals cannot be assigned to vocational education for more than twelve months. Additionally, no more than 20 percent of heads of households receiving public assistance may meet the work participation requirements through either vocational education or school attendance by teenagers. Thus, an increase in the number of teenage heads of households attending school would decrease the number of vocational education placements a state could make. These requirements were modified by Congress during the summer of 1997, but the ability of states to rely on vocational education remains limited.

While the FSA reflected a presumption in favor of educational and training placements, the PRWORA adopts a presumption against them. A state that seeks to adhere to the long-term employability strategy of the FSA will encounter numerous obstacles, including the cap on the number of vocational education placements and the disqualification of secondary and post-secondary educational placements. If an individual over age twenty wishes to complete a high school equivalency program, and the state agrees that such a course would improve the long-term employability of that individual, the educational assignment will not count as work activity. Moreover, other forms of educational placements, such as English as a second language programs, appear to be precluded as well. The only indication that the PRWORA places any value on adult education is that it specifically authorizes states to sanction families with adults between the ages of twenty and fifty who have not completed high school and who are not working toward diplomas.

. . .

Accordingly, under the PRWORA a state can assign an individual to sweep streets without any consideration of whether such an assignment will improve the individual's long-term or short-term employment prospects. The state can also continue such assignments indefinitely without periodic review of any kind. Moreover, the PRWORA contains no requirement that ties work assignments to the minimum or prevailing wages. Thus, a state with a benefit level of $390 a month can assign recipients to sweep streets for 120 hours a month, equivalent to an hourly rate of $3.25, without violating the PRWORA.

. . . [W]elfare recipients may be assigned to work in the private sector as a condition of receipt of their grants. Although such a situation could connect recipients with potential employers, it also creates the possibility that state and local governments will simply supply politically powerful employers with a cost-free work force. Thus, an unemployed secretary could be assigned to work off her TANF grant by performing secretarial work for a corporation that, in essence, receives her services for free.

. . .

Moreover, the PRWORA reflects the view that it is inappropriate to permit welfare recipients to remain out of the workforce while they gain skills or training to improve their long-term employability. In this respect, the PRWORA rejects the premise of the FSA that welfare recipients can fulfill their social obligation to reciprocate for the receipt of benefits by striving to improve their employment prospects. Instead, the PRWORA's supporters viewed education and training as additional benefits, rather than as demands placed on recipients. Alternatively, PRWORA supporters saw education and training simply as a means of shirking the obligation to work. In discussing the PRWORA's limitation on the states' ability to assign recipients to vocational training, Senator [Phil] Gramm explained:

[W]ork does not mean sitting in a classroom. Work means work. Any farm kid who rises before dawn for the daily chores can tell you that. Ask any of my brothers and sisters what "work" meant on our family's dairy farm. It didn't mean sitting on a stool in the barn, reading a book about how to milk a cow. "Work" meant milking cows.[3]

. . .

III. Work Requirements and Shifting Social Messages

. . .

Work requirements provide an inadequate lever on the economic problems that poor mothers face in joining the labor force. They do nothing to address the long-term trends in the job market over the past twenty years, which, despite the recent upturn in the economy, have been characterized by a sharp decline in wages for workers at the bottom end of the labor market, a decline in the availability of jobs for less skilled workers, and a loss of jobs in inner cities where many welfare recipients reside. The suggestion of PRWORA supporters that education and training are unimportant is contradicted by a wealth of data showing that education and job skills are increasingly critical to success in the labor market. Although the FSA's education and training initiatives were no substitute for school systems that educate the first time through, the emphasis on training showed some appreciation of the obstacles that welfare recipients face in the job market.

Programs directed at helping recipients attain immediate employment by improving job search and retention skills may also have some positive impact, but their potential is limited by the larger economic context in which they operate. To the extent that they increase employment, these programs do so by placing recipients in low paying, unstable jobs that are unlikely to provide health benefits. Moreover, such jobs are unlikely to serve as footholds that enable former recipients to secure better employment. Instead, such jobs often lead only back to welfare.

. . .

[T]he work requirements of the PRWORA curtail the notion that society's interest in protecting the children of welfare recipients warrants special treatment of mothers. Although the Democrats obtained some concessions in the area of child care, the new law has dropped the guarantee of child care created by the FSA. While the FSA exempted mothers with children under the age of three from the JOBS program, the PRWORA does not require states to exempt any mothers based on the age of children, and only permits states to exclude mothers of infants under the age of one from calculation of work participation rates.

By foreclosing opportunities for training, the PRWORA drops any commitment to supply mothers with the skills necessary to earn a wage that can support a family. By removing all of the restrictions that the FSA placed on work experience programs, the PRWORA permits states to use deterrence-oriented work programs designed to drive recipients away, rather than to assist them in securing employment. Moreover, the PRWORA's time limits on receipt of benefits indicates that the goal of protecting children has become subservient to the goal of policing the work effort of mothers.

Although the PRWORA does contain some vestiges of the idea that the obligation to work should be different for mothers than for the general population, it has shifted federal policy closer toward the deterrence-oriented approach to work requirements characteristic of programs for childless adults. In this sense, the work requirements of the PRWORA deter not only welfare receipt, but also child bearing. Single women who have children can expect few accommodations of their needs as parents. Like childless adults, they are expected to be able to obtain and survive on unstable and low-paying jobs, with little regard for the added burdens of supporting and raising children. In this way, the work requirements of the PRWORA reflect Congress's overall purpose of discouraging single parenthood.

IV. The PRWORA and the Creation of Workfare Caste

The PRWORA allows states to create large workfare programs in which recipients labor for their public assistance grants without any return commitment by the state to promote their employability. Although such programs were always permitted in state general assistance programs, and were used in that context, the potential to expand such workfare to mothers raises vast new possibilities. Given the work requirements of the PRWORA, states will be looking for ways to put poor mothers to work. In short, large-scale workfare programs may become a permanent feature of American society and workfare assignments may be constrained only by the time limits on receipt of benefits. This development has the potential to change the social institution of work in American society and to undermine traditional employment.

Absent a training component, the principal moral justification for workfare programs is that they are based on a principle of reciprocity—the notion that recipients should provide useful services in return for their benefits. Underlying this view is an implicit analogy to employment—the exchange of work for wages that occurs in the labor market. Moreover, the issue is often presented as one of parity: People who are not welfare recipients must work to keep a roof over their heads, and so should welfare recipients. The analogy is false, or at best incomplete. Although the work performed by workfare workers is analogous to the labor of employees, the terms and conditions under which workfare workers labor and the benefits that they receive are seldom comparable to those enjoyed by employees.

Although at-will employment remains the cornerstone of the employer/employee relationship, a body of laws provide a number of important rights and protections to workers. The extent to which workfare workers will receive the benefits of these safeguards has become the subject of intense debate. In May 1997, the Department of Labor issued a policy interpretation stating that workfare workers may be considered employees for purposes of federal employment laws. The interpretation makes the minimum wage and federal occupational safety and health requirements applicable to workfare workers. The policy statement, however, was immediately criticized by governors, congressional leaders, and the American Public Welfare Association, the organization of welfare administrators. In fact, disagreement over the issue was one of the last issues resolved prior to passage of the Balanced Budget Act of 1997, which in the end, is silent on the matter. Congressional leaders have promised to continue their efforts to overturn the Department of Labor ruling.

Whether the Department of Labor ruling stands or is undercut by statutory amendment, there are a host of additional rights and protections accorded to workers, including workers' compensation; the right to organize and bargain collectively; Social Security coverage for retirement, death, and disability; unemployment insurance; and the Earned Income Tax Credit. The availability of many these protections is not resolved by the Department of Labor policy statement. Ultimately, resolution will depend on the definition of terms such as "employee" or "wage" used in each of the state or federal laws establishing these protections.

As the debate over the applicability of the minimum wage demonstrates, any application of the basic package of protections to workfare workers is strongly contested. Moreover, because minimum wage protection is one of the most rudimentary of all employee rights, application of other workplace protections is likely to be even more bitterly opposed. Thus, most states have declined to provide unemployment insurance coverage to workfare workers, and a number of courts have concluded that benefits paid to welfare recipients engaged in workfare are not "wages" for such purposes. Social Security coverage and the Earned Income Tax Credit are not available to workfare workers. Efforts of labor leaders to unionize workfare recipients have met with widespread opposition on the ground that recipients who work for municipalities are not "employees."

Moreover, states and localities have sought to avoid the provision of workers' compensation to workfare workers injured or killed in performing their assignments. State courts are split on the issue; although court decisions in Maine and Rhode Island have rejected claims that workfare workers must be covered, decisions in California and Iowa have mandated inclusion. Most recently, the Ohio Supreme Court required workers' compensation coverage for a widow whose spouse died from an illness contracted through contact with pigeon excrement on his workfare assignment.[4] The Court found an equal protection violation in the state's refusal to treat the plaintiff like other survivors of workers killed on the job who would have been entitled to significantly better benefits under Ohio's workers' compensation program.

In sum, state and local governments are seeking to have it both ways: Workfare workers are required to work on the rationale that they should be treated like individuals who do not receive welfare, but once in the workplace states are unwilling to treat welfare recipients like other workers.

. . .

Accordingly, the larger question is whether mothers who labor in workfare programs will receive the social status traditionally accorded to those who work—will workfare be regarded as the social and moral equivalent of a job? The debate over application of workplace rights to welfare workers is in part a debate over this question. Even aside from the resolution of these issues, the answer is clearly no. Workfare workers are still stigmatized as welfare recipients, a status perceived as a mark of social failure in society. Moreover, a pay check is not comparable to a welfare check. Welfare recipients receive none of the freedom and control over their lives enjoyed by individuals who receive wages. Instead, the welfare system rigorously monitors and regulates almost all aspects of their lives.

. . .

Under the PRWORA, TANF recipients must assign their rights to receive child support on behalf of their children to the state. Although the AFDC program required states to pass on to recipients the first fifty dollars of child support collections each month, the PRWORA permits states to keep all child support payments. Alternatively, the arrangement could be viewed as one in which the child support payments are remitted to the recipient in the form of a public assistance grant. But if the public assistance grant is composed of child support payments, then the work done by the workfare worker is uncompensated. Under the PRWORA, if the TANF recipient refuses to cooperate in this process, she is subject to sanction. The PRWORA also authorizes states to dock the recipient if her children fail to attend school. As noted above, a TANF recipient may be docked for her own failure to finish high school. In addition to these conditions that are now common or are becoming common, under the PRWORA the state may impose virtually any other condition on TANF recipients, and is limited only by the porous and uncertain boundaries of the unconstitutional conditions doctrine.

It may be argued that these conditions are not new—they have characterized welfare administration for decades. In this sense a "welfare caste" is not a new development. But the PRWORA changes the relationship between the recipient and the state in a fundamental way. Ongoing oversight and control of welfare recipients was always justified on the ground that recipients were accepting benefits from the state. Because recipients took money from the state, the state could impose conditions in return. Indeed, such conditions were viewed as necessary to ensure the proper allocation of state money. But if recipients are working in exchange for benefits, these conditions become much more difficult to justify, particularly because the conditions imposed on public assistance recipients are not generally imposed on other workers. If a recipient is working to maintain the cleanliness of city parks, what is the justification for taking her child support? The continued existence of these welfare rules and requirements means that workfare cannot be justified simply by analogy to employment. Welfare recipients required to sweep streets and clean parks do not receive a benefit for their labor that is comparable to a wage.

. . .

In sum, the analogy to employment that underpins workfare under the PRWORA is a one-way street. Recipients are required to fulfill the obligations of employees without receiving the same legal protections and rights, social standing, or degree of control over their lives that employees enjoy. Recipients are not rewarded for their efforts with salaries. Instead, they continue to be subject to a larger system designed to communicate the message that recipients are social failures rather than productive members of society.

This social arrangement is a threat to the traditional social understanding of work because it is likely to expand at the expense of traditional jobs. As workfare workers become broadly available, public and private employers can satisfy their need for labor without hiring traditional employees. For state and local governments this prospect may prove particularly tempting because in their governmental capacities they establish the terms of workfare. At the same time, in their proprietary roles they are major employers. Thus, they can establish workfare programs designed to supply themselves with workers at low cost and partially subsidized with federal TANF funds.

In this regard, the PRWORA contains a "nondisplacement" provision that would be more aptly described as a "displacement promotion" provision. Although the provision is presumably intended to ensure that workfare does not supplant traditional wage work, it begins with a general rule that TANF recipients may be assigned to fill job vacancies. The "anti-displacement" protection consists of an exception to this general rule which provides that work assignments under TANF cannot be made to fill any position for which an individual is on layoff or if the employer has terminated an employee in order to replace him or her with a workfare worker. In other words, the PRWORA protects the jobs of individual employees, but not job availability in general. When employees leave through retirement or resignation, they can be replaced with workfare workers. Thus, employers can replace their staff of employees with workfare workers simply through the process of attrition. Moreover, employers can fill any new jobs with workfare workers rather than employees.

The PRWORA creates both the incentive and the authority for state and local government to replace their workforces with public assistance recipients. Such a course may enable government to save money in a number of ways. First, workfare workers need not be paid at the prevailing wage rate. Second, funds for these payments can be drawn from federal TANF funds, providing a new source of federal funding for municipal services. Third, the potential to use workfare workers undermines the bargaining power of traditional employees, thereby creating the potential for even larger reductions in labor costs. In addition to these fiscal advantages, the use of workfare can be presented as innovative social policy.

For these reasons, the PRWORA has the potential to dramatically expand a social arrangement for the provision of work in our society that is separate and distinct from the institution of employment. Moreover, from the point of view of workers, it is inferior to employment in almost every respect.

. . .

NOTES

1. Pub. L. No. 104-193, 110 Stat. 2105 (codified as 42 U.S.C.A. § 601-1788 (West 1997).

2. Pub. L. No. 100-485, 102 Stat. 2343.

3. 141 Cong. Rec. S13788 (Sept. 19, 1995).

4. *State ex rel. Patterson v. Industrial Commission of Ohio*, 672 N.E.2d 1008 (Ohio 1996).

Equality, of the Right Sort

Edward J. McCaffery

. . .

Far from having already reached the promised land and attaining equality of the right sort, a strong case can be made that we, as a society, have only taken the easiest and most visible first steps on what will be a long road toward purging patriarchy. My scholarly work in the field of tax has been important in opening up my mind to this insight. When one examines tax from the perspective of gender and justice—as Grace Blumberg began to do a quarter of a century ago—it is hard not to be struck by the depth and breadth of gender bias.[1]

. . . What is important about the gender biases in the tax system has little to do with "tax" per se. It is true that the tax system is deeply biased against working wives and mothers. Working wives in upper-middle income households sacrifice, on average, two-thirds of their salaries to tax- and work-related expenses. This is indeed a problem for distributive justice, a traditional domain for tax analysis. These biases are most important, however, not because they result in some improper orderings of tax burdens among otherwise similarly situated families, or some such hollow, static formulation of a distributive norm, but because they impact behaviors and play a large role in shaping our various life plans and projects. The biases of tax make it hard to be a working wife, and discourage many from the attempt. This plays into social attitudes and stereotypes and the rational planning of market actors, and so is multiplied across the social space. The same forces push men to work more and serve to entrench the dominant model of full-time, full-commitment work. Women who want to work are given limited models of how to do so. None of this has much to do, directly, with who pays what amount of tax; it has everything to do with patterns of social behavior. It is time to get this message out to "nontax" people, which means the overwhelming majority of Americans.

. . .

[My book] *Taxing Women* begins with the long and interesting history of the movement towards the system of joint filing under the income tax, which became a fixed feature of the American system in 1948. Joint filing, which most democratic countries have since moved away from, creates a problem known as the "secondary earner bias." Because husband and wife are treated as one in the tax system, there is a push for spouses to think of one earner as "primary" and the other as "secondary," so that a burden is placed on the secondary earner, who will almost always be the lesser earning wife. The bias is created because this spouse enters the workforce at a marginal tax rate dictated by the primary earner's salary. Under current tax rates, for example, if a husband earns $25,000, his wife faces an income tax rate of 15 percent on her first dollar of earned income; if the husband earns $60,000, the wife enters at a 28 percent rate. Social security and state and local taxes add considerably to the total burden.

There are many interesting things to say about joint filing and the secondary earner bias, both before and after the pivotal 1948 year, but I'll pass over that subject here. (Actually, Carolyn Jones has written wonderful legal history about just this topic.) One point is worth noting, however: The secondary earner bias has no necessary connection to the so-called "marriage penalty." This penalty refers to the fact that some couples see their federal income taxes increase when they marry because the rate structure for married persons is less favorable than double the individual structure. Under the joint filing system put in place in 1948, which persisted until 1969, there were no marriage penalties but a potentially severe secondary earner bias. A rate change in 1969, designed to appease single taxpayers, created the marriage penalty, which has generated increasing attention recently. For those couples who face a penalty—about a third—it falls, strictly by definition, in equal numbers on men and women. The secondary earner bias is far more narrowly the wife's problem. Yet we have paid almost no attention to the secondary earner bias, either politically or intellectually. This is another example of a pattern of limited social cognition of gender-based problems. The tax laws were designed to foster and reward traditional, single-earner families, where the man as breadwinner worked outside the home and the woman as homemaker worked inside it. This bias towards single-earner families has had remarkable salience and persistence, right down to the present age. The contemporary Contract with America, for example, is heavily centered around a tax reform proposal to entrench traditional families.

Taxing Women also considers five other tax-related factors, in addition to joint filing, that are heavily biased against working wives or modern two-earner families. Social security turns out to be a larger tax for most Americans, and even more gendered—and consciously so—than the income tax. Bias is also evident in the failure to tax the "imputed" income from self-supplied services, such as child care; the inadequacy of the law's provision for child care and other work-related expenses of working parents; the fringe benefit system; and state and local taxes. All of these factors compound the bias in favor of traditional, single-earner families. When all of this is added up, it adds up indeed. In a wide range of circumstances, wives simply and flatly lose money, in a cash flow sense, by working. The bias is especially severe at the upper and lower economic classes, in the latter case because the loss of benefits as families move from lower- to middle-class status operates like a tax and has a devastating impact on two-earner families. Everywhere, it is hard to make much money at part-time work. There are strong incentives for wives simply to stay home, where their household services are not taxed, rather than to struggle to pay child care and other work-related expenses out of a salary cut in half, or more, by taxes.

Looking closely at tax gives a good look at the intersection between gender and class, and the way that social choices have shaped the intersecting space. A basic theme is that a bias against two-earner families cuts differently at different income levels. It is a bias against families themselves among the poor, where a strong need for money income often compels both parents to work. But, ironically and cruelly, working wives among the lowest income classes often face tax rates in excess of 50 and sometimes 100 percent, because the family is being taxed by losing welfare benefits, like the earned income tax credit. The very same general bias—in favor of single-earner families—is a push against working wives among the wealthiest classes, who can indeed afford to have one spouse stay home. Among the richest Americans, potentially working wives also face tax rates well over 50 percent, at a level where more money, alone, may not be all that much needed. Women in the vast middle are put to hard and stressful choices, between trying to work outside the home full-time as well as doing a good deal of work in it, or staying home full-time and sacrificing workplace skills, as well as possibly greater autonomy, independence, and variety.

These biases map up with the picture of households sketched above: Twenty-four percent of American children live in households headed by their mothers and almost half of these families are below the poverty level; 40 percent of American children live with two working parents, typically both working full-time; 23 percent live in single-earner, dual-parent households, many of them wealthy. A recent study of top executives at large American corporations, for example, revealed that some 80 percent were men with stay-at-home wives.

All of this has disconcerting effects across the income ranges, as lower-class women are left in unstable family structures, middle-class women are placed under tremendous stress, and upper-class women stay home. Poor women struggle to enter the middle class; in the middle class, women juggle the competing demands of work and family; and if they reach the upper classes, women are pushed back into the home. The problems of lower- and middle-income women are quite serious, indeed—and the tax system compounds these—but tax also gives a good look at what is happening among the upper classes and why this should matter to issues of gender justice. Feminists often neglect the problems of rich women, because they are rich, but this might be a mistake, insofar as they are women. The loss of prestigious positions at the top of the income ranges deprives all women of power and symbolically important roles. Women are being both taxed and deprived of the positions of wealth and power that we think of as going along with the price, however unwanted, of being taxed. Meanwhile, women see their ranks broken up by class, as women in every income range struggle with different problems and issues that point them in different directions; it is as if the forces of patriarchy had pursued a clever "divide and conquer" strategy.

Taxing Women also develops what I take to be a large and important part of the story, the theory of "optimal tax." I won't get too technical here, choosing instead to just set out the basic insight of this longstanding public finance theory. In order to maximize utility (or, sometimes, wealth), optimal tax theory recommends that we tax actors in inverse proportion to their "elasticity" or degree of commitment to an activity. The idea is rather common-sensical. If Dick just loves candy, so that he would buy it at any price, his candy habit is a good object of taxation; if Jane is close to being indifferent about soda, there is little point taxing her soda consumption, because she'll just quit. Analogously, if Jack is going to work just as hard no matter how much we tax him, we might as well do so; if Jill is going to call it quits and leave the paid workforce if we tax her too heavily, we should be wary of doing so.

There are, of course, many questions about the social theoretic implications of optimal tax theory, and many reasons to believe that we should not turn over fundamental questions of public policy to utility-maximizing social scientists, which I explore at some length in *Taxing Women*. But the main reason I am drawn to optimal tax theory in the tax context is that it has a precise recommendation for taxing married men and women: We should tax married men more, much more, than married women. Michael Boskin, a rather conservative economist who became chairperson of President Bush's Council of Economic Advisors, published a paper with Eytan Sheshinski in 1983, suggesting that married men should be taxed twice as much as married women.[2] I find this very interesting material, for what we do in practice is completely, purposely, and perversely the opposite: We tax married women more—much more—than married men. There's plenty of evidence that we like things that way. But I am interested mostly, and exclusively here, in other aspects of the story.

Optimal tax theory also tells us that we are burdening the behavior of married women far more than married men. Married women, by many statistical measures, are conflicted about their roles, while married men are not. Given this, we should lessen the burden on women. We can put all of this high theory in the form of a simple example. Imagine a married woman who has recently given birth to her first child, sitting around the kitchen table with the family accountant. The woman is conflicted about just what to do; she feels some pull to stay home with her new baby, but also some desire to stay in the paid workforce, partly because she knows that the family could use money to save for things like the child's education. It is a close call and she's on the margin, unsure of what to do.

Now the accountant informs our exemplary new mother that, were she to go back to work, income, social security, and state and local taxes would eat up about one-half of her salary; the family would have to pay for child care and get only limited tax relief for this; and there are many other, somewhat hidden, costs of working—two-earner families spend more money on restaurant meals, dry cleaning, and commuting costs, for example. The average working wife in a middle- to upper-income family sacrifices two-thirds of her pay to taxes and these extra costs. Many women sacrifice still more, and no one has yet figured out a reliable way to calculate how many married mothers of young children stay home full-time with their children because of this financial calculus. What is apparent is that a close and difficult call under any circumstances gets a strong shove from the tax system.

Meanwhile, what is the husband to do, except apply himself all the more, hoping to get a raise, or put in overtime, or take on a second job to help out with both the new costs of child rearing and the loss of the wife's labor market earnings? Primary-earning men enter the workforce at a zero percent income tax rate; their social security contributions, unlike their wives', add to the family's well being; their work, alone, does not occasion child care costs, nor do their extra hours at work add to commuting expenses. For example, a primary-earning husband can add as much to the family's bottom line, take-home pay by earning $4,000 as his wife could by taking a job paying $30,000: Seven and one-half times the pretax salary yields the same amount after taxes. Tax is no small matter. This story also helps to show how men, too, are shaped and constrained by the tax system. The push to keep women at home is also a push for men to stay away from it.

. . . [T]he history of the evolution of the tax system, combined with the economic and utilitarian insights of optimal tax theory, show that it was a patriarchic society that committed the original sin: It set up a tax system with the implicit and, surprisingly frequently, explicit goal of keeping women at home and preserving the traditional, single-earner family as the model. Optimal tax theory now shows us, precisely and exactly, that the tax system is distorting and coercive vis-à-vis women's preferences. If we truly want a minimally burdensome government, optimal tax theory shows us how to set up the tax system. That is exactly the mission of optimal tax: to minimize the distortions and coercion of tax. Optimal tax tells us to tax married men much more than married women. We do the opposite, and current conservative political proposals, like the Contract with America, would make it all worse.

. . .

Optimal tax theory gives us a third way. It suggests that we tax men more, precisely on account of their insistence on working as they always have and precisely until their behavior, in the aggregate, becomes as variable and susceptible to social and other pressures as women's behavior is. We will compel men to look for choices. Meanwhile, optimal tax suggests that we should lessen the burdens on married women because life has burdened them enough already. This will enable them to choose more freely.

There are ways to make the generally impractical recommendations of optimal tax practical and sensible. We should move to the system of separate filing that most Western democracies have now adopted. We should reform the social security system and rethink fringe benefits. We should give more generous child care and secondary earner relief. All of these proposals have been advocated by feminists for a long time, and most of them would be rather easy to implement. It is high time to pay them heed.

. . .

We have been confused over much of this because we are not looking in the right places, in the right way. Much of the focus on gender discrimination—both coming from conservative skeptics and liberal activists—has focused on the firm, or demand-side, of labor markets. Conservatives like [Richard] Epstein rest their case for doing nothing on the rationality of firm action and the absence of obvious market failures, such as monopoly power. Many liberals remain convinced that something must be wrong with firms, and so they would mandate top-down, demand-side solutions: better part-time work, more generous maternity leave, or antidiscrimination laws. But there is good reason to believe that many of such policies, when they fly in the face of economic rationality, will be of limited and possibly even counterproductive effect.

. . .

Tax gives a perfect and precise way out of this bind. First, optimal tax is indeed based on private preferences, and these in fact reveal a greater elasticity among married women. This also means, again quite precisely, that tax shapes and affects women's behavior more than men's behavior; something is wrong—is unfair and unequal—on the supply-side. Since we play the whole game out on a wide canvas, dynamic effects are set in motion: Tax pushes men to work more and many women to work less, and this pattern perpetuates social stereotypes and rational firm calculations. Optimal tax theory affords a mechanism of empowering women by lessening or removing coercive, paternalistic constraints—presumably, what many libertarians and other conservatives want. We can do more than mandate top-down policies or engage in exhortatory rhetoric. We can change the institutional structures in which individual preferences are formed, in the direction of removing a lingering burden from an historically burdened group and placing some of it on the historically oppressing group. It all sounds fair and just. Optimal tax theory also tells us that it is efficient—that is, that we could increase national wealth and productivity, those endlessly chanted mantras of the supply-side crowd, by taxing women less. All of this, of course, leaves us with the puzzle of why no one is advocating this particular progrowth policy, but I'll leave that for another day.

. . .

Letting women work like men have always worked and paying them equal wages for doing so is not going to do the whole trick. Equality of the right sort is deeper than that, more complicated, and less easy to define: It turns always, as it must, on an equality of concern and respect, on a recognition of our mutual statuses as free and equal citizens and participants in society, which can never be too specific or numeric. Perhaps the most definite and optimistic thing that can be said about what equality of the right sort for gender justice means is that, while we have no extant models of it to point to or to learn from, we'll know it when we see it. Our children, or our children's children, should be so lucky.

Notes

1. Grace Blumberg, *Sexism in the Code: A Comparative Study of Income Taxation of Working Wives and Mothers*, 21 Buffalo Law Review 49 (1971–72).

2. Michael J. Boskin and Eytan Sheshinski, *Optimal Tax Treatment of the Family: Married Couples*, 20 Journal of Public Economics 281, 291 (1983).

19

African-American Women and Economic Justice: A Preliminary Analysis of Wealth, Family, and African-American Social Class

Patricia Hill Collins

. . .

II. Wealth and African-American Social Class

Scholarship on African-American social class continues to be influenced by two classic approaches. . . . [S]tratification models treat social class as a system of hierarchical social positions. From this perspective, innate individual capacities such as talent and motivation, when combined with achieved qualities such as educational qualifications and employment experiences, constitute individual "human capital." Individuals exchange their accumulated human capital for income in competitive labor markets. Those individuals possessing superior human capital garner greater rewards while those lacking human capital fall behind. Grounded in the concept of a meritocracy, social class becomes measured by some combination of education, occupational status, and income, and groups are defined in response to their possession or absence of these criteria. Both the "equal opportunity exists" and some versions of structural discrimination perspectives on inequality can be accommodated within the assumptions of stratification models. "Equal opportunity exists" approaches routinely attribute African-American poverty to a lack of human capital, even though the lack of human capital remains an outcome of discriminatory practices in housing, education, and employment. Structural discrimination thinkers are more likely to identify institutionalized racism as a deficiency in the system that prohibits African-Americans free access to the means of acquiring human capital. Whether the emphasis lies in the lack of human capital or in challenging institutionalized discrimination in social institutions, the very concept of stratification treats social class as a hierarchical array of social positions with the main purpose of classifying individuals.

In contrast to stratification models, conflict models view social class as a system of power and privilege. Identifying the ownership and control of property as a central feature of social-class formations, this literature takes a historical perspective on social-class formations across different societies. Conflict among varying groups with competing property interests operates as a central feature in social organization. In contrast to stratification models that treat the top and bottom 20 percent of American households as representing two ends of a continuum developed as a classification device—the top 20 percent's share of income and wealth is not inherently connected to the absence of income and wealth in the bottom 20 percent of households—conflict approaches view these two groups as having connected and opposed, or conflicting, interests. One group of households has income and wealth because the other does not, a fundamentally unjust situation. Thus, from a conflict approach, social class is less a thing than a relationship among competing groups. Despite the dominance of stratification models in American social science, efforts to draw upon the insights of conflict theory have yielded some fruitful analyses among structural discrimination analysts concerning social-class processes and race. Specifically, literature describing the uneven development of African-American and white neighborhoods, as well as labor market segmentation and split labor market approaches, have provided some important insights concerning race and social-class formation.

Although conflict models identify group conflict as central to social-class relations, these approaches typically do not perceive African-American women as a group with interests in their own right. Instead, African-American women are treated either as female members of African-American collectivities or as African-American members of working-class or poor people's collectivities. . . . Stratification and conflict approaches to social class also have difficulty identifying women's placement in social-class relations. In both approaches, women's social-class classification emanates not only from traditional social-class measures such as education, employment, and occupation, but from their attachment to family units, either as dependent daughters within male-headed households or as wives of male breadwinners. Women as independent agents in social-class formation typically remained neglected. Given the high participation of African-American women in the labor force, particularly after emancipation, and the centrality of African-American women's earnings to African-American family well-being, this omission is especially problematic for understanding the gendered dimensions of African-American, social-class formations. . . .

Although the literature on race and wealth typically underemphasizes theoretical reconceptualizations of social class, it does offer provocative new insights for developing an intersectional analysis of African-American social class generally and of African-American women's economic status in particular. . . . Arguing that the existing emphasis on income as a measure of African-American progress be supplemented with wealth as a measure of African-American economic capacity, [Melvin] Oliver and [Thomas] Shapiro suggested not only that wealth is unevenly distributed within the United States, with African-Americans disproportionately clustered at the bottom of the wealth hierarchy, but that this inequality of wealth reproduces itself through intergenerational processes.[1] Income refers to a flow of money over time, typically through salaries, wages, and payments periodically received as returns from an occupation, investment, or government transfer. Typically referring to one year, income refers to a rate of dollar accumulation, like a rate per hour, week, or year. In contrast, wealth describes the total extent of the accumulated assets and access to resources owned by an individual, family, or some other social unit at a particular time. Referring to the net value of assets—stocks, money in the bank, businesses, and real estate—less debt held at one time, wealth is anything of economic value that is bought, sold, stocked for future disposition, or invested to bring an economic return. Income is what people receive for work, retirement, or social welfare. Wealth is what people own.

Although related, income and wealth address different dimensions of African-American economic well-being. Relying exclusively on income as a measure of social inequality can reveal some trends while simultaneously obscuring others. For example, Oliver and Shapiro reported that income gaps have decreased for African-American and white married-couple families in which husbands and wives both worked; these are the households comprising the most advantaged segment of the African-American population. In 1984, African-American families in this category earned 77 percent of white income, or $34,700 as compared to $40,865 respectively. Despite the persistence of a fifteen percent racial gap in income, one could justifiably argue that, over time, the combination of being employed and being married would constitute a sufficient remedy for African-American economic disadvantage. But wealth data tell a different story. For African-American and white married couples in which the husband and wife both worked, African-American families own $17,375 in net worth, and their white counterparts own $56,046; figures that give whites more than three times the net worth of similarly situated African-American couples.

Emphasizing income as a measure of social inequality works especially well with stratification models of social class in at least three ways. First, an individual's social-class status is typically measured by combining her income with other variables defined as measures of social-class status, such as educational attainment, occupation, and years of experience. Once classified, individuals can be grouped according to researcher-defined criteria of what constitutes a social class. In this sense, social class is defined according to researcher preferences. Thus, social class does not represent actual social relations as much as it represents theoretically derived, artificial categories constructed by social scientists. Second, stratification approaches to social class that rely on income mask pre-existing social relations of race and gender. Because race and gender are both designated as residing in the bodies of individual African-Americans or individual women, they both become defined outside of social-class relations and, thus, remain examined as part of other seemingly natural phenomena. Therefore, African-American women and other seemingly "naturally" occurring social groups can be measured according to the amount of income (and by implication, other human capital variables) earned by each group. Finally, the emphasis on "income linked to stratification" models fosters an ahistorical view of social class. The relatively short time frames attached to income flows—hour, week, month, or year—both obscure actual total lifetime income and remove individuals from the social-class system itself when they do not earn incomes.

Shifting to wealth links discussions of African-American social class much more closely to conflict models that view social-class relations as an outcome of systems of power and privilege. Emphasizing wealth as the measure of African-American well-being has several implications for reconceptualizing African-American social-class formations. First, measures of wealth refocus attention to ownership of property as an indication of social-class formations. Although income comes and goes, wealth is more constant. The possession and disposition of wealth is institutionalized through laws of property ownership, transmission, inheritance, and consumption. Thus, tracking the property and who owns it becomes another way of determining social-class composition. Rather than focusing on the individual and her attributes, examining wealth and its owners allows for construction of social-class categories around actual material relations. Individuals come and go, but groups control property rights. In this view, differential distributions of occupations and of income among individuals are less causes of disparities in wealth than outcomes of property ownership. Thus, in contrast to social-class analysis, which is organized around individual earnings at one point in time and which builds models of social structure on findings about individual social locations, tracing social class through wealth gets at the stability of social-class formations.

Second, this shift to a social-class model that emphasizes property provides a social-class framework grounded not in researcher-created categories, but in actual material relations. African-American women and other historically specific groups can be located within the framework of ownership and control of actual property. This shift would follow property ownership across longer time periods in order to determine which historically specific groups of people routinely control property. Rather than making individuals the object of class analysis, the distribution of property becomes the focal point. Thus, group classification flows from property relations, not vice versa. This perspective allows categories of race and gender to be examined in light of how they actually operate. Gender specific differential distributions of African-Americans and whites within a system of wealth become more visible.

Third, this approach leads to a more historical analysis of the processes of social-class formation, and this analysis accommodates actual racialized patterns of white privilege and African-American disadvantage. This historical transmission of wealth, poverty, and the related opportunities that wealth and poverty provide has substantial implications for understanding patterns of African-American disadvantage as a continuation of a historical pattern of institutionalized racism organized through, and simultaneously shaping, American social institutions. As Oliver and Shapiro pointed out:

> [W]hat is often not acknowledged is that the same social system that fosters the accumulation of private wealth for many whites denies it to blacks, thus forging an intimate connection between white wealth accumulation and black poverty . . . since wealth builds over a lifetime and is then passed along to kin, it is . . . an essential indicator of black economic well-being.[2]

Emphasizing wealth allows models of African-American social class to illustrate the cumulative disadvantage of inherited wealth.

Finally, because wealth is typically possessed and transmitted through family, focusing on wealth fosters a shift from the individual to the family as the fundamental unit of social-class analysis. Within models using the individual as the unit of social-class analysis, women and children are often not treated as independent actors in social-class analyses because they do not consistently produce income. However, women and children are never outside the system of property ownership. Because real property never disappears, but is transferred from one owner to another, this shift from individual to family introduces gender and age into social-class analysis. Depending on their families of origin and procreation, women and children are differentially positioned to inherit and pass on wealth. Emphasizing wealth reintroduces family organization into social-class analysis in a distinctively new way. Focusing on family as a raced, gendered, age-stratified social institution that is central in intergenerational wealth transmission redefines family as a building block of social-class formations.

. . .

IV. African-American Families and Intergenerational Wealth Transmission

By shifting to wealth as a measure of family organization and by coupling this with an understanding of family as a gendered site of wealth transmission that is grounded in assumptions about marriage, new directions are provided in which the family is viewed as a key site of inheritance. This inheritance is not limited solely to cultural values, but extends to the ability to produce certain outcomes in the economy. Wealth matters because it is directly transferable from generation to generation, thus, assuring that positions and opportunity remain in the same families' hands. Families use wealth to create opportunities, to secure a desired standard of living, and to pass their social-class status along to their children. Wealth taps not only contemporary resources, but also the historic origins and the reproduction of material assets. As Oliver and Shapiro observed, "Private wealth thus captures inequality that is the product of the past, often passed down from generation to generation."[3]

For whites, the familiar transmission of property from parents to children within middle-income and upper-income family units is fairly straightforward. This is the group identified as property owners whether property accrues from inherited wealth or from the nouveau riche of professionals and managers who garnered considerable incomes that they brokered into property that could be transmitted to their children. Over time, these structural inequities mean that married couples have more material resources for their children and that children growing up in married-couple families inherit more wealth and have more wealth to pass on to their children. Moreover, traditionally high rates of marriage meant that white children living in two-parent families enjoyed considerable economic benefits. Children raised by two married adults enjoy a huge resource advantage over those raised by single parents. "This is not a moral, psychological, or developmental advantage," Oliver and Shapiro observed, "[r]ather, it involves a recognition that these families generally can draw from a larger stockpile of resources, and that may translate into expanded choices and opportunities."[4]

However, when it comes to intergenerational transfer of wealth for middle-class, African-American families, several significant features emerge. First, African-American, middle-class households control far fewer assets than their white counterparts. In other words, the African-American middle class remains structurally different than white, middle-class families—there is much less wealth with which to begin in the African-American middle class. Second, entrenched patterns of institutional racism often mean that middle-class African-Americans cannot benefit from the wealth they do control in the same way as whites. For example, home ownership comprises one of the key assets for family wealth. However, restrictions on segregated housing markets mean that homes owned by African-Americans appreciate more slowly than those owned by whites. Because a host of city services are linked to home ownership, racial segregation has a snowball effect. Third, retrenchment in civil rights enforcement coupled with a dramatically changed global economy since 1980 has effectively stopped social mobility of working-class African-Americans into the African-American middle class. Because of the absence of mobility, the intergenerational transfer of property to middle-class children becomes especially significant. Moreover, fertility data from married-couple, African-American, middle-class families suggests that these families average one child per household. Because approximately one-half of all African-American children live below the official poverty level and many more African-American children live in poverty, but are not officially classified as doing so, one can speculate that the actual numbers of middle-class, African-American children may not be increasing and, in fact, might actually be decreasing. Thus, the greatest assets within African-American populations, however limited when compared to white middle-class assets, are passed on to a relatively small number of children. Obviously, this has immense implications for the intergenerational transfer of wealth in African-American communities.

The intergenerational transmission of wealth through family also operates among working-class families. Both stratification and conflict models of social class typically view working-class families purely in wage-earning terms. Such families are thought to have no property to pass on to their children and are seen as mere employees or producers of wealth within capitalist political economies. From this perspective, neither white nor African-American, working-class families have much property or wealth to pass on to their children. Instead, these families are involved in a constant struggle to procure income.

However, a race-sensitive analysis of working-class family organization challenges this view of property transmission. White working-class families may view their status as inheritable in ways that disadvantage African-Americans. In her analysis of how racism undermined the 1960s War on Poverty Program, Jill Quadagno described the resistance that craft unions in particular put forth when confronted with political pressure to change entrenched patterns of racial discrimination. As Quadagno pointed out, the right of unions to select their own members was seen as a "property right of the working class."[5] "This was a very compelling argument for nepotism—the tradition of passing on the craft from fathers to sons."[6] Among Philadelphia plumbers, 40 percent of apprentices were sons of members who wanted their sons to be trained as plumbers and eventually to continue in the business. Practices such as these virtually ensured that African-Americans and other groups remained excluded from these and other lucrative positions from generation to generation. Quadagno quoted one construction worker who explained the concept of property rights and property transmission in white working-class families:

> Some men leave their sons money, some large investments, some business connections and some a profession. I have none of these to bequeath to my sons. I have only one worthwhile thing to give: my trade. . . . For this simple father's wish it is said that I discriminate against Negroes. Don't all of us discriminate? Which of us when [the time] comes to [choose] will not choose a son over all others?[7]

Attitudes like this one suggest that white working-class males perceive their positions in the economy as inheritable property. In effect, racial discrimination in education, employment, and housing may reflect white working-class treatment of these social locations as "property" that can be disposed of as inherited wealth. Although it certainly may reflect attitudes of personal prejudice, racial discrimination may be more closely attached to property rights and to concerns about the value of inheritable property than to actual attitudes toward African-Americans. Examples such as these demonstrate how family becomes a key social institution for distributing wealth and, in this capacity, serves as a building block and mechanism for reproducing the social-class system.

Gender complicates these race and social-class specific relationships. Despite considerable rhetoric claiming that American marriages are fundamentally egalitarian institutions, feminist scholarship suggests that most working, married women still face a double day of working outside of the home while simultaneously doing considerably more household labor than their spouses. Moreover, women and men in marital relationships may not have equal access to control over family assets. As Oliver and Shapiro pointed out:

> Earnings provide the conventional measure of the material well-being of women in comparison to men. A resource perspective, by contrast, shifts the question away from the value of women in the labor market and toward control over assets. . . . But determining control of assets in the family is a difficult matter. While we are convinced that households and families are the appropriate units to analyze when the focus is on wealth, because it is families who accumulate and plan how to use their economic resources, we are less certain about the relative control that women have over nonincome resources. A household perspective may assume more gender equality in economic matters within families than exists.[8]

Despite a rhetoric of complementarity claiming that women and men make separate but equal contributions to family well-being, families organized around the nucleus of married, heterosexual couples may mask and, therefore, collectively naturalize a system of male authority and dominance. Thus, although families organized around married, heterosexual couples form a site for intergenerational control over, and transfer of, racialized wealth, these same social locations simultaneously constitute an important site for intergenerational male control of property.

Varying gendered configurations of different types of African-American family organization participate differently in intergenerational wealth transfer. Although African-American families remain disadvantaged as sites of wealth transmission when compared to white families, differences between African-American, married-couple families and African-American, female-headed families reveal the added dimension of gender. Andrew Billingsley reported that, prior to 1960, the vast majority of African-American families were two-parent families, typically over 80 percent.[9] While 20 percent of African-American family households with children were headed by women in 1960, 33 percent fit this profile by 1970, 49 percent by 1980, and a majority of 57 percent were female-headed by 1990. While data like this provides a sense of trends, it simultaneously tells little about the significance of gender in explaining these trends for intergenerational transfer of wealth.

Assumptions about marriage and, by implication, desired family forms remain supported by governmental policy, corporate policies, and the legal system. Just as the sedimented disadvantages of institutionalized racism are passed on intergenerationally to African-Americans as a collectivity, the benefits accruing to families fitting state-sanctioned marital patterns encounter comparable cumulative advantages or disadvantages. African-American women's status regarding entitlement criteria for 1930s Social Security programs illustrate how institutionalized racism combines with gender-specific public policies that reward and punish families based on marriage patterns. Originally designed as a social insurance program for employed workers, Social Security initially contained no provisions for wives or widows. In 1939, Congress added spousal and widow benefits. The eligibility rules rewarded women who remained in marriages and were supported by their husbands, but penalized women who became separated or divorced or who remained single and earned their own way. Thus, African-American women who were not in stable marriages lacked access to spousal and widow benefits that routinely subsidized white women. Moreover, both married and unmarried African-American women who worked lacked access to the social insurance benefits extended to working people. Two occupational categories were expressly excluded from Social Security coverage—agricultural and domestic workers. Not surprisingly, those two categories formed the majority of employment for African-Americans. When combined, the effects of these allegedly race- and gender-neutral social policies had direct effects on African-American women in the 1930s. Moreover, these policies also have had cumulative effects because African-American women's children and grandchildren bear the costs of exclusionary practices like these. In this case, the combination of race-targeted policies concerning occupational category and of gender-targeted policies concerning marital state of applicants worked to exclude African-American women then and now.

. . .

The growth of female-headed households and the increasing numbers of African-American children growing up in such households certainly have great implications for the intergenerational transmission of wealth. However, current approaches that collapse all African-American, female-headed households with children under age eighteen into one fairly stereotypical category obscure the differential ways that African-American, female-headed households are formed across social classes, as well as the potential intergenerational wealth transmission within such families. Material on African-American women heading households who are working-class, middle-class, or affluent remain noticeably absent in literature on African-American, female-headed households. Moreover, the over-attention given to households headed by adolescent unmarried mothers has obscured households formed through other processes.

Because of these limitations in the existing literature, the effects of the differential treatment of African-American, female-headed households formed through various marital configurations also remain less known. Like all female-headed households with children, African-American women heading households are either widowed, separated, divorced, or never-married. Households with children that were formed through these different routes have substantially different levels of assets available to children. Not only does the tax system favor married couples, but it also discriminates among categories of women heading households and uses former and current marital status as a yardstick for determining citizenship rights and benefits. . . . Moreover, because so many African-American, female-headed households are below the poverty level and, thus, participate to varying degrees in government transfer programs, questions concerning tax policies and African-American, female-headed households are rarely asked. However, what about African-American working-class and professional women who head households? These women control some assets, and the question of how effectively American taxation policy aids these families in building assets is important.

V. African-American Women, Economic Inequality, and Economic Justice

. . .

Overall, given the centrality of families in the intergenerational transmission of material wealth, actual patterns of family organization become especially germane to understanding both African-American social class and the more general reality of economic inequality in the United States. Current levels of economic inequality raise deep-seated moral questions concerning race, gender, and economic justice. If African-American children confront a level playing field, yet falter through their own lack of merit or barriers internal to African-American civil society, then economic inequality of whites and African-Americans constitutes economic justice. However, if the emerging literature on the significance of racial differences in the intergenerational transfer of wealth is any indication, the level playing field remains more illusion than reality. In this case, in the absence of social policies dedicated to asset redistribution, economic justice for current and future African-Americans will remain elusive.

Notes

1. Melvin L. Oliver and Thomas M. Shapiro, Black Wealth/White Wealth: A New Perspective on Racial Inequality 5 (1995).

2. *Id.* at 5–6.

3. *Id.* at 2.

4. *Id.* at 78.

5. Jill Quadagno, The Color of Welfare: How Racism Undermined the War on Poverty 65 (1994).

6. *Id.*

7. *Id.*

8. Oliver and Shapiro, supra note 1, at 77.

9. Andrew Billingsley, Climbing Jacob's Ladder: The Enduring Legacy of African-American Families 334–40 (1992).

20

How Should Human Rights and Development Respond to Cultural Legitimization of Gender Hierarchy in Developing Countries?

Celestine I. Nyamu

Introduction

Human rights and development are the two fields of international law that have addressed gender and culture in developing countries. Human rights scholars and practitioners have invoked domestic and international human rights standards to eradicate certain Third World cultural practices, particularly with regard to women. Similarly, the field of development has predominantly treated culture as an obstacle to women's full participation in society. These approaches have highlighted specific negative cultural practices such as female genital surgeries. Human rights and development have, however, made minimal contributions to building a dialogue balancing the goals of gender equality and cultural identity. As long-term strategies, the approaches of these two fields are limited in their ability to address forms of gender hierarchy that cannot be easily characterized as cultural oppression. In this [a]rticle the specific issue of gender hierarchy in property relations will be used to evaluate and critique the approaches of these two fields. Emerging approaches—as opposed to the conventional approaches—will be used to suggest more effective ways of conceptualizing and remedying cultural justifications for practices that reinforce gender hierarchy in the Third World.

. . .

I. Overview of Development and Human Rights Approaches

. . .

A. Trends in Development and Gender Equity

The history of development practitioners' and scholars' concern with Third World women may be classified into three phases:

- Women in Development (WID) (early 1970s, influenced by the modernization framework);

- Women and Development (WAD) (mid-1970s through early 1980s, influenced by Marxist class analysis and dependency theory); and
- Gender and Development (GAD) (1980s, influenced by post-modernism)

. . .

4. Influence of WID, WAD, and GAD on Institutional Practice

At the institutional level, WID has had the deepest impact of the three approaches. In the 1970s and 1980s, WID spawned "Women in Development" desks at bilateral and multilateral development agencies, as well as at government ministries. The World Bank established the post of Adviser on Women in Development in 1977, and the United States Agency for International Development (USAID) established the Office of Women in Development as a direct result of the Percy Amendment to the Foreign Assistance Act of 1961.

In addition, both the WID and liberal feminism movements impacted international law with the United Nations Convention on the Elimination of All Forms of Discrimination Against Women (CEDAW). First proposed at the UN Decade for Women Conference in Mexico City in 1975, the Convention was opened for signature at the mid-decade conference in Copenhagen in 1980 and entered into force in 1981.

WAD, in contrast, has not had a significant impact on institutional practice. Its focus on poor women resonated with the emphasis on poverty alleviation adopted by multilateral and bilateral agencies in the early 1980s, but this concern overlapped with the predominant WID approach. WAD was, however, able to draw attention to the unusually high levels of poverty experienced by female-headed households. Additionally, non-governmental organizations (NGOs) run by WAD proponents work toward implementing this WAD approach.

The GAD influence on institutions is fairly recent and began after the 1985 UN World Conference on Women held in Nairobi, Kenya. Yet, in several important institutions, such as the World Bank, analysts have pointed out that despite the shift from WID-oriented to gender-oriented discourse, little has changed in practice. GAD has, however, substantially influenced the research and training practices of some NGOs, national institutions, bilateral development agencies, and multilateral agencies. For instance, the Kenya Agricultural Research Institute (KARI) incorporates gender analysis in its programs and conducts gender training for its agricultural extension staff in projects funded by the European Union and the Netherlands.

GAD also appears to have strongly influenced the United Nations Development Programme (UNDP), as indicated by the UNDP's annual Human Development Report—particularly the 1995 report that focuses on gender equality. The report addresses traditional WID issues such as the devaluing or undervaluing of women's work and the exclusion of women from the development process. Overall, however, the report is centrally concerned with engendering the entire development paradigm and moving beyond the limited discussion of equal participation within existing asymmetrical institutional structures. The report advocates comprehensive policy reforms and strong affirmative action to remove the legal, economic, political, and cultural barriers that prevent the exercise of equal rights by women and men. Underscoring the need for institutional transformation, the report notes that, despite marked improvement in women's access to education and health, there has not been a corresponding improvement in economic and political opportunities for women.

The report appears to have been influenced by GAD's advocacy of an approach that integrates productive and reproductive activities and is not restricted to the public sphere. For instance, the key recommendations to broaden the choices of men and women in the workplace aim to encourage men to increase their participation in family care: parental leave, flexible work hours for both men and women, and public day-care facilities. The UNDP seems to have adopted the ideology of the gender framework, but it is still unclear whether the framework has been implemented in practice.

. . .

B. Trends in Human/Women's Rights

1. *The Abolitionist Approach*

. . .

In practice, human rights is a state-oriented discipline that focuses on rights violations within the public sphere, particularly state violations of civil and political rights. Violations within the private sphere are often ignored. But feminists have challenged this public/private distinction, noting that violations against women occur mainly in the private sphere, and refusal to intervene perpetuates structures that deny women equal enjoyment of rights. Furthermore, states have refrained from criticizing cultural activity within another state's borders.

Thus, in order to promote accountability for private acts committed against women, human rights advocates have attempted to find a basis for state responsibility. The human rights community often focuses on the state's failure to regulate the area in question by prosecuting perpetrators, and advocates emphasize the state's own direct or indirect participation in facilitating violations. Articles 2(f) and 5(a) of the United Nations Convention on the Elimination of All Forms of Discrimination Against Women[1] (CEDAW) provide a basis for state accountability by calling upon states to take appropriate measures to modify or abolish customs and practices that constitute discrimination against women. Many Third World states, especially those with an Islamic majority, have, however, made reservations to these articles. Thus, human rights actors also use alternative human rights language, such as torture, to address state responsibility for harms suffered by women.

Most human rights groups have adopted an abolitionist approach and call for an end to cultural practices that contravene international human rights norms. This strategy is similar to WID's abolitionist approach in characterizing culture as an obstacle to development that must be overcome in order for women to participate effectively in the economy.

Some critics have pointed out that these abolitionist responses create the impression that women's rights do not exist in custom or local practice, and the solution therefore lies in substituting custom and local practice with alternatives offered by national legislation or the international human rights regime. Furthermore, the abolitionist approach does not encourage a holistic understanding of the context in which these practices are embedded, and as a result, prevents comprehensive solutions. The abolitionist approach has also suffered counteraccusations of cultural imperialism from interested Third World states.

2. Toward a Cross-Cultural Dialogue:
Moving away from the Abolitionist Approach

Critics of the abolitionist approach argue that culture is dynamic, responds to social change, and undergoes transformation over time. Such cultural change necessarily includes improvement in women's rights. People are not simply "the naive product of a rigid and static society"[2] except in the uninformed imagination of some people in Western societies who view Third World societies as "stable, timeless, ancient, lacking in internal conflict, [and] premodern."[3] However, social transformation does not always create improvement in women's lives. It is quite possible for matters that are central to women to remain bound by tradition even after other aspects of social life have undergone significant change.

Scholars point to the abolitionists' treatment of culture as a theoretical construct and their failure to grasp the meaning and daily existential experience of culture. Third World critics view abolitionist proposals as decontextualized, hegemonic, and counterproductive for gender equality in practice.

The non-abolitionist approach, therefore, calls for a non-hegemonic human rights practice that incorporates the two simultaneous processes of internal discourse and cross-cultural dialogue, in order to find legitimacy for human rights principles within all cultures. Internal discourse suggests some active deliberation on such issues as: recognizable standards of cultural legitimacy; responsibility for selecting standards; allowable action and reaction to divergent and competing views; and power relations between groups with different views.

Cross-cultural dialogue, in turn, calls for the pursuit of a global consensus viewing the relationship between international human rights and local culture as "a genuinely reciprocal global collaborative effort."[4] This two-way sharing of perspectives draws on the cultures' respective internal discourses. Through cross-cultural dialogue, external actors can support and influence internal discourse, but they must take care not to undermine internal discourse.

. . .

II. *Human Rights and Development Challenges to Cultural Legitimization of Gender Hierarchy in Property Relations*

. . .

A. Background: Why Property Relations Are Important

The example of property relations illustrates the interaction between formal law and policy and cultural normative orders in a plural legal setting. Whereas both women and men have access to land, women, in their capacity as wives, widows, or daughters (married or unmarried), generally have less control over land. Women are regarded as lacking the authority to make major decisions concerning land use and cannot inherit land or acquire a share of land following marital dissolution if they were married under customary law. In the conventional view, women's land interests extend only to use and not to ownership. African customary laws are used as the primary justification for this exclusion of women: national land registration programs have replicated these socio-cultural conventions. Using the concept of "male head of household" as the criterion for title registration, most, if not all, title to registered land is individually held in men's names. Joint registration between spouses is rare.

The ongoing process of individualization and formalization of title to land is shaped both by contemporary cultural perceptions of men as the proper authority in land matters and by narrow, individualistic conceptions of ownership in the formal legal regime. This process is set within a climate of free market reforms that promotes strong protection of an individual's private property. The convergence of these factors transforms the nature of property rights. The increased commodification of land weakens the position of women in relation to property officially held by their husbands and male relatives. The restructuring measures dictated by international financial institutions to Third World countries similarly emphasize a legal regime that strongly protects private property rights. In some countries, the World Bank and USAID finance programs geared toward individualization of land ownership. Regardless of gender, family members without a registered land interest experience insecurity as a result of the transformation in the property regime.

The male bias in land registration causes many difficulties for women. For example, women are often denied a share of marital property after divorce since title to their property is held in their husband's name. The male bias in land registration also impedes obtaining independent credit. Without evidence of land ownership, women cannot offer adequate collateral to secure a loan.

Land is the economic base in rural areas where women constitute the majority of the population. Beyond its economic significance, land also supports and defines a network of kin relationships. A discussion of property relations and gender is, therefore, a key component in addressing the issues of gender justice, women's identity, and social status.

B. Conventional Responses to Gender Hierarchy in Property Relations

. . .

In challenging the gender hierarchy in property relations, human rights activists also rely on international law, primarily the principle of non-discrimination in CEDAW. Specific articles of CEDAW relevant to property discrimination include:

- Article 2(f) which calls upon governments to abolish or modify laws and customs that discriminate against women;[5]
- Article 16(h) which calls on governments to ensure the same rights for both spouses in the ownership, acquisition, management, administration, enjoyment, and disposition of property;[6] and
- Article 14(g) which requires states to guarantee rural women equal access to agricultural credit and equal treatment in land and agrarian reform and in land resettlement schemes.[7]

Some human rights scholars have also sought to rely on regional human rights instruments, such as the African Charter on Human and Peoples' Rights. Within Western-based international women's human rights scholarship and practice, however, the issue of control of economic resources (including land) by women has not gained prominence. This omission stems from a bias in the human rights practice that emphasizes civil and political rights over economic, social, and cultural rights. Furthermore, the minimal presence of women's rights NGOs in rural areas, where the issue of land has greatest significance, perpetuates the political/economic rights dichotomy.

The WID response to gender hierarchy in property relations emphasizes the inconsistency between denying women control of property and the role of women as the primary producers in the agricultural sector. Cultural biases that prevent women from controlling land must be eliminated before women can participate fully in the development process; additionally, excluding women from land ownership and effective participation in economic development defeats the economic goals of the country and the utilitarian good.

Thus, both human rights and WID approaches view culture as the problem and recommend the application of remedial legal rights provisions. Proponents of gender equality generally adopt this view when debating the operation of personal laws alongside national statutes in societies described as legally and culturally pluralistic. According to this conventional view, formal laws addressing issues such as succession and marital property do not overtly discriminate against women, but customary law, which has a more immediate impact at the grassroots level, does discriminate against women. This analysis suggests that culture, not law, is the primary problem. Law is a problem only to the extent that it is not implemented properly. Since human rights and WID literature adopts this conventional view, actors in these fields will be referred to collectively as "proponents of gender equality" in the course of this discussion.

C. Difficulties Presented by the Conventional Approach

Conventional human rights and WID approaches attribute existing gender inequality to a vague notion of culture and presume a radical disjunction between the spheres of formal law and culture. Even though formal law and policy also disadvantage women, the emphasis on custom overshadows the mutually reinforcing relationship between formal law and policy and cultural interpretation of property relations. The cultural explanation is easily accepted and remains a recurring theme in conventional analysis by proponents of gender equality.

. . .

1. Obscuring the Overlap between Formal Law and Culture

Formal laws and cultural norms are modes of social control that play an important role in constructing social arrangements. Formal law may operate to give a natural and immutable appearance to dominant articulations of custom, and custom may be invoked to legitimize formal law. Attributing gender hierarchy to a vague notion of culture masks the role played by formal legal institutions in creating those conditions. A vague notion of culture provides a convenient scapegoat for government institutions and obscures the state's responsibility in redressing inequalities. A government can easily avoid addressing inequalities by claiming that it is powerless to alter social structures within the cultural sphere.

An example of government avoidance of responsibility for inequality can be seen in the framework adopted by some Anglophone African constitutions to accommodate cultural and religious pluralism. The Kenyan constitution, for example, exempts customary and religious laws in the areas of marriage, divorce, devolution of property on death, and other personal law matters from the anti-discrimination provision in section 82. In addition, any customary law limited to members of a particular race or tribe cannot be labeled discriminatory under the constitution.

Similar provisions are contained in the constitutions of Zimbabwe, Zambia, and Ghana. In Zimbabwe, the Supreme Court applied such a constitutional provision in a 1999 case and ruled that a Shona customary law barring a daughter from administering her deceased father's estate, solely on the basis of her sex, was not discriminatory. This Shona customary law was protected from constitutional scrutiny. In Kenya, a similar constitutional provision was applied to the highly publicized case of S. M. Otieno. The constitutional exception was invoked to justify the application of Luo customary burial law, denying a widow any role in deciding where her husband would be buried.

These exceptions insulate practices carried out in accordance with customary or religious law from constitutional scrutiny. Aggrieved citizens within those religious or cultural communities are thus left without formal legal or constitutional remedies. Through these exemption provisions, the state facilitates the establishment and preservation of asymmetrical social arrangements by denying some citizens a voice in shaping social norms.

. . .

2. *Implicit Endorsement of Dominant Articulations of Culture*

When gender-biased social arrangements are defended in the name of culture, the purported cultural norms need to be challenged. Arguing on the basis of their inconsistency with human rights standards and ideals of gender equity in development does not go far enough. Scholars and practitioners must ask: Do the cultural norms reflect actual social practice? Are they representative of the community, or are they simply a generalization of the narrow interests of a few? Whose power is preserved through the use of cultural norms? Is the label of culture being deployed to stifle a desirable and necessary political debate?

Human rights advocates need to understand the process of cultural legitimization and change within a political context. Assertions of culture in family law reform are best viewed as a matter of current politics, rather than descriptions of age-old tradition. Scholars warn that rigid and exclusionary statements about customary property entitlements must be viewed in the context of increased socio-economic pressures, such as unemployment, and the increased competition over family resources, such as land. GAD scholars, in particular, emphasize the need to question political, social, and economic institutions involved in the production of culture and the shaping of gender relations.

Community practices vary and the best indication of living cultural norms can be found in an analysis of the everyday interactions between social actors. Assertions of culture will often fail to capture the entire social reality. In fact, the incongruity between social reality and ideological systems, which include laws, procedures, customs, rituals, and symbols, is a feature of social life. Customs, laws, rituals, symbols, and rigid procedures serve as a cultural framework that attempts to capture and represent social life. Social life is, however, difficult to define due to continuous cultural and social change. General statements often present cultural norms in a rigid manner, as immutable, inflexible, and applicable in all situations. Yet these assertions, presented for the purpose of political debate and court-based arguments, often overlook variations and the conflicts inherent within actual practice. Proponents of gender equality could counteract broad and generalized statements about custom with evidence of alternative practices and social change, especially where such change and variation are observable but not explicitly acknowledged.

In legal disputes or political debates, stated cultural norms are not neutral descriptions of a community's way of life. Rather, such articulations should be read as competing efforts to preserve certain social, economic, and political arrangements. Articulations of cultural norms are expressions of power relations that are often limited to the dominant voices in a specific social interaction. Scholars of legal anthropology and legal history have shown that the colonial period was crucial in defining what is now considered customary law in African countries. The specific customs that were officially recognized and applied in the colonial courts and administrative tribunals represented the outcome of conflicts between diverse social practices. The institutionally recognized customary law rules merely reflected the versions of custom endorsed by the colonial structures of authority.

. . .

3. Precluding a Positive Role for Culture in the Pursuit of Gender Equality

. . .

The current emphasis on individual land ownership has grown out of a commitment to market-friendly policies that place a premium on well-defined and secure property rights, deemed synonymous with absolute and individual ownership. An official switch from a system that recognizes multiple and overlapping interests in land to one that overemphasizes individual and absolute title has devalued the unregistered claims of many family members. When ownership disputes have arisen following registration, the majority of courts have maintained that the registered proprietor holds the only valid interests. All other interests stemming from customary law are extinguished.

The negative effects on women's property rights implied by such a position are illustrated in a 1988 case involving two widows whose husbands had died before repaying loans secured on the family's land. The widows, whose husbands were brothers, attempted to prevent the auctioning of the land by arguing that their rights as occupants under customary law had not been taken into account. The Court of Appeal, the highest court in Kenya, held that registration of a husband as sole proprietor extinguished a wife's right of access under customary law, acquired through marriage.

In a few cases, judges have ruled that any person registered as the sole proprietor of land previously held under customary tenure must be presumed to be a trustee on behalf of people with interests in the land. This line of argument, however, represents a minority view and is not favored by courts. The High Court last used this reasoning to decide a case in 1978 and only one Court of Appeal decision has upheld this approach.

In addition to the threat posed by individual ownership and registration, women's interests are also jeopardized by the diminishing importance of social/customary mechanisms for supervising the exercise of male authority over land. For instance, the sale of land previously required approval by the larger family network. In a system of registration, however, titles facilitate the free transfer of land, thus weakening protection of the unregistered interests of family members.

The language of customary rights to land is the only defense that has challenged the trend of marketization of land and its dangers for women's unregistered interests. The language of customary rights can accommodate multiple or overlapping claims and makes it possible to articulate obligations owed to family members.

Often such obligations are neither recognized nor enforceable in formal law. For example, the principle is widely accepted in some communities that unmarried or divorced daughters, particularly if they have children, are entitled to a piece of their family's land for cultivation and, in some cases, for construction of a home. A strong ethic of care creates a social expectation that natal families will care for such daughters and their children, regardless of legitimacy/illegitimacy notions. A divorced daughter bringing such a claim against her family in formal court is, however, unlikely to succeed. Although some court interpretations of customary law do recognize certain limited rights for daughters, they appear to restrict such recognition to daughters who have never married, thus jeopardizing the claims of divorced daughters.

Proponents of gender equality must take the lead in shaping the language of customary rights to land. Otherwise, the space opened up for challenging the marketization process can easily be appropriated to argue in favor of customary arrangements that would be unwilling to question gender disparities. Yet, because the conventional human rights and WID approaches place proponents of gender equality in opposition to culture, these actors are noticeably absent from the discourse of customary rights. Proponents of gender equality may fear that arguing on the side of custom will work against them in other cases in which custom is deployed to displace women's claims. This tension will be discussed further in the following [p]art.

III. Lessons toward Effective Responses to Cultural Legitimization of Gender Hierarchy in a Plural Legal Context

. . .

B. Critical Pragmatic Approach to Plural Normative Orders

Critical pragmatism provides a framework that is helpful in meeting the challenge presented by the apparent tension between gender equality and cultural identity in plural contexts. . . .

In concrete terms, a critical pragmatic approach would challenge the constitutional framework that shields customary and religious laws from questioning, in order to create room for more voice and inclusiveness in the shaping and articulation of community norms. Marriage, divorce, and death are key events for defining and reconstituting property rights of women and children, whose access to economic resources heavily depends on relationships to fathers or husbands. The absence of constitutional protection for women and children in marriage, divorce, and death has far-reaching consequences in a social context that makes it easy for opportunistic individuals to justify (on the basis of custom) negative treatment of widows or divorced women and their children.

. . .

The South African constitution recognizes the validity of traditional authority, as well as the right to enjoy and practice one's culture, but it subjects the exercise of these rights to the constitution. The exercise of traditional authority and the operation of customary law can therefore be challenged under the South African Bill of Rights. According to Justice Yvonne Mokgoro of the South African Constitutional Court, political necessity required the recognition of traditional authority but justice demanded that the exercise of such power be subjected to constitutional scrutiny.

The constitution of Ghana employs a similar model and recognizes a right to practice one's culture while also prohibiting customary practices that dehumanize or injure the physical or mental well-being of a person.

The Ugandan constitution strikes a balance that explicitly addresses the tension between women's rights (article 33) and the right to practice culture (article 37). Article 33(6) prohibits "laws, cultures, customs or traditions which are against the dignity, welfare or interest of women or which undermine their status."[8]

. . .

Critical pragmatists should also work toward strengthening informal social processes and mechanisms that protect the interests of family members by restricting the power of the official owner (usually the father/husband). In most communities in Kenya, it is generally understood that family land must be sold in consultation with family members. In the Akamba community, for example, various clans have rules requiring a seller to notify and make the first sale offer to members of the extended family, particularly when the land was originally inherited, not purchased. The seller can only offer the property on the open market if no one in the extended family or clan is willing or able to buy the land. In addition, the seller must show that the family will have sufficient land to meet its needs before selling that portion of the land. Informal measures such as these help to enforce the obligations owed to family members.

. . .

C. Critical Pragmatic Engagement with the Politics of Culture

. . .

2. Invoking a Community's Own General Principles of Fairness and Justice
A rule of custom may be widely accepted, but may not apply to all situations. In a given situation, the application of this rule may be objectionable in light of commonly held notions of fairness and justice. For instance, the conventional understanding that girls do not inherit their families' property is widespread in Kenya. Research conducted in the Makueni District of Eastern Kenya, however, established that people generally favor providing for daughters who may not marry or whose marriages may not work out. People also make provisions for such a contingency in the future. The people interviewed frequently reinforced that view with the remark: "Nengi na ni mwana ta aangi, na ndekw'a itheka i!" which means, "Indeed she is a child, just like the others, and she cannot be cast away!" The overarching principles of providing sustenance and taking responsibility for every child justify this flexible practice, qualifying the conventional notion that male children are the only ones entitled to their families' property.

. . .

These suggestions would greatly improve the conventional methodology of human rights practice in which advocates criticize inconsistencies between cultural practices and human rights standards but do not attempt to reconcile the two. The fact that articles 2(f) and 5(a) of CEDAW call upon governments to abolish or modify customs that discriminate against women does not mean that in all situations the only way to achieve desired change is through lobbying for legislation aimed at outlawing those customs. Although CEDAW's strong abolitionist language is arguably an important reflection of the Convention's aspirations, abolition is not conducive to a positive dialogue that achieves a balance between gender equality and cultural identity.

. . .

D. Dilemmas Presented by a Critical Pragmatic Approach

. . .

The critical pragmatist approach of taking up the enforcement of customary obligations in local forums and in courts may also pose dilemmas for proponents of gender equality alluded to earlier in the [a]rticle. For instance, gaining cultivation and occupancy rights for an unmarried or divorced daughter with children will, clearly, bring immediate benefits to her. For long-term gender equality, however, this recognition of customary rights is not a real victory. It is premised on the perception that women's interests in property belonging to their natal families are contingent. Daughters do not achieve full control of resources on an equal basis with their brothers, who are seen as the real or permanent members of the family. Daughters are only accommodated in exceptional circumstances, namely when they fail to marry, or when their marriages fail. Furthermore, the prevalence of the practice highlights the inadequacy of spousal support for women following marital breakdown. Gains for individual women in such circumstances leave intact the gender hierarchy in landholding and the ineffective spousal support mechanisms in family law.

This dilemma is not resolved, however, by choosing not to support such customary law claims by daughters who may need them. Rather, it is important to appropriate the openings present in local cultural or religious traditions, while simultaneously working toward changing the larger social matrix of national legislation, constitutions, and administrative institutions. By finding the space that local contexts provide for the recognition of women's rights, proponents of gender equality avoid creating the impression that the only solution lies in substituting local custom with the alternatives offered in national legislation or by the human rights regime.

Conclusion

In plural contexts, responses to cultural legitimization of gender hierarchy must take account of the symbiotic relationship between formal law and culture and the role of formal institutions in the shaping of culture. Formal law may lend a natural appearance to dominant articulations of custom, and custom may be invoked to lend legitimacy to formal law. The symbiotic relationship between law and custom is exemplified by the special accommodation of customary laws in the national constitutions of some African countries. Granting customary laws immunity from anti-discrimination provisions in constitutions amounts to systemic state-sanctioned stifling of debate and denial of voice in the process of determining cultural norms. Challenging this setup is crucial to facilitating a positive cultural dialogue and to challenging the use of culture to justify gender hierarchy in plural societies.

Proponents of gender equality must engage with the specific politics of culture. Situations in which culture is deployed to end political debate and preempt the questioning of unjust social arrangements must be challenged. Assertions of the rigid notions of custom must be met with empirical evidence of the flexibility, variety, and richness of contemporary local practice. Such critical pragmatic engagement recognizes that normative orders, including human rights regimes, in a plural legal context offer setbacks to gender equality, as well as resources for challenging such inequality. A critical pragmatic approach to pluralism calls upon local and international actors to engage at multiple sites and to assess the most successful methods of redressing gender hierarchies in diverse contexts.

NOTES

1. Convention on the Elimination of All Forms of Discrimination Against Women, Dec. 18, 1979, 1249 U.N.T.S. 13, 19 I.L.M. 33 (entered into force on Sept. 3, 1981) [hereinafter CEDAW].

2. Katha Pollitt, *Whose Culture?* in Is Multiculturalism Bad for Women? 28 (Joshua Cohen et al., eds., 1999).

3. *Id.* at 29.

4. Abdullahi An-Na'im, *State Responsibility under International Human Rights Law to Change Religious and Customary Laws*, in Human Rights of Women: National and International Perspectives 173 (Rebecca J. Cook, ed., 1994).

5. CEDAW, supra note 1, art. 2(f).

6. *Id.* art. 16(h).

7. *Id.* art. 14(g).

8. Uganda Constitution art. 33(6).

Part III

Women, Children, Well-Being, and the State

Introduction

Feminist theory centered on family and children epitomizes the process of bringing the margin to the center in several respects. Families, caregiving, and domestic work have not been a core focus for feminist theory, which overwhelmingly has focused on work rather than family, on the public sphere rather than the private. Bringing family to the center reorients priorities and connections between the presumed place of family and the other spheres of life. Bringing women to the center requires thinking about caregiving, unpaid family work, children's rights and needs, caretaking of other family members, and the construction of adult relationships in both intimate and nonintimate contexts. Bringing marginalized women to the center orients issues, priorities, perspectives from those with the greatest needs while allowing different voices to be heard and different models and lessons to be presented. If those most marginalized are the model for policy, then those with the greatest privilege are more easily served. If, by contrast, those most privileged drive theory and policy, then it is easy for real needs to be rendered invisible or blamed on marginalized women as the consequences of their faults.

Family is a strongly defining structure for most women. Reproductive rights, especially the right to choose an abortion, have been a primary focus for feminists for decades. But the controversial nature of abortion has arguably pulled resources and attention from other equally demanding issues. The construction of motherhood, the ability to become a mother, and the lived-out reality of caregiving and its consequences for women's lives are all critical topics for feminist theory. Defining who is a "mother" in the context of evolving reproductive technologies has become more complex and destabilized, even as it has exposed differentiations that privilege already-privileged women. A different kind of challenge to motherhood norms arises in the context of adoption and is rendered more difficult in the context of transracial and international adoption.

Valuing all mothers, regardless of the form of their families or the changes in family forms over women's lifetimes, is an area of policy that as yet remains poorly developed. Divorce reform has been the subject of legislative activity and scholarly attention throughout the last quarter of the twentieth century and into the new millennium, but with mixed results with respect to women's economic status.

Formal equality has rarely translated into substantive equality and, perversely, has often meant an even less equal outcome than under patriarchal legal regimes. The typical situation of women after divorce, with a disproportionate responsibility for the care of children and a disproportionate lack of economic resources, remains common, while the structure of decision making and control favors shared connections with ex-spouses.

Welfare reform has also been a target of policy makers but often is totally separated from divorce. Single mothers who have never married similarly are often separated from divorced mothers and commonly are more strongly penalized and controlled within the welfare structure than in the divorce structure. The challenge for feminists remains resistance to this tendency to separate mothers into "good" mothers and "bad" mothers along lines of class and race and linking motherhood across these lines of division and across various family structures.

The liberty to choose whether to construct an intimate partnership is particularly an issue for lesbians. The classic feminist critique of marriage as a patriarchal institution, and its stubborn retention of that characteristic despite the redefinition of marriage as an equal partnership, exists in tension with the desire for public recognition and private commitment, as well as the associated legal protections and respect for privacy of marital relationships. Whether patriarchal tools can be utilized to dismantle the patriarchal house of marriage, to paraphrase Audre Lorde's classic question, is an enduring feminist issue epitomized by the current debate among lesbian and gay couples over the desirability of the right to marry.

Women's health also has been largely unexplored, subsumed under race and gender norms than the right to marry, but has become the focus of recent feminist attention. The disproportionate attention to abortion may have contributed to this lacuna. Recent work has begun to document pervasive discrimination in medical research and practice. Challenges to hospital procedures for poor mothers also have highlighted women's needs.

The readings in this part revolve around these topics. They also focus on the role of the state as either intruder or supporter, as a negative force regulating the lives of women or a necessary source of the redistribution of goods and services to ensure the health and well-being of women and their dependents. Because of the interconnection of families and work, these selections have many connections to the preceding section, on workplace-related issues. Because of the presence of violence in women's domestic lives, the readings also connect to Part 4, on women's experiences with violence in public and private spheres. Equality remains a core concern, but in the area of families, privacy and liberty are also critical conceptual issues, with the meaning of those terms contested and reconfigured by feminist analyses.

Overview of the Readings

Maxine Zinn's overview of families provides a rich picture of the diversity of families and their transitions over the life course. Her construction of the context sets the stage for theoretical perspectives from Martha Fineman, Barbara Woodhouse, and Anita Allen. Fineman has challenged the underlying assumptions of family law as well as the orientation of feminist analysis and has contributed significantly to the development of both feminist theory and the structure of family law. She has been particularly critical of the orientation of family law in the intimate adult heterosexual marital pair and has argued for a reorientation of family law in structures of dependency, especially the mother-child relationship. She has made visible and central the existence of dependency and how dependency is viewed and dealt with in law. She argues for the necessity of legal support for those who care for others and, by virtue of that care, are economically dependent, as well as those inevitably dependent by virtue of age or incapacity.

Barbara Woodhouse suggests a equally radical reorientation and rethinking of family law, revolving around children's needs and rights. Woodhouse has argued for the importance of centering notions of family on generative parenting—that is, caregiving to children on a model of fiduciary obligation—to replace economic notions of parenthood. Her generative model, based on interdisciplinary research and evaluation of children's needs, also requires a reorientation of the place of children in law. Rather than presume that parents or the state can best serve their interests, Woodhouse would require that children be listened to and involved in the construction of their lives to the extent that they are capable. She also argues for a standard of care of all children that would support their caregivers regardless of the structure of the family in which they are situated.

Finally, Anita Allen reconsiders privacy in light of feminist critique and argues for the importance of privacy for women's autonomy. Feminists have seen privacy as a dangerous protection for inequalities and violence within the family but at the same time have used privacy as the basis for individual choice and protection from state intrusion into family life. Allen suggests a reorientation of privacy concepts that takes account of feminist critiques of privacy without rejecting its usefulness and importance in the lives of women.

The readings that follow touch on specific substantive areas. The central role of the legal structures of divorce and welfare in women's lives and whether those structures serve women well are the focus of the readings by Nancy Dowd and Tonya Brito. Dowd highlights the gulf between the equality assumptions of the divorce structure and the inequalities in family life before and after divorce. Brito points out the dissonance between what we know about poor families and the assumptions of welfare reform and suggests that telling the real stories of poor women is essential to undermining the discourse of stigma that justifies harsh treatment and control of poor women on welfare. Nancy Polikoff analyzes the arguments for and against marriage as a goal for gays and lesbians and, in particular, considers whether gay marriage could revolutionize marriage as we know it. Adoption has been an underdeveloped subject of feminist analysis, but the work of Lorie Graham and Twila Perry brings powerful insights to this issue. Graham evaluates the effectiveness of policies designed to prevent the adoption by non–Native Americans of Native American children, emphasizing the distinct parenting culture of

Native Americans and its critical role in creating and sustaining cultural identity. Perry examines the issues surrounding transracial and international adoption and what they suggest about assumptions about mothers and mothering practices.

Health issues have long been a focus of feminists, particularly reproductive issues, but the overall health of women and their place in the health care system constitute a relatively recent topic of academic and political attention. Karen Rothenberg outlines the consequences of a health care system that revolves around a male norm. Lisa Ikemoto further fleshes out the health care structure by looking to the reproduction of race and gender hierarchies even within the adoption of race and gender categories of data and analysis. Reproductive issues, particularly the control of the reproductive choices of poor women of color based on persisting attacks on their mothering, are Dorothy Roberts's focus.

The two final pieces in Part 3 focus on the interaction between feminism and culture. Leti Volpp examines the constructions of culture and their impact on the evaluation of family behavior, comparing the perception and treatment of white families and immigrant families of color who engage in similar practices. Practices perceived as deviant are simply treated as individual differences for whites, while they are viewed as cultural (read "racial") manifestations for families of color. Cultural bias and paternalistic feminism are also the concern of Amede Obiora, who discusses the controversial issue of female genital mutilation and the reactions and strategies of feminists to this issue.

21

Family, Feminism, and Race in America

Maxine Baca Zinn

. . .

The Feminist Revision

Feminist challenges to traditional family theory have been accomplished by decomposing the family, that is, by breaking the family into constituent elements so that the underlying structures are exposed. In doing so, feminists have brought into relief three aspects of that structure: ideologies that serve to mystify women's experiences as wives and mothers, hierarchical divisions that generate conflict and struggle within families, and the multiple and dynamic interconnections between households and the larger political economy. An understanding of family dynamics has been transformed by exposing gender as a fundamental category of social relations both within and outside the family.

First evolved as a critique of functionalism and its emphasis on roles, the crucial impact of feminist scholarship on family research has been to recast the family as a system of gender stratification. Because roles neglect the political underpinnings of the family, feminists have directed attention outside the family "to the social structures that shape experience and meaning, that give people a location in the social world, and that define and allocate economic and social rewards."[1] Once feminist scholars made it clear that gender roles are not neutral ways of maintaining order in family and society but benefit some at the expense of others, virtually everything about the family looked different. . . . Rather than viewing the family as a unit shaped only by affection or kinship, we now know that families are settings in which people with different activities and interests often come into conflict with one another.

. . . Feminists have challenged the monolithic ideology of the family that elevated the contemporary nuclear family with a breadwinner husband and a full-time homemaker wife as the only legitimate family form. We now give equal weight to the varied family structures and experiences that are produced by the organization of the economy, the state, and other institutions. Some of these alternative family structures and living arrangements are nonmarital cohabitation, single-parent households, extended kinship units and expanded households, dual-worker families, commuter marriages, gay and lesbian households, and collectives.

Revisions in Race-Relations Scholarship

The revisioning of American scholarship on racial ethnic families [as] different from those of the White middle class has run a similar but not intersecting course with feminist scholarship. Like feminist scholarship, this revisioning began with a critique of functionalist accounts of racially and ethnically diverse families as dysfunctional units that acted as barriers to their groups' mobility. . . .

The model of the backward and culturally deviant minority family originated within the sociology of race relations in the United States and its then guiding framework of assimilation and modernization. The preoccupation in race relations with "traditional" and "modern" social forms fit well with family sociology's preoccupation with the nuclear family, its wage-earner father, and domestic-caretaker mother. Minorities and others whose family patterns differed from the ideal were explained as cultural exceptions to the rule. Their slowness to acculturate and take on the normal patterns of family development left them behind as other families in American society modernized. They were peripheral to the standard family and viewed as problems because of their failure to adopt the family patterns of the mainstream.

. . .

Scholars of various disciplines have long refuted this culturally deviant model of family, arguing that alternative family patterns do not reflect deviance, deficiency, or disorganization and that alternative family patterns are related to but not responsible for the social location of minorities. Revisionist approaches have emphasized the structural conditions giving rise to varied family forms, rather than the other way around. Differences in family patterns have been reinterpreted as adaptations to the conditions of racial inequality and poverty, often as sources of survival and strength.

Assessing the Revisions

. . .

Despite such fundamental similarities in their intellectual roots, the feminist revision and the racial ethnic studies revision have not been combined, nor have they had the same impact on theories of the family. Feminist scholarship with its gender-as-power theme has had a far greater impact.

. . .

Social Location and Family Formation

In our quest to understand the structural sources of diversity in family life, we must examine all of the "socioeconomic and political arrangements and how they impinge on families."[2] Like class and gender hierarchies, racial stratification is a fundamental axis of American social structure. Racial stratification produces different opportunity structures that shape families in a variety of ways. Marriage patterns, gender relations, kinship networks, and other family characteristics result from the social location of families, that is, where they are situated in relation to societal institutions allocating resources.

Thinking about families in this way shifts the theoretical focus from cultural diversity or "ethnic lifestyles" of particular groups to race as a major element of hierarchical social relations that touches families throughout the social order. Racial stratification is a basic organizing principle in American society even though the forms of domination and discrimination have changed over time. . . . As racial categories are formed and transformed over time, the meanings, practices, and institutions associated with race penetrate families through the society.

Social categories and groups subordinate in the racial hierarchy are often deprived of access to social institutions that offer supports for family life. Social categories and groups elevated in the racial hierarchy have different and better connections to institutions that can sustain families. Social location and its varied connection with social resources thus have profound consequences for family life.

. . . Instead of treating diversity as a given, or as a result of traditions alone, we must treat racial stratification as a macrostructural force situating families in ways requiring diverse arrangements. These macrostructural forces can be seen in two periods of economic upheaval in the United States—industrialization and the current shift from manufacture to information and services. . . . Industrialization and deindustrialization are not neutral transformations that touch families in uniform ways. Rather, they manifest themselves differently in their interaction with race and gender, and both periods of transition reveal racial patterning in family and household formation. . . .

Industrialization and Family Structure

The past two decades of historical research on the family have revealed that industrialization has had momentous consequences for American families because of massive changes in the way people made a living. The industrial revolution changed the nature of work performed, the allocation of work responsibilities, and the kind of pay, prestige, and power that resulted from various positions in the economy. The effect of industrialization on American family life was uneven. Instead of a linear pattern of change in which families moved steadily to a more modern level, the pattern of change was checkered. Labor force exploitation produced various kinds of family and household adaptations on the part of slaves, agricultural workers, and industrial workers.

Both class and race were basic to the relations of production in the United States in this period. Race was intertwined with class; populations from various parts of the world were brought into the labor force at different levels, and racial differences were utilized to rationalize exploitation of women and men. European ethnics were incorporated into low-wage industrial economies of the North, while Blacks, Latinos, Chinese, and Japanese filled labor needs in colonial labor systems of the economically backward regions of the West, Southwest, and the South. These colonial labor systems, while different, created similar hardships for family life.

All these groups had to engage in a constant struggle for both immediate survival and long-term continuation of family and community, but women's and men's work and family patterns varied considerably within different racial labor structures, with fundamentally different social supports for family life. [Bonnie] Thornton Dill[3] has compared patterns of White families in nineteenth-century America with those of racial ethnics and identified important racial differences in the social supports for family life. She finds that greater importance was accorded Euro-American families by the wider society. As primary laborers in the reproduction and maintenance of family life, these women were acknowledged and accorded the privileges and protections deemed socially appropriate to their family roles. Although this emphasis on family roles denied these women many rights and privileges and seriously constrained their individual growth and development, it also revealed public support for White women's family roles. Women's reproductive labor was viewed as an essential building block of the family. Combined with a view of the family as the cornerstone of the nation, this ideology produced experiences within the White dominant culture very different from those of racial ethnics. Because racial ethnic men were usually unable to earn a "family wage," their women had to engage in subsistence and income-producing activities both in and out of the household. In addition, they had to struggle to keep their families together in the face of outside forces that threatened the integrity of their households.

During industrialization, class produced some similarities in the family experiences of racial ethnic women and those of White working-class immigrants. As Smith has argued, working-class women during this period were often far removed from the domestic ideal. The cults of domesticity and true womanhood that proliferated during this period were ideals attained more frequently by those Euro-American women whose husbands were able to earn enough to support their families.

This ideal was not attainable by Blacks, Latinos, and Asian Americans, who were excluded from jobs open to White immigrants. For example, in most cities, the constraints that prevented Black men from earning a family wage forced Black married women into the labor market in much greater proportions than White immigrant women. By 1880, about 50 percent of Black women were in the labor force, compared with 15 percent of White women. Furthermore, the family system of the White working class was not subject to institutional assaults, such as forced separation, directed against Black, Latino, and Chinese families.

Racial ethnic women experienced the oppressions of a patriarchal society but were denied the protections and buffering of a patriarchal family. Their families suffered as a direct result of the labor systems in which they participated. Since they were a cheap and exploitable labor force, little attention was given to their family and community life except as it related to their economic productivity. Labor and not the existence or maintenance of families was the critical aspect of their role in building the nation. They were denied the social and structural supports necessary to make their families a vital element in the social order. Nevertheless, people take conditions that have been thrust upon them and out of them create a history and a future. Using cultural forms where possible and creating new forms where necessary, racial ethnics adapted their families to the larger social order. These adaptations were not exceptions to the rule; they were instead variations created by mainstream forces. One family type was not standard and the others peripheral. Different forms existed at the same time.

. . .

De-Industrialization and Families

Vast changes in the social organization of work are currently transforming the American family across class and race groups. Not only are women and men affected differently by the transformation of the economy from its manufacturing base to service and high technology, but women and men in different racial categories are experiencing distinctive changes in their relationship to the economy. This transformation is profoundly affecting families as it works with and through race and gender hierarchies.

In the current American economy, industrial jobs traditionally filled by men are being replaced with service jobs that are increasingly filled by women. Married White women are now entering the labor force at a rate that, until recently, was seen exclusively among women of color. The most visible consequences of the increased labor force participation among White women include declining fertility and changes in marriage patterns. American White women are delaying marriage and childbearing and having fewer children over their lifetimes, living alone or as heads of their own households—living with neither parents nor husbands. The new economy is reshaping families as it propels these women into the labor force.

In minority communities across America, families and households are also being reshaped through new patterns of work and gender roles. The high level of female-headed families among Blacks and Hispanics (especially Puerto Ricans) is the outgrowth of changes in the larger economy. The long-term decline in employment opportunities for men is the force most responsible for the growth of racial ethnic families headed by women. [William Julius] Wilson's compelling work has shown that the shortage of Black men with the ability to support a family makes it necessary for many Black women to leave a marriage or forgo marriage altogether. Adaptation to structural conditions leaves Black women disproportionately separated, divorced, and solely responsible for their children.

Families throughout American society are being reshaped by economic and industrial change. . . . Families mainly headed by women have become permanent in all racial categories in America, with the disproportionate effects of change most visible among Blacks and Latinos. While the chief cause of the increase in female-headed households among Whites is the greater economic independence of White women, the longer delay of first marriage and the low rate of remarriage among Black women reflects the labor force problems of Black men. Thus race creates different routes to female headship, but Whites, Blacks, and Latinos are all increasingly likely to end up in this family form.

Conclusion

Knowing that race creates certain patterns in the way families are located and embedded in different social environments, we should be able to theorize for all racial categories. Billingsley suggests that the study of Black families can generate important insights for White families: Families may respond in a like manner when impacted by larger social forces. To the extent that White families and Black families experience similar pressures, they may respond in similar ways, including the adaptation of their family structures and other behaviors. With respect to single-parent families, teenage childbirth, working mothers, and a host of other behaviors, Black families serve as barometers of social change and as forerunners of adaptive patterns that will be progressively experienced by the more privileged sectors of American society.

While such insights are pertinent, they should not eclipse the ways in which racial meanings inform our perceptions of family diversity. As social and economic changes produce new family arrangements, alternatives—what is sometimes called "family pluralism"—are granted greater legitimacy. Yet many alternatives that appear new to middle-class White Americans are actually variant family patterns that have been traditional within Black and other minority communities for many generations. . . .

In much popular and scholarly thinking, alternatives are seen as inevitable changes, new ways of living that are part of an advanced society. In other words, they are conceptualized as products of the mainstream. Yet such alternatives, when associated with racial ethnic groups, are judged against a standard model and found to be deviant. Therefore, the notion of family pluralism does not correctly describe the family diversity of the past or the present. Pluralism implies that alternative family forms coexist within a society. In reality, racial meanings create a hierarchy in which some family forms are privileged and others are subordinated, even though they are both products of larger social forces.

Treating race as a basic category of social organization can make the feminist reconstruction of the family more inclusive. The implications of this approach are also provocative and uncomfortable because they challenge some of our basic sociological and feminist assumptions about how families in different races (and classes) are related to the larger society, to each other, and how they are all changing as a result of ongoing social and economic changes. These are important issues for social scientists, policymakers, and others to ponder, understand, and solve.

NOTES

1. *Introduction* in Analyzing Gender 11 (B. Hess and M. Marx Ferree, eds.) (Newbury Park, CA: Sage, 1987).

2. L. Mullings, *Anthropological Perspectives on the Afro-American Family*, 6 American Journal of Social Psychiatry 11, 13 (1986).

3. B. Thornton Dill, *Our Mother's Grief: Racial Ethnic Women and the Maintenance of Families*, 13 Journal of Family History 415–31 (1988).

22

Cracking the Foundational Myths:
Independence, Autonomy, and Self-Sufficiency

Martha Albertson Fineman

. . .

Perhaps the most important task for those concerned with the welfare of poor mothers and their children, as well as other vulnerable members of society, is the articulation of a theory of collective responsibility for dependency. The idea of collective responsibility must be developed as a claim of "right" or entitlement to support and accommodation on the part of caretakers. It must be grounded on an appreciation of the value of caretaking labor. A further important concern is to ensure that any theory of collective responsibility not concede the right of collective control over individual intimate decisions, such as whether and when to reproduce or how to form one's family.

The rhetorical and ideological rigidity with which contemporary policy debates have been conducted makes the claim of collective responsibility a particularly difficult task. . . . Core components of America's founding myths, such as the sacredness of individual independence, autonomy, and self-sufficiency have been ossified, used as substitutes for analysis, and eclipsed rather than illuminated debate.

I do not reject these core concepts. I do, however, insist that we have a responsibility to reexamine them in the context of our present society and the needs and aspirations of people today.

. . .

IV. Dependency and Social Debt

Historic ideals of independence and self-sufficiency are complementary themes in our political discourse. These aspirational ideals are applied to individuals as well as to families. Their dichotomous terms, dependence and subsidy, are also complementary, viewed as occurring in tandem. Both dependence and subsidy have been successfully used in a simplistic and divisive manner by politicians, social conservatives, and advocates of small government to control and limit contemporary policy discussions.

Dependence is negatively compared with the desirable status of independence—subsidy with the meritorious self-sufficiency. Independence and self-sufficiency are set up as transcendent values, attainable aspirations for all members of society. Simplified pejorative notions of dependence and subsidy are joined, and condemnation or pity are considered appropriate responses for those unable to live up to the ideals, particularly those who are dependent and in need of subsidy.

In fact, dependency is assumed if an individual is the recipient of certain governmental subsidies. Furthermore, the mere label of dependency serves as an argument against governmental social welfare transfers. Policy makers argue that the goal should be independence, and favor the termination of subsidy so the individual can learn to be self-sufficient.

It is puzzling, as well as paradoxical, that the term "dependency" has such negative connotations. Its very existence prompts and justifies mean spirited and ill-conceived political responses, such as the recent welfare "reform." Far from being pathological, avoidable, and the result of individual failings, dependency is a universal and inevitable part of the human development. It is inherent in the human condition.

All of us were dependent as children, and many of us will be dependent as we age, become ill, or suffer disabilities. In this sense, dependency is "inevitable" and not deserving of condemnation or stigma. Note that the examples I have chosen to illustrate this category of inevitable dependency are biological or physical in nature. Biological dependencies, however, do not exhaust the potential range of situations of dependence. For example, in addition to biological dependence, one may be psychologically or emotionally dependent on others. In fact, these other forms of dependence may even accompany the physiological or biological dependence, which I have labeled inevitable. But economic, psychological, and emotional dependency are not generally understood to be universally experienced. As a result, assertions about their inevitability in each individual's life would be controversial. It is the characteristic of universality (which indisputably accompanies inevitable dependence) that is central to my argument for societal or collective responsibility. In other words, the realization that biological dependency is both inevitable and universal is theoretically important. Upon this foundational realization is built my claim for justice—the demand that society value and accommodate the labor done by the caretakers of inevitable dependents.

I argue that the caretaking work creates a collective or societal debt. Each and every member of society is obligated by this debt. Furthermore, this debt transcends individual circumstances. In other words, we need not be elderly, ill, or children any longer to be held individually responsible. Nor can we satisfy or discharge our collective responsibility within our individual, private families. Merely being financially generous with our own mothers or duly supporting our own wives will not suffice to satisfy our share of the societal debt generally owed to all caretakers.

My argument that the caretaking debt is a collective one is based on the fact that biological dependency is inherent to the human condition, and therefore, of necessity of collective or societal concern. Just as individual dependency needs must be met if an individual is to survive, collective dependency needs must be met if a society is to survive and perpetuate itself. The mandate that the state (collective society) respond to dependency, therefore, is not a matter of altruism or empathy (which are individual responses often resulting in charity), but one that is primary and essential because such a response is fundamentally society-preserving.

If infants or ill persons are not cared for, nurtured, nourished, and perhaps loved, they will perish. We can say, therefore, that they owe an individual debt to their individual caretakers. But the obligation is not theirs alone—nor is their obligation confined only to their own caretakers. A sense of social justice demands a broader sense of obligation. Without aggregate caretaking, there could be no society, so we might say that it is caretaking labor that produces and reproduces society. Caretaking labor provides the citizens, the workers, the voters, the consumers, the students, and others who populate society and its institutions. The uncompensated labor of caretakers is an unrecognized subsidy, not only to the individuals who directly receive it, but more significantly, to the entire society.

V. Institutions and Dependency

Society-preserving tasks, like dependency work, are commonly delegated. The delegation is accomplished through the establishment and maintenance of societal institutions. For example, the armed services are established to attend to the collective need for national defense. But delegation is not the same thing as abandonment. The armed services are structured simultaneously as both the responsibility of only some designated members (volunteers or draftees) and of all members of society (taxpayers and voters).

This dual and complementary responsibility is consistent with our deeply held beliefs about how rights and obligations are accrued and imposed in a just society—collective obligations have both an individual and a collective dimension. Certain members of society may be recruited, volunteer, or even be drafted for service, but they have a right to be compensated for their services from collective resources. They also have a right to the necessary tools to perform their assigned tasks and to guarantees that they will be protected by rules and policies that facilitate their performance. Caretakers should have the same right to have their society-preserving labor supported and facilitated. Provision of the means for their task should be considered the responsibility of the collective society.

Society has not, however, responded this way to caretaking. The most common form of social accommodation for dependency has been its assignment to the institution of the private family. Within that family, dependency has been further delegated as the individual responsibility of the family equivalent of volunteer or draftee—the person in the gendered role of mother (or grandmother or daughter or daughter-in-law or wife or sister). But the resources necessary for caretaking have not been considered to be the responsibility of the collective society. Instead, each individual private family is ideally and ideologically perceived as responsible for its own members and their dependency. A need to call on collective resources, such as welfare assistance, is considered a family as well as an individual failure, deserving of condemnation and stigma.

VI. Derivative Dependency

The assignment of responsibility for the burdens of dependency to the family in the first instance, and within the family to women, operates in an unjust manner because this arrangement has significant negative material consequences for the caretaker. This obvious observation allows me to introduce an additional, but often overlooked, form of dependency into the argument—"derivative dependency." Derivative dependency arises on the part of the person who assumes responsibility for the care of the inevitable dependent person. I refer to this form of dependency as derivative to capture the very simple point that those who care for others are themselves dependent on resources in order to undertake that care. Caretakers have a need for monetary or material resources. They also need recourse to institutional supports and accommodation, a need for structural arrangements that facilitate caretaking.

Currently, neither the economic nor the structural supports for caretaking are adequate. Many caretakers and their dependents find themselves impoverished or severely economically compromised. Some of their economic problems stem from the fact that within families, caretaking work is unpaid and not considered worthy of social subsidies. There are also, however, direct costs associated with caretaking. Caretaking labor interferes with the pursuit and development of wage labor options. Caretaking labor saps energy and efforts from investment in career or market activities, those things that produce economic rewards. There are foregone opportunities and costs associated with caretaking, and even caretakers who work in the paid labor force typically have more tenuous ties to the public sphere because they must also accommodate caretaking demands in the private. These costs are not distributed among all beneficiaries of caretaking (institutional or individual). Unjustly, the major economic and career costs associated with caretaking are typically borne by the caretaker alone.

Further, most institutions in society remain relatively unresponsive to innovations that would lessen the costs of caretaking. Caretaking occurs in a larger context and caretakers often need accommodation in order to fulfill multiple responsibilities. For example, many caretakers also engage in market work. Far from structurally accommodating or facilitating caretaking, however, workplaces operate in modes incompatible with the idea that workers also have obligations for dependency. Workplace expectations compete with the demands of caretaking—we assume that workers are those independent and autonomous individuals who are free to work long and regimented hours.

In discussing the costs and impediments associated with undertaking the tasks of caretaking, it is important to emphasize that, unlike inevitable dependency, derivative dependency is not a universal experience. In fact, many people in our society totally escape the burdens and costs that arise from assuming a caretaking role, perhaps even freed for other pursuits by the caretaking labor of others. The status of derivative dependency is structured by and through existing societal institutions, culturally and socially assigned according to a script rooted in ideologies, particularly those of capitalism and patriarchy. These scripts function at an unconscious (and therefore, unexamined) level, and channel our beliefs and feelings about what is considered natural and what are appropriate institutional arrangements. When individuals act according to these scripts, consistent with prevailing ideology and institutional arrangements, we say they have chosen their path from the available options. The construction of this notion of individual choice allows us to avoid general responsibility for the inequity and justify the maintenance of the status quo. We ignore the fact that individual choice occurs within the constraints of social conditions. These constraints include ideology, history, and tradition, all of which funnel decisions into prescribed channels and often operate in a practical and symbolic manner to limit options.

As it now stands in this society, derivative dependents are expected to get both economic and structural resources within the family. The market is unresponsive and uninvolved, and the state is perceived as a last resort for financial resources, the refuge of the failed family. A caretaker who must resort to governmental assistance may do so only if she can demonstrate that she is needy in a highly stigmatized process.

VII. Subsidy

In popular and political discourse, the idea of "subsidy" is viewed as an equally negative companion to dependence, the opposite of the ideal of self-sufficiency. But a subsidy is nothing more than the process of allocating collective resources to some persons or endeavors rather than other persons or endeavors because a social judgment is made that they are in some way "entitled" or the subsidy is justified. Entitlement to subsidy is asserted through a variety of justifications, such as the status of the persons receiving the subsidy, their past contributions to the social good, or their needs. Often, subsidy is justified because of the position the subsidized persons hold or the potential value of the endeavor they have undertaken to the larger society.

Typically, subsidy is thought of as the provision of monetary or economic assistance. But subsidy can also be delivered through the organization of social structures and norms that create and enforce expectations. Taking this observation into account, along with the earlier discussion of inevitable and derivative dependency, it seems obvious that we must conclude that subsidy is also universal. We all exist in context, in social and cultural institutions, such as families, which facilitate, support, and subsidize us and our endeavors.

In complex modern societies no one is self-sufficient, either economically or socially. We all live subsidized lives. Sometimes the benefits we receive are public and financial, such as in governmental direct transfer programs to certain individuals like farmers or sugar growers. Public subsidies can also be indirect, such as the benefits given in tax policy. Private economic subsidy systems work in the forms of foundations, religions, and charities. But a subsidy can also be non-monetary, such as the subsidy provided by the uncompensated labor of others in caring for us and our dependency needs.

It seems clear that all of us receive one or the other or both types of subsidy throughout our lives. The interesting question in our subsidy shaped society, therefore, has to be why only some subsidies are differentiated and stigmatized while others are hidden. In substantial part, subsidies are hidden when they are not called subsidy (or welfare, or the dole), but termed "investments," "incentives," or "earned" when they are supplied by government, and called "gifts," "charity," or the product of familial "love" when they are contributions of caretaking labor.

VIII. A More Responsive State

In order to rethink how we might constitute a just system for handling dependency, our society must move beyond simplistic catch words and engage in a nationwide debate. What types of mechanisms can generate and sustain such a series of discussions? Shaped by the successes of early feminist consciousness raising techniques, which proved powerful in challenging entrenched ideas and assumptions about gender roles, I advocate for a national consciousness raising process. We need a forum for vigorous debate. The forum must not only be public in the sense that it will be created and supported by government, but also public in the sense that it will be participatory and beyond governmental control, inclusive and not politically partisan in composition.

It is important that the forum be a public responsibility (as antiquated and quaint as that idea seems at this point in our national history).

. . .

[I]mportant questions that need to be resolved and discussed in a very public forum . . . [include:]

1. How should the need for caretaking resources be satisfied so that caretakers can act independently, make decisions, and fulfill societal expectations in ways that best respond to their individual circumstances?
2. Should caretakers be primarily dependent on the family in this regard?
3. Given the tenuous status of marriage in this society (where the divorce rate hovers near 50 percent and women are expected to be wage earners, as well as wives and mothers) how can we continue to have a traditional model of the family served up by politicians as the solution for poverty?
4. Shouldn't the richest country in the history of the world have a family policy that goes beyond marriage as the solution for dependency?
5. Specifically, doesn't the family as it exists today require substantial assistance from other societal institutions?
6. Is it fair that the market and the state (which are totally dependent on caretaking labor and in no way self-sufficient or independent from caretaking) escape responsibility for dependency and continue to be freeloaders (or free riders) on the backs of caretakers and families?
7. Isn't it time to redistribute some responsibility for dependency, mandating that state and market bear their fair share of the burden?

As a result of such discussion, the very terms of independence and self-sufficiency might well be redefined or re-imagined in the public mind. . . . Independence, as well as justice, requires that those who are assigned a vital societal function are also provided with the wherewithal to do those tasks. This is a state of collective responsibility and may not be relegated to potentially exploitative private institutions.

. . .

23

Children's Rights

Barbara Bennett Woodhouse

. . .

Americans tend to sort children into two categories. There are "our own children" and "other people's children." Our children are coddled and spoiled by adoring parents. They certainly do not need rights. They already know how to wrap us around their little fingers. Other people's children, especially if they are inner city children of color, are predatory monsters and are totally out of control. While our children are spoiled by too many luxuries and not enough work, other people's children work at jobs just to meet their basic needs for clothing, food, and shelter. While our children shuttle between two parents battling for custody, other people's children become state-created orphans when their parents' rights are terminated without any prospective adopter in sight.

This divide between our children and other people's children is an illusion. It ignores a fundamental tenet of human rights: All people are my brothers and sisters, parents and children. Human rights violations know no territorial, tribal, or family boundaries. . . . [T]here is nothing funny or trivial about trying children in adult criminal courts and executing them for crimes committed as juveniles. There is nothing amusing about children torn from or forced out of their families by family breakdown, poverty, and domestic violence, or about children who labor in sweatshops instead of hanging out in malls. These rights violations cry out for legal reform.

How can we transmute children's suffering and exploitation into legal rights for children? To borrow NYU Professor Peggy Cooper Davis' terms, we must look for and invoke in our legislatures, in our advocacy, and in our research, the motivating stories of children's rights. . . . Also critical in this effort is the construction of a written document; a basic text for describing rights. While Americans have resisted the notion of children's human rights, the rest of the world has been hard at work creating such a text and using it as a template for these new rights.

The United Nations Convention on the Rights of the Child is only ten years old. Introduced in 1989, it is the most rapidly and universally accepted of all human rights charters. The Convention is a charter not only of negative liberties but also includes positive rights. Not only does the Convention commit its signatories to advancing due process, fundamental rights for children, the protection of children from exploitation and abuse, but also to sustenance of children's basic physical, educational, and medical needs. It recognizes rights as belonging to the child, even though he or she lacks capacity, and casts parents, families, and the community in the role of trustees of children's birthrights.

Peoples around the world now look to the UN Convention as a blueprint for constitutional and legislative reform. Presently only two countries, Somalia and the United States, have failed to adopt it. Somalia lacks a functioning government and the United States lacks a governing body that truly believes in children's rights or in the obligation to meet the needs of children. Why has the United States remained the lone holdout in embracing this convention?

There are many reasons. First, as I have suggested, is the trivialization and invisibility of children's rights violations in our own culture. . . . We have not identified children as a discrete class of persons targeted for focused persecution. We have tended to view harms to children as simply collateral damage in the endless wars between adults.

Additionally, we have not adequately recognized children as actors in the larger drama of human rights and as individuals of courage who fought and prevailed against their own destruction and refused to accept assaults on their human dignity. We have tended to see them, instead, as passive victims, not as role models and freedom fighters.

. . .

Throughout history, all children, and especially the children of poor and minority communities, have suffered disproportionately from famine, war, plague, religious persecution, racism, genocide, social dislocation, and economic exploitation. . . . [T]hese harms did not seem like targeted assaults on children. They appeared to adult observers as tragic, but somehow collateral effects.

. . .

The importance of recognizing children's systematic persecution, as well as their spiritual victories, was first made real to me in a visit several years ago to Anne Frank's house in Amsterdam. As I toured the cramped and darkened attic rooms where Anne wrote her famous diary, it struck me that children were not merely swept up in the Holocaust, they were singled out as children for destruction. When the Franks' hiding place was betrayed and she and her family were shipped to the concentration camps, Anne narrowly escaped immediate extermination. On arrival children under fifteen were automatically separated from their parents and sent to their deaths. Anne, however, had celebrated her fifteenth birthday on June 12, 1944, a few months earlier. She was no longer classified as a child, completely dispensable and useless to the Nazi machine and her life was spared, if only for a few months.

Separated from both her parents, weakened by typhus, starvation, and grief, Anne died in March 1945. A school friend who was the last to see her in the camps reported, "It was so terrible. She immediately began to cry and she told me, 'I don't have parents anymore.' I always think if Anne had known that her father was still alive, she might have had more strength to survive."

For Anne Frank, unlawful imprisonment, harsh labor, untreated illness, and starvation were the final chapters of a long story. Three years earlier, Anne's world began to crumble when she was banned from the school she had always attended and segregated from her classmates. Soon Jewish children could not ride a bicycle or a tram, although Anne wrote in her diary that she learned to make do cheerfully with "shank's mare."

As the persecution deepened, like all Jewish children in Holland six and over, Anne was forced to wear a yellow star, could not shop in stores, associate with non-Jews, or go freely in public streets. One diary entry concerns her father's terror and anger when Anne came home at ten minutes past 8:00, violating the Nazi curfew laws. For three years Anne and her sister were terrorized relentlessly, deprived of freedoms of education, association, and speech, and subjected to religious and ethnic persecution. The event that sent the family into hiding occurred in July 1942. Sixteen-year-old Margo was ordered to report for transportation to a labor camp in Germany. Finally, in September of 1944 Anne suffered her greatest loss: [w]hen she was forcibly separated from the person whom she most loved, Otto Frank, her father, and soon thereafter from her mother.

Anne Frank is only the most famous of the children of the Holocaust.
. . .
[This] narrative remind[s] us of the importance to children of the abstract rights that the 1989 UN Convention recognizes and protects. Persecution and separation of communities and families violate the human rights of adults, but even more acutely they violate the rights of children. Far more than adults, children are damaged by an environment that stunts their physical and mental growth, compromising their sense of self and their prospects for the future. Their growth to autonomy depends on the care and guidance provided by bonded caregivers in the intimacy of the family, and children rely on these supportive relationships for their very survival.

Other charters of human rights recognize the importance of basic liberties to adults. These liberties include protection of intimate family relationships. However, as the stories of these children demonstrate, while food, shelter, medical care, religious and ethnic tolerance, and particularly the right to nurturing family relationships may be important to grown-ups, they are a matter of life and death to children.

We recognize Anne Frank's autobiography as a child's story because Anne's life was taken before she reached adulthood. Often the stories of children as heroes are hidden in the autobiographies of famous adults. How many of you recognize the name Fred Bailey? Do you recognize the name Frederick Douglass?

The great abolitionist writer and orator was born Fred Bailey in Eastern Shore, Maryland, in 1818. Although Fred Bailey knew nothing of such laws, the laws of slavery controlled his destiny from birth. Separated from his mother so she could work in the field, he was raised by his grandmother, and grieved as an adult that he could capture no memory of his mother's face.

His childhood ended abruptly at age six when Fred's grandmother was forced to turn him over to his owners in the big house. He felt terrified and abandoned. At eight he was uprooted again to be a house servant in the bustling port city of Baltimore. Here, a new world opened to this bright and curious child, who made friends of all colors among the working children of the Fells Point shipyards. Challenged by his master's chance comment that learning to read would "forever unfit him to be a slave," Fred defied the laws which prohibited slave children from learning to read. Hiding this newfound weapon against oppression, he studied anti-slavery tracts in secret and surreptitiously read discarded newspapers for news of the abolitionist movement. By the time he turned fifteen, Fred Bailey was no longer a precocious little boy, but a young man who had learned a trade and was flexing his physical, economic, and mental powers. He openly began to question the injustice of racial slavery and the laws that forced him to labor to enrich his master.

To punish Fred for challenging authority, his master sent him back to the plantation, where he was bound out to a wheat farmer with a reputation as a slave breaker. Worked to exhaustion, yearning for freedom, in his bleakest moments he consoled himself with this thought: "I am but a boy, and all boys are bound to someone." Like other boys of his times, Fred was resigned to the inevitability of children's bondage, but he was determined not to be, in his own words, "a slave for life." Fred Bailey ultimately escaped to freedom, took the name of Frederick Douglass, and wrote the powerful narrative of a life in slavery that galvanized abolitionist resistance. Few readers paused to realize that the entire story of this man's bondage and escape to freedom takes place while Frederick Douglass was still legally a child.

Fred Bailey's story reminds us of the continuing influence of a long and discredited tradition, the tradition of treating children as property. The tenacious power of this property theory is not surprising. The concept of human property, [of] which slavery was the most notorious vestige, had ancient roots. The notion of children as their father's property flowed naturally from the story of procreation as told by a patrilineal society.

According to the ancients, it was the father's seed which, once planted in the mother's womb, grew into his likeness within the woman's body. Flesh of their father's flesh, children rightly belonged to the patriarch, to be worked, traded, and given in marriage in exchange for money. Had you tried to engage Aristotle in debate over the question of parental powers versus justice for children, the debate might have ended almost before it began. He would have contended, as he did in the Nichomachean Ethics, "There cannot be injustice towards that which is one's own. And a chattel or a child, until it is at a certain age and has attained independence, is, as it were, a part of one's self. And nobody chooses to injure himself. Hence there can be no injustice towards oneself. And so neither can there be any conduct towards them that is politically just or unjust."[1]

Subsequent Western European political theorists, such as Thomas Hobbes and John Locke, attempted to map out other arguments justifying adult power over children. Hobbes argued that parental power was based on an implicit contract. The infant agrees to obey the parent in exchange for the parent's forbearance from allowing the helpless infant to perish. Locke contended that God was the true owner of children. God created children and gave them into their parents' care. Parental powers were a form of trusteeship of the Creator's property.

. . .

Fred Bailey's story not only speaks of the evils of child labor, but also reminds us of the critical importance of children's inclusion in the intellectual community of rights bearers. Virtually every one of the human rights of children articulated in the UN Convention was violated on a daily basis under the legally sanctioned regime of racial slavery. What saved Fred from internalizing the message of his own powerlessness and inferiority was the conviction, born in his own spirit and nurtured by access to the written word, that his oppression was neither natural nor deserved. He confronted and rejected racism as fundamentally unjust. Frederick Douglass the man owed his life to Fred Bailey the child, who refused to be enslaved.

In much the same way, all of us owe a debt as Americans to the teenagers of Little Rock and the young plaintiffs in *Brown v. Board of Education*.[2] We must never underestimate children's rights to freedom of thought, education, association, and especially to personhood and ownership of their own lives. Fred Bailey, Anne Frank, and the children who challenged Jim Crow were surely heroes of human rights, despite their young ages. They are fitting icons for those who seek to preserve the rights of children at risk of separation from their families, and of those who fight to end the economic exploitation of children. However, what about the bad children, the predatory children, the ones who join gangs, run wild in the streets, murder each other catching innocent bystanders in the crossfire? "If they want rights," say American legislators, "we'll give them rights," the same rights we gave Miranda and Gideon. "We'll try them as adults and they'll get adult time for adult crime." Surely these predators have no claim to special treatment. To the contrary, these children are the ones most in need of our unflagging commitment to children's human rights. A core principle of children's rights is the notion that children have not only the rights preserved to all persons, but may also claim special rights because of their youth. The notion is that they are young risk-takers, impulsive, feel no fear, and because they are young, they have not yet learned about the connection between acts and consequences.

Adolescents are learning to operate a dangerous vehicle: their own untested personal autonomy. We must give them the benefit of a learner's permit in spite of the potential for disaster. Can we fairly hold them to the same standards of culpability or require them to pay for the damage they inflict as we would an adult offender who fully understood his crimes? I am not an apologist for juvenile violence. To temper our anger, however, let me invoke the story of a group of children who committed many lawless and violent acts and are yet recognized by their elders as victims and even heroes of the human rights struggle. I spoke not long ago with Yvonne Mokgoro, a justice of the South African Constitutional Court, . . . [and] the very first Black woman judge in South African history. Justice Mokgoro spoke movingly of the huge debt owed by the new South African Republic to the youths that took [to] the streets in protest in townships torn by rioting and strife.

I will try to paraphrase her message, although I cannot match her eloquence. "So many of our nation's children," she told me earnestly, "lost their childhood in detention. Their schools were battlegrounds and their communities were destroyed. They grew up without parents because of the Group Areas Act, which forced mothers and fathers to leave home to find work. These children had to kill or be killed before they had ever been young. We must make reparation for their stolen childhood."

I believe these words could fairly describe the lives of many youths incarcerated in American juvenile prisons and institutions. Unlike Americans, however, South Africans responded to the crisis of this lost generation by enacting a constitution with a children's bill of rights that gives especially strong protections to juveniles in criminal or delinquency proceedings: [f]or example, a right to counsel in all proceedings, including quasi-criminal and civil cases, and rights not to be detained with adults and to age-appropriate conditions of confinement and rehabilitation. This bill of rights is drawn in large part from the Convention on the Rights of the Child as well as from the African Children's Charter, and it explicitly recognizes that children have all the rights guaranteed to other persons, plus additional enumerated rights of their own.

. . .

It seems clear that they need help, not condemnation. Perhaps, if we make more real and vivid our own children's stories as displaced refugees, as children armed by adults, as children exploited in sweatshops, and treated like human property, we can generate sufficient political commitment to meet their needs through domestic humanitarian aid, income transfers, reunification and rehabilitation programs, and through law reform.

. . . [T]he story of human rights violations and of human rights victories belongs to children, as well as to adults. Look for such stories, and I guarantee you will find them everywhere. In *The Autobiography of Malcolm X*, who spoke searingly of the destruction of his family and of the pain of being raised as a "state child"? In the emerging feminism of Willa Cather, who wrote of the hard lives of Nebraska's immigrant daughters and sons? In the caged bird song of Maya Angelou, who wrote about a child's brutal rape and her triumphant spirit? And in the book, *Fist Stick Knife Gun*, by Geoffrey Canada, who makes real to us the fear and courage of a little boy traversing the four blocks of enemy territory between his home and his school in New York City?

These are the motivating stories of . . . working children, of displaced refugees, of abused children, of children who grow up amid violence, learning to fight and kill or be killed. As lawyers and policy makers, we must look for the stories of children's heroism, suffering, and survival, in our own clients and in our research. We must bring these children's stories out of hiding and into the courtrooms, legislatures, and newsrooms of America.

NOTES

1. Aristotle, Nichomachean Ethics 188 (J. A. K. Thomson, trans., 1986).
2. 347 U.S. 483, 495 (1954).

24

Coercing Privacy

Anita Allen

Introduction

. . .

The liberal conception of privacy is the idea that government ought to respect and protect interests in physical, informational, and proprietary privacy. By physical privacy, I mean spatial seclusion and solitude. By informational privacy, I mean confidentiality, secrecy, data protection, and control over personal information. By proprietary privacy, I mean control over names, likenesses, and repositories of personal identity. . . . The liberal conception of privacy overlaps considerably with the liberal conception of private property. We associate privacy with certain places and things we believe we own, such as our homes, diaries, letters, names, reputations, and body parts. At the core of the liberal conception of privacy is the notion of inaccessibility. Privacy obtains where persons and personal information are, to a degree, inaccessible to others.

The liberal conception of private choice is the idea that government ought to promote interests in decisional privacy, chiefly by allowing individuals, families, and other nongovernmental entities to make many, though not all, of the most important decisions concerning friendship, sex, marriage, reproduction, religion, and political association. The liberal conception of private choice informs normative understandings of the First Amendment and the substantive due process requirements of the Fourteenth Amendment.

The concept of private choice seems to presuppose that social life is divided into distinguishable public and private spheres, the private sphere being a realm of individual decisionmaking about sex, reproduction, marriage, and family. . . .

Privacy, on the one hand, and private choice, on the other, restrain and obligate government. Government must leave us alone as a matter of government restraint. Government also must protect us from interference and invasion as a matter of government obligation.

. . .

The impossible ideal of a private sphere free of government and other outside interference has currency despite the reality that, in the United States and other Western democracies, virtually every aspect of nominally private life is a focus of direct or indirect government regulation. Marriage is considered a private relationship, yet governments require licenses and medical tests, impose age limits, and prohibit polygamous, incestuous, and same-sex marriages. Procreation and child-drearing are considered private, but government child abuse and neglect laws regulate how parents must exercise their responsibilities. The liberal ideal of a private sphere can be no more than an ideal of ordinary people, living under conditions of democratic self-government, empowered to make choices about their own lives that are relatively free of the most direct forms of governmental interference and constraint.

The first proposition that I will advance against the preceding background is this: although the liberal conception of private choice is flourishing, as evidenced by the growing acceptability of homosexual unions and abortion rights, the liberal conception of privacy is not flourishing similarly. One detects signs of an erosion of the taste for and expectation of privacy. . . .

The second proposition that I will advance relates to the first: traditional liberal conceptions of privacy and private choice have survived appropriately strenuous feminist critique, re-emerging in beneficially reconstructed forms. As a result of the feminist critique, we understand that the conditions of confinement, forced modesty, obedience, and unaccountability that once constituted the private sphere are not a model of privacy worthy of the name. Ironically, just when meaningful, unoppressive forms of privacy and private choice are becoming imaginable and available to women, privacy is losing its cachet.

. . . I suggest that imposing privacy norms to undergird the liberal vision of moral freedom and independence is generally consistent both with liberalism and with the egalitarian aspirations of feminism.

. . .

III. Feminist Reconstruction

. . .

Feminist critics equate traditional ideas of privacy and private choice with (1) barriers to escaping confinement in traditional roles; and (2) ideals of isolation, independence, or individualism that conflict with the reality of the encumbered self and with ideals of ethical care, compassion, and community. Not all feminists, however, believe in the possibility of reconstructing privacy and private choice consistent with gender equality. When all is said and done, some feminists retain a decidedly negative stance toward privacy, professing the need to relegate privacy and private choice to the trash bin of outdated ideology. By contrast, I accept the basic feminist critique of privacy and private choice, but I also believe worthwhile, egalitarian conceptions of privacy and private choice survive the critique.

A. Overcoming Under-Participation

Feminists exploded the assumption that the proper role of women is to live under the authority of men as daughters, wives, and mothers.

. . .

A felicitous balance between privacy and disclosure can come about if lessons about exploiting privacy and lessons about exploiting the new openness in public life are offered in tandem. Some feminists seem to assume that privacy and disclosure are differing models of how one might live. Privacy and disclosure are better understood, however, as important and necessary dimensions of a range of good lives one can elect to live.

B. Overcoming Violence

Liberal society thrives on open government and closed personal relations. Feminists have stressed that closed personal relations make it more likely that serious harm will go undetected. A parent-child relationship may involve sexual abuse or neglect; a marital relationship may involve beatings or rape. Government cannot protect vulnerable citizens from domestic violence if unbreachable boundaries of legally sanctioned privacy surround the family.

. . .

The solution to domestic violence and the . . . problem of public neglect of private violence is not to end families and seclusion, but to make better use of evidence of chronic violence and imminent peril. The act of making better or different use of evidence regarding what occurs among family members and cohabitators is a way of reconstructing privacy—redrawing lines of public and private. The line between public and private already has been redrawn substantially in the criminal law of rape where, in many jurisdictions, "marital privacy" no longer immunizes married men from prosecution for unconsensual sex with their wives.

C. Righting the Conservative Tilt

Some feminists view the concept of privacy as having an inherently conservative tilt in the Western liberal societies where it has had the greatest currency. The privacy banner waves away beneficial public intervention calculated to reinvent customary standards of behavior that lead to female under-participation and male aggression or harassment. Legal feminists commonly argue that the liberal ideology of "privacy" is inherently conservative and has slowed the growth of egalitarian laws beneficial to vulnerable classes of women. Another argument posits that a conservative ideology of privacy supports the notion that gays and lesbians belong, if at all, silent and repressed in the "closet."

. . .

In an attempt to reconceive public and private, a number of feminists have argued that certain privacy rights for the poor entail public support. These efforts strike me as exactly right. There is no need to concede the battle to liberalism's most conservative exponents. The liberal theorists who see the privacy case for abortion funding as doomed to fail because of the supposed inherent conservative tilt of privacy rights talk lack the will to impose a new construction of privacy over the old conception of negative freedom. The idea that privacy is simply a negative liberty—a freedom from, as opposed to a claim to—can be challenged, and has been challenged, on its own terms.

. . .

Feminist critiques of privacy leave the liberal conceptions of privacy and private choice very much alive. The longing for personal time and personal decisionmaking can linger long after the grip of patriarchy over women's bodies and lives is loosened. Feminists need not reject the language of public and private or the broad principles of inaccessibility, control, and decisional autonomy that undergird privacy rights. They do need to stress that the lines between public and private should be renegotiated and redrawn as necessary to further dignity, safety, and equality. Feminists have good reason to be critical of what the privacy of the private sphere has signified for women in the past and what the rhetoric and jurisprudence of privacy rights can signal for the future. At the same time, there is little doubt that women seeking greater control over their lives already have begun to benefit from heightened social respect for appropriate forms of physical, informational, proprietary, and decisional privacy.

IV. Liberalism and the Politics of the Good

. . .

The version of liberalism to which I subscribe understands persons as shaped partly and substantially by social forces not of their own choosing, but also and importantly by their own choices—their own decisions, commitments, and compromises. Education is vital to the formation of persons who understand human capacities for choice and the limits of those capacities. Persons are educated by families, schools, and religious institutions, and increasingly by exposure to television, radio, print media, films, and the Internet. The direct and indirect education they receive from these sources varies in content and intensity. Not all of what they learn contributes constructively and beneficially to liberalism's "formative project."

My conception of privacy (and private choice) is distinctly liberal in its assumption that individuals are and should be well-informed, morally autonomous choosers. My conception is also egalitarian and feminist in its assumption that a background of educational, economic, and sexual equality is a requirement of meaningful choice. In a just and liberal democracy, one's ability to choose how one shall live will be constrained through taxation and regulation so that others can achieve a comparable palette of choices. The "old" civic republican conception of privacy rights as public recognition of obligations generated by encumbrances of identity may well have been what Warren and Brandeis had in mind. So much the worse for them. Surely my privacy means more than that others should let me alone to be the best darn African-American, Methodist, suburban wife and mother I can be. Privacy is also a matter of freedom to escape, reject, and modify such identities. I should be free to make and remake myself.

Privacy is a matter of escaping as well as embracing encumbrances of identity. Without adequate privacy, there can be no meaningful identities to embrace or escape, and no opportunities to engage in meaningful reflection, conversation, and debate about the grounds for embracing, escaping, and modifying particular identities. Undergirding the liberal democratic way of life will require public policies mindful of the cumulative threat to privacy.

Government will have to intervene in private lives for the sake of privacy and values associated with it. Protecting privacy, however, rarely will require government to proscribe specific categories of conduct. The men who sunbathe in the nude on warm Sundays in Berlin's Tiergarten are as morally autonomous as their friends and neighbors who do not. The threat to liberalism is not that individuals sometimes expose their naked bodies in public places, display affection with same-sex partners in public, or broadcast personal information on national television. The threat to liberalism is that in an increasing variety of ways our lives are being emptied of privacy on a daily basis, especially physical and informational privacy.

Government already, and with minimal controversy, interferes with individual privacy in the interest of protecting third parties or children from serious harm. In the near future, liberal government may have to proscribe and regulate disclosures and publications precisely in the interest of preventing cumulatively harmful diminutions of the taste for or the expectation of privacy. So empowered, there is a risk that government will make mistakes and engage in discrimination. Proscribing breast-feeding, while permitting men to go about bare-chested, is one example of error and discrimination with which we are all familiar. Government could use its power to single out particular groups for repression, and one legitimately worries that public policies will penalize certain behaviors unfairly. Consider prohibitions against public displays of affection by same-sex partners and "Don't ask, [d]on't tell" policies. Coercing privacy in the strong sense of dictating what people must always keep to themselves and what they may disclose to others would threaten the liberal egalitarian ideal of tolerance. A plurality of notions and opportunities for privacy must be permitted to flourish.

When it comes to government, coercing privacy may be as much a matter of self-restraint as restraint of others. Government's greater and greater ability to demand, access, and manipulate information about us contributes to the increasingly lowered expectations of privacy. It may also be a matter of regulating the corporate sector more aggressively, requiring fair information practices that give employees and consumers greater control over what information is collected and how it is used.

Fear of a government misstep is sometimes a reason for recommending government inaction. There is both empirical evidence and normative philosophical argument supporting the proposition that paradigmatic forms of privacy (e.g., seclusion, solitude, confidentiality, secrecy, anonymity) are vital to well-being. It is not simply that people need opportunities for privacy; the point is that their well-being, and the well-being of the liberal way of life, requires that they in fact experience privacy.

Coming up with public policies that are responsive to the aggregation problem—the problem of many small privacy losses cumulating into a large overall loss—will require special creativity on the part of those responsible for making policy. It may require a mode of thinking environmental policy analysts engage in all the time, namely, broad, long-term multi-factored assessments of costs, benefits and non-quantitative values. We ultimately may need a national privacy "czar" to promote the ideal of policies and practices that encourage and protect essential forms of privacy without intolerance or undue paternalism.

Suppose there is no efficient way to make public policy that is responsive to the aggregation problem because, for example, it would require mutual knowledge and coordination within a large and varied group of institutional actors. My observations about the importance of privacy to liberalism would hold, as a matter of principle, even if the transaction costs of regulatory approaches to "coercing privacy" are prohibitive in practice. Moreover, if we can do no better than to leave things precisely as they are, then the seriously liberal way of life is in jeopardy. I am hopeful that we can do at least a little better than leaving things as they are. My proposal is that public policymakers begin to take account of the cumulative effects of eroding privacy tastes and expectations, and weigh the risks of either doing something or doing nothing. . . . We are very much at the beginning, not the end, of a fresh line of thinking about privacy, culture, and regulative norms.

25

In Defense of Single-Parent Families

Nancy E. Dowd

. . .

Family Law

At divorce, the single-parent structure that exists *within* marriage is reconstituted as a devalued family form. The structure of divorce law creates and perpetuates poverty as the price of creating single-parent families. The law also permits the abandonment of caretaking responsibilities, usually by fathers, allowing the surrender of all responsibility to one parent, usually mothers, who often take on *de jure* what has been *de facto* sole caretaking responsibility. The emergence of the typical single-parent family at divorce is entirely predictable, based on the context of work and family relationships during marriage and the way in which law structures families at divorce.

General Principles of Divorce Law

Certain identifiable principles, varying by degree in particular jurisdictions but consistent overall, inform the current divorce structure. Although the vast majority of divorce is resolved by agreement, in the form of settlement, those rules nevertheless affect the shape of settlement as well as our social vision of the form and function of the post-divorce family. Those principles consist of the following: that no party will be held at fault; that each party should leave the marriage with a roughly equal share of property created or acquired during the marriage by financial or other contributions; that neither party has a long-term financial obligation to the other party as a result of the marriage; that the parties will continue to share in the parenting and financial support of minor children; and that neither finances nor children will be allocated other than on gender neutral principles.

These principles presume that marriage is a partnership among equals who share work and family responsibilities equitably and who have equal opportunities to structure their private lives, as well as to choose from an equal range of options in the wage workforce. Any variation from an equal (meaning similar) division of roles and responsibilities is understood as the product of choice.

With respect to post-divorce conditions, the principles presume that each spouse can function independently on the same terms as he or she did during the marriage, limited only by his or her individual effort and accomplishments in the labor market. A spouse with a shortfall of income can compensate by taking advantage of opportunities in the wage labor market. A spouse with a shortfall of time for domestic work can purchase childcare and housework services. A spouse with an excess of childcare responsibilities can rely on income provided pursuant to shared financial support of children to supplement income or finance care of children in order to do wage work, and can also rely on the other parent to provide childcare as part of shared parenting. This post-divorce model presumes that any interruption of wage work or modification of work behavior in response to family responsibilities during the marriage can be overcome by making different choices in labor market work after divorce. In other words, each partner resumes the position he or she had before the marriage, as modified by his or her responsibility for parenting children. Since parenting responsibility is shared, as it is presumed was done during the marriage, the burden of parenting is presumed to be equally distributed between two independent self-supporting adults.

The realities of divorced single-parent families are starkly at odds with these presumptions. The pattern of divorce is one of striking inequality, split along clear gender lines. Men and women continue to emerge from divorce at opposite economic poles: men's financial position improves, while women's sharply declines. The labor market does not correct these inequalities; instead, the marked pattern of sex segregation and wage inequity frustrates women's attempts to equalize the economic imbalance of divorce, despite the divorce system's reliance on the ability of each parent to generate additional income if needed.

The caretaking patterns are equally gendered. Sole or primary custody is overwhelmingly granted to mothers. Most estimates still put mother custody at about 90 percent. The vast majority of custody is designated by agreement rather than by litigation. In contested custody cases, however, there is evidence that fathers are surprisingly successful.

Many fathers without custody, however, abandon their relationships with their children, usually within two years of divorce.

> Nonvisitation seems to occur in about fifty percent of the cases. . . . For about one-third of the children of divorce, it means that they will not see their noncustodial parent at all after the first year of separation. Very few ever sleep at the home of the noncustodial parent or do daily activities with them. Instead, their contact is sporadic and primarily social. Fewer than one-fifth will have contact with the noncustodial parent on a weekly basis.[1]

According to another study, only one child in six saw their father weekly; another one in six saw their father less often than once a month but more often than once a year; and nearly half of the children had not seen their father in the previous twelve months. Ten years after divorce, according to the same study, only one in ten children had contact, while nearly two-thirds had no contact in the prior year. When fathers abandon their nurturing relationship, they also, usually, abandon economic support of their children. The level of paternal abandonment is high, and the lack of discussion about it disturbing.

Rather than supporting equality, the structure of divorce law seems designed to create stigma or at least to do nothing to prevent it. Current divorce rules create poverty by ignoring social roles created within marriage and barriers to opportunity and choice in the labor market. Under the guise of equality and choice, divorce law has recreated, or even worsened, the explicit gender hierarchy of earlier legal regimes. Single custodial parents, especially single mothers, are penalized for divorce by impoverishment. In turn, they are blamed for the consequences of poverty for their children. At the same time, until recently, the legal system has largely permitted non-custodial parents, mostly fathers, to escape financial responsibility without consequence, blame, or stigma.

The experience of single parenting for women and men after divorce is remarkably different, and that difference is accepted within the equality regime. Arguably, that very inequality is structured *by* the equality regime. Under the current legal regime, what is missing is the role of unwaged work in the family economy and the consequences of children's dependency. What also seems to be missing is a reconceptualization of work and family to reflect more accurately the consequences of an economy in which more than one income is essential for the support of most families. Finally, the legal regimes lack a vision of gender equality and non-subordinating gender roles, and instead reveal the striking persistence of traditional, patriarchal gender roles despite the rhetoric of gender-neutral equality.

Economic/Financial

The financial consequences of divorce can be subdivided into alimony, property division, and child support. Alimony has shifted from a duty of support for life to a short term transitional form of financial support. It is presumed that the labor market provides equal opportunity to both spouses; that both spouses likely will work during the marriage; and that any hiatus from the market can be overcome, or a shift from part time to full time work can be accomplished, without major difficulty or impact upon long range earning capacity. The ideal is autonomy and self-reliance. Alimony is available only upon a showing of need, dependency, or incapacitation. Current inability to be self-supporting is cured by "rehabilitating" the dependent spouse into an independent wage earner. Care of children, even young children, is not usually a sufficient reason for even short-term alimony.
. . .

Property division and child support are the primary sources of private support between divorced parents. In these areas of divorce law, the principle of equality is strongly expressed. In property division, the principle of equitable distribution, with a presumption of equal contribution, by monetary or non-monetary means, is the guiding principle. The goal is a one-time settlement of finances, a clean financial break. Although the concept of marital property has dramatically expanded (e.g., pensions, business and professional goodwill), that which is available to be divided is not, in most cases, a sufficient economic base on which to support a family. Most marital estates do not have much property to divide, and what property they do have is heavily mortgaged. A large proportion of displaced homemakers lose their house in the divorce process. Furthermore, the presumed equality of contribution does not address the inequality of post-divorce consequences if one spouse, usually the woman, has foregone opportunities in the labor market which have lifelong consequences. It focuses, rather, on losses during the marriage, not their post-divorce implications. The property division model presumes an ability to supplement marital property with employment. As a consequence, the dominant pattern is that women's income declines as their needs increase, while the reverse occurs for men. These patterns persist for years after divorce especially if women do not remarry.

Between alimony and property division, therefore, most spouses receive little or no resources. Child support, then, is the primary financial consequence of divorce where minor children are involved. Divorce law conceives of child support as an entitlement which runs to the child, a conception that ignores the interdependence of the child with the primary or sole caretaker. The law of child support treats children as an independent economic unit. Although equality is the ideal, with each parent expected to support the child, courts calculate the amount of child support pro rata based on income, and consequently parental obligations are not likely to be equal given typical male and female wage-earning patterns. Support is calculated by the income of both parents, and then applying child support percentage, prorated for each parent's income. At upper income levels the court has discretion how much above the guidelines to award.

Support amounts are characteristically lower than actual expenses and lower than typical families of the same income level would spend on their children. The guidelines do not vary the percentage of income required to be devoted to children, yet studies show that as income rises, families spend more on children. Since this is not taken into account, and the average percentage may therefore be considerably lower than resources expended pre-divorce. For example, for two children, 25 percent of income is appropriate according to the guidelines, while two income middle class families actually expend 40 percent of their income on their children.

Change in support is not usually automatic. Few parents can afford to return to court to seek a modification of the initial child support order. Payments commonly decrease as children age, and often end at age 18. Not surprisingly, there is a clear trend of downward economic and social mobility for children awarded support under the guidelines.

The level of support actually paid is very low. A common pattern is non-payment, coexisting with the lack of regular contact with children.

. . .

The divorce structure fails to provide sufficient economic resources to the typical single-parent family. By defining equality of parental responsibility in a narrow way which takes a snapshot of resources at one moment in time, current and future needs of the family are ignored. The consequences for children are disastrous. The typically drastic decline in income most immediately affects housing and education, which has both short- and long-term consequences. Education is the single most critical factor in children's future opportunities.

Many believe that the labor market is the answer to the problem of impoverishment among single mothers. However, . . . the labor market provides no assurance to women that it will operate any more fairly at divorce than it did during marriage. Regardless of one's parenting status, jobs which respect and support parenting responsibility, or that adequately support a family on a single income, are scarce or non-existent. Furthermore, to the extent that mothers work full time or attend school full time in order to improve their competitiveness in the workforce, the workforce solution poses the risk of losing custody. Some courts have sanctioned single parents' choices to work full time or attend school by using such choices as justification for an award of custody to the other parent.

Parenting/Custody

Just as the economic principles unequally allocate resources, the divorce structure distributes actual caregiving and other responsibilities on a highly unequal basis. Moreover, the inequality is as strongly gender-differentiated as the economic consequences of divorce. Despite gender-neutral rules and a preference in most jurisdictions for joint custody, most women continue to provide primary or sole nurturing for their children after divorce. Although men have increased their share of parenting, the overall pattern has not changed significantly. Furthermore, the theoretical predisposition for joint custody has resulted in lower levels of child support under that custody framework, even if actual custody becomes entirely or predominantly vested in the mother.

. . .

Socially, the common phenomenon of the uninvolved divorced father is widely accepted. This may simply reflect the social acceptance of maternal caregiving. Data on the impact of fathering post-divorce may also, ironically, reinforce father absence. Increased contact by fathers post-divorce does not translate into better outcomes for children. In part, researchers suggest, this is because the nature and quality of post-divorce fathering is characteristically minimal, more like a visitor or a relative than a parent. In part, it is because fathering in marital families similarly is mother-centered and fathers' role is minimal.

Family law arguably is not the primary culprit, then, in widespread father abandonment. Admittedly, some courts, out of misplaced gender stereotyping, deny custody or visitation to deserving fathers, or fail to enforce fathers' rights of access to their children. Some evidence suggests that the legal system continues to favor mothers in terms of custody outcomes. One study indicates that mothers simply more strongly assert their preferences regarding custody in the legal system. But other research indicates the contrary pattern of men's significant success when seeking custody, suggesting that family law strongly supports fathers' rights to parent if and when those rights are asserted. Furthermore, as noted earlier, the norm of some form of shared or joint custody is widespread. If voluntary abandonment of relationships with children, not legal denial of such relationships, determines most caretaking patterns, then family law appears, to a great extent, to protect maintenance of father-child relationships if and when fathers elect to continue parenting.

The failure of family law with respect to fathers is not that it has failed to increase fathers' rights, but rather that it does not require that fathers fulfill their nurturing responsibilities, nor impose consequences for the failure to do so. Any version of custody short of joint physical custody presumes less than equal paternal involvement. On the other hand, an imposed structure of joint physical custody defies existing caretaking patterns, and both joint legal and joint physical custody can too easily perpetuate patterns of dominance and control rather than mutual sharing of care. In addition, if the right to custody exists without a corresponding duty or responsibility of caretaking, and is coupled with a gendered pattern of marital household and childcare responsibility, then custodial rights may be twisted into a weapon to deny support, rather than protection of fathers' relationships with their children. Indeed, many fathers have used their custody rights as bargaining chips in order to reduce their economic obligations. The power imbalances between men and women at divorce have long been documented, yet we have done little in the equality structure to deal with it.

In addition, most custody structures do not impose penalties on fathers who fail to fulfill even limited nurturing responsibilities. Custody arrangements which permit fathers to abandon nurturing responsibilities without economic or other compensation for the lack of caretaking leaves fathers free to be "take it or leave it" parents.

The law has, to a great extent, moved in the direction of acknowledging the equal ability of men and women to raise children, at least in theory. The legal structure need not abandon this position, but it need not stigmatize those families, currently the majority, in which parenting responsibilities are unequally divided. Indeed, it is ironic that the law permits many fathers to be parents in little more than name (or genes) only, while condemning single-parent families for, among other things, the absence of a father. Instead of seeing the single-parent family as inherently dysfunctional, the law should recognize the prevalence and importance of single-parent families. Critical to that recognition is an understanding of the actual division of caregiving during marriage and after divorce, as well as understanding the scope of children's needs, children's dependency, and the nature of caregiving and household work. This is not to say that men's parenting is not important, but rather that single-parent parenting has been the most common pattern of parenting within marriage as well as after divorce.

The vast gulf between family law's theory of equality and the reality of unequal caregiving is ignored by placing blame on single-parent families. Single parents are blamed for the phenomena of financial impoverishment and the breakdown of parent-child relationships, focusing attention away from the structure of family law and its impact upon a highly unequal familial structure. To the extent inequity is recognized at all, it is viewed as the product of choice capable of change by new choices. The ability to change especially presumes the availability of opportunity in the workplace, reinforcing the focus away from the equality and choice issues within family law. Expecting single parents to resolve their financial difficulties in the workforce, where structural constraints and shortcomings confound their ability to succeed, simply creates further blame of single-parent families. Shifting expectation to the workplace not only moves attention away from dealing with dependency and unwaged work, but also shifts evaluation of single-parent families toward an arena where choice again can be blamed for individualized problems.

NOTE

1. Karen Czapanskiy, *Volunteers and Draftees: The Struggle for Parental Equality*, University of California at Los Angeles Law Review 38:1415, 1449 (1991).

From Madonna to Proletariat: Constructing a New Ideology of Motherhood in Welfare Discourse

Tonya L. Brito

I. Introduction

The story of America's welfare system is the story of transformed images of women and their roles in society. At the inception of welfare, the dominant image of women on welfare was that of the Madonna-like mother whose role in society was to care for and nurture her child. Society believed that mothering was a full-time vocation and, as a result, it excused welfare mothers from workforce participation. Over time, the maternal image waned as the complexion of the welfare population became darker and increasingly included unmarried mothers. A less idealized image of motherhood has characterized this new generation of welfare mothers. The stereotype that emerged—the "Black Welfare Queen"—reflects negative societal attitudes toward Black women, toward women who have children out of wedlock, and toward poor women who must resort to welfare to support their families. This devastating image has been instrumental in smoothing the way for conservative reformers to impose work requirements, strict time limits, and other punitive reform measures on welfare mothers.

The recent welfare reforms connote an image of mother as a worker first—a reluctant worker, to be sure, but a worker nonetheless. The new welfare mother fulfills her societal obligations by providing for her children economically through her wages rather than emotionally through her caregiving. Some might view this change—the transformed image of welfare mothers from Madonna to proletariat—as a reflection of changes in women's lives that have occurred more generally in society over time. Certainly, the steadily increasing participation of mothers in the labor force has been well documented and publicized. A closer look at the history and politics of the American welfare state, however, reveals that demographic change does not solely account for the dramatic shift in image. Rather than simply reflecting social realities, the images of women on welfare have been constructed, and these constructed images result from a coupling of deliberate political strategy and the enduring influence of racial and patriarchal ideology.

. . . [B]ecause the prevailing images of welfare mothers are pejorative, it has been difficult to win broad-based political support for progressive welfare reform proposals, including universal programs that aim to benefit all low income families. I suggest that it is first necessary to use narrative approaches (as a complement to the prevailing quantitative approach) to construct a new, positive ideology of motherhood in welfare discourse. A positive image of mothers who receive welfare could be developed if it were possible to appropriate for these mothers one of the several existing cultural conceptions of working motherhood—the "Soccer Mom" or the "Superwoman," for example. I conclude with the suggestion that a new ideology be constructed and offer as a possibility the image of the "Second Shift Mom."

. . .

The early AFDC [Aid for Families with Dependent Children] program scrutinized women's situations to determine if they qualified for assistance. The focus of these eligibility determinations was not solely economic need. Through enforcement of "suitable home" provisions, local welfare officials guaranteed aid for mothers who satisfied the moral and parenting standards imposed by public agencies. Consequently, poor single mothers routinely did not receive benefits due to a perceived "flaw" in their motherhood.

This system of exclusion persisted until the 1960s, when federal court decisions, civil rights lawyers, and welfare rights activists forced states to end arbitrary eligibility restrictions and other barriers to welfare. Welfare became a statutory "right" and a uniform means test was implemented for determining eligibility. As previously excluded women in need joined the rolls, the demographics of the welfare caseload changed dramatically. By 1967, a welfare population once 86 percent white had become 46 percent non-white. Overall, the size of the program exploded, growing from 3.5 million beneficiaries in 1961 to 11 million beneficiaries in 1971. The maintenance costs of AFDC soared as the rolls expanded and many perceived that welfare was growing out of control. Congress and the states reacted by narrowing eligibility, reducing benefits, implementing work programs, and trying to increase support from absent fathers. Expenditures, however, continued to rise. . . . The welfare system became a major public issue and a source of political controversy and conflict; thus, it became a proposal for reform.

. . .

The new federal welfare law, the Personal Responsibility Act, overhauled the fundamental structure of the more than 60-year-old welfare system. The Personal Responsibility Act abolished AFDC, ended an individual's entitlement to welfare benefits, and replaced AFDC with the new block-grant program TANF [Temporary Assistance to Needy Families]. . . .

Even in the face of the abundant reliable empirical data and findings . . . policymakers have created a sweeping new welfare system that accepts wholesale the negative assumptions and beliefs about welfare and its recipients. The Personal Responsibility Act further reinforces these stereotypes by implementing a number of measures that coerce women on welfare into conforming to prescribed gender and family norms. Both the findings set out in the Personal Responsibility Act and its stated purposes exemplify this purpose. The first three findings are particularly telling and state, "(1) Marriage is the foundation of a successful society; (2) Marriage is an essential institution of a successful society which promotes the interests of children; (3) Promotion of responsible fatherhood and motherhood is integral to successful child rearing and the well-being of children."[1]

TANF, the new "welfare" program, includes among its stated goals preventing non-marital births and promoting the formation and maintenance of two-parent families. Further, TANF attempts to bolster the above findings by reciting statistics regarding the increase in single-parent families at length and associating single-parent families with increased crime, poverty, and welfare dependency.

With these changes to the welfare system, there is no longer a system that purports to honor motherhood and finds value in poor single women caring full-time for their children to ensure that they grow up to be productive citizens. Instead, a system exists that characterizes families on welfare as deviant and characterizes mothers as irresponsible. Welfare again stigmatizes "undeserving poor" those whose personal behavior does not conform to putative middle-class norms. "This stigmatizing process makes mothering outside the context of a two-parent, traditional family susceptible to extensive legal regulation and supervision."[2]

Thus, in response to the "deviance" of welfare families and their "dysfunctional" lifestyle, a major component of welfare has been an effort to regulate the marital, childbearing, and parenting behavior of women on welfare. The message of the behavior modification efforts comes across loud and clear—women on welfare should get married, stop having children, and go to work to support the children they already have. The measures implemented to facilitate these goals include Bridefare, Family Cap, and increasingly strict work requirements.

. . . The meaning of . . . work rules, however, must be understood in the broader context of welfare reform measures designed to regulate women and their family life, particularly the Bridefare and Family Caps programs implemented by a number of states. Bridefare promotes marriage by giving monetary incentives to mothers who marry the fathers of their children. Bridefare, which pushes poor women toward marriage, views marriage as a viable exit from poverty. . . . Bridefare reinforces the family values ideology of welfare detractors by preferring two-parent households over single-parent households and claiming that "legitimate families can only be built upon the foundation of a traditional marital tie."[3]

. . .

Family Caps, another program implemented by a number of states to discourage women on welfare from having additional children, regulates childbearing. It eliminates the incremental increase in welfare benefits that a family would otherwise receive from AFDC after the birth of an additional child. . . .

The rationale underlying Family Caps programs is straightforward and rather simplistic. Giving birth to a child while on welfare is "irresponsible" reproductive behavior. Family Caps measures create economic disincentives to childbirth. The expectation is that welfare mothers are dissuaded from having more children while on welfare because of the unavailability of an increase in public assistance upon the birth of an additional child. . . .

In addition to these marriage and childbearing regulations, the Personal Responsibility Act prescribes parenting behavior through its work requirements. The rhetoric surrounding welfare requires parents to take "personal responsibility" for their children—for mothers on welfare this means entering the paid labor force and for the fathers of welfare children this means paying child support. Since its inception, welfare has reflected a tension between the desire to provide economic support to needy children and the expectation that parents should provide for their children themselves. The Personal Responsibility Act unequivocally resolves that tension in favor of work. Now, the clear message is that children need financial support from their parents, rather than from the state, and that financial support trumps the parental nurturing role.

The paramount emphasis of the law is on parents supporting their families. Because employment is the only "responsible" option for poor, single mothers, the Personal Responsibility Act moves these women off welfare and into the paid labor force. Under the act, parents and other caretakers must engage in "work activities" (as defined by the legislation) after no more than twenty-four months of receiving benefits (whether or not consecutive) and, unless a state opts out, it must require recipients to perform community service after two months of receiving cash benefits. To encourage fulfillment of obligations, the Personal Responsibility Act allows states to terminate benefits to a family for not complying with work requirements.
. . .

To facilitate the labor force participation of women on welfare, the PRA includes provisions regarding transitional child care and health care. . . . Children have only been considered in the welfare reform debate through the growing recognition that working mothers need reliable child care to get and keep a job. Work programs necessitate decisions about who will care for children while their mothers are employed outside the home. Children are no longer the object of welfare policy; rather, they are now just another impediment, such as lack of transportation, that exclude poor women from the workforce.

Not only does the law emphasize work over nurturing, it completely fails to recognize the value of mothering. . . .

In addition, poor mothers have received little attention for the objective difficulties they face when combining employment and caregiving. Compelling poor mothers on welfare to work outside the home leaves them with significantly less time for their maternal duties. They will have less time for mother work, which includes nurturing, teaching values, guiding children through difficult times, protecting, nursing sick children, reviewing children's homework, toilet training, meeting teachers, participating in school events, meeting children's friends, taking children to after school activities, and so on. By compelling work outside the home, the Personal Responsibility Act requires poor mothers to relinquish many of these duties. The founders of Mothers' Pensions understood the importance of work that poor mothers perform every day in their homes and realized that children benefit from their mothers' presence. . . .

The devaluation of mothers' work is reflected in welfare critics' inability to see the contribution women on welfare make to society through their role in child care. In addition, welfare rhetoric suggests that children are better off under the care of someone other than their mothers. The rhetoric blames mothers on welfare for being poor and for transmitting a "culture of dependency" to their children. Their mothering is deemed pathological and unworthy of subsidy.

Although gender dynamics have taken center stage in welfare reform, the racial politics have been more subtle. Racial politics continue to infect welfare reform efforts even though today, race-neutral terms pervade the public debate about welfare. Unlike when Mothers' Pensions and AFDC won passage, race-based discrimination is no longer legally acceptable. Explicit race claims are rare and ultimately unnecessary because welfare is widely viewed as a "code word" for race. Welfare has become a coded issue whereby politicians who attack welfare can exploit whites' racial animosity and resentment while diminishing the appearance of race baiting. Political use of race-neutral language hides welfare's racial subtext and insulates politicians from criticism. If a public figure makes race-based charges, his or her claims would be challenged and refuted. Because "Blacks are linked with . . . welfare . . . only implicitly, such links are less likely to be challenged . . . [and] [t]he public is left to draw its own conclusions, based on existing stereotypes."[4]

The racial imagery of welfare has significant force in welfare policy. "Part of the reason that maternalist rhetoric can no longer justify public financial support is that the public views this support as benefitting primarily Black mothers."[5] . . . [T]he welfare queen prevails as the stereotype of a typical welfare recipient. . . .

These types of unspoken racial images shape public understanding of welfare. Such misleading perceptions of welfare mothers permit the public to think of welfare recipients as "them" and not "us."

. . .

As we look to the future of welfare, it is hard not to remain pessimistic. Americans have inherited a welfare state with racist and gendered origins. History shows that welfare law originates from negative assumptions about economically needy women and their families. This legacy had enormous influence during the recent effort to reform welfare. Rather than recognizing the commonalities that all mothers share, welfare programs emphasize the differences between classes of mothers (i.e., poor mothers, Black mothers, and unwed mothers). Misguided policies magnify and exaggerate these differences severely enough to isolate poor mothers from the mainstream of society. Poor mothers are put on a different track with different rules.

Yet, a more general examination of family processes reveals that welfare families are only one variation of families struggling to balance work and home. Although their economic situation is dire, welfare families face the same time and money pressures that working-class, single parent, and even many middle-class families face. Reformers who favor universal programs have not overlooked these commonalities. For example, advocates of universal programs—such as increases in the minimum wage, universal health care, government subsidized day care, and a strengthened earned income tax credit—recognize that the situation of welfare families is not unique and that many families need assistance. Some reformers have promoted universal programs in the hope that such programs will garner greater public support than traditional welfare programs. They believe that universal programs, although designed to serve a broader population with common interests, will still provide much needed benefits to their intended target—the poor.

. . .

Constructing a new identity of welfare motherhood can be accomplished by using the real experiences of poor women's lives to contest, and ultimately replace, the caricatures. Such stories undoubtedly will resemble the stories heard from working mothers from all socio-economic strata. The storytelling will reveal that the collective experience of balancing work and family demands with little support eclipses the differences between these groups. The public may listen to these stories in a way they failed to do when confronted with empirical data. Of course, despite the authenticity of the storytelling, efforts to alter public discourse to recognize welfare motherhood as simply one variant of working motherhood will meet resistance.

. . .

I suggest that welfare activists inject into the discourse the ideology of welfare mothers as "Second Shift Moms." The image Second Shift Mom conveys is that of the working mother who comes home tired from work to face a "second shift"—running the household and caring for the children. Although the term derives from studies of dual-earner couples, which found that women perform more of the caretaking and housework than their husbands, the term applies equally to working single mothers who must raise children under time constraints and social and economic disadvantages.

The ideology of the Second Shift Mom addresses three central concerns. First, it legitimates welfare mothers by reflecting their status as workers and by leaving behind the destructive elements of current welfare discourse. This discourse vilified women on welfare as lazy for not working outside the home to support their families. As a consequence, the Personal Responsibility Act imposes mandatory work requirements on welfare recipients. Although some commentators continue to oppose the work requirements, it is not my purpose here to rehash that debate because all indications are that they are here to stay. Progressive reformers should not let defeat on the work issue obscure the potential benefits that attend its passage. The potential exists for welfare mothers to claim credit for the work they have been doing all along. Indeed, early reports from corporate executives who have hired former welfare recipients are quite positive. The respect and benefits that flow to workers in the United States should now be extended to welfare mothers. Equally significant is the effect the work requirements may have on welfare ideology and discourse. Enacting mandatory work requirements is precisely the type of structural change that can undermine the prevailing image of women on welfare and, to some degree, facilitate the enormously difficult task of changing this ideology. Politicians who have feasted on the image of welfare mothers as lazy and lacking in personal responsibility can no longer convincingly make such accusations.

Second, the term "Second Shift Mom" itself shifts emphasis from the labor market role of working mothers to their parental role. It suggests that families are being shortchanged because the childrearing duties are relegated to the second shift and mothers can only devote to their families the energy that has not been expended at their workplace. Further, it implicitly rejects both the Progressive Era glorification of ideal motherhood and Personal Responsibility Act's devaluation of motherhood as an impediment to employment.

Third, political activism and legal reform premised on the ideology of the Second Shift Mom have potential, not simply because the term provides an appealing slogan that attempts to alter widely shared assumptions about welfare motherhood. The true strength of this construction of motherhood lies in the potency of the symbol. It reflects the collective experience of working mothers—women who are forever juggling their work and home responsibilities—and it references these generally held norms. By acknowledging the shared complexity of the lives of working mothers (welfare, single, working-class, and otherwise), the term possesses an authenticity that should resonate with other lower income, working mothers and mobilize them to join the political struggle for universal programs that aid working mothers in their parental function.

Just as welfare reformers did during the Progressive Era, activists today must deliberately project this image of welfare motherhood. This task is not solely lawwork. Indeed, law reform efforts have been ineffectual in the face of the contemptuous tales crafted by welfare detractors. To sell "stories" about mothers on welfare, activists must adopt a public relations strategy involving community outreach, marketing efforts, and a media campaign. Such efforts have occurred in a piecemeal fashion. For example, in Illinois, the Jewish Council on Urban Affairs organized a "Welfare Truth Squad" to combat stereotypes. The Welfare Truth Squad has seven former welfare recipients, who are goodwill ambassadors and tell their stories to church groups, synagogues, rotary clubs and other organizations to put a human face on the often cold-blooded debate over welfare reform. In addition, on an individual level, some former welfare recipients have spoken out and told their stories to increase public awareness of welfare's successes. For these stories to penetrate the public consciousness and take hold, activists from a variety of fields should work together in a coordinated manner. Only after this narrative rebuts the conservative rhetoric that welfare mothers and their families are deviants can reformers successfully advance more dignified social welfare programs that address the caretaking needs of working, poor mothers.

Notes

1. Personal Responsibility Act § 101(1)-(3), 42 U.S.C. § 601 (1996).

2. Martha Albertson Fineman, The Neutered Mother, The Sexual Family 68 (1995).

3. Martha L. A. Fineman, *Masking Dependency: The Political Role of Family Rhetoric*, 81 Virginia Law Review 2181, 2190 (1995).

4. Martin Gilens, *"Race Coding" and White Opposition to Welfare*, 90 American Political Science Review. 593, 602 (1996).

5. Dorothy E. Roberts, *The Value of Black Mothers' Work*, 26 Connecticut Law Review 871, 873 (1994).

27

We Will Get What We Ask For:
Why Legalizing Gay and Lesbian Marriage
Will Not "Dismantle the Legal Structure
of Gender in Every Marriage"

Nancy D. Polikoff

The arguments for and against making marriage a priority for the lesbian and gay rights movement have been presented extensively. Attorney Tom Stoddard justifies aggressively pursuing same-sex marriage on three bases. First, Stoddard cites practical reasons, including the right to obtain direct economic benefits (e.g., social security benefits, health insurance), the advantages of tax and immigration laws, and protection of the relationship from outside interference.[1] Stoddard next addresses the political justifications, asserting that only by marrying will gay and lesbian couples validate the significance of their relationships. . . . "[M]arriage is . . . the issue most likely to lead ultimately to a world free from discrimination against lesbians and gay men."[2] Finally, Stoddard articulates a number of philosophical arguments to convince skeptics that the desirability of the right to marry does not require that one approve of that institution's current state. Indeed, Stoddard suggests that legalizing same-sex unions might even transform marriage into a state divested of its sexist base.

In contrast, Stoddard's colleague, Paula Ettelbrick, contends that "[m]arriage runs contrary to two of the primary goals of the lesbian and gay movement: the affirmation of gay identity and culture and the validation of many forms of relationships."[3] She argues that justice for lesbians and gay men depends upon accepting our differences from mainstream culture and the many choices we make about our relationships. Lesbian and gay marriage would not alter the current system . . . but would instead create a double standard for lesbian and gay sex—accepted if one is married, outlawed if one is not. In addition, Ettelbrick insists that the economic benefits lesbians and gay men would obtain by marrying . . . help primarily those who already enjoy relative economic security. . . . We should instead focus our efforts, she argues, on obtaining economic security and adequate health care for everyone, regardless of marital status or sexual orientation.

Let me acknowledge my own position in this debate. I "came out" as a lesbian feminist in the early 1970s, and my lesbian identity was intertwined with a radical feminist perspective. . . . I believe that the desire to marry in the lesbian and gay community is an attempt to mimic the worst of mainstream society, an effort to fit into an inherently problematic institution that betrays the promise of both lesbian and gay liberation and radical feminism.

The only argument that has ever tempted me to support efforts to obtain lesbian and gay marriage is the contention that marriages between two men or two women would inherently transform the institution of marriage for all people. . . . Nan Hunter . . . states:

> What is most unsettling to the status quo about the legalization of lesbian and gay marriage is its potential to expose and denaturalize the historical construction of gender at the heart of marriage. . . . Certainly marriage is a powerful institution, and the inertial force of tradition should not be underestimated. But it is also a social construct. Powerful social forces have reshaped it before and will continue to do so. . . . [T]he impact [of lesbian and gay marriage] . . . will be to dismantle the legal structure of gender in every marriage.[4]

It is in the context of responding to the view that lesbian and gay marriage will transform the otherwise marred institution of marriage that I examine Professor Eskridge's research on the historical and cross-cultural evidence of socially and/or religiously approved same-sex marriages. . . .

Professor Eskridge's research does substantially contribute to the debate on lesbian and gay marriage. The first clue to the significance of his work lies in the context within which it was generated. Professor Eskridge represents two District of Columbia men who were denied a marriage license and are challenging the District's action under the D.C. marriage statute and the D.C. antidiscrimination ordinance. The superior court judge, after hearing argument on the claim, requested that both sides research the history of marriage. In meeting this challenge, Professor Eskridge extensively researched scores of historical and anthropological materials. Upon concluding his study, he asserted that marriage has not at all times and for all peoples been a union of a man and a woman, and that same-sex unions have not always been condemned.

In the context of this litigation, the evidence that same-sex marriages have existed and been accepted in numerous communities has a distinctly conservative tone; most of the marriages Eskridge uncovered support rather than subvert hierarchy based upon gender. His historical and anthropological evidence contradicts any assumption that "gender dissent" is inherent in marriage between two men or two women. Rather, most of the unions reported were in fact gendered. Although both partners were biologically of the same sex, one partner tended to assume the characteristics and responsibilities of the opposite gender, with both partners then acting out their traditional gender roles. Thus, early observers of the Native American berdache noticed that some men "marry other men who . . . go around like women, perform their duties and are used as such and who cannot carry or use the bow,"[5] and that some women "give up all the duties of women and imitate men, and follow men's pursuits as if they were not women. . . . [E]ach has a woman to serve her, to whom she says she is married, and they treat each other and speak with each other as man and wife."[6] Contemporary scholarship on the berdache, such as Walter Williams' acclaimed study, *The Spirit and the Flesh: Sexual Diversity in American Indian Culture*, supports the conclusion that marriages between men and berdache followed the gendered division of labor observed in traditional Native American marriages, with the man taking on the role of husband and the berdache taking on the role of wife.[7] Similarly, female berdache hunted and headed the household, assuming traditional male responsibilities. Eskridge quotes from a scholar of female berdache that "the cross-gender female's partner . . . was always a traditional female; that is, two cross-gender dominant females did not marry,"[8] demonstrating that these same-sex partners assumed the traditional gendered roles of different-sex couples.

Eskridge's compilation is filled with many similar examples of same-sex relationships whose structure reinforces traditional notions of marriage as gendered and hierarchical. For example, Greek same-sex relationships are described by historian Kenneth Dover as including a courtship by the dominant party, the "husband/man," toward the receptive party, the "wife/boy," in which the receptive party responds coyly. "Boy wives" among the Azande (now in the Sudan) were similarly described as performing the services normally rendered by women. Among Eskridge's examples of traditionally gendered same-sex unions from Asia is the Chuckchee, whose "soft men" married men. While the other men hunted and fished, the "soft men" took care of the house and performed other domestic tasks. Indian hijras, emasculated men with female dress and demeanor, likewise married "traditional" men and assumed the historical female role.

Female couples likewise assumed conventional gendered roles. For example, marriages between women in Southern China in the nineteenth century resulted in the designation of one partner as "husband" and the other as "wife." Similarly, African "woman-marriage" is an institution in which a woman gives "bridewealth for, and marries, a woman over whom and whose offspring she has full control."[9] Eskridge cites one scholar whose assessment of this practice is that it allows powerful, wealthy women to assume the social roles of men and thus serve as leaders in a male-dominated society.

The vision of same-sex marriage presented in the research Professor Eskridge proffers is a profoundly constricted one. In some instances, the relationships he describes do not seem to be same-sex unions at all, as the relevant culture appears to recognize a third gender, such as the berdache and the hijras. Marriage within each gender did not exist. Furthermore, hierarchy was a component of all such ostensibly same-sex marriages, with the partner embodying the most male characteristics accorded higher status and greater control. Accordingly, an argument based on continuity between lesbian and gay marriage today and same-sex marriages of other eras and cultures is not one that makes deconstruction of gender the core reason to fight for the ability of lesbians and gay men to marry. Should public debates arise as to whether to legislate in favor of contemporary lesbian and gay marriage, this type of historical research would probably be used to advance the proposition that there is nothing new or truly unconventional about same-sex marriage. Indeed, that was the precise assertion made by Professor Eskridge in the litigation sparking his research. Similarly, the political and public relations campaign to legalize same-sex marriage would likely contend that our relationships are no different from heterosexual marriages. In other words, the pro-marriage position would accept, rather than challenge, the current institution of marriage. I believe this process would be profoundly destructive to the lesbian and gay community.

Professor Hunter acknowledged this danger in her article advocating same-sex marriage in the hope that it would deconstruct gender. She writes:

> The impact of law often lies as much in the body of discourse created in the process of its adoption as in the final legal rule itself. . . . The social meaning of the legalization of lesbian and gay marriage . . . would be enormously different if legalization resulted from political efforts framed as ending gendered roles between spouses rather than if it were the outcome of a campaign valorizing the institution of marriage, even if the ultimate "holding" is the same.[10]

Everything in our political history suggests that a concerted effort to achieve the legalization of lesbian and gay marriage will valorize the current institution of marriage. Just as Professor Eskridge was propelled toward a litigation strategy that accepted marriage—even grossly hierarchical, gendered marriage—as a good, any effort to legitimize lesbian and gay marriage would work to persuade the heterosexual mainstream that lesbians and gay men seek to emulate heterosexual marriage as currently constituted.

Demands for social change often have begun with a movement at first articulating the rhetoric of radical transformation and then later discarding that rhetoric to make the demands more socially acceptable. The movement's rhetoric is modified or altered when those opposing reform explore the radical and transformative possibilities of that rhetoric, causing its advocates to issue reassurances promising that such transformation is not what the movement is about at all.

Within the arena of eliminating gender hierarchy, women's access to abortion provides one such example of a movement redefining its goals to make them more politically palatable. Early abortion activists spoke of women's liberation and women's entitlement to sexual fulfillment, viewing access to abortion as part of a larger struggle to end male dominance. As abortion became a major political issue, however, and with the battle to win public opinion in full gear, the rhetoric changed, adopting its current pro-choice vocabulary. In the judicial arena, the prevailing arguments spoke of privacy. In fact, it became fashionable to say that while one was not in favor of abortion, one was nonetheless in favor of choice, to imply—if not to state—that abortion was an evil but a necessary one. In the face of conservative voices decrying abortion as a facilitator of unchecked sexual freedom, "pro-choice" voices denied or downplayed the relationship between women's access to abortion and women's ability to enjoy guilt-free sexual pleasure.

By shifting their strategy, abortion rights activists lost the transformative potential of women's ready access to abortion. Supporters of abortion rights no longer link it to ending male supremacy or to affirming sexual pleasure for women. Indeed, "abortion on demand" is no longer the call of abortion supporters but the specter brought forth by antiabortion voices.

. . .

Similar analyses apply to the lesbian and gay rights movement. Specifically, the current rhetoric voiced in the campaign to end the military's practice of excluding lesbians and gay men is useful in imagining how a campaign to end the exclusion of lesbians and gay men from marriage would be shaped. Those challenging the military exclusion neither critique the military as an institution nor acknowledge the transformative potential of allowing lesbians and gay men to serve openly. I believe those campaigning for lesbian and gay marriage would adopt a similar strategy, neither critiquing the institution of marriage nor acknowledging the transformative potential of allowing lesbians and gay men to enter into state-sanctioned unions.

The vehemence of military and congressional opposition to President Clinton's proposal to lift the ban caught most of the lesbian and gay rights lobby by surprise. In response, an ad hoc organization was formed to work exclusively on this issue on behalf of the lesbian and gay community. The name adopted by the organization, the Campaign for Military Service, was not an arbitrary or random choice. At the meeting at which the name was selected, a public relations professional cautioned the group that the words "justice" and "equality" should be avoided. Interestingly enough, the words "lesbian," "gay," "homosexual," "discrimination," and "rights" were also omitted. Instead, the emphasis is on military service, the willingness to enter the revered institution that is charged with this country's defense. It is a campaign that meets and embraces the military on its own terms, the implicit message being that the military is accepted as it now exists. The name serves to assure military leaders and mainstream society that there will be nothing transformative about allowing lesbians and gay men to serve their country openly.

The strategy that lesbian and gay rights activists have pursued in their quest to eliminate the military exclusion is filled with rhetoric professing respect for the armed services.

. . .

There is no room in this campaign for the community's internal debate about the military's proper role.

. . .

By the same token, I believe that an effort to legalize lesbian and gay marriage would make a public critique of the institution of marriage impossible.

. . .

If my hypothesis about the process of change is correct, then we must measure the value of the work it will take to legalize lesbian and gay marriage by how closely the arguments we make in advocating this change match what we really believe about and want for our relationships and our community. For those who support lesbian and gay marriage because it would allow us access to the package of benefits now associated with heterosexual marriage, or because it would demonstrate that our relationships are as valuable as their heterosexual counterparts, advocating lesbian and gay marriage is an obvious choice. I do not share that vision. Advocating lesbian and gay marriage will detract from, even contradict, efforts to unhook economic benefits from marriage and make basic health care and other necessities available to all. It will also require a rhetorical strategy that emphasizes similarities between our relationships and heterosexual marriages, values long-term monogamous coupling above all other relationships, and denies the potential of lesbian and gay marriage to transform the gendered nature of marriage for all people. I fear that the very process of employing that rhetorical strategy for the years it will take to achieve its objective will lead our movement's public representatives, and the countless lesbians and gay men who hear us, to believe exactly what we say.

NOTES

1. Thomas B. Stoddard, *Why Gay People Should Seek the Right to Marry*, in Lesbian and Gay Marriage 13, 14–16 (Suzanne Sherman, ed., 1992).

2. *Id.* at 17.

3. Paula L. Ettelbrick, *Since When Is Marriage a Path to Liberation?* in Lesbian and Gay Marriage, supra note 1, at 20, 21.

4. Nan D. Hunter, *Marriage, Law and Gender: A Feminist Inquiry*, 1 Law and Sexuality, 9, 18–19 (1991).

5. Francisco Lopez de Gomara, Historia General de las Indeias (1552), translated in Francisco Guerra, The Pre-Columbian Mind 85 (1971).

6. 2 Pero de Magalhaes, The Histories of Brazil 88–89 (John B. Stetson, Jr., trans., Cortes Society 1922) (1576).

7. Walter L. Williams, The Spirit and the Flesh: Sexual Diversity in American Indian Culture 112 (1986).

8. William N. Eskridge, Jr., *A History of Same-Sex Marriage*, 79 Virginia Law Review 1419, 1457–58 (1993).

9. *Id.* at 1460–61.

10. Hunter, *supra* note 4, at 29.

28

"The Past Never Vanishes":
A Contextual Critique of the
Existing Indian Family Doctrine

Lorie M. Graham

. . .

I. Introduction

"I don't know my own culture, . . . I am going to need your help in understanding [it]. . . . Teach me, teach my children." These are the words of a forty-three-year-old Navajo woman on her first visit back to the Navajo Nation since her birth. Stolen as an infant, along with her twin brother, and adopted out on the black market, she was recently reunited with her family and community. Her journey home comes at a time when Native American nations are fighting proposed legislation and court-made rules that seek to limit the reach of the Indian Child Welfare Act of 1978 (ICWA).

Congress passed the ICWA in response to the massive displacement of Native American children in this country. Prior to the law's passage, one-third of all Native American children were being separated from their families and communities and placed in non-Indian adoptive homes, foster care, and educational institutions by federal, state, and private child welfare authorities. While there were a myriad of interrelated factors that led up to this Indian child welfare crisis, at its core was the failure of mainstream society to recognize and respect the cultural values and social norms of Native American nations. . . .

This assimilative attitude that Native American children were better off growing up in a non-Indian environment did not surface overnight. Rather it percolated from centuries of U.S. sanctioned policies—from boarding schools, to "placing out" programs, to Indian adoption projects—aimed at the erasure of Native American cultures.

The passage of the ICWA marked a reversal in federal Indian policy toward one of self-determination for Native American nations. The law recognized the sovereign authority of tribes to address Indian child welfare issues. Tribal courts were designated as the exclusive forum for certain custody proceedings involving Native American children domiciled or residing on the reservation or a ward of the tribal court, and the preferred forum for proceedings involving non-domiciliary children. Additionally, in state cases involving the termination of parental rights, foster care, and adoption, the law sought to protect the rights of Native American children to be raised and nurtured, whenever feasible, in their families and communities of origin through the establishment of minimum federal standards and procedural safeguards. The law is limited to Native American children who are members of or eligible for membership in a federally recognized tribe. As one ICWA attorney noted, "the hopeful vision" for the ICWA was a future "in which the states, tribes, and federal government work[ed] together . . . to protect Indian children and to reaffirm the value of Indian family life."[1]

While the law is not flawless, it provides vital protection to Native American children, their families, and tribes. Yet recent studies suggest that one-fifth of all Native American children "are still being placed outside of their natural tribal and family environments."[2] Courts, social welfare agencies, and attorneys who fail to follow the letter and spirit of the law have all contributed to this ongoing crisis. The "Existing Indian Family" doctrine, a state judicially created exception to the ICWA that has received some recent congressional support, is one such example. While the doctrine varies slightly from state to state, the end results are the same: to cut off a number of Native American children from their extended families and cultural heritages by thwarting the express language and goals of the ICWA and ignoring indigenous views of what constitutes an "Indian family." It is in this way that the doctrine is reminiscent of past U.S. policies. Indeed, these recent challenges to the ICWA cannot be properly evaluated without placing them in the larger historical context of U.S. Indian policy toward American Indian children. The legacies of these policies remain with us today as Native American nations struggle to reconnect with their lost loved ones and maintain a sense of community for their children and their children's children. To ignore the past . . . is to risk reversing all that has been achieved by Native American nations in the past twenty years with respect to familial self-determination.

. . .

II. The Historical Realities of American Indian Children

If we do not understand each other, if we do not know the culture or the history of each other, it is difficult to see the value and dignity of each other's societies.[3]
—Chief Justice Yazzie, Navajo Nation Supreme Court, 1993

A. Some Indigenous Views of Family and Community

Indigenous nations, tribes, or communities are "culturally distinctive groups" that have "their ancestral roots imbedded in the lands in which they live, or would like to live, much more deeply than the roots of more powerful sectors of society living on the same lands or in close proximity."[4] It is estimated that there are some 5,000 indigenous nations and 500,000,000 indigenous peoples in the world. In this country alone, there are over 550 federally recognized Native American nations and some 1.9 million people who identify with their American Indian ancestry. These indigenous nations are not defined by any "racial" category, but rather by their distinct histories, cultures, governments, economic institutions, languages, philosophies, and senses of spirituality.

. . . Certainly, the child-rearing traditions of indigenous peoples are as diverse as the communities that embody them. Moreover, as Greg Sarris so aptly points out, "tradition itself is not fixed, but an on-going process."[5] Yet subsumed within these traditions are unifying concepts that are important to a fuller understanding of Indian family life. A brief look at some of these concepts and traditions will help to establish a contextual framework for evaluating past U.S. policies aimed at destroying the cohesiveness of the Indian family and the more current existing Indian family doctrine.

For many Native American nations, "family" denotes extensive kinship networks that reach far beyond the Western nuclear family. It is a "multi-generational complex of people and clan and kinship responsibilities"[6] that extends to past and future generations. According to Vine Deloria, Jr., "[K]inship and clan were built upon the idea that individuals owed each other certain kinds of behaviors and that if each individual performed his or her task properly, society as a whole would function."[7] As Evelyn Blanchard explains, Indian people have two relational systems:

> They have a biological relational system, and they have a clan or band relational system. It is the convergence, if you will, of these two systems in tribal society that creates the fabric of tribal life. And each of us as an Indian person has a very specific place in the fabric. Those responsibilities are our rights, individual rights. And even our mother has no right to deny us those rights. We want that. We know ourselves, and that is necessary for these children.[8]

Understanding this interplay between "collective responsibility" and "individual rights" is essential to understanding indigenous familial relations. Where children and community are concerned, they are actually two sides of the same coin. For instance, a child's right to love and nourishment (e.g., cultural, emotional, spiritual, and physical) is the community's responsibility. "Those [collective] responsibilities are our individual rights."[9] To place a child outside the kinship community absent culturally relevant safeguards, as was the case before the ICWA was passed, would be to deny that child certain rights otherwise recognized by her tribe.

The kinship community plays an integral role in the care and education of Native American children, from newborn infants to those on the threshold of adulthood. While parents might assume responsibility for the basic guidance of the child, extended family members often have distinct child-rearing responsibilities. For instance, according to Blackfoot tradition, it is not uncommon for grandparents to raise one of their grandchildren. Moreover, if a small child should lose her mother, a grandmother or elderly widow in the community often steps in to care for the child. In the Navajo culture, when a child is born into a family, the whole clan has child-rearing responsibilities. This is reflected in the Navajo language.

There are no Navajo words for aunt or uncle, niece or nephew. When a young boy addresses his mother he refers to her as shima' (mother). When the boy addresses his mother's sister he refers to her as shima' ya'zhi' (which means little mother). And the aunt addresses the boy as shiyazov (her little child or little son). Other indigenous nations have similar customs. According to Comanche custom, a child's paternal aunt might assume the role of mother when the child's mother is unavailable. These customs and traditions continue to serve as important guideposts for determining appropriate placement of American Indian children in need of care and supervision.

. . .

[C]hild-rearing and indigenous education practices often go hand in hand. Within the context of the home and community, a child learns to develop her full potential as an individual and to harmonize that individuality with communal needs. This is done through a holistic system of education that teaches the child that all things in life are related. Children are taught from an early age to pay close attention to the "constructive and cooperative relationships"[10] that make up the universe. It is in this way that they learn how their survival and that of the community are dependent upon maintaining a proper balance between the earth and all living things.

. . .

A community's spiritual and cultural practices, such as initiation ceremonies that mark different stages of one's life, are equally important to a child's education and upbringing. These practices have been described as the "wellspring" of instructions for Native peoples, as individuals and collectively as societies. Such knowledge is often interwoven into the land and language of the community.

. . .

[T]he "cumulative knowledge" that is passed from community to child and from generation to generation is the lifeblood of Native American nations. When a child is removed from the kinship community without appropriate safeguards, it breaks the cycle of indigenous life.

. . .

B. Some Effects

The massive displacement of American Indian children has had long-lasting effects on the well-being of Native American children, families, and tribes. One of the most devastating consequences has been the unusually high rate of suicide among American Indian children placed in foster care, adoptive homes, and institutions—a rate twice that of the reservation suicide rate and four times that of the general population. At U.S. congressional hearings on the Indian child welfare crisis, experts testified that Native American children were more likely to face significant social problems in adolescence and adulthood as a result of the displacement. The American Academy of Child Psychiatry agreed, stating in a 1975 report that

[t]here is much clinical evidence to suggest that Native American children placed in off-reservation non-Indian homes are at risk in their later development. Often enough [the children] are cared for by devoted and well-intentioned foster or adoptive parents. Nonetheless, particularly in adolescence, they are subject to ethnic confusion and a pervasive sense of abandonment.[11]

Other studies have corroborated these findings. Moreover, children raised in boarding schools or other educational institutions knew very little of life in a "family." As parents themselves, they had no patterns to follow in rearing their own children. Many had to learn to live and cope with harsh experiences, such as physical and mental abuse. In addition, they were being educated in systems that devalued their Native cultures, resulting in further alienation from community and loss of self-esteem. High dropout rates and low employment were the norm for many of these students. The large number of American children raised in foster care similarly perpetuated the destruction of the American Indian family. "Stricken by a 'constant sense of not knowing where they will be or how long they'll be there,'"[12] these children found it difficult in adulthood to establish permanent roots. Additionally, because society frowned upon their cultures, many American Indians sought to deny their own heritages. This denial caused further distress, often leading to some form of substance abuse. Some of the consequences of the removal process for the individual child were not easily quantifiable, such as the loss of opportunity to learn about one's heritage from one's elders.

Studies did show that when the child was removed from the home without the benefits of proper cultural, political, and social safeguards, it affected the entire kinship community. AAIA [Association on American Indian Affairs] related studies indicated that removal of a child "effectively destroyed the family as an intact unit . . . exacerbat[ing] the problems of alcoholism, unemployment, and emotional duress among parents."[13] The consistent threat of losing one's child created a sense of hopelessness and powerlessness that made it difficult for the adults to function well as parents. Many feared emotional attachment because of the inevitable loss. One psychologist noted that American Indian parents had become so conditioned to the removal process that they would often place their own children in boarding schools as a matter of course. Others would place the children with social service agencies and hospitals, rather than entrusting them to the care of extended family members.

Moreover, since the community's economic and social well-being were built around kinship networks, the destruction of the family unit perpetuated the dire socioeconomic conditions existing on many reservations. The Indian child welfare crisis also chipped away at the cultural heritages of tribes. As Chief Calvin Isaac of the Mississippi Band of Choctaw Indians noted in a 1978 hearing before the Senate:

Culturally, the chances of Indian survival are significantly reduced if our children, the only means for the transmission of the tribal heritage, are to be raised in non-Indian homes and denied exposure to the ways of their People. Furthermore, these practices seriously undercut the tribes' ability to continue self-governing communities. Probably in no area is it more important that tribal sovereignty be respected than in an area as socially and culturally determinative as family relationships.[14]

C. Congress' Response

Once the Indian child welfare crisis had been brought to the forefront, Native nations and Congress were faced with the daunting task of developing legislation that would prevent further abuses and help remedy the years of damage that had already been done to Native American children, families, and tribes. In 1978, Congress passed the Indian Child Welfare Act, declaring:

> It is the policy of this Nation to protect the best interests of Indian children and to promote the stability and security of Indian tribes and families by the establishment of minimum Federal standards for the removal of Indian children from their families and the placement of such children in foster or adoptive homes which will reflect the unique values of Indian culture, and by providing for assistance to Indian tribes in the operation of child and family service programs.[15]

The ICWA was designed to achieve a number of interrelated goals. First, the law seeks to reverse the historical policies and practices that led to the massive removal of American Indian children to institutions, foster care, and adoptive homes. The law is an official acknowledgment by the federal government that Indian children are not necessarily "better off" far from the influence of family and community. The law similarly recognizes that an Indian child's best interests may be inextricably connected to that of the tribe. While the law could not dictate a change in the attitudes of social workers, educators, and judges, it could establish minimum standards and procedures for the placement of American Indian children outside the home.

Second, the ICWA seeks to recognize and respect the familial traditions and responsibilities of Native American nations. When viewed in the context of indigenous family and community, the law recognizes the importance of the traditional kinship system and the role of the extended family in the rearing of children. For instance, it recognizes foster care and adoptive placement preferences with extended family members and other tribal members, and requires state courts to consider the social and cultural standards of tribes when making placement determinations. It also seeks to protect the individual rights of Native American children to be raised, whenever feasible, in their families and communities of origin by mandating that families receive culturally appropriate remedial services before a placement occurs. Prior to the law being passed, American Indian families were less likely to receive any supportive services as an alternative to removal of their children as compared to non-Indian families. Additionally, the Act was designed to be sufficiently flexible to meet the diverse cultural interests and complex social needs of American Indian children. Evidence of this flexibility can be found in the opinions of several state and tribal courts, as well as various tribal and state programs.

Third, it seeks to promote Indian self-determination in the area of child welfare. The doctrine of tribal sovereignty holds that the "powers of Indian tribes are . . . inherent powers of a limited sovereignty which has never been extinguished."[16] The ICWA recognizes the sovereign powers of Native American nations to develop indigenous systems of child welfare. This goal is in line with studies indicating a link between the welfare of Native American children and the extent to which tribes are able to control their own political, social, and economic development. The law reaffirms the jurisdiction of tribal courts over certain child custody proceedings, and extends that jurisdiction to children living away from their communities. It ensures that tribes and extended family members will have an opportunity to be heard through notification provisions and the ability to intervene in the proceedings. Finally, it encourages the development and implementation of tribal child welfare services. These provisions recognize the symbiotic relationship between tribe and child, including the child's right to participate in the "fabric of tribal life" and the tribe's right to exist as a distinct political community.

Despite some limitations in the law, there is a general consensus among Native American nations and organizations that the ICWA provides "vital protection to American Indian children, families and tribes."[17] Yet the Act continues to be ignored in many instances. The Existing Indian Family Doctrine is a prime example of how certain state courts are circumventing the mandates of the law. As the next section demonstrates, this judicially created exception to the ICWA, which some politicians have advocated should be incorporated into the Act itself, constitutes a significant retreat from the purposes and goals of the ICWA.

IV. A Return to Assimilationist Thinking?

The Indian culture is foreign to me, and I don't think it is valid.[18]
—Adoption Attorney, 1987

A. The Existing Indian Family Doctrine

The current legal and political challenges to the Indian Child Welfare Act pose a number of important questions: Does the judicially recognized "Existing Indian Family" exception represent a return to the assimilationist attitudes of the past? What are the dangers inherent in the "social, cultural, or political affiliation" standard of the "Existing Indian Family" Doctrine? And what are the future implications to Indian children, their families, and their tribes should this Doctrine become settled law?

In 1996, a bill was introduced into the House of Representatives that would have excluded from the coverage of the ICWA any child whose parents did not maintain "significant social, cultural, or political ties with the tribe of which they are a member."[19] This amendment passed through the House of Representatives as part of The Adoption Promotion and Stability Act without any input from Native

American nations or organizations. Although the amendment was later deleted from the Senate version of the bill, the debate over the ICWA continues in Congress with a series of new amendments being proposed each term. The original House amendment was an attempt to codify a judicially created exception to the ICWA known as the Existing Indian Family Doctrine. Some state courts have refused to apply the ICWA to any case not involving the "removal" of an Indian child from an "existing Indian family or home." State courts that have adopted this exception contend that Congress never intended ICWA to apply to American Indian children who had not lived in an Indian cultural environment or bonded with an Indian parent, or whose parent has no apparent connection with his or her community.

Courts and advocates alike have maintained that the Doctrine violates the plain meaning of the ICWA, which states that the law will apply to "custody proceedings" involving "Indian children" who are either a member of their tribe or eligible for membership. There is no statutory requirement that the child or parent meet any additional test of "Indian-ness" beyond membership. As one judge aptly noted, "When a court ignores the clear provisions [of the Act] . . . in reliance on what the court believes the legislature must have meant to say, the court is improperly engaging in judicial lawmaking."[20]

The Doctrine also violates basic principles of tribal sovereignty. Native American nations, as distinct political communities, have the authority to determine their own membership. Membership in a tribal nation is conceptually equivalent to citizenship, although not always synonymous with "enrollment." Every Indian nation has its own membership or citizenship criteria which may be determined by "written law, custom, intertribal agreement, or treaty with the United States."[21] The Existing Indian Family Doctrine, which allows state courts and agencies to substitute their views of what "belonging" to a tribal family means for that of the tribe's views, thwarts this essential function of tribal sovereignty. Tribal membership determinations and issues of domestic relations between tribal members are two areas of American Indian law in which the Supreme Court continues to support the autonomous self-determining status of tribes even as it seems to chip away at other aspects of tribal sovereignty. For instance, in *Santa Clara Pueblo v. Martinez*,[22] the Court held that there was no federal court review beyond habeas corpus of tribal governmental actions under the Indian Civil Rights Act (ICRA). By construing the provisions of the ICRA narrowly to exclude federal court review of tribal membership determinations, the Court sought to ensure a "proper respect both for tribal sovereignty itself and for the plenary authority of Congress."[23]

These are just two of several arguments advanced against the application and codification of the Existing Indian Family Doctrine. Perhaps the most dangerous aspect of this Doctrine, however, is that it perpetuates, while maybe not consciously so, the very type of assimilationist thinking that led to the crisis in the first place.

. . .

B. Whose "Family" Is It Anyhow?

Simply put, the Existing Indian Family Doctrine is reminiscent of the assimilationist policies of the past. First, it substitutes indigenous views of "family" for that of the individual state. Although the Existing Indian Family Doctrine varies from state to state, all of the cases turn on state court interpretations of "Indian-ness" and "family." Some state courts focus on the relationship of the child to the Indian parent, others on the relationship of the parent to the tribe. . . . The potential relationship of the child to the kinship community and the tribes' views of what it means to be "Indian" or part of an "Indian family" are not determinative. In this sense, the Doctrine completely thwarts Congress's goal, codified in the ICWA, "to recognize the essential tribal relations of Indian people and the cultural and social standards prevailing in Indian communities and families."[24] Moreover, rather than viewing the notion of "family" as a "multi-generational complex of people and clan and kinship responsibilities," courts . . . have chosen to apply a narrower definition of family, which they proclaim is the "fundamental social unit" of any "civilized society." Besides being offensive, this interpretation directly conflicts with Congress' intent to respect "the unique [familial] values of Indian culture[s]."[25] The difficulty of applying state standards to these cases is . . . [aptly described by Christine Metteer]:

> [I]n asking both whether the child is "Indian" enough to be embraced under the Act, and if so, whether the child was part of an existing Indian "family," the courts fail to see that from the Indian perspective, the two questions are one. To be an Indian under [the ICWA] requires, at a minimum, eligibility for tribal [membership]. And to be eligible for tribal [membership] means that the tribe has embraced the child as part of the whole, the tribal family.[26]

At issue here is the relationship of the individual to the kinship community. . . . American Indian children have a unique symbiotic relationship with their tribe. . . . In many respects, these laws and customs serve the same overarching goals that family laws of individual states serve in "protecting the best interest of a child." Citizens of those states must abide by state law just as members of American Indian nations are similarly bound by tribal law and custom.

Second, the Existing Indian Family Doctrine fails to recognize the important role that extended family members play in the care and upbringing of children. . . .

C. International and National Debates on the Individual versus the Group

A child's right to be raised and nurtured in her family and community of origin has been increasingly recognized in international legal discourse. For instance, in 1988, the Hague Conference on private international law expressed concern for the "world-wide phenomenon [of inter-country adoption] involving migration of children over long geographical distance and from one society and culture to another very different environment."[27] In 1995, the Hague Inter-Country Adoption

Convention came into force. The Preamble to that Convention recognized, among other things, that: (1) "a child, for the full and harmonious development of his or her personality, should grow up in a family environment in an atmosphere of happiness, love, and understanding"; (2) "each State should take, as a matter of priority, appropriate measures to enable a child to remain in the care of his or her family of origin"; and (3) "measures [should be taken] to ensure the inter-country adoptions are made in the best interests of the child and with respect for his or her fundamental rights, and to prevent the abduction, the sale of, or the traffic in children."[28] Additionally, individual countries that experienced a dramatic increase in the number out-of-country adoptions during recent times, such as Guatemala, El Salvador, and Romania, have begun to enact domestic laws and regulations aimed at curtailing the number of foreign adoptions. Other international instruments, such as the United Nations Convention on the Rights of the Child, have similarly sought to recognize "the right of the child to preserve his or her identity, including nationality, name, and family relations."[29]

At the same time, indigenous peoples have been fighting for greater international affirmation of their right to thrive as distinct political and cultural communities. For instance, the Draft United Nations Declaration on the Rights of Indigenous Peoples affirms, among other things, the rights of indigenous peoples to self-government, control of lands and resources, and basic human rights, as well as the freedom to develop their identities and cultures without assimilation. Article 6 of the Declaration states that indigenous peoples have "the collective right to . . . full guarantees against genocide . . . including removal of indigenous children from their families and communities under any pretext."[30] Studies indicate that abuses similar to those committed in the U.S. against American Indian children have occurred in other countries. For instance, a recent study on Aborigine children in Australia documented "the horror of a regime" that took 100,000 children from their families and communities, and tried to instill in them "a repugnance of all things Aboriginal."[31] In light of these and other abuses, indigenous peoples are pushing for new international procedures and norms beyond existing human rights laws that would address the "historically rooted grievances of indigenous peoples."[32]

While there seems to be broad international support for the idea of a declaration on indigenous rights, the process has been hampered by a perceived conflict between individual and group identities. Similarly, while the rights of children vis-à-vis their families and communities of origin have received heightened awareness internationally, they seem to have clashed with national conceptions of individualism. Legal scholar Barbara Bennett Woodhouse states that the "very notion of preserving children's cultural or ethnic identity seems to conflict with liberal conceptions of parents' and children's individual rights, ideals of color-blind equality, and a peculiarly American kind of liberty consisting in the freedom to reinvent oneself as a new citizen of a new world."[33]

. . . On closer examination, it may be that the ideological conflicts over the ICWA are merely a continuation of the cultural misunderstandings that have plagued this country for centuries.

. . .

The ICWA does seek to protect what Woodhouse refers to as a child's "identity of origin."[34] Yet it does so within the "the generally accepted premise that the first and best choice is to preserve and protect the child's . . . family and community of origin from disruption."[35] The reason the ICWA was necessary in the first place was to counter the abusive practices aimed at destroying American Indian families and stripping children of their indigenous identities and heritages. In fulfilling its trust responsibility to Native American nations, Congress sought to promote the stability and security of tribes and families by providing them with greater control over Indian child placement decisions. The Existing Indian Family Doctrine, on the other hand, seeks to disrupt American Indian families and tribes by failing to recognize a child's ties to the kinship community and the tribe's notion of what it means to be part of an "Indian family."

Woodhouse aptly demonstrates that missing from the debate over individual versus group identity "is a coherent schema for articulating children's rights to preservation of their identity" in placement determinations.[36] She offers a compelling case for looking at issues of identity and kinship through the children's eyes. "Drawing upon stories from children's lives, as well as stories about children and for children," she demonstrates how a child develops her identity from "individual caregivers" as well as from "family and group membership."[37] She sees the first relationship as constituting the child's "personal identity rights," defined as a right to "a safe and secure caregiving relationship in order to survive infancy and to begin forming any identity at all."[38] The second relationship is the child's "identity of origin," defined as a right to "explore her identity as a member of the family and group into which she was born."[39] Woodhouse states that from these dual needs "a theory of children's rights, including rights to protection of identity," can be developed. She further advocates for the development of "a full array of flexible tools" beyond the "traditional" nuclear family adoption to meet the complex needs of children and their caregivers, including open adoption, kinship adoption, kinship foster care, foster care with tenure, and visitations with biological siblings, extended family, and community.

. . . [T]he provisions of the ICWA, and the indigenous concepts they embody, are consistent with Woodhouse's "child-centered perspective" on identity. The ICWA is not a law of absolutes. It does not seek to protect the rights of the group at the expense of the rights of the individual. Indeed, Native American communities do not view issues of childcare and custody in such stark terms. The law does recognize that it is in the best interest of American Indian children to maintain ties with their extended families and tribes whenever feasible. Moreover, it does so in a way that acknowledges the unique political status of tribes in this country and their ability to either make child custody determinations in the first instance or be involved in those determinations through a right of intervention. In either case, the child may end up being removed from the home and even perhaps permanently placed outside the kinship community. However, the law ensures that this does not happen because of a court or agency's unwillingness to "recognize either the vitality or validity of contemporary American Indian cultures and values."[40] Nor does the law threaten the "personal identity" or immediate survival needs of the children. Indeed, by its very terms, it is designed to prevent improper removals, strengthen Indian families and tribes, and ensure that when placement is necessary the child's familial and tribal options are considered and explored. . . . The ICWA protects the "identity rights" of American Indian children within the context of their own historical and cultural realities and therefore should not be lightly disregarded.

. . .

NOTES

1. Bruce Davies, *Implementing the Indian Child Welfare Act*, 16 Clearinghouse Review 179 (1982).

2. Introduction to The Indian Child Welfare Act: Unto the Seventh Generation: Conference Proceedings (Troy R. Johnson, ed., 1993).

3. Lisa Driscoll, *Tribal Courts: New Mexico's Third Judiciary*, 32 New Mexico Bar Bulletin, Feb. 18, 1993, at A5 (quoting Chief Justice Robert Yazzie).

4. James Anaya, *Indigenous Peoples*, in International Law 3 (1996).

5. Greg Sarris, Keeping Slug Woman Alive: A Holistic Approach to American Indian Texts 179–80 (1993).

6. Vine Deloria, Indian Education in America 22 (1991).

7. *Id.*

8. Indian Child Welfare Amendments: Hearings on S. 1976 before the Senate Select Committee on Indian Affairs, 100th Cong. 97 (1988) (statement of Evelyn Blanchard).

9. *Id.*

10. Vine Deloria, Indian Education in America 22 (1991).

11. Indian Child Welfare Act of 1977: Hearing on S. 1214 before the Senate Select Committee on Indian Affairs, 95th Cong. 538, 603 (1977), at 114 (statement of Drs. Carl Mindell and Alan Gurwitt, American Academy of Child Psychiatry).

12. Russel Lawrence Barsh, *The Indian Child Welfare Act of 1978: A Critical Analysis*, 31 Hastings Law Journal 1287, 1291 (1980).

13. Margaret Plantz et. al., Indian Child Welfare: A Status Report, Final Report of the Survey of Indian Child Welfare and Implementation of the Indian Child Welfare Act of 1978 and Section 428 of the Adoption Assistance and Child Welfare Act of 1980 ES-1 (1988), at 54.

14. Hearings before the Subcommittee on Indian Affairs and Public Lands of the House Committee on Interior and Insular Affairs, 95th Cong. 193 (1978).

15. 25 U.S.C. § 1902 (1994).

16. *United States v. Wheeler*, 435 U.S. 313, 322–23 (1978).

17. Amendments to the Indian Child Welfare Act: Hearings before the Senate Committee on Indian Affairs, 104th Cong. 303 (1996) (statement of Jack F. Trope, for AAIA).

18. Thomas B. Rosensteil, *Whites Adopt Navajo: Sovereignty on Trial in Custody Case*, Los Angeles Times, Feb. 11, 1987, at A1.

19. H.R. 3275, 104th Cong. (1996).

20. *In re N.S.*, 474 N.W.2d 96, 100 (S.D. 1991) (Sabers, J., concurring).

21. *Santa Clara Pueblo v. Martinez*, 436 U.S. 49 (1978) (citing *Delaware Indians v. Cherokee Nation*, 193 U.S. 127 [1904]).

22. *Id.*

23. *Id.*

24. 25 U.S.C. § 1901(5) (1994).

25. 25 U.S.C. § 1902 (1994).

26. Christine Metteer, *Pigs in Heaven: A Parable of Native American Adoption under the Indian Child Welfare Act*, Arizona State Law Journal 589, 614 (1996).

27. Gonzalo Parra-Aranguren, *An Overview of the 1993 Hague Inter-Country Adoption Convention*, in Families across Frontiers 567 (Nigel Lowe and Gillian Douglas, eds., 1996).

28. *Id.* at 567.

29. Barbara Bennett Woodhouse, *Protecting Children's Rights of Identity across Frontiers of Culture, Political Community, and Time*, in Families across Frontiers 259 (Nigel Lowe and Gillian Douglas, eds., 1996).

30. Draft United Nations Declaration on the Rights of Indigenous Peoples, reprinted in James Anaya, Indigenous Peoples in International Law at 209 (1996).

31. J. H. Wooten, Royal Commission into Aboriginal Deaths in Custody, Report of the Inquiry into the Death of Malcolm Charles Smith 20 (1989).

32. James Anaya, Indigenous Peoples in International Law 184 (1996).

33. Barbara Bennett Woodhouse, *Protecting Children's Rights of Identity across Frontiers of Culture, Political Community, and Time*, in Families across Frontiers 260 (Nigel Lowe and Gillian Douglas, eds., 1996).

34. *Id.* at 269.

35. *Id.* at 262.

36. Barbara Bennett Woodhouse, *"Are You My Mother?" Conceptualizing Children's Identity Rights in Transracial Adoptions*, 2 Duke Journal of Gender Law and Policy 108 (1995).

37. *Id.* at 114–29.

38. *Id.* at 273–74.

39. *Id.*

40. Donna Goldsmith, *Individual vs. Collective Rights: The Indian Child Welfare Act*, 13 Harvard Women's Law Journal 1, 10 (1990).

29

Transracial and International Adoption: Mothers, Hierarchy, Race, and Feminist Legal Theory

Twila L. Perry

. . .

[A] feminist analysis of adoption must view adoption as more than an individual transaction in which one or two adults legally become the parent or parents of a particular child. Just as feminists view marriage as an institution warranting an analysis that goes beyond individual couples, adoption must be approached with a similarly broad perspective. Adoption, like marriage, involves issues of hierarchy and power; unlike marriage, however, adoption involves these issues among women. These issues must be retrieved from the background, where they have existed largely in silence, and must be confronted in the open.

Because my focus is on issues of hierarchy and privilege, I have chosen to place Black women, other women of color, and poor women at the center, rather than at the margin of my analysis. . . . In placing poor women of color at the center, I argue that a feminist analyzing adoption must take into account the political and economic circumstances in which parenting takes place and the difficulties that often lead to the surrender of children. It requires taking into account the political and cultural meaning of motherhood and it must confront the possibility that women from minority groups may have ambivalent or negative feelings about transracial or international adoptions. A feminist analysis must consider the past and present effects of racism, capitalism, colonialism, neocolonialism, and patriarchy, and recognize that elimination of racism, patriarchy, and poverty would likely diminish the availability of adoptable children. Ultimately, a feminist approach should have the goal of working toward a world in which the choice of women to place their children for adoption is not dictated by oppressive circumstances.

. . .

Prior to World War II, adoption was not a common event among whites in America. A child born out of wedlock was considered a "child of sin" and the product of a genetically flawed, mentally deficient mother. The child was considered tainted and undesirable, and the mother was expected to raise the child herself, with both the mother and child marginalized and stigmatized by society.

After World War II, when more and more Americans sought to adopt children, and white newborns became scarce, the white, unwed mother was transformed in public consciousness from a genetically tainted individual to a person who happened to be psychologically maladjusted and was therefore unsuited to raise her own child. Society erased the stigma that white newborns previously carried and they became marketable commodities.

. . .

The history of adoption among Blacks is different from that of whites. During and after slavery, Black children orphaned by the sale or death of their parents were often taken in by the families of slaves or former slaves—among Blacks, informal adoption has a very long history. At the same time, relinquishment of children for adoption because of birth outside marriage has been rare. For many years the formal adoption system utilized criteria for adoption that excluded most Black families. Also, although birth within marriage may have been considered the ideal, because of the rape and sexual exploitation of Black women by their white masters during slavery, historically Black children born out of wedlock have never been stigmatized in the same way as the children of white women. As sociologist Joyce Ladner has observed, the Black child born out of wedlock was considered a child who had a right to live in the community without stigmatization.

. . .

Black Women and Transracial Adoption

Race is a factor that affects the experiences of Black women and white women in very significant ways. Racial differences can be found in the experiences of women in terms of employment, income, and economic status, the statistical chances of being married or divorced, and access to health services, among other areas of life. Not surprisingly, the experiences of Black women frequently lead them to have different perceptions of the society than those that might be held by women who are white.

. . .

There are probably many reasons why Black women often appear to be ambivalent or even hostile toward transracial adoption. Some of the reasons certainly involve perceptions about the needs of individual Black children—there is skepticism about whether white women can provide Black children with the skills they need to survive in a racist society. Some Black women may also feel that white women often raise white children with a sense of superiority over Blacks and that they will naturally raise Black transracially adopted children to feel the same way. Some Black women may simply believe that white people cannot love a Black child the same way they would love a white one. They understand that however precious Black children may be to Black people, for many whites seeking to adopt, a Black child is a second, third, or last choice, behind children that are white, Asian, or Hispanic. Some Black women are quite critical of the mothering skills displayed by white mothers with respect to their own children, and thus view arguments of some advocates of transracial adoption that white families may be able to parent Black children better than Black families with amused contempt. Others may be concerned that white women are interested in adopting Black children to fulfill their own desires to parent, but have no interest in the condition of Black children in general or in conditions that threaten the stability of so many Black families.

I offer two additional explanations for the feelings some Black women may have toward transracial adoption—feelings unrelated to concerns about the competence of white women to raise Black children. I argue that many Black women feel that arguments in favor of transracial adoption that minimize the role of race in parenting devalue an important part of what motherhood means to them—a historical and contemporary struggle to raise Black children successfully in a racist world. In addition, many Black women may also resent transracial adoption because they see it as part of a larger system of racial hierarchy and privilege that advantages white women while it devalues and subordinates women of color.

. . .

Mothering Children in a Racist Society

Because women play a dominant role in caring for children, a subtext in the debate over transracial adoption involves the issue of mothering. Thus, a question underlying the debate about giving Black children "survival skills" is: [W]ho is qualified to mother children in a society that even the advocates of transracial adoption admit is racist? It is interesting that there are ways in which this issue is discussed, and ways in which it is not discussed. . . . [S]ociety's perceptions of the competence of women to mother children is intricately tied to the racial hierarchies among women in this society and these perceptions are reflected in the controversy concerning transracial adoption. All too often, Black women are seen as inadequate to the task of mothering Black children, while white women are seen as competent to raise children of any race.

I view this racial hierarchy among mothers as having a number of troubling ramifications. First, if society values the mothering of some women more than it values the mothering of others, the separation of the devalued mother from her children is less likely to be a cause of concern. Indeed, children transferred from devalued women to valued women are deemed to have received a lucky break. Second, women who know that they are devalued as mothers are likely to resent a pattern of adoption in which children from their group are always transferred to the women of higher status. Finally, the perception of the more valued group of women as competent to mother all children may deflect other important inquiries. In the context of the controversy over transracial adoption, assumptions about the ability of white women to mother Black children avoid a different inquiry about mothering, race, and racism that deserves attention.

. . . I identify four different racial combinations of mothers and children. . . . [P]erceptions of the adequacy of mothering in these different contexts reflects the racial hierarchy that exists in this society and is reflected in the transracial adoption controversy. . . .

A. Black Women Mothering Black Children in a Racist Society

The idea that Black parents must teach Black children how to survive in a racist society was not invented in response to the controversy over transracial adoption. Instead, this view represents the acknowledgment by many Black people of a long history of struggle to ensure that Black children are able to survive physically and emotionally in a racially hostile world. Many Blacks would agree that Black parents face unique challenges in raising Black children, and they celebrate the fact that generations of Black children have been successfully raised against the odds.

However, white society's view of Black women mothering Black children is often at odds with this perspective. A number of scholars have written extensively about society's devaluation of Black mothers, noting the widespread stereotypes of the emasculating matriarch, the lazy welfare mother, and the licentious Jezebel. In recent conservative discourse, Black mothers are portrayed as raising a future generation of welfare cheats, violent criminals, and absent fathers.

. . . [T]he mothering of Black children by Black women has been devalued in both the public and the legal discourse surrounding transracial adoption. The media frequently presents the public with scenarios in which screaming, crying Black children are ripped from the arms of loving white foster parents who want to adopt them only to be returned to out of control, drug-addicted Black mothers destined to abuse, or even kill them. Some legal scholarship advocating transracial adoption incorporates and reifies this approach to promote the argument that the use of race as a factor in adoption is harmful to Black children.
. . .

Although Black women may often see themselves as successfully mothering against the odds, this is often not the perception of the larger society. The legal discourses on both foster care and transracial adoption . . . are examples of a widespread negative view of the competence of Black mothers in raising Black children.

B. Black Women Mothering White Children in a Racist Society

. . . Black women have long worked as domestics and nannies for white families. The image of a Black woman as the caretaker of white children is a part of the story of America portrayed on television, in the movies, and in literature. It is also, unfortunately, a part of the reality of America. The fact that many Black women still hold these kinds of jobs should be obvious to anyone from even the briefest observation of playgrounds in many upper or upper-middle class neighborhoods.

Women who work as nannies clearly serve a mothering function. The nanny's job is to provide the children in her charge with affection, discipline, and physical care. In many instances, a nanny may, in effect, raise the children in the employer's family, and this may be particularly true where both parents work at demanding, time consuming jobs. It would not be unfair or inaccurate, then, to say that there are many white children who, essentially, have been raised by Black women.

However, the relationship of a nanny to the children in her care is not a legal one. A nanny has neither the legal rights nor the social status that society accords to a child's own mother. Indeed, the relationship between the nanny and the children in her care can be severed at any time by the woman who wields the real power in this context—the child's mother, who is the nanny's employer. The nanny thus has no legal rights with respect to a child with whom she may have developed strong emotional bonds. It is interesting then, that although many Black women have functionally served as the mothers of white children, the idea of a Black woman raising a white child as an adoptive mother is one that is seldom explored in the literature on transracial adoption, even for the limited purpose of exploring perceptions about race and parenthood. The mere contemplation of such a scenario seems to exceed our cultural imagination.

. . .

[T]ransracial adoption is, in practicality and also in conception, a one-way street. The mothering of a white child by a Black woman is seen as acceptable, perhaps even desirable, as long as the Black woman occupies the subordinate position of domestic servant. It is far more difficult for many whites to imagine what it would mean for a Black women to mother a white child in a racist society, not as a nanny, but on an equal status to a white woman—as a bona fide legal adoptive mother.

C. White Women Mothering Black Children in a Racist Society

In support of their argument that white adults can effectively raise Black children in a racist society, advocates of transracial adoption sometimes rely on the work of researchers on transracially adopted children who seem to unanimously conclude that transracial adoption is not detrimental to Black children. Another argument that has been advanced is that transracial adoption cannot be detrimental to Black children because many white women have successfully mothered Black children who are their biological children as the result of interracial marriages or relationships.

America has had a long history of thinking of biracial individuals as "tragic mulattos," people painfully caught between the white world and the Black world, and not fully accepted by either. . . . No longer seen as tragic misfits, biracial people are now seen by some as being on the cutting edge of the evolution of a rich, multicultural society.

Psychologists have challenged the earlier, negative image of biracial people and have argued instead that the lives of such individuals, although complex, can be rich and satisfying. . . .

The skills of white women in mothering Black children in a racist society continue to be the subject of inquiry and discussion. Relatively speaking, it is still a rare phenomenon. Certainly there are white women who have successfully mothered Black children. Moreover, all children who are considered Black in this society must learn to negotiate the question of race if they are to succeed, whether their mothers are white or Black. The focus in this discussion is not on the question of whether or not white mothers actually are or are not competent to raise Black children. Rather this discussion addresses the question of society's perceptions of mothers of different races, and it does seem clear that there is no widespread assumption that white women are not up to the task of mothering Black children, whether adopted or not. Certainly the world faced by white women and their biracial children is a different one, and a more tolerant one, than that confronted by Black women and their biracial children in earlier times. Still, the positive images of white women raising Black children can be contrasted to the view of many in this society that any problems Black children may have are the fault of the Black mothers who have raised them.

D. White Women Mothering White Children in a Racist Society

It is interesting that the question of what it means to raise children in a racist society is generally raised in the context of discussions about the rearing of Black children or other children of color. Black mothers, and indeed, Black fathers, are constantly put on the defensive. Advocates of transracial adoption argue that white parents are able to give Black children a healthy racial identity and the skills they need to survive in a racist society. At the same time, very little attention is given to the question of what it means to raise white children in a racist society. The assumption seems to be that race is not an important issue in the rearing of white children. Given caring parents who love them and who are willing to make the expected parental sacrifices, white children are expected to take their places of privilege within the status quo and thrive.

The question posed by the controversy over "survival skills"—the ability of white parents to give Black children the tools to cope with a racist society—is an important one. However, there is a more important question that needs to be addressed. What does it mean for white women to mother white children in a racist society? If race is a factor when Black women raise Black children, is race also not a factor when white women raise white children? Is mothering in America ever colorblind? In making the argument that white parents can raise Black children with a healthy racial identity, the question is often asked as to what it means to have a Black identity and how such an identity is acquired. But we also need to ask: What is a white identity and how is it acquired?

. . .

Although people may derive their racial identities from a variety of sources, parents clearly must play some significant role in their development. In examining the question of how white children acquire a white identity, feminists must be willing not only to engage in theoretical discussions about the welfare of children and the need for social justice, but also to examine their own lives and to reflect on the choices they make that influence their own children's development of a racial identity and racial consciousness. Obvious issues include decisions about neighborhoods, schools, and personal social relationships. For white feminists committed to social change, the question is whether it is enough to have the goal of simply raising a "well adjusted" individual who can assume his or her place of racial privilege by becoming a doctor, lawyer, or other professional person, or whether the goal in raising a white child in a racist society is to nurture the kind of person who will see racism as a problem he or she has a commitment to address.

Perhaps there should be less concern about whether white mothers can teach Black children about what it means to be Black and more concern about what white mothers teach white children about what it means to be white. And finally, if we are willing to question the skills of white mothers in imparting ideas about race and racial justice to children who are white, why should we assume that they can do this effectively with children who are Black? This slant on the "survival skills" issue warrants further discussion by the advocates of transracial adoption.

. . .

The Links of Poverty, Racism, and Patriarchy

There are important links to be drawn between the transracial adoption of Black children in the United States and the adoption of children of color from Asia and Latin America. The factors of racism and economic discrimination that result in large numbers of Black children being separated from their biological parents in this country have counterparts in the international context, where a history of colonialism, neocolonialism, cultural imperialism, and economic exploitation often results in mothers being unable to keep the children to whom they have given birth. Thus, both domestically and internationally, transracial and international adoption often result in a pattern in which there is the transfer of children from the least advantaged women to the most advantaged women. Despite the differences between the specific circumstances of Black women in America and some other third world women, there is a connection in terms of a struggle by both to function as mothers under political and economic conditions which severely challenge their ability to adequately parent their own children. Moreover, many transracial adoptions, international adoptions, and adoptions in which racial and ethnic differences are not a factor, also share another connection—a link to the institution of patriarchy. Because poverty, racism, and patriarchy are often factors when children become available for adoption, consideration of each of them is essential to the development of a feminist approach to adoption.

. . .

In the domestic context, a feminist analysis of adoption must conceptualize adoption as more than either an individual act of altruism or the fulfillment of individual desires to parent. Most importantly, an analysis that focuses on issues of race and class should lead to an understanding that the interests of individual Black children cannot be separated from the conditions that Black children as a whole face in this society. It means a commitment to better the lives of Black children as a whole in order to decrease the kind of family disruption that results in disproportionate numbers of children being placed in foster care and having their legal relationships with their parents involuntarily terminated. This goal, rather than a simple focus on the narrow goal of providing white adoptive homes for a small number of children, must merit a higher place on the agenda.

. . .

In thinking about international adoption, I do not contend that American women alone have the power to change the complex circumstances that result in so many children needing homes. These circumstances stem from a complex mix of history, economics, patriarchy, and racism that has roots going back many centuries, and they admit of no easy solution. I do believe, however, that a feminist analysis must consist of more than the simple willingness to adopt the children of women who cannot care for them. Instead, there must be some acknowledgment that a Western woman's happiness in transacting an adoption may have been built upon a third world woman's misery, and this must lead to some commitment to change the conditions that have created that state of affairs.

What might be the benefits of thinking about transracial and international adoption in this kind of a wider context? First of all, it might lead to action to improve the lives of children of color, both in this country and in some of the foreign countries from which many internationally adopted children come. Secondly, the demonstration of concern about the groups and societies from which adopted children come might diminish some of the reservations that women of color in this country and third world countries sometimes express about the white, Western feminist movement not appearing interested in the problems faced by poor women of color. Any resulting improvement in solidarity between women, both worldwide and in this country, could increase the power of women to address a wide range of issues. . . .

> Feminism is the political theory and practice that struggles to free all women: women of color, working class women, poor women, disabled women, lesbians, old women— as well as white, economically privileged heterosexual women. Anything less than this vision of total freedom is not feminism, but merely female self-aggrandizement.[1]

. . .

NOTE

1. Barbara Smith, *Racism and Women's Studies*, in All the Women Are White, All the Blacks Are Men but Some of Us Are Brave 48, 49 (Gloria T. Hull et al., eds., 1982).

30

Gender Matters: Implications for Clinical Research and Women's Health Care

Karen H. Rothenberg

. . .

Gender Bias: Realities and Reasons

. . .

For the most part, the lack of knowledge about women's health has resulted from our failure to research women's health issues. Commentators point to the reinforcement of gender attitudes and the history of protectionism that have led to current gaps in medical knowledge. Several notions associated with gender have contributed to the systematic exclusion of women from clinical research. These factors include the perception of men as the "norm," the idea that hormonal differences in women will "complicate" research results and increase costs, the traditional role of women, and the primarily male-dominated research community. For pregnant women, these barriers are also entangled with potential risks to the fetus and the associated liability that might follow.

Science has a long history of viewing men as the standard by which all things are measured. "Like the pronoun 'he,' it was taken for granted that the white male subject stood for all of us."[1] Because the research community views men as the norm, they see differences in women as unknown variables that tend to confound results. For example, women present factors such as menstrual cycles, pregnancy, teratogenic liability, and menopause. Some researchers argue that these factors complicate research and add excess costs to experimentation. Paradoxically, "scientists seem to be confirming that women's bodies are different and more difficult to study. But then by simply extending their male-drawn conclusions to women, they are implying that—with a few obvious exceptions—women's bodies are the same as men's."[2] These assumptions have discouraged studies on females and have fostered ignorance concerning the special needs of women.

The perception of the middle-aged white male as the normal economic distributor and an emphasis on the economic costs of health care also may have led to this disproportionate concern for the health of men. In addition to outnumbering women in positions of political influence, men also dominate in the medical research community. Although the proportion of women in medical schools has risen steadily in the last decade to approximately 40 percent, women still constitute a minority of medical researchers and a small percentage of those making funding decisions. Naturally, policymakers and researchers prioritize issues according to their most personal interests. As a result, women's concerns, as well as the underlying variables of race, ethnicity, socioeconomic status, and sexual orientation, have not been given the attention they deserve. Because men dominate the decisionmaking community, the social worth judgments of how to allocate funds also favor research on men.

The Public Health Task Force on Women's Health Issues concluded that many methodological problems, as well as lack of data, limit the ability to understand the status of women's health and women's particular health care needs. In study after study of health issues important to women, women have been excluded or seriously underrepresented.

A. Gender Gaps in Clinical Research

Perhaps the most shocking example of the exclusion of women from the clinical study of a health condition that almost exclusively affects women was a project that examined the impact of obesity on breast and uterine cancer. The study participants were all men. For twenty years, women were also excluded from the Baltimore Longitudinal Study of Aging, one of the largest studies of the natural process of aging. Six years after women were permitted to participate, a report of the study findings entitled "Normal Human Aging" was published. It is considered the definitive study of aging in the United States. It contains no data on women.

Women were also frequently left out of clinical trials of experimental AIDS therapies, yet women now represent the fastest growing population with AIDS. Of the 28 trials of drugs designed to fight HIV, only 131 of 2,634 participants were women. In addition, when the FDA approved AZT in 1987, not one of the 63 federally sponsored studies had analyzed its effects on women.

The effects of exclusion from clinical research are far reaching. All women suffer the consequences of studies that include only men, or that include women, but do not adequately analyze any gender-related differences. Because of the research gap, "physicians now frequently lack adequate evidence on whether women . . . will be helped, harmed, or not affected at all by numerous therapies now endorsed as promoting 'human health.'"[3]

. . .

Several well-known studies of cardiovascular disease considered only male subjects. Although they have had a significant impact on the treatment and prevention of heart disease in men, these studies have not produced definitive information about prevention and treatment of women's heart disease. In fact, the lack of research on women's health and gender-blind health conditions in women may have a dangerous effect. Based on the findings of studies of heart disease and cholesterol that included men only, the American Heart Association recommended a diet that could actually elevate the risk of heart disease for women. . . .

In 1988, the results of a government funded study of 20,000 male physicians revealed that small doses of aspirin would help prevent heart attacks. Physicians were thought to be the ideal subjects, knowledgeable and disciplined, and able to comply with complicated research protocols. Women, who comprised 10 percent of physicians in the United States at the time, were excluded from the study. Nurses, the vast majority of whom were women, apparently weren't considered up to the task.

B. Gender Disparities in Clinical Decisionmaking

Gender bias extends beyond clinical research into all areas of health care: "[I]t pervades medicine, beginning with medical-school admissions and education, encompassing research facilities and medical journals, and culminating in how women are treated as patients in clinics, hospitals, and physicians' offices across the country."[4] For example, men are more likely to be referred for diagnostic testing for lung cancer than women, even where risk factors are equal between the two genders. Women in need of kidney dialysis are approximately 30 percent less likely to receive a transplant than men. Men are 6.5 times more likely to be referred for cardiac catheterization than women. At the same time, 26 percent of men versus 14 percent of women receive clot-dissolving drugs after a heart attack. Further, another study indicated that physicians are twice as likely to attribute symptoms of heart disease in women to psychiatric and noncardiac causes.

With respect to AIDS, it was not until 1993 that the Centers for Disease Control (CDC) amended its presumptive definition of AIDS to include those manifestations most common in women, i.e., cervical cancer, pelvic inflammatory disease, and vaginal yeast infections. After the change, thousands more women were classified as having AIDS. Even after being diagnosed and entering treatment, women still receive fewer services than men. For example, a male injection drug user (IDU) with AIDS is 20 percent more likely to be hospitalized than a woman with AIDS, and then the hospital costs of treating a male IDU with AIDS are over $9,000 more per year than the hospital care costs of treating a woman with AIDS. . . .

C. The Role of Gender in the Physician-Patient Relationship

Bias has also been reported in studies that evaluate the relationship between the gender of a physician and the offering of gender-sensitive diagnostic practices, such as breast exams, pap smears, and mammograms. Women who reported having a male physician as their usual provider were less likely to receive pap tests and mammograms than women who reported having a female physician as their usual care provider. There was a similar but insignificant trend for breast exams. These results persisted after "multivariate adjustment for patient age, race, education, income, insurance status, subjective health status, other health behaviors, and attitudes toward health care and health insurance."[5]

In another study, rates of pap smears and mammograms ordered were consistently higher for female physicians than for male physicians. The difference was particularly significant between physicians in internal medicine and family practice. Women physicians may be more likely to exercise greater diligence in initially and repeatedly offering screening tests. They also may communicate the risk of cancer more effectively. Women patients may be more likely to follow through in obtaining tests suggested by women physicians because they are more comfortable discussing issues of concern with female physicians.

. . . Because communication is the fundamental instrument by which physician and patient relate to each other and attempt to achieve therapeutic goals, the relationship between physician and patient is central to the process of health care delivery. Physicians must promote trust—they must hear the patient's story.

As one author has observed, "[I]nstitutional authority of the physician and acquiescence to that authority by the patient, fostered frequently by gender expectations, can make it difficult for patients to assert their informational needs."[6] For example, women who believe they have serious diseases may present their worries in a vague manner in an effort to avoid being labeled hypochondriacs.

The most difficult physician-patient relationships tend to be between male physicians and female patients. Some research has shown that male physicians may discourage information exchange with female patients. For example, compared to male physicians, female physicians engage in significantly more positive talk, partnership-building, question-asking, and information-giving. Similarly, when with female physicians, patients talk more during the medical visit and appear to participate more actively in the medical dialogue. The longest visits are between female physicians and female patients and the shortest between male physicians and female patients.

Both male and female patients are more willing to disclose symptoms to a physician of the same sex than to a physician of opposite sex. Research has shown that female-female interactions are characterized by fewer interruptions of patients by physicians. Fear and embarrassment may in fact be further barriers to health care, especially among special population groups, including low income Blacks, hispanics, and women over 50.

A few recent studies have, in fact, surveyed women's attitudes about physician-patient communication. In the 1993 Commonwealth Fund study of over 2,500 women and 1,000 men, 1 out of 4 women (compared to 12 percent of men) said that they had been "talked down to" or treated like a child by their physician. Nearly 1 out of 5 women (compared to 7 percent of men) had been told that a reported medical condition was "all in (your) head."

A recent Gallup survey of 833 women aged 45–60 found that the physical and emotional effects of menopause most frequently cited as the greatest concerns were osteoporosis, emotional well-being, and heart disease. Of the women who reported these conditions, only about half said their physicians had discussed emotional symptoms or heart disease with them, while two-thirds said that their physicians had discussed osteoporosis. Instead, physicians were more likely to discuss short-term physical symptoms such as hot flashes and night sweats.

Communication barriers may be of particular concern to the older female population. In addition to sensory losses and concerns about the use of medical jargon, psychosocial factors were a major concern. Older women may fear being labeled as a nuisance, hypochondriac, or "crabby old woman." Many older women report being intimidated by doctors and consider them as god-like entities who are busy with important matters and should not be bothered with their trivial aches and pains. Older women may feel particularly timid about private or embarrassing information and are likely to accept poorly communicated explanations, believing they are the ones who are at fault.

In another study, health care professionals' impressions of women with cancer were compared with their impressions of women with other serious diseases. All the professionals thought they would feel more tense treating a woman who had been diagnosed with breast cancer or lung cancer or who had been burned severely than a woman who had experienced a heart attack. The study also examined how different categories of health care professions perceive emotional issues surrounding serious illness. It concluded that nurses and psychologists perceived more need for psychological counseling than did physicians.

In the context of contraception and reproductive health, the contrast becomes clear between the provider's biomedical assumptions based on physiological orientation and the woman's contextual understandings based on knowledge of their social lives. Of even more importance is that medical dominance over the parameters of interaction produces inadequate communication, which in turn leads to inadequate medical care. Physicians may cut off women when they try to raise topics that are not directly medical in nature. Women come to physicians for help and understanding on how to adjust their bodies to their social lives, whereas the medical model assumes that women should adjust their social lives to their bodies.

Gender differences may be further compounded by the dependency and inequality inherent in the provider-patient relationship. When the power between the parties is unequally distributed, effective participation is undermined and control of the ultimate decision is minimized. Without power, patients cannot give effect to their own values without difficulty, whether on a personal, cultural, religious, or otherwise group-defined basis. When patients find themselves unable to control decisionmaking, the likelihood increases that unwanted risks may be imposed on them.

Ironically, all this medical attention may harm women, as evidenced by recent concerns about high rates of hysterectomies and cesarean sections. In the area of mental health, women are consistently treated more frequently and more aggressively than men. For example, numerous studies conducted over the last 20 years have shown that when men and women present the same physical or emotional complaints, women are significantly more likely to receive antidepressants, tranquilizers, and other psychotropic drugs.

In fact, women do use health services more than men. Nevertheless, the effects of gender on the doctor-patient relationship may undermine the value of the health care they receive. Even though women use more health services and report more symptoms, we still do not know whether women and men seeking health care differ in the number or types of symptoms they disclose to the physician. Women may ask more questions, but we do not know why. It could be attributed to greater exposure to sources of health information, to greater acceptance of health-seeking roles, or to less clear information women receive from their physicians.

. . .

All of these gender-based obstacles increase exponentially for pregnant women, who face the added consideration of balancing their own health needs with associated risks to the fetus. Society has created the expectation that a woman must always place the well-being of her child before all other concerns. Thus, the pregnant woman bears the highest moral, ethical, and legal responsibilities to her fetus. Furthermore, society may stigmatize a woman who does not make an "acceptable" decision concerning her own health and its relation to that of the fetus. . . .

By establishing protectionist policies in clinical research and health care, society has wrested the decisionmaking power away from women and reinforced the pregnant woman's obligation to conform to social expectations concerning traditional gender roles. In essence, protectionism devalues women as individuals and characterizes them as vulnerable vessels of reproduction, incapable of making the correct choices concerning their health and that of their own offspring. It is this premise, in fact, that puts into context the evolution of regulatory barriers that excluded women from clinical research.

. . .

NOTES

1. Rebecca Dresser, *Wanted: Single, White Male for Medical Research*, 22 Hastings Center Reporter 24, 24 (1992).

2. Leslie Laurence and Beth Weinhouse, Outrageous Practices: The Alarming Truth about How Medicine Mistreats Women 4 (1994).

3. Dresser, *supra* note 1, at 24.

4. Laurence, *supra* note 2, at 5.

5. Peter Franks and Carolyn M. Clancy, *Physician Gender Bias in Clinical Decisionmaking: Screening for Cancer in Primary Care*, 31 Medical Care 213, 213 (1993).

6. M. Robin DiMatteo, *The Physician-Patient Relationship: Effects on the Quality of Health Care*, 37 Clinical Obstetrics and Gynecology 149, 153 (1994).

31

The Fuzzy Logic of Race and Gender in the Mismeasure of Asian American Women's Health Needs

Lisa C. Ikemoto

. . .

Gender and Race as Important Categories

The standard methods of measuring health acknowledge that gender and race are important categories of assessment. A first step in the logic of health assessment starts from the premise that gender and race are important categories of assessment. For example, federal and state government health status reports provide gender- and race-specific data on birth, fertility, death, disease, and injury rates. Race and gender have long been used as standard categories in measuring health, explicitly as physical descriptors and implicitly as means of reinforcing, privileging, and subordinating race- and gender-based norms. In 1985, the federal government seemed to acknowledge that gender and race were not simply categories of physical description, but categories drawn by the operation of racialized and gendered norms and practices that, in turn, interact with health. In that year, two events occurred. The Public Health Service Task Force on Women's Health Issues reported that the dearth of research data on women restricted the understanding of women's health needs. In addition, the Task Force on Black and Minority Health issued its report, which echoed the report on Women's Health Issues by identifying the lack of data, the lack of racial minorities in health care, and other biases that contribute to disparities in access and quality of care. In both instances, it seemed clear that the problem—the lack of information and, therefore, the inability to adequately address the health needs of gender and racial minorities—arose from biases operating at the social, political, and economic level. This moment provided an opportunity to change the use of race and gender in measuring health.

. . .

B. The Standard and the Deviation

Acknowledging the links between race, gender, and health care can, but does not necessarily, lead to a more equitable distribution of health care. In part, the reason for this depends on the distinction between efforts that use race and gender solely as categories of difference and efforts that are race- and gender-conscious. Using race and gender solely as categories of difference tends to assume that, for health care purposes, the categories and the differences among them need only be assessed in biological terms. Therefore, race- and gender-specific health assessment does not consistently take social and political context into account. For example, government reports do not coordinate health and class data. Most of the efforts to address race- and gender-linked variations in health status and health care use race and gender solely as categories of biological difference.

Built into the premise that race and gender are important categories are the paired assumptions that race categories and gender categories are mutually exclusive and that the necessary information derives from comparing the health status and the needs of different groups. These assumptions are necessarily paired in the logic of exclusion by the implicit use of white men as the normative standard in the comparisons.

. . .

The fact that white males are the point of comparison in health data puts the status and the needs of this group at the center of attention. Even if the justification for using the white male category as the norm is apparently neutral—white males form the numerically largest population—the racialized and gendered content of the comparisons perpetuates the acceptability of a race and gender hierarchy. In addition, the arrangement of the data may encourage the use of majoritarianism in health policy making. . . . The fact that the message is expressed as empirical data, which is presumptively neutral in the social construction of knowledge, gives the message greater weight.

. . .

In contrast to efforts using race and gender as points of difference, race- and gender-conscious health care efforts use contextualized understandings of those categories. That is, these efforts take the social and political significance of race and gender into account; they perceive race and gender as operatively linked with, for example, income and wealth. In their most effective forms, these efforts also acknowledge the following: (1) race and gender categories are socially constructed and, therefore, are dynamic; (2) these categories are complex so that, for example, efforts must take ethnicity as well as race into account; and (3) the experiences and perspectives of the people in these categories must direct the assessment and the care. Not surprisingly, most of the race- and gender-conscious health efforts are being made at the community level where there is the least funding, where top-level policy decisions have the most harmful impact, and where there is the least reciprocal influence.

. . .

IV. Outside the Measured Boundaries

A. Expanding the Categories

Measuring efforts that provide a useful understanding of health must acknowledge that health status is as complex as the people being measured and that health status is interactive. Health status cannot be fully or accurately measured by comparing race and gender groups on the basis of biological variability alone. As the preceding discussion indicates, the limitations on reaching a full understanding of Asian Pacific American women's health have been multiple. These limitations are linked primarily by flattened, but shifting, definitions of race and gender. These limitations include defining race and gender as biological categories, comparing these categories using the white male as the naturalized norm, addressing the health concerns of women and of people of color with separate efforts, using the two-sided oppositional white and Black paradigm for racial difference with the result that race means Black and that Latino and Asian Pacific American fall into the totalizing Other category, and using the claims of statistical insignificance or model minority to justify exclusion.

Recent efforts, such as those reflected in the passage of the Disadvantaged Minority Health Act, have begun to shift the way we measure health. When the National Center for Health Statistics began collecting ethnic specific data, it used race codes for Chinese, Japanese, Hawaiian, Filipino, other Asian and Pacific Islander, and other races. The National Center for Health Statistics has begun to collect data for the race categories used in the 1990 Census; therefore, Asian Indian, Korean, Vietnamese, Cambodian, Hmong, Laotian, Thai, Indonesian, Pakistani, Samoan, Tongan, Guamanian, and Melanesian have been added to the list. However, data are coded for this longer list of categories for only a few health issues. Additional race and health categories have been added as funding has become available. However, the expanded list of categories is not being used in most geographic regions. Thus, many Asian Pacific Americans, including Burmese, Ceylonese, Chamorro, Dutch East Indian, Fijian, Gilbertese, Javanese, Malaysian, Maori, Marshallese, and Ponapean, are still in the Other category for most health assessment purposes.

Even if data collection efforts acknowledge the ethnic heterogeneity of the Asian Pacific American communities, the information will fall short of measuring health status, particularly for Asian Pacific American women. The question of how race and gender operate within the structures of Asian Pacific American lives is critical to understanding health status in its fullest sense. Understanding health status as interactive with the operational categories of race and gender, in turn, is necessary to developing accessible and effective means of addressing health needs.

. . .

Acknowledging how race and gender interact with health means taking the lives of Asian Pacific American women into account. At a series of discussions in which Asian Pacific American women described and evaluated the links between self-identity, majority culture, and the structures in which they live, several focal points emerged—self-identity, ethnic identity, and family roles. Much of the discussion was about the cultural gaps and contradictions between these focal points and majority culture and institutions. In addition, consider the significance between health, economics, and work. Work largely determines income and access to, or exclusion from, health insurance and, therefore, access to health care. The conditions in which one works also directly affect health. Work opportunities, which are significantly formed by race and gender, provide an important point of class analysis. Accordingly, I recommend that Asian Pacific American women's health be measured in the context of the structures surrounding these focal points. Health should be examined within the structures of the individual, the community, the family, and the relevant labor markets.

Others have provided useful health assessment approaches by focusing on barriers to access. Among the barriers identified are financial barriers, including poverty levels in the Asian Pacific American communities and the fact that "Asian Pacific Americans were among the groups least likely to have access to employer-provided benefits";[1] immigration status barriers; ethnic-specific barriers formed by the failure to provide linguistically and culturally appropriate care; linguistic barriers; cultural barriers; system-wide barriers, such as lack of data; and the lack of linguistically and culturally competent providers. These assessments add essential information for understanding the health status of Asian Pacific Americans. They are useful because they point to specific, concrete changes that can be made to improve access and care.

. . .

Locating these barriers within the structures in which they operate would add several things. First, a structural approach more clearly enables a gendered analysis. It is more obvious that, within the structures of self, family, community, and work, gender plays a role. Second, a structural approach allows an analysis that exposes the connections between class, race, gender, and health. Focusing on barriers tends to describe socioeconomic issues as a category unto themselves, separate from culture, language, race, and ethnicity. Third, although identifying specific barriers leads to concrete solutions, the solutions tend to be fairly discrete in scope. They may eliminate specific effects of practices such as racism, sexism, and xenophobia, but they seldom expose larger institutional and industry practices that premise these effects. For example, disparities among Asian Pacific American women, between Asian Pacific women and men, and between Asian Pacific American women and other women result from how race, ethnicity, and gender operate in the labor market. Employers use hiring formulas based on race-, ethnic-, and gender-specific stereotypes. Industries target labor forces for exploitation based on race, gender, and ethnic stereotypes, and they do so in a way intended to maintain tension along these group lines. The transformation of the garment industry, leading to the prevalence of sweatshops, consciously relied on Asian and Latino immigrant labor. Addressing Asian American women's health within these kinds of analyses not only suggests, for example, that Asian American women may be susceptible to certain work-related injuries and illnesses, but also that addressing health means addressing problems outside the body and beyond the medical profession. Finally, . . . the structural approach shifts the presumption that the locus of knowledge and power in health care is in the medical profession. The critical knowledge is held by those whose health is at stake—Asian Pacific American women. Because the structural approach makes the operation of race, class, and gender obviously dynamic and does so in contexts in which Asian Pacific American women act, solutions considering Asian Pacific American women as actors should be more apparent.

. . .

NOTE

1. Association of Asian Pacific Community Health Organizations, Taking Action: Improving Access to Health Care for Asians and Pacific Islanders 19 (April 1995).

32

Representing Race:
Unshackling Black Motherhood

Dorothy E. Roberts

When stories about the prosecutions of women for using drugs during pregnancy first appeared in newspapers in 1989, I immediately suspected that most of the defendants were Black women. Charging someone with a crime for giving birth to a baby seemed to fit into the legacy of devaluing Black mothers. . . . My hunch turned out to be right: a memorandum prepared by the ACLU [American Civil Liberties Union] Reproductive Freedom Project documented cases brought against pregnant women as of October 1990 and revealed that thirty-two of fifty-two defendants were Black. By the middle of 1992, the number of prosecutions had increased to more than 160 in twenty-four states. About 75 percent were brought against women of color. . . . Taking race into account transformed the constitutional violation at issue. . . . [T]he problem with charging these women with fetal abuse was not that it constituted unwarranted governmental intervention into pregnant women's lifestyles—surely a losing argument considering the lifestyles of these defendants. Instead, . . . the prosecutions punished poor Black women for having babies. Critical to my argument was an examination of the historical devaluation of Black motherhood. Given this conceptualization of the issue and the historical backdrop, the real constitutional harm became clear: charging poor Black women with prenatal crimes violated their rights both to equal protection of the laws and to privacy by imposing an invidious governmental standard for childbearing. Adding the perspective of poor Black women yielded another advantage. It confirmed the importance of expanding the meaning of reproductive liberty beyond opposing state restrictions on abortion to include broader social justice concerns. . . . [A]ttorneys have successfully challenged the prosecutions of prenatal crimes in appellate courts without relying on arguments about the race of the defendants. But failing to contest society's devaluation of poor Black mothers still has negative consequences. . . . Some lawyers and feminist scholars have tried to avoid the degrading mythology about Black mothers by focusing attention on issues other than racial discrimination and by emphasizing the violation of white, middle-class women's rights. I argue, however, that we should develop strategies to contest the negative images that undergird policies that penalize Black women's childbearing.

I. The South Carolina Experiment

Despite the fact that most prosecutors renounce a punitive approach toward prenatal drug use, South Carolina continues to promote a prosecutorial campaign against pregnant crack addicts. The state bears the dubious distinction of having prosecuted the largest number of women for maternal drug use. Many of these cases arose from the collaboration of Charleston law enforcement officials and the Medical University of South Carolina (MUSC), a state hospital serving an indigent, minority population. . . . MUSC instituted the "Interagency Policy on Cocaine Abuse in Pregnancy" ("Interagency Policy"), a series of internal memos that provided for nonconsensual drug testing of pregnant patients, reporting results to the police, and the use of arrest for drug and child abuse charges as punishment or intimidation.[1] . . . The Interagency Policy resulted in the arrests of forty-two patients, all but one of whom were Black. Disregarding the sanctity of the maternity ward, the arrests more closely resembled the conduct of the state in some totalitarian regime. Police arrested some patients within days or even hours of giving birth and hauled them to jail in handcuffs and leg shackles. The handcuffs were attached to a three-inch wide leather belt that was wrapped around their stomachs. Some women were still bleeding from the delivery. One new mother complained, and was told to sit on a towel when she arrived at the jail. Another reported that she was grabbed in a chokehold and shoved into detention. At least one woman who was pregnant at the time of her arrest sat in a jail cell waiting to give birth. Lori Griffin was transported weekly from the jail to the hospital in handcuffs and leg irons for prenatal care. Three weeks after her arrest, she went into labor and was taken, still in handcuffs and shackles, to MUSC. Once at the hospital, Ms. Griffin was kept handcuffed to her bed during the entire delivery. . . .

A former slave named Lizzie Williams recounted the beating of pregnant slave women on a Mississippi cotton plantation:

> "Its seen nigger women dat was fixin' to be confined do somethin' de white folks didn't like. Dey [the white folks] would dig a hole in de ground just big 'nuff fo' her stomach, make her lie face down an whip her on de back to keep from hurtin' de child."[2]

Thinking about an expectant Black mother chained to a belt around her swollen belly to protect her unborn child, I cannot help but recall this scene from Black women's bondage. The sight of a pregnant Black woman bound in shackles is a modern-day reincarnation of the horrors of slavemasters' degrading treatment of their female chattel.

. . .

The blatant racial impact of the prosecutions can be overlooked only because it results from an institutionalized system that selects Black women for prosecution and from a deeply embedded mythology about Black mothers. These two factors make the disproportionate prosecution of Black mothers seem fair and natural, and not the result of any invidious motivation. These factors also make it more difficult to challenge the prosecutions on the basis of race. . . . Prosecutors . . . do not announce that they plan to single out poor Black women for prosecution. Rather, they rely on a process already in place that is practically guaranteed to bring these women to their attention. The methods the state uses to identify women who use drugs during pregnancy result in disproportionate reporting of poor Black women. The government's main source of information about prenatal drug use comes from hospital reports of positive infant toxicologies to child welfare authorities. This testing is implemented with greater frequency in hospitals serving poor minority communities. . . . One common criterion triggering an infant toxicology screen is the mother's failure to obtain prenatal care, a factor that correlates strongly with race and income. Worse still, many hospitals have no formal screening procedures, and rely solely on the suspicions of health care professionals. This discretion allows doctors and hospital staff to perform tests based on their stereotyped assumptions about the identity of drug addicts. . . .

Even more than a "metaphor for women's alienation from instinctual motherhood,"[3] the pregnant crack addict was the latest embodiment of the bad Black mother. The monstrous crack-smoking mother was added to the iconography of depraved Black maternity, alongside the matriarch and the welfare queen. For centuries, a popular mythology has degraded Black women and portrayed them as less deserving of motherhood. Slave owners forced slave women to perform strenuous labor that contradicted the Victorian female roles prevalent in the dominant white society. One of the most prevalent images of slave women was the character of Jezebel, a woman governed by her sexual desires, which legitimated white men's sexual abuse of Black women. The stereotype of Black women as sexually promiscuous helped to perpetuate their devaluation as mothers. This devaluation of Black motherhood has been reinforced by stereotypes that blame Black mothers for the problems of the Black family, such as the myth of the Black matriarch—the domineering female head of the Black family. White sociologists have held Black matriarchs responsible for the disintegration of the Black family and the consequent failure of Black people to achieve success in America. Daniel Patrick Moynihan popularized this theory in his 1965 report, The Negro Family: The Case for National Action, which claimed, "At the heart of the deterioration of the fabric of Negro society is the deterioration of the Negro family."[4] Moynihan blamed domineering Black mothers for the demise of their families, arguing that "the Negro community has been forced into a matriarchal structure which, because it is so out of line with the rest of the American society, seriously retards the progress of the group as a whole."[5] The myth of the Black Jezebel has been supplemented by the contemporary image of the lazy welfare mother who breeds children at the expense of taxpayers in order to increase the amount of her welfare check. This view of Black motherhood provides the rationale for society's restrictions on Black female fertility. It is this image of the undeserving Black mother that also ultimately underlies the government's choice to punish crack-addicted women.

The frightening portrait of diabolical pregnant crack addicts and irreparably damaged crack babies was based on data that have drawn criticism within the scientific community. The data on the extent and severity of crack's impact on babies are highly controversial. At the inception of the crisis numerous medical journals reported that babies born to crack-addicted mothers suffered a variety of medical, developmental, and behavioral problems. More recent analyses, however, have isolated the methodological flaws of these earlier studies. The initial results were made unreliable by the lack of controls and the selection of poor, inner-city subjects at high risk for unhealthy pregnancies. Maternal crack use often contributes to underweight and premature births. This fact alone is reason for concern. But many of the problems seen in crack-exposed babies are just as likely to have been caused by other risk factors associated with their mothers' crack use, such as malnutrition, cigarettes, alcohol, physical abuse, and inadequate health care. Researchers cannot determine authoritatively which of this array of hazards actually caused the terrible outcomes they originally attributed to crack, or the percentage of infants exposed to crack in the womb who actually experience these consequences. In addition, the claim that prenatal crack use causes irreparable neurological damage leading to behavioral problems has not been fully substantiated. An article by a team of research physicians concluded that "available evidence from the newborn period is far too slim and fragmented to allow any clear predictions about the effects of intrauterine exposure to cocaine on the course and outcome of child growth and development."[6]

The medical community's one-sided attention to studies showing detrimental results from cocaine exposure added to the public's misperception of the risks of maternal crack use. For a long time, journals tended to accept for publication only studies that supported the dominant view of fetal harm. Research that reported no adverse effects was published with less frequency, even though it was often more reliable. The point is not that crack use during pregnancy is safe, but that the media exaggerated the extent and nature of the harm it causes. News reports erroneously suggested, moreover, that the problem of maternal drug use was confined to the Black community. A public health crisis that cuts across racial and economic lines was transformed into an example of Black mothers' depravity that warranted harsh punishment.

. . .

The best approach for improving the health of crack-exposed infants, then, is to improve the health of their mothers by ensuring their access to health care and drug treatment services. Yet prosecuting crack-addicted mothers does just the opposite: it drives these women away from these services out of fear of being reported to law enforcement authorities. This result reinforces the conclusion that punitive policies are based on resentment toward Black mothers, rather than on a real concern for the health of their children. The medical profession's new information regarding the risks of prenatal crack exposure has had little impact on the public's perception of the "epidemic." The image of the crack baby—trembling in a tiny hospital bed, permanently brain damaged, and on his way to becoming a parasitic criminal—seems indelibly etched in the American psyche. It will be hard to convince most Americans that the caricature of the crack baby rests on hotly contested data.

IV. Strategies for Unshackling Black Motherhood

Given the mountain of structural and ideological hurdles that pregnant crack addicts must surmount, their attorneys have a difficult task in presenting them as sympathetic parties. One strategy in opposing a punitive approach to prenatal drug use is to divert attention away from these women and the devaluing racial images that degrade them.

. . .

Attorneys and scholars have suggested three alternative [ways] . . . to replace attention to the racial images that make their clients so unpopular—concern for the health of the babies exposed to prenatal drug use, the potential expansion of state interference in pregnant women's conduct, and claims of middle-class white women who have been prosecuted for using drugs during pregnancy.

. . .

One of the greatest assets on the defendants' side is the opinion of major medical and public health organizations about the health risks created by the prosecution of substance-abusing mothers. Most leading medical and public health organizations in the country have come out in opposition to the prosecutions for this very reason. . . .

2. The Parade of Horribles

A second avoidance tactic is to steer attention to more sympathetic middle-class white women. A common criticism of the prosecution of drug-addicted mothers is that the imposition of maternal duties will lead to punishment for less egregious conduct. Commentators have predicted government penalties for cigarette smoking, consumption of alcohol, strenuous physical activity, and failure to follow a doctor's orders. If harm to a viable fetus constitutes child abuse . . . then an endless panoply of activities could make pregnant women guilty of a crime.

. . .

3. Relying on White Women's Claims

Feminist strategists have also suggested that challenging the charges brought against white drug users will benefit Black defendants. . . . This view, while recognizing the special injury to women of color, proposes a strategy of challenging governmental intrusion in women's reproductive decisions by demonstrating how they thwart the liberties of middle-class women. Again, the rationale is that calling attention to the harm to privileged women is more likely to generate change than decrying the harm to poor minority women. It is based on the hope that the benefit of establishing a strong theory of reproductive liberty for middle-class white women will trickle down to their poor, less privileged sisters. . . .

B. Focusing on Race

. . .

1. Telling the Whole Story

The diversionary strategy might be worth the neglect of Black women's particular injuries if it presented the only feasible route to victory. Yet this tactic has other disadvantages that weaken its power to challenge policies that devalue Black childbearing. By diverting attention from race, this strategy fails to connect numerous policies that degrade Black women's procreation. In addition to the prosecutions, for example, lawmakers across the country have been considering schemes to distribute Norplant to poor women, as well as measures that penalize welfare mothers for having additional children. Viewed separately, these developments appear to be isolated policies that can be justified by some neutral government objective. When all are connected by the race of the women most affected, a clear and horrible pattern emerges. Lynn Paltrow recently stated, "[F]or the first time in American history . . . what a pregnant woman does to her own body becomes a matter for the juries and the court."[7] Paltrow is correct that the criminal regulation of pregnancy that occurs today is in some ways unprecedented. Yet it continues the legacy of the degradation of Black motherhood. A pregnant slave woman's body was subject to legal fiat centuries ago because the fetus she was carrying already belonged to her master. Over the course of this century, government policies have regulated Black women's reproductive decisionmaking based on the theory that Black childbearing causes social problems. Although the prosecution of women for prenatal crimes is relatively recent, it should be considered in conjunction with the sterilization of Black welfare mothers during the 1970s and the promotion of Norplant as a solution to Black poverty.

2. Telling Details about Black Women's Lives

. . . Although the image of the monstrous crack-addicted mother is difficult to eradicate, it will be hard to abolish the policies that regulate Black women's fertility without exposing the image's fallacies. Describing the details of these women's lives may help. Crystal Ferguson, for example, was arrested for failing to comply with Nurse Brown's order to enter a two-week residential drug-rehabilitation program. Her arrest might appear to be justified without knowing the circumstances that led to her refusal. Ferguson requested an outpatient referral because she had no one to care for her two sons at home and the two-week program provided no childcare. Ferguson explained in an interview that she made every effort to enroll in the program, but was thwarted by circumstances beyond her control:

> I saw the situation my kids were in. There was no one to take care of them. Someone had stolen our food stamps and my unemployment check while I was at the hospital. There was no way I was going to leave my children for two weeks, knowing the environment they were in.[8]

3. Highlighting the Abuse of Black Women's Bodies

... [A] complaint [was filed] with the National Institutes of Health alleging that the . . . South Carolina policy constituted research on human subjects, which MUSC had been conducting without federally mandated review and approval. . . . Under threat of losing millions of dollars in federal funding, the hospital halted its joint venture with the solicitor's office and the police. One advantage of the complaint was that it made the Black mothers claimants rather than defendants. Instead of defending against charges of criminality, they affirmatively demanded an end to the hospital's abusive practices. Instead of fending off a host of negative images, claimants can accuse the government of complicity in a legacy of medical experimentation on the bodies of Black women without their consent.

In past centuries, doctors experimented on slave women before practicing new surgical procedures on white women. Marion Sims, for example, developed gynecological surgery in the nineteenth century by performing countless operations, without anesthesia, on female slaves purchased expressly for his experiments. In the 1970s, doctors coerced hundreds of thousands of Black women into agreeing to sterilization by conditioning medical services on consent to the operation. More recently, a survey published in 1984 found that 13,000 Black women in Maryland were screened for sickle-cell anemia without their consent or the benefit of adequate counseling. Doctors have also been more willing to override Black patients' autonomy by performing forced medical treatment to benefit the fetus. A national survey published in 1987 in the New England Journal of Medicine discovered twenty-one cases in which court orders for cesarean sections were sought, and petitions were granted in eighteen of these cases. Eighty-one percent of the women involved were women of color; all were treated in a teaching-hospital clinic or were receiving public assistance.

Given the durability of disparaging images of Black mothers, particularly those who smoke crack, it is understandable that lawyers would search for ways to avoid these images altogether. One strategy, then, is to try to make judges forget that the prosecutions of prenatal crimes are targeted primarily at crack-addicted mothers. But I believe that leaving these images unchallenged will only help to perpetuate Black mothers' degradation. A better approach is to uproot and contest the mythology that propels policies that penalize Black women's childbearing. The medical risks of punitive policies and their potential threat to all women only enhance an argument that these policies perpetuate Black women's subordination.

NOTES

1. Plaintiffs' Memorandum in Support of Their Partial Cross-Motion for Summary Judgment and in Opposition to Defendants' Motion for Summary Judgment at 10–11, *Ferguson v. City of Charleston*, No. 2:93-2624-2 (D.S.C. Oct. 1995).

2. Dorothy E. Roberts, *Punishing Drug Addicts Who Have Babies: Women of Color, Equality, and the Right of Privacy,* 104 Harvard Law Review 1419, 1420 (1991).

3. Cynthia R. Daniels, At Women's Expense: State Power and the Politics of Fetal Rights 116 (1993).

4. Office of Policy Planning and Research, U.S. Department of Labor, The Negro Family: The Case for National Action 5 (1965).

5. *Id.* at 29.

6. Linda C. Mayes et al., *Commentary: The Problem of Prenatal Cocaine Exposure: A Rush to Judgment,* 267 JAMA 406 (1992).

7. Rivera Live (CNBC television broadcast, July 16, 1996).

8. Barry Siegel, *In the Name of the Children: Get Treatment or Go to Jail, One South Carolina Hospital Tells Drug-Abusing Pregnant Women,* Los Angeles Times, Aug. 7, 1994 Magazine at 14.

33

Blaming Culture for Bad Behavior

Leti Volpp

Introduction

When do we call behavior "cultural"? And when do we not? Why do we distinguish behavior in this way? And what are the consequences of this difference in recognition and naming? . . . [N]arratives . . . emerge in cases of forced and voluntary adolescent marriage. These narratives suggest that behavior that we might find troubling is more often causally attributed to a group-defined culture when the actor is perceived to "have" culture. Because we tend to perceive white Americans as "people without culture," when white people engage in certain practices we do not associate their behavior with a racialized conception of culture, but rather construct other, noncultural explanations. The result is an exaggerated perception of ethnic difference that equates it with moral difference from "us."

. . .

Selectively blaming culture leads to the misapprehension that certain immigrant cultures are fundamentally different from "our" culture. Ethnic difference is equated with moral difference, with which we must struggle in a multicultural state. Specifically, commentators depict the sex-subordinating practices of certain immigrants as creating an irreconcilable tension between the values of feminism and multiculturalism. The presumed existence of this conflict leads to policy proposals and theoretical conclusions that exaggerate differences between "us" and "them." Such misreadings prevent us from seeing, understanding, and struggling against specific relations of power—both within "other" cultures and our own.

. . .

C. Nation, Gender, and Sexuality

Why are the child marriages of nonwhite immigrants but not white Christian sects perceived as threatening Western cultural traditions? Contrasting "progressive" Western traditions to the "primitive" and "barbaric" lends credibility to the idea that Western culture is progressive. . . .

The contrast between the cultural traditions of the West and those of immigrants with "backward, primitive values" is somewhat ironic, as Western cultural traditions include child marriage and early sexuality. Ten years of age was the age of consent under English common law, as well as the age of consent in most states in 1885, when agitation to reform statutory rape law first began in the United States. At that point the age of consent in Delaware was only seven years of age.

Despite this, many commentators . . . point to cases of forced marriage, Asian immigrant parent-child suicide, Hmong marriage by capture, female genital mutilation, and "wife killing" by nonwhite immigrants to assert that multiculturalism has gone too far. In their view, multiculturalism and feminism cannot coexist[;] [m]ulti-culturalism must give way, and feminism must triumph.

. . .

What appears truly to underlie the assumption of a peculiarly misogynistic immigrant culture is the relationship between nationalism, gender, sexuality, and race. National identities, expressed here as "American values," often coalesce around women's bodies. Racializing sex-subordinating practices allows problematic behavior to be projected beyond the borders of a nation and located on the bodies of racialized immigrant subjects.

The interaction of these factors deserves scrutiny. The control of women and their sexuality is crucial to maintaining and reproducing the identity of communities and nations. . . . [I]mages of nations are constructed in terms of familial and domestic metaphors, where women are located as the symbolic center and boundary marker of the nation. In this scheme, women are mothers of the nation and guardians of its purity and honor. Purity and honor survive when women engage only in sexual relations that are heteronormative and occur within the confines of state-sanctioned marriage that controls the reproduction of the state's citizenry. The nation also depends on the family as a unit through which the stability of gender roles is preserved. Adolescent premarital sexuality creates anxiety, so the state seeks to direct this prohibited sexuality into appropriate channels, such as early marriage. Thus, we find statutes that legislate the acceptability of marriage at ages as young as thirteen with proof of pregnancy and/or parental consent, and reluctance to increase the age of consent lest the law promote promiscuity or illegitimate births.

What is the role of race in this process? Nationalist ideologies are often concerned with racial purity and subject women to reproductive and other forms of control to achieve this aim. In the cases of forced and voluntary adolescent marriage discussed here, the racialized bodies and community control over the sexuality of immigrant girls appear to rupture a national fabric that is presumptively both white and progressive. The sexuality of immigrant adolescent girls of color is marked as a racialized threat to a national cultural consensus about appropriate female sexuality and responses to that sexuality.

Women's bodies serve as "boundary markers of the nation"[1] in the context of charting societal progress. In nationalist discourse the figure of the woman acts as a primary marker of an essential communal identity or tradition. Women, home, family, and nation become conflated so that women serve to signify a community's culture and tradition. As a result, perceptions of the relative treatment of women have historically been used to assess the progress of a culture and to justify subjugation of different populations in the name of a racialized gender uplift. . . .

A nation can consolidate its identity by projecting beyond its own borders the sexual practices or gender behaviors it deems abhorrent. Thus, even while voluntary or forced adolescent marriages occur within white American communities, we do not conceptualize these practices as cultural phenomena characterizing white America. Rather, this undesirable behavior is projected beyond U.S. borders and characterized as an abhorrent practice imported by immigrants that undermines enlightened Western norms. This projection allows the United States to maintain a self-image as a progressive state with a progressive culture—especially in the arena of women's rights—by naming as "other" the source of backward behavior. This process occurs even when such practices are not unique to immigrants of color but in fact are legally condoned by statute, as is the case for voluntary adolescent marriage, or, if illegal, appear among native-born whites as well as immigrants.

III. Feminism and Multiculturalism

Advocates and scholars have attempted to problematize the conflation of racialized immigrant communities and regressive sex-subordinating culture in a variety of contexts, including female genital surgeries and so-called cultural defenses. These individuals have recognized that culture is neither static nor homogenous and that culture is experienced and described variously by individuals situated differently within a particular community. Further, these commentators have argued that every community is characterized by both patriarchy and resistance to patriarchy, and that women are agents, not just passive subjects of their culture.

But these attempts to create a complex and accurate understanding of culture often go unheard. Susan Moller Okin recently used the Iraqi case as a launching pad to criticize multiculturalism in an essay titled, *Is Multiculturalism Bad for Women?* (Her answer: "Yes.")[2] Okin asserts that there are fundamental conflicts between a commitment to gender equity and a multiculturalist respect for minority cultures, as illustrated by the Al-Saidy case, French schoolchildren wearing headscarves, African immigrant polygamous marriages, female clitoridectomy in immigrant communities, Hmong marriage by capture, parent-child suicide by Japanese and Chinese immigrants, and "wife murder by immigrants from Asian and Middle Eastern countries whose wives have either committed adultery or treated their husbands in a servile way."[3] In Okin's account, these examples reflect ethnic difference, which in turn represents moral difference. Okin then argues that we must choose universalist values that respect women rather than succumbing to the multiculturalist or relativist disinclination to judge difference.

To assert that these cases reveal a tension between multiculturalism and feminism is not only to rely upon a caricature of the culture of immigrant communities and communities of color, but also to posit very specific and problematic versions of feminism and of multiculturalism. These discussions assume a feminism that replicates the colonialist feminism of a century ago. In the colonialist paradigm, native women were completely passive subjects of a native male subordination that grossly exceeded that experienced by women in the West. Colonialist feminism emerged, in this account, in order to uplift the suffering women of the "East." This brand of feminism was used to justify colonization as part of a civilizing process, along with the rule of law, education, and Christianity.

The assumption of this strand of feminist theory, reflected in Okin's perspective, that immigrant women require liberation through induction into the progressive social mores and customs of the metropolitan West, has been subjected to significant criticism. Critics have pointed to the manner in which feminists describe "other" women as "always/already victim," passively waiting to be rescued from cultural norms that mysteriously impose no restraints on Western feminists.

Just as these discussions perpetuate a distorted feminism, they assume a multiculturalism that resembles crude cultural relativism. Under a multicultural regime, this discourse suggests that we as a society would be unable to critique any culture and would be forced to accept the bizarre customs and behaviors of nonwhites at the expense of long-cherished American principles. This portrayal of multiculturalism relies on problematic assumptions. First, it invents a homogenous, "American" tradition of principles, a monoculturalism of transcendent values with a "we" or "us" at an unwavering center of rationality. This assumption is historically inaccurate, relying upon distortions and marginalizations for its narrative coherence. Second, this account confuses the multiculturalist valuation of ethnic particularity with a defense of cultural relativism. Valuing difference does not destroy our ability to judge among differences. We need not rely upon "long-cherished Western principles" that masquerade as universal values in order to make critical judgments about gender-subordinating practices.

As Homi Bhabha has recently written, the construction of a conflict between feminism and multiculturalism relies on the monolithic characterizations of minority, migrant cultures. Such a construction mistakenly presumes the "Western" domestic scene to be egalitarian and empowering; depicts minorities as abject "subjects" of their cultures of origin "huddled in the gazebo of group rights, preserving the orthodoxy of their distinctive cultures in the midst of the great storm of Western progress";[4] and assumes that Western liberal values—utterly foreign to immigrant communities—will lead to their salvation.

Juxtaposing these narratives of similar stories differently perceived illustrates how distinctive interpretative lenses are applied to virtually identical behavior according to the actors' identity. Our society considers the voluntary pregnancy and marriage of a young teenage girl to an older man to be the act of an aberrant individual when the girl is white, but considers it to reflect a more primitive culture when the girl is a Mexican immigrant. Under the prevailing view, a father forcing his young teenage daughters into marriage is a cultural act demonstrating the evils of multiculturalism when the actors are Iraqi immigrants, but not when they are white and Mormon. Society presumes that immigrants of color are passive victims dominated by their cultural traditions, in contrast to the rational actors of Western liberalism.

The consequences of selectively blaming culture in this way are striking: These discursive practices cause us to overlook specific relations of power, both in "other" cultures and in our own society. In hasty expressions of distaste for other cultures perceived as primitive and backward, we miss the complex ways in which power actually functions in particular communities.

A specific example may help to clarify this point. In a recent article, Katherine Franke examines how our choice to label certain practices as "sexual" eclipses important implications of behavior.[5] One of her examples is the anthropological report of ritualized practices in a community where boys must fellate older men as part of the process of becoming a man. It is easy to feel disgust at the daily ingestion of semen by seven-year-old boys—to label this practice as a symptom of a horrifically bad culture, and to dehumanize those who would engage in such practices. Alternatively, one could, as various commentators have, describe these practices as fundamentally homoerotic, as evidence of an exotic manifestation of homosexual behavior. Both of these responses distance the observer from the culture observed, connecting the evaluation of the "other" culture to the observer's self-image. One interpretation is condemnatory, the other laudatory; one unreflectively says "[T]hat is not me," the other says "[T]hat is me." The former calls the practice culture, the latter calls it sex. Both miss the way this sexual practice signifies and enforces power relations.

As Franke describes, the fellatio is accompanied by nose-bleeding through the use of sharp grasses, as well as cane-swallowing to induce vomiting and defecation. The purpose of these rituals is to purge female body fluids that the male child inherited from the mother. Boys are isolated from all women and taught that women are polluters who will deplete their masculine substance, which they must ingest in the form of semen required for boys to grow. Franke writes that, rather than considering these practices principally homoerotic and calling them "sexual," we can more appropriately understand them as part of a larger indoctrination process whereby boys learn and internalize gender norms premised upon misogyny and male superiority. We could therefore argue that what is eclipsed in the selective labeling as sexual—or as cultural—is the relation of these practices to the specific manner in which gender structures social relations.

The condemnatory reaction, which distances the observer from the practice and defines the observer as the antithesis of that practice, relies upon and perpetuates a failure to see subordinating practices in our own culture when, for example, young girls are forced to engage in nonconsensual sex or are battered in the process of "becoming a woman." When we gaze with condemnation at other cultures, we can miss the fact that "our" culture is also characterized by problematic, sex-subordinating behavior. The cases of adolescent marriage should make us rethink the belief that culturally based subordination of women and girls is a phenomenon particular to immigrant communities of color. So long as we chalk up sexist behavior in other communities to their "culture," we must critically examine the fact that American culture is characterized by, for example, epidemic rates of male violence against women. Alternatively, if we say that we reject sexism as part of "our culture"— that some of us claim that domestic violence, for example, has no part of "our culture"—we should similarly recognize that segments of other communities are also engaged in a process of rejecting sexism as part of "their culture."

Extraterritorializing of problematic behavior by projecting it beyond the borders of "American values" has the effect both of equating racialized immigrant culture with sex-subordination, and denying the reality of gendered subordination prevalent in mainstream white America. The failure to interrogate these effects has real-life consequences. These assumptions about gender, race, culture, and nation do not solely raise questions of descriptive representation; they result in shifts in material reality and in distributions of power. While the sexist culture of immigrants of color is used to justify calls for immigration exclusion (some race-based, some not), there appears to be little headway against the shocking incidence of domestic violence in nearly one-third of intimate relationships in the United States. To be perfectly clear, I am not pointing out the problematic discursive representations of racialized communities in these cases in order to assert that these cultures are not sexist. Rather, I am calling for an approach to combat gendered subordination across communities, an approach that neither attacks the cultures of communities of color based on racial assumptions, nor presumes that the United States is always a site of liberation.

NOTES

1. Editorial, 44 Feminist Review 1 (1993).

2. Susan Moller Okin, *Is Multiculturalism Bad for Women?* in Is Multiculturalism Bad for Women? 9 (Joshua Cohen et al., eds., 1999).

3. *Id.* at 18.

4. Homi K. Bhabha, *Liberalism's Sacred Cow*, in Is Multiculturalism Bad for Women? 79 (Joshua Cohen et al., eds., 1999).

5. Katherine Franke, *Putting Sex to Work*, 75 Denver University Law Review 1139 (1998).

34

Bridges and Barricades:
Rethinking Polemics and Intransigence in the
Campaign against Female Circumcision

L. Amede Obiora

. . .

A. On Cultural Self-Determination: Whose Culture? Which Self?

. . .

Conceptualizing individual and collective rights in terms of mutual checks and balances creates definite quandaries, one of which is the implicit suggestion that individual and collective rights are binary opposites. To the contrary, individual and collective rights are not binary opposites. They do not merely function to threaten and repudiate each other. In many respects they affirm and reproduce each other; they can be convergent, interdependent, and mutually reinforcing. Insofar as the individual's formation of a sense of humanity, self, and identity is invariably contingent on a cultural context, respect for the totality of individual human rights necessarily entails some degree of respect for the variability and specificity of culture. In a non-linear perspective in which the individual is constructed as a cultural being, the rights of peoples to self-determination then becomes a complement of individual liberty and self-expression. Yet, to acknowledge the relationship between individual and collective rights is not to refute the points of dissonance that exist between them.

. . .

One may appreciate the value of attending to cultural specificities without discounting the problems that arise from essentializing culture. To the extent that culture is socially constituted, it tends to be structured by disparate power configurations, shot through with vested interests, and experienced differently by members of the same community. Social stratification means that culture is seldom neutral. Consequently, prioritizing or espousing the inviolability of culture runs the risk of foisting contested claims as universal and consensual, the risk of occluding real social inequities and tensions, the risk of perpetuating the voicelessness and powerlessness of persons who do not have an equitable input in the constitution of the culture in question precisely because their marginalization had rendered them voiceless and powerless.

This explanation is the classic understanding that informs the concerns articulated at the United Nations Women's Conference in Beijing. Feminist scholars and activists are commendably united in the struggle to eliminate gender-based discrimination. In keeping with the feminist objective, the Declaration and the blueprint for action that were issued in Beijing furnish a framework for challenging situations in which the rights of women are compromised for the benefit of cultural traditions that institutionalize and reproduce patriarchal hegemony, gender asymmetry, violence, and oppression. The Declaration can also be read as implicating certain cultural practices that women themselves deliberately appropriate and celebrate. The following discussion is motivated by the dilemmas presented by the international campaign against female circumcision.

The discussion attempts to engage questions such as: What does the preference of some women for a cultural practice such as female circumcision which has been adjudged problematic by diverse parties connote? Whose culture are these women really affirming? Does such affirmation have significance for their self-determination as individuals or for the proscription of the practice in question? How can we achieve a semblance of balance between validating a multiplicity of cultural expressions and realizing the global commitment to protect the cardinal rights of women? The following is an attempt to engage these and related questions.

B. The Anti-Circumcision Campaign in Africa

Western legislation and cultural criticism have placed female circumcision at the center of a worldwide controversy concerning how states may best act to protect the interests of women within a universal framework of human rights. Emotional charges and symbolism combined with an overwhelming emphasis on individualistic assumptions about the body, lead critics to insist that all African practices of genital markings and reconstructions be designated a crime against women. The debate is divided between universalists, who invoke monolithic categories and constructions of dignity, integrity, and empowerment to condemn genital surgeries, and relativists, who argue for locally autonomous and culturally sensitive reformatory strategies.

Female circumcision does not easily fall within the traditional definition of a gender-specific human rights violation, nor does it seem completely analogous to violent coercion of women by men. It is usually performed for socio-cultural reasons by predominantly female private actors with the apparent consent of the circumcised or her proxy. In moderate forms, only a drop of blood or the prepuce is extracted from the clitoris—and with medical supervision the procedure need not engender health complications.

. . .

[I seek] . . . to reconcile conflicting positions in the circumcision controversy by elaborating a middle course underscoring how an acute sensitivity to cultural context and indigenous hermeneutics balances efforts to protect the interests of women. This assertion of local context compensates for an emerging radical feminist consensus that overwhelmingly ignores the incommensurability of cultural motivations and meanings by projecting Western understandings of female circumcision onto African cultures.

[I argue] . . . that positions opposed to the modification of female circumcision are more appropriate for drastic forms of the practice. Although there is a dearth of scientific research on female circumcision, the available data do not implicate mild forms of the practice as dangerous. Without compelling health hazards, the case for total prohibition loses its force. . . . [T]he value of eliminating mild forms of circumcision, in spite of the affirmative meanings they may express for the women and the cultures concerned, remains to be seen.

. . .

II. Definitions

A. What Is Female Circumcision?

Genital scarification and reconstruction are time-honored and worldwide practices. As extant cultural traditions, the practices are particularly prevalent in Africa where they are reported to occur in about twenty-six countries; the exact number of women affected is unknown, but it is estimated between 80 and 110 million. Within the African context, the age at which it is performed varies between localities and it is possible to distinguish at least four major forms of incidence. The ritualized marking of female genitalia begins with the mildest forms of the procedures, where the clitoris is barely nicked or pricked to shed a few drops of blood. This procedure is innocuous and has a strictly symbolic connotation.

The next range of surgeries extend to the removal of the clitoral prepuce, hood, or outer skin. This is the form that ritual Muslims refer to as sunna, and medical data indicates that it poses minimal health risks if scientifically performed and monitored. Sunna is most comparable to male circumcision and there is some suggestion that it may serve the purpose of hygiene and cleanliness. A more radical form of female genital surgeries is known as excision or clitoridectomy. In this procedure, the clitoral glans and some of the nympha or labia minora, the narrow lip-like enclosures of the genital anatomy, are severed. The most extreme form of the surgeries is called infibulation, and it has been identified as the form that presents the most significant risks and hazards. This procedure entails scraping the labia majora, the two rounded folds of tissue that contour the external boundaries of the vulva, and stitching the remaining raw edges together in a manner that ensures that only a tiny opening will be left after the surgery heals.

. . .

III. The Quest for Lost Origins

. . .

The only restrictions on a woman who makes a rational and self-interested choice within her limited field of options are external, not internal. The basic discovery of feminist studies is that women, insofar as they are oppressed by a culture, are rarely oblivious of their grievances. Instead of existing as acquiescent pawns of historical forces and cultural transactions, women engage and interact with their material conditions as agents; they negotiate gender constructs and asymmetries in studied resistance and acquiescence to claim a significance that is at least complementary to men's. In this vein, Janice Boddy argues that even circumcision and its social implications are counter-hegemonic efforts by women to negotiate ascribed subaltern statuses.

Female genital scarring or reconstruction epitomizes the tenuousness and artificiality of the boundaries of agency and critical thought. Depending on the angle of vision, it has ramifications that both oppress and empower women to manipulate oppressive structures. On one level, it is plausible to suggest that mature participants in genital surgery exhibit a considerable degree of awareness and instrumentality. At the very least, they are deploying cultural constructs within the confines of their realities to reach compelling self-affirming ends. On another level, it is conceivable that their ratification of, and complicity in, a potentially coercive transaction to validate culturally imputed values bespeak the gravity of their oppression. From this perspective, the exaltation of agency over submission is circular, insofar as a gender-based culture dictates the utilitarian and aesthetic values celebrated in circumcision. This dilemma underscores the inherent risk of polarizing the issues of agency and submission as if they are mutually exclusive absolutes. Women, like men, are culturally situated beings of inevitably relative autonomy; their responses are, to some extent, necessarily determined. As such, a more pressing consideration is the question of the circumstance and degree of determinism.

. . .

Law alone seldom changes behavior. Although it is certainly a key determinant of change, it is not a panacea, nor is it a brooding omnipresence in the sky. It is instead a mechanism that is integral to, and contingent on, a broader societal scheme. Against this backdrop, it is reasonable to infer that law can wield considerable influence over actions and attitudes where it is accepted as legitimate authority. A corollary view is that legal control is affected by social influences; the greater the social consensus the higher the chances of observance and punishment for violations. As exemplified by the aggressive posture of the French judiciary, there will be more interventions in jurisdictions where there is concerted public outrage against female circumcision than where it is considered normal. The court's documented ambivalence in sentencing, in addition to its uniqueness of posture, demonstrates the legal dilemmas of circumcision.

These dilemmas are even more complicated if the law that "jumps the gun" to "legislate morality" is perceived as an outraged regimen with scant organic root or regard for local logic. In such a case, the law lacks minimal prospect for meaningful enforcement and becomes a mere rite de passage to which governments acquiesce out of formal deference to powerful instigators. Not even the police are immune from the tentacles of social forces; to the contrary, they typically share the values and moral code of the community and may be inclined to conform to local patterns and preferences for social control, instead of to the ideals of law. Thus, given budgetary constraints and the demands on their schedule, they may adjust their enforcement priorities to approximate not the ideal of law, but the community's sense of justice or its evaluation of propriety.

In the case of circumcision, the lack of political will and an impotent enforcement structure, will be compounded by the cultural embeddedness of the practice and by the fact that it is deeply fossilized in women's psyches. Because the criminal justice process depends largely on the participation of victims, if the complainant is not willing to testify, there will often be no basis for prosecution and conviction. A circumcised woman who is well-adjusted by the standards of her reference group may, notwithstanding the physical pain involved, not perceive circumcision as a wrong to be vindicated. Since the official classification of female circumcision as illegal may not immediately alter this view of morality, such a woman is unlikely to facilitate prosecution or to disclose the identity of the parties to be charged. The high probability of grave repercussions, such as jeopardizing a close relationship, risking the incarceration of her care-giver, and being alienated from the community, are further disincentives for complaining.

. . .

V. Orchestrating Change: Extra-Legal Alternatives

. . . Critical consciousness is an outcome one must define, develop, and appropriate for oneself, as opposed to something done "to" or "for" someone. . . .

By virtue of education for critical consciousness, women can articulate and assess the burdens and benefits of circumcision in order to determine how best to serve their interests. One way of maximizing critical consciousness may be to integrate circumcision into a mainstream discourse of health and to encourage women to explore the possibility that the notion of femininity encapsulated in circumcision may well be a metaphor, not just for internalized identity, but for externally imposed stricture. In this respect, medical facts that are not readily discountable on the basis of subjective experience may be marshaled to explicate the adverse implications of the practice for the practitioners' overarching values and objectives. For example, it may be necessary to employ this avenue to demonstrate that circumcision is potentially inimical for pronatalistic aspirations. In the event that the women are successfully persuaded, they may decide to abandon the practice entirely or to salvage its redeeming features.

. . .

Although rooted in the past, female circumcision has contemporary relevance that is believed to enhance personal fulfillment and social continuity. In view of indigenous justifications for circumcision, many avid participants perceive outsiders' intervention as surreptitiously intent on corrupting and ultimately disintegrating the social fabric.

. . .

Regulating female circumcision, even as an interim response, reconciles the need to protect women with a respect for embodied socio-cultural identities. It also underscores the relevance of claims of cultural specificity to overriding questions of justice, liberty, and diversity. In conclusion, it is important to emphasize that the argument for a middle course . . . [is] neither a case for nor a case against female circumcision. Essentially, the argument seeks to give voice to perspectives that have heretofore remained unarticulated or muted, and to enrich pertinent academic debates and policy strategies.

Part IV

Women and Violence:
Individuals, the State, and Other Actors

Introduction

Unfortunately, violence is a factor in the lives of women in almost every culture. As is evident from historical studies of the common law, normative standards in the law revolved around men's perceptions of rights and justice. Women's perceptions were largely ridiculed at worst and treated as less serious than men's at best. As a result, it became difficult, if not impossible, to protect women's rights in certain areas, such as the right to be free from violence. A man's home was his castle, and actions taken in the confines of the home were viewed as private matters, shielded from public scrutiny. When women experienced violence at the hands of husbands or male relatives, the law was loath to interfere. And women faced similar dangers outside the home. A woman's right to the integrity of her own body was never firmly secured. If she had a male relative, he could claim and protect her virtue. But that virtue was easily lost if she was raped or assaulted by a stranger or even a male relative. The plight of African American women was even more precarious. During the period of slavery, the law authorized and encouraged white slave owners to exercise complete control over the bodies of enslaved African women. Whites could torture, rape, sexually assault, and murder Black women without fear of any criminal sanction whatsoever.

A number of rationales are posited for the historical absence of legal protection from rape for enslaved African women. First, such rapes often produced new slave offspring, which resulted in an economic benefit to the white slave owner and, by extension, to white society. Second, it was not considered proper for white men to exercise their sexual urges upon chaste white women; therefore African women were considered a "legitimate" outlet for male sexual urges. Finally, allowing the rape of Black women to go unpunished was a political tactic used both to demoralize and to break the resistance of enslaved Black women, as well as to demoralize the entire Black community. The law still has difficulty conceptualizing violence against Black women as a crime. The historical legacy of slavery, with its attendant stereotypes about the brutish or lascivious nature of Black women, leaves them particularly vulnerable to violence. Stereotypes about other women of color

(Latinas are hot-blooded, Asian women are sexually exotic) combine with the law's perceptions of Black women, making it difficult for these women to gain the protection of law as well.

The grassroots feminist movement alone has been responsible for drawing the eyes of the nation to the problem of violence in the lives of women. Throughout the late 1960s, the 1970s, and into the 1980s the feminist movement challenged evidentiary rules, jury instructions, and law enforcement and judicial attitudes that made it difficult for women who were raped or assaulted to come forward with their stories and to demand prosecution of men who violated them. At the same time, feminists challenged the belief that what happened to women at home, behind closed doors, was a private matter and not an appropriate area of inquiry for law enforcement. Many positive gains have been made that are helping curtail violence against women. The passage of state and federal legislation focusing solely on the issue of domestic violence marks a major victory for feminists. Yet, as in other areas of feminist theory, much remains to be done. Many strategies that have been considered successful in the fight against violence, such as mandatory arrest policies, have been critiqued by feminists of color who allege the strategies work against the interests of women of color and their communities. It is still difficult for women of color to have their needs recognized in the same way that middle-class white women's needs are addressed. In addition, it is fair to state that feminist theories about violence are still basically rooted in the paradigm of individual male violence perpetrated against individual females and fail to address the broader issue of gendered constructs that lead to the occurrence of same-sex violence and violence that, though caused by men, creates victims who are also males.

It is fitting, therefore, to open this part with two selections that depart from the paradigm of male-on-female violence. Angela Harris's insightful essay on the Abner Louima police brutality case explores whether violence is a necessary component of contemporary masculine identity and therefore gendered. That males constantly feel the need to establish their own masculinity, whether publicly, in the company of other males, or privately, when subjected to some perceived "humiliation" at the hands of a woman, lends credence to the argument that the traditional paradigm of male-to-female violence is inadequate to explain the frequency and intensity of male violence. Harris argues that policing practices thrive on a cult of hypermasculinity, where male violence thrives. She suggests approaches the state can endorse that can help separate policing from gender violence. Rachel Toker's article continues the thread of examining the concept of masculinity in the context of same-sex harassment. She explores the threat that men perceive when confronted with nonconforming gender behaviors from other males. Traditional analyses of male-on-female violence are simply ineffective in explaining same-sex harassment or violence, which is rooted in a broader internalization of gender roles and gendered power relations. Toker proposes a concept of multiple masculinities that is intended to offer options to gauge masculinity and help men avoid gendered violence.

The readings then move to an examination of institutional actors who help perpetrate state violence. Cassandra Shaylor's article details how state prisons create and maintain environments in which female inmates are subjected to physical and emotional violence that is either explicitly approved or tacitly endorsed by the state. By examining common trends among female inmates, she analyzes how violence in correctional institutions exacerbates many of the problems that bring women to prison in the first place. Amy Ray examines the nation-state actor and the use of rape as a weapon of war. Ray explores how the state can intentionally use rape as a method of subjugating, terrorizing, and cleansing an enemy population. While there are international mechanisms to hold states accountable for war crimes, Ray highlights how and why some of these mechanisms are ineffective to address war injuries women have experienced as women, as opposed to merely as one aspect of war crimes against a nation. The institutional-actor section concludes with Sylvia Law's article on commercial sex workers. Law proposes that state efforts to continue criminalizing prostitution support an environment where violence against sex workers flourishes. Commercial sex workers are deprived of the legitimate protection of law enforcement. In addition, feminists are still ambivalent toward sex workers. Consequently, assistance normally extended to female victims of violence, such as access to shelters, is denied to sex workers who are also victims of violence.

We then return to a more traditional analysis of issues of violence. The selections examine sexual and domestic violence from the vantage point of women of color. Sumi Cho's essay on sexual harassment of Asian women presents an excellent segue between institutional violence and traditional male-on-female violence. In this selection, she discusses not only traditional legal principles of sexual harassment but also the difficulties of successfully challenging offensive male behavior when the complainant must also overcome stereotypes about the sexuality of Pacific Asian women. Using the university setting, Cho navigates through two cases of sexual harassment of Asian women professors and discusses the difficulty of bringing litigation in an environment where university officials openly supported the harassers. Jenny Rivera analyzes the opportunity for intersectional work between feminists and civil rights activists presented by the enactment of the Violence Against Women Act (VAWA). At the same time, through the lens of a Latina woman, she identifies provisions of VAWA that work against the interests of women of color. To enhance opportunities for coalition work, Rivera encourages the mainstream feminist movement to consider the realities of women of color who experience violence.

Altering the focus slightly, Holly Maguigan discusses feminist reaction to attempts to introduce what has become known as a "cultural defense," or offering a culturally based explanation for defendant violence, in criminal trials. Many feminists have argued that admitting cultural evidence allows men to kill women under the guise of cultural entitlement. Maguigan argues that feminists who believe cultural evidence condones violence against women have rejected its use without performing a complete analysis. Maguigan examines cultural defenses in several cases, including two where women successfully used culture as part of their defense strategy, one when she used violence to protect herself against an abusing man and another to excuse abuse of children. Maguigan cautions feminists that total rejection of cultural defenses can result in the denial of legitimate defenses to marginalized women. The excerpt from Darren Hutchinson pinpoints another deficiency in mainstream analyses of violence. His work focuses on homophobic forms of racial violence against gay, lesbian, bisexual, and transgendered people of color. The traditional violence analysis is brought to a close by Michelle Jacobs's article which explores the intersection of domestic violence and child abuse through prosecutions under "failure to act" statutes. Jacobs identifies two populations, abused children and abused mothers, that compete for the sympathies of mainstream feminists. She argues that battered mothers are subject to particularly harsh murder prosecutions when spouses or significant others kill the women's children because feminists have not fully developed a legal theory that explains the complexity of domestic violence when an individual other than the abuser dies. Mothers are subsequently held liable for deaths they are powerless to prevent. Jacobs challenges feminists to resist comparing the relative worth of battered mothers to that of abused children and to work toward a comprehensive theory that acknowledges the effects of violence on the fabric of the entire family.

The final two pieces in Part IV are by Martha Minow and Donna Coker. Minow addresses feminist responses to violence, pointing out their inconsistencies. Mainstream feminism tends to endorse traditional criminal-justice punitive treatment of individuals who are violent toward women. At the same time, she argues that mainstream feminists endorse excusing or lenient treatment of women who respond violently to spouses, lovers, and children. Using examples from the South African Truth and Reconciliation Hearings, Minow raises the possibility that feminists can begin to adopt a restorative-justice model in response to some incidents of violence against women. Minow suggests that the restorative-justice model may help address some of the concerns women of color have with regard to increased correctional presence in their communities. Donna Coker's article moves from theory to practice and therefore serves as a fitting conclusion to the series of essays. She analyzes Native American attempts to offer one indigenous community, which exists outside of the bounds of traditional law, an opportunity to help shape a restorative-justice model that can work in the domestic violence context: the Navajo peacemaking process. While Coker indicates the model is not perfect, she offers it as one that feminists everywhere can study to help them begin the process of challenging their own assumptions and rigidity with respect to responding to violence in our communities, in a way that both protects the violated member and seeks to restore the harmony of the community.

35

Gender, Violence, Race, and Criminal Justice

Angela P. Harris

. . .

Introduction

One early morning in August 1997, New York City police officer Charles Schwarz forcibly held down a Haitian immigrant named Abner Louima in a bathroom in the 70th Precinct while Schwarz's fellow officer Justin Volpe rammed a broken broomstick into Louima's rectum, rupturing his bladder and his colon, and then jammed it into his mouth. Approximately twenty officers were working in the area while Louima was attacked, but no one came forward during the attack or demanded medical attention for Louima. "Instead, Louima was left to wait nearly three hours, bleeding in a holding cell, until an officer was assigned to accompany the paramedics to the hospital."[1] Meanwhile, officers saw Volpe brandishing a feces-stained stick around the stationhouse and bragging about how he had humiliated Louima. Four officers eventually came forward to report what had happened, but many suspected they did so only because of a widening federal investigation.

In the end, Officer Volpe confessed and pleaded guilty to a civil rights violation; Officer Schwarz was convicted of violating Louima's civil rights. Three other officers—two accused of beating Louima in a police car before he got to the stationhouse and one, their supervisor, accused of trying to cover up the beating—were acquitted. Volpe said that he sodomized Louima because he mistakenly believed that Louima had punched him during a disturbance at a nightclub; as it turned out, the assailant at the nightclub was actually Louima's cousin. . . .

The racial meanings of incidents of police brutality such as the Louima beating and torture have been well explored. Less well explored have been the charged gender relations among men that make intelligible the manner of the Louima attack as well as its target. The attack on Louima can be understood not only as an act of racial violence but also as a racial attack accomplished through a peculiarly male language of sexual violence. On other occasions, the charged gender relations among men have made it possible for racial hostilities to be temporarily transcended by gender loyalty: the loyalty, for instance, to the "boys in blue" that protected Volpe and Schwarz for so long. In these and other ways, gender violence sometimes creates and sometimes shatters racial community.

Feminist legal theorists, of course, are well familiar with the concept of "gender violence," but for the most part they have focused only on violence against women. Feminist and queer theorists working in the area of sexual harassment law have recently demonstrated, however, that the concept of "sex-based" aggression is difficult, if not impossible, to confine to the heterosexual, cross-sex context in which it began. Similarly, gender violence does not produce only female victims; indeed, since most victims of violent crime are male, it may be that more men than women suffer from gender violence. This does not mean that the traditional feminist focus on violence against women is wrong; the gender system operates precisely to disempower women as a class. But this recognition should not obscure the fact that hierarchies of race, class, sexual orientation, and gender itself also mark out groups of men as vulnerable to the violence of other men. Exploration of the violence in the criminal justice system—the violence of both private and public actors—begins to reveal the extent to which masculine identity is shaped by relations of repulsion and desire between men. That Volpe would sodomize Louima, when to be a heterosexual man is precisely to be terrified of homosexuality, presents a puzzle that is best understood not by reading Louima as symbolically female but by recognizing the powerful feelings men have for other men. These feelings, in turn, are shaped by cultural fantasies of race, nation, and sexuality. In this Commentary, then, I want to suggest that investigations of violence and community, including investigations of racial violence, are incomplete without paying attention to gender violence among men.

. . .

Manliness is one of those ideas that is often made real with violence. Violent acts often carry idiosyncratic moral or emotional meanings to the perpetrator. But violent acts are also, sometimes, the result of the character of masculinity itself as a cultural ideal. In these cases, men use violence or the threat of violence as an affirmative way of proving individual or collective masculinity, or in desperation when they perceive their masculine self-identity to be under attack.

. . .

While social stratification along lines of race and class separates men from one another and engages them in relations of competition, envy, and desire, masculinities of all varieties share in common the requirement that men establish themselves on the ground of what they are not. One of the great contributions of feminism has been to make plain that men achieve masculinity at the expense of women: at best by being "not a woman," at worst by excluding, hurting, denigrating, exploiting, or otherwise abusing actual women. Even in male-male relations, the domination of men over women arguably continues to function: Men in all-male groups often prove their individual and collective manhood by symbolically reducing others in the group to women and abusing them accordingly. Men's need to defend themselves at all costs from being contaminated with femininity can be found in as mundane and seemingly trivial phenomena as children's play and the reluctance of married men to do housework or take care of the children.

The feminist movement has focused critical attention on woman-hating as a cornerstone of masculinity. But queer theorists have recently begun to argue that relationships between men are as important as those between men and women in forming masculine identity. The argument is that not being a "faggot" is as important to being a man as not being a woman. Yet disavowing homosexuality is not as simple as it might seem. First, of course, many men, whether they define themselves as straight, gay, or something else, may feel desire for other men. Even if this is not the case, however, in order to achieve success as a man one must often establish the very close emotional and physical bonds with other men that make one vulnerable to the charge of homosexuality. The result, queer theorist Eve Kosofsky Sedgwick argues, is a constant state of anxiety:

> [A]t least since the eighteenth century in England and America, the continuum of male homosocial bonds has been brutally structured by a secularized and psychologized homophobia, which has excluded certain shiftingly and more or less arbitrarily defined segments of the continuum from participating in the overarching male entitlement—in the complex web of male power over the production, reproduction, and exchange of goods, persons, and meanings. . . . Because the paths of male entitlement, especially in the nineteenth century, required certain intense male bonds that were not readily distinguishable from the most reprobated bonds, an endemic and ineradicable state of what I am calling male homosexual panic became the normal condition of male heterosexual entitlement.[2]

Sedgwick's argument is that Western masculinity from the eighteenth century onward has placed men in a double bind: In order to be true men, they must not be homosexual; yet many paths toward hegemonic masculinity—such as sport, battle, and mentorship—involve just the sort of close, emotionally intense, and frequently physical and sexually charged relationships that subject men to the suspicion that they are homosexual. According to Sedgwick, there are two main results of this double bind: "[F]irst, the acute manipulability, through the fear of one's own 'homosexuality,' of acculturated men; and second, a reservoir of potential for violence caused by the self-ignorance that this regime constitutively enforces."[3]

The military provides one such example. As Sedgwick points out, the military is a place where both men's manipulability and their capacity for violence are at a premium. As is true elsewhere in the culture, the privileges of masculinity require that one establish intimate relationships with other men; yet the very closeness of these bonds provokes the terror of being marked homosexual and of losing one's masculine privileges. The instability of masculine identity under these circumstances makes insecure men easily manipulable (anxious and eager to prove their masculinity) and potentially violent (for not only status but also personal identity itself is at stake). The military both exemplifies and shrewdly exploits the internal structure of masculinity: Military culture, like prison culture, both seeks to make men doubt their own masculinity and encourages them to prove their manhood through violence and casual sexuality.

This account of contemporary hegemonic masculine identity suggests that violence—whether directed at women, at other men, or at oneself—is never far below the surface. Men must constantly defend themselves against both women and other men in order to be accepted as men; their gender identity, crucial to their psychological sense of wholeness, is constantly in doubt. . . .

II. *Crime and Punishment as Gender Performance*

. . .

A. Gender Violence and Lawbreaking

The link between doing crime and doing gender has received a fair amount of attention from sociologists. For example, Jack Katz argues that the violent crimes of some men are part and parcel of a masculine persona to which these men aspire, the desired image being that of the impervious coldness of the "hardman" or the crazy, unpredictable "badass." But gender-based criminal violence is not limited to such men. Ordinarily law-abiding and peaceful men may find themselves committing violent criminal acts when (in public settings) their manhood is threatened by conflict with other men or when (in private settings) women threaten to reveal them as sexually inadequate, fail to submit to their patriarchal authority, or threaten to leave them. In these situations, the potential loss of masculinity brings shame and humiliation, and the man who finds these emotions intolerable may turn them into rage and act violently in expression of that rage.

. . .

Criminal law casebooks are full of homicides that emerge from seemingly trivial encounters between men who are strangers to one another, interactions that would seem inexplicable unless it is understood that manhood is at stake.

Another distinctively masculine form of humiliation that may quickly lead to rage and then criminal violence occurs not in public among other men, but in "private" in connection with women. For example, both actual humiliation by women and the fear of being humiliated play a large role in men's accounts of why they rape women. Rapists tend to experience themselves as the humiliated victims of female sexual power. As one man succinctly noted, "Just the fact that they can come up to me and just melt me and make me feel like a dummy makes me want revenge."[4] Similarly, researchers of domestic violence interpret the actions of some men who batter women as efforts to establish and maintain male dominance. In other instances, men beat or kill their wives or girlfriends when the women attempt to leave the relationship. In these cases, criminal violence emerges not simply out of the desire to control, but out of an extreme emotional dependence, coupled with an unwillingness or inability to see the woman as a separate and independent person. In this form of love, masculine style, a woman's attempt to end the relationship is experienced as an intolerable threat to the self: "If I can't have her, no one can" is the response.

. . . Another dynamic that produces criminal gender violence emerges from the behavior of men in groups. The violence of street gangs provides an example. Katz argues that these gangs, which are usually made up of very young men, use violence as a way of heightening the drama of their moral and sensual lives and as a way of demanding that others take them seriously as adults rather than children.

. . .

Wealthier, more privileged young men have their own brotherhoods from which violence may emerge. Criminologists Patricia Yancey Martin and Robert A. Hummer argue, for example, that campus "fraternities create a sociocultural context in which the use of coercion in sexual relations with women is normative and in which the mechanisms to keep this pattern of behavior in check are minimal at best and absent at worst."[5] Because fraternities promote masculine brotherhood as the center of campus social life and treat the casual use of women as an important element of the brotherhood, date rapes and even occasional gang rapes can be expected to occur with depressing regularity.

Finally, men in groups may engage in "hate crimes" and other spontaneous violent attacks as a way of performing their gender. In one survey of gay men and lesbians who were the victims of bias crimes, it was noted that the perpetrators commonly boasted about their own alleged hyperheterosexuality while attacking men, and derided feminism and women in general while attacking women. This violence was, then, as much about the perpetrators' purportedly secure and superior masculinity as it was about bigotry. . . .

In a wide variety of situations, then, male criminal violence is gender violence. The term "gender violence" should not be used to ignore the currents of race, ethnicity, religion, and sexuality that shape who becomes a victim and who a perpetrator. But I want to suggest that, when studying racial violence and other kinds of bias crimes, we should not forget about the codes of gender that make this violence explicable; similarly, when studying violence against women, we should place it in the context of gender violence as a whole.

B. Gender Violence and Law Enforcement

. . .

Hypermasculinity also characterizes the policing style favored by most departments. As the NCWP [National Center for Women and Policing] argues, "Law enforcement agencies continue to promote an outdated model of policing by rewarding tough, aggressive[,] even violent behavior. This 'paramilitary' style of policing results in poor community relations, increased citizen complaints, and more violent confrontations and deaths."[6] Class provides the energy for much of this hypermasculinity: Beat cops tend to be working-class men, men denied the masculinity of wealth, power, and order giving. The dynamic of competing masculinities—hegemonic, authoritative masculinity versus rebellious, physical masculinity—is indicated by the gendered language cops use to distinguish types within police work itself. [James] Messerschmidt notes, for example, that police construct "office cops" and the work they do—public relations and administration—as feminine while "street cops" are masculine.

The experience of street policing is deeply steeped in a masculine culture of brotherhood that rests on the division between "us" and "them." Although "us" is supposed to refer to honest citizens and "them" to lawbreakers, often "us" becomes simply a mirror image of "them": our guys against their guys.

. . .

Finally, the hypermasculine culture of policing is reflected in the treatment of women by many police officers, both on and off the job. The NCWP reports that, as of 1998,

> [e]ight out of ten municipal police agencies with the largest percentage of sworn women officers are currently under, or have been under, consent decrees to hire women or minorities. . . . This demonstrates that nearly all of the largest gains for women in policing have been achieved only as a result of lawsuits initiated by women in law enforcement and women's organizations to force agencies to hire more women or minorities.[7]

Sexual harassment of women within police departments is reportedly rampant. As in other working-class, predominantly male work environments, police departments are often characterized by the stuff of which "hostile environment" sexual harassment suits are made: pornography, attempts at inappropriate touching, and hostile sexual joking and teasing. The report of the Los Angeles Police Commission released after examination of the Mark Fuhrman tapes confirmed the existence of a clandestine organization within the LAPD called "Men Against Women." According to two police force critics, "[T]his male-only rogue group's purpose [was] to wage an orchestrated campaign of ritual harassment, intimidation[,] and criminal activity against women officers with the ultimate objective of driving them from the force."[8] Given the dynamics of heterosexual hypermasculinity, it is not surprising that men perceived as gay are also particular targets for harassment. Messerschmidt, for example, describes several studies suggesting that "policing gay men may actually be central to routine police procedures and practices."[9]

Sexual harassment is not the only problem in law enforcement agencies; so too is domestic violence. Indeed, the report of the NCWP indicates that law enforcement agencies have shown little or no commitment to investigating and punishing domestic violence. In fact, studies have found that as many as 40 percent of male law enforcement officers commit domestic abuse themselves.

The hypermasculinity of policing leads to a culture in which violence is always just below the surface. Moreover, eruptions of excessive force and brutality at the street level are commonly condoned or excused by higher-ups. A recent report on police brutality issued by Human Rights Watch concludes: "Police or public officials greet each new report of brutality with denials or explain that the act was an aberration, while the administrative and criminal systems that should deter these abuses by holding officers accountable instead virtually guarantee them impunity."[10]

. . .

This lack of interest in controlling brutality signals that the line between brutality and "business as usual" is extremely fine. And police brutality is not random. It follows the vectors of power established in the larger society in which white dominates nonwhite and rich dominates poor. Police often, and not without justifica-

tion, understand their charge as the protection of "nice" neighborhoods and "decent" people against those perceived to be a threat. In practice, this often means that male power and state power converge on the Black and Latino "underclass."
. . .

Police officers in poor urban minority neighborhoods may come to see themselves as "law enforcers in a community of savages, as outposts of the law in a jungle."[11] In such a situation, race, gender, and nation converge. "Us versus them" collapses into "us versus the nonwhites," and rogue police officers, like private perpetrators of hate violence, are provided with ample opportunity to prove not only their patriotism but also their masculinity.

The hypermasculine culture of policing helps explain how it is possible for African American police officers to be just as brutal and abusive toward African American citizens as white police officers. Like military work, police work offers individuals a chance at all the privileges of hegemonic masculinity in exchange for embracing and excelling at the job. It thus offers a powerful lure to African American men otherwise denied hegemonic masculinity; and because police work does not explicitly set whites against nonwhites, but rather law-abiders against law-breakers, citizens against "scum," an African American police officer can experience full acceptance as a man without feeling that he has betrayed his race.

We are now in a better position to understand the logic of the feces-smeared broomstick that Officer Justin Volpe proudly displayed around the station house. Abner Louima was a direct threat to the masculinity of the officer he was thought to have assaulted; by extension, he was a threat to the masculinity of the officers in Volpe's unit and to the masculinity of New York's finest as a whole. Abner Louima was also a racialized threat: He stood for the Black and brown people who constitute the presumed majority of the criminal element on New York City's streets and for the mindless savagery of Black masculinity. In challenging this threat, Volpe adopted a hypermasculine stance of his own. Sodomizing Louima—not using his penis but an even bigger "stick"—showed Louima who was the bigger man, who ruled the night. It also showed Louima the superiority of white masculinity, invigorated by a touch of savagery yet retaining the superiority of mastery and control.

I have argued that the concept of gender violence helps make sense of police brutality and of attacks like the one on Abner Louima. Though police abuse is often analyzed through a racial lens, and correctly so, it is important to see as well the thread of hypermasculinity that runs through racism. Acts of violence can be ways of doing race as well as gender. The notion of gender violence as a broader term than "violence against women" also brings to light the powerful currents of fear, hostility, and desire that run among men. Gender violence both set Officer Volpe against Louima and engaged the officer and his unit in a bloody community.

III. Disengaging the Criminal Justice State from Gender Violence

. . . Both the criminals who break the law and the police and legislators who make and enforce it understand violence as the lingua franca of men, and in this masculine language, violence must be countered with more violence lest manhood be reduced or lost. The result is an arms race of punitive treatment perpetuated by the criminal justice state.

. . .

A. Gender Violence and the Criminal Justice State

In liberal democracies, the exercise of state violence, both in the domestic realm and in foreign relations, is justified by reference to the values of protection, security, and order. These values are indeed compelling: Everyone wants to be protected, and certainly neither political citizenship nor social happiness can be pursued without order and security. Yet the language of protection and security provokes a feminist suspicion that a deal with patriarchy has been made somewhere. Political theorist Wendy Brown argues that there is such a deal and that it is a two-part arrangement:

> In the first [part], the state guarantees each man exclusive rights to his woman; hence the familiar feminist charge that rape and adultery laws historically represent less a concern with violations of women's personhood than with individual men's propriety over the bodies of individual women. In the second, the state agrees not to interfere in a man's family (de facto, a woman's life) as long as he is presiding over it (de facto, her).[12]

Questioning the characterization of this arrangement as "security" begins to uncover gender violence perpetrated in the name of the state.

. . .

The conflation of criminal justice with gender violence is facilitated by the public's own investments in the romance of hypermasculinity. As the inexhaustible appetite for books, movies, and television series about criminals, police, and criminal attorneys indicates, Americans have a fascination with criminal justice. . . .

The fictionalized criminal justice system endlessly examined in the popular media provides an ideal forum for the public enjoyment of violence. . . .

The violence dramatized in media portrayals of the criminal justice system may appeal to public tastes because it dramatizes the conflicts within heterosexual masculinity. Or public enjoyment of representations of violence may have to do with the frustrations of living in a world in which freedom and choice are extolled, yet many people find themselves anything but free. Here, the argument is that the obscure sense of shame, humiliation, and resentment at not having achieved enough, at being continually held "responsible" for one's circumstances, may result in rage and the desire to see someone pay.

Finally, another speculation about the popularity of gender violence when perpetrated by fictional cops is that the frequent portrayals of weary and hardbitten, yet heroic white law enforcement officers under siege provide an important vehicle for the contemplation of white masculinity at a time when white men feel they are an endangered species, "losing ground."

Regardless of its sources, however, one effect of the public appetite for depictions of gender violence in the criminal justice system is the perception that a certain amount of gender violence is necessary for law and order. Violence may indeed be necessary for society to exist. Yet the amount and kind of violence necessary to enforce the law and the amount and kind of violence necessary to sustain heteropatriarchal masculinity may not be identical. The public's taste for male gender violence confirms Fuhrman's vision of the police officer as someone who needs to "beat people down" and reinforces the tastes of citizens and politicians for more and more punitive treatment of criminals. But we should not confuse the necessary violence of the criminal justice state with the violence demanded of a certain kind of man.

B. Separating State Violence from Gender Violence

. . .

1. Rethinking Criminal Justice in Theory

Scholars and policymakers, many concerned specifically with criminal justice, have recently begun to argue for the need to use social norms as well as legal rules in the project of influencing behavior. The suggestion that violence is often a form of gender performance brings both good news and bad news to these efforts to take norms into account. The good news is that, as norm theory suggests, the expensive and disappointingly inefficient business of trying to control crime solely with more police, more laws, more punitiveness, and more prisons may not be our only chance for security. Rather, changing and reinforcing nonlegal norms can prevent some crimes and help to properly remedy others.

The bad news is that, as social constructionists have come to realize, the fact that something is conventional rather than innate does not necessarily make it any easier to change. If violent behavior often finds its roots in conventions of masculine gender performance, making a significant dent in America's violence problem may involve not merely changing norms about gun possession or lawbreaking, but altering the rules of gender itself—as feminists will testify, not exactly an easy task.

Nevertheless, the folly of our present criminal justice system has not blocked all ambitious thinking. For example, one project for revamping our criminal justice system calls for replacing punitive justice with restorative justice. [Editors' note: See Chapter 45, Martha Minow's "Between Vengeance and Forgiveness: Feminist Responses to Violent Injustice," for a further discussion of restorative justice.]

. . .

2. Rethinking Criminal Justice in Practice

The identification of gender violence as an endemic problem in policing suggests that ending pervasive police brutality requires not simply more punishment for "rogue" officers or a greater commitment to the vague idea of "community policing," but rather a disruption of the entire gendered culture of policing. A recent community policing initiative in New Haven, Connecticut, provides an example of the kind of thoroughgoing practical changes that such disruption requires.

Nicholas Pastore served as chief of the New Haven Police Department from 1990 to 1997. His tenure is described by one observer in the following way:

> To Pastore, the transition to community policing was an acknowledgment of the growing complexity of the role of the officer. It was no longer enough to be big, strong, male[,] and tough. Instead, reading, writing, talking, listening, solving problems, caring about people, being part of the community, being "nice" and acting respectfully to felons as well as to elected officials were now what the job was to entail and, therefore, what should be taught in the [police] academy.[13]

K. D. Codish, recruited in 1992 to be the director of training and education at the New Haven Police Academy, brought her feminist values to the job of collaborating with Pastore. In order to "de-militarize" the academy, Codish and Pastore adopted the institutional model of a university. They replaced disciplinary calisthenics with assignments in research and writing, eliminated the physical training requirement, and turned trainees from "cadets" or "recruits" into "students." Codish even replaced militaristic and sexist language in police academy materials with gender-neutral language: "Police force" became "police department," "men" became "officers," "manning" became "staffing," and so on.

The substance of the curriculum changed as well. Codish reports:

> Sergeant Proto and I added to the state's "human relations" inservice training requirements a course in the Yale Child Study Community Policing Program, which teaches our officers to identify and refer young witnesses of violence to a specially trained interdisciplinary crisis intervention team. With faculty from the Yale School of Medicine, we developed an inservice program on "special populations," exploring police interactions and referrals for citizens with memory and seizure disorders. We added inservice classes on problem solving and decision making, diversity, HIV/AIDS, and the Americans with Disabilities Act. We replaced mace, the nightstick[,] and blackjack with the less aggressive OC pepper spray and PR-24 defense baton as well as instruction in the non-violent Management of Aggressive Behavior (MOAB).[14]

Finally, Codish attempted to alter the pool from which police officers were selected. Under her leadership, the police academy undertook a special program to recruit women, people of color, and sexual minorities. Codish and Pastore also tried to break down the traditional "us against them" mentality: The new recruitment slogan became "Police Others As You Would Have Others Police You."[15]

It is not clear whether these efforts to "feminize" New Haven policing will have any lasting effect. Pastore left his position in a cloud of scandal in 1997, and the new chief of police is reportedly far more traditional-minded. But the New Haven initiative indicates that the masculinist culture of policing is not unassailable and suggests some practical ways to disrupt that culture. Like the theory and practice of restorative justice, the New Haven initiative points the way toward disentangling the criminal justice state from the practices of gender violence.

. . .

NOTES

1. Allyson Collins, *Justice Won't Prevail until Blue Wall of Police Silence Comes Down*, Houston Chronicle, June 13, 1999, available in 1999 WL 3995543.

2. Eve Kosofsky Sedgwick, Epistemology of the Closet 185 (1990).

3. *Id.* at 186.

4. Timothy Beneke, Men on Rape 42 (1982).

5. Patricia Yancey Martin and Robert A. Hummer, *Fraternities and Rape on Campus*, in Criminology at the Crossroads: Feminist Readings in Crime and Justice 157, 158 (Kathleen Daly and Lisa Maher, eds., 1998).

6. National Center for Women and Policing, Equality Denied: The Status of Women in Policing: 1998, at 3 (visited Oct. 31, 1999) http://www.feminist.org/police/status1998.html.

7. *Id.* at 2.

8. Katherine Spillar and Penny Harrington, *The Verdict on Male Bias: Guilty*, Los Angeles Times, May 16, 1997, available in 1997 WL 2211349.

9. James W. Messerschmidt, Masculinities and Crime: Critique and Reconceptualization of Theory 182 (1993); *Gender Differences Found*, York Daily Record, Dec. 6, 1999, available in 1999 WL 22798825.

10. Human Rights Watch, Shielded from Justice: Police Brutality and Accountability in the United States 25 (1998).

11. Angela P. Harris, *Criminal Justice as Environmental Justice*, 1 Journal of Gender, Race and Justice 1, 17 (1997).

12. Wendy Brown, States of Injury: Power and Freedom in Late Modernity 189 (1995).

13. K. D. Codish, The New Haven Police Academy: Putting One Sacred Cow Out to Pasture or, Policing Others the Way You Would Have Others Police You 1 (1996) (unpublished pamphlet) (on file with author).

14. *Id.* at 4.

15. *Id.* at 4–5.

36

Multiple Masculinities:
A New Vision for Same-Sex Harassment Law

Rachel L. Toker

. . .

III. Theories of Title VII

Although the Supreme Court has clarified the simplest elements of sexual harassment, there appears to be little consensus on what harm Title VII was created to prevent. Many argue that Title VII was enacted to prevent the domination of one sex by another in the workplace. But this statement merely raises further questions. Does Title VII protect against domination of a person because they are of a particular sex, regardless of who the aggressor is—does it focus purely on the sex of the victim? Can we reasonably expect Title VII to promote the equality of the sexes by combating the growing influence of entrenched masculine supremacy—or must it go further and erode the masculine supremacy that already exists?

In an attempt to aggregate different voices in the debate over the meaning and significance of Title VII, this Note categorizes theories about the appropriate scope of Title VII protections based upon their understandings of the harm inflicted and of the means by which that harm is carried out. There are three categories in all.

The first category subsumes two major feminist theories about sexual harassment in the workplace. Both theories conceptualize the harm that Title VII was designed to combat as male dominance of women in the workplace, although they may disagree about the extent of that dominance. That is, both theories view sexual harassment as defined by sex relations and sexuality (in other words, sexual desire and/or power disguised as sexual desire or aggression) as the mode through which female inequality and/or subordination is accomplished.

While both theories assume that male sexuality is predatory and heterosexual, one proposes that the use of masculine power in sexual ways defines "sexual harassment." This theory, articulated and advocated by Catharine MacKinnon, explains that male dominance is perpetrated through the use of sexualized power. Power acts through sexuality, and sexuality shapes gender. The two-sex scenario, in which one dominates the other, produces two polar gender ideals, which are shaped by the profound inequality between the sexes.

The second theory within the first category targets unwanted sexual advances, the means by which men preserve their power over women in the workplace. These unwanted sexual advances produce male hierarchy because they are uniquely debilitating and dehumanizing in the context of workplace hierarchies. This version assumes the presence of sexual desire on the part of the harasser, and asserts that the act of objectifying the victim functions as a form of discrimination through sexualized power. It focuses on women as victims primarily because they are more often the objects of unwelcome sexual desire, but this focus is not theoretically required.

The second category, developed by Vicki Schultz, treats gender segregation (or gender guarding) as the primary harm that Title VII should address. The premise is that a significant portion of sexual harassment is motivated by the desire "to maintain the most highly rewarded forms of work as domains of masculine competence."[1] Schultz argues that this harm is carried out through competence-undermining behavior (nonsexual, aggressive behavior). In this category, sexual harassment occurs when competence-undermining behavior is used to discriminate against a person because their sex, gender, and/or sexuality threaten the male dominance of a particular workplace.

Under this theory, Title VII should block attempts to delineate work and work competence along masculine and feminine lines. Schultz attempts to escape the heterosexual presumption and the problematic issue of "desire" by focusing on the profound tensions that cause men (predominantly) to harass women (predominantly) to prevent them from becoming equally proficient in traditionally male spheres of competence. In her view, [Catharine] MacKinnon and [Susan] Estrich fail to recognize that harassment that is motivated by aspirations for a gender-segregated workplace is actually more damaging to women than harassment motivated by sexual desire.

The third category seeks to prohibit all forms of gender regulation through Title VII because it produces sex stereotypes that deny people the liberty of exercising human agency in the creation of their selves. Katherine Franke and Kathryn Abrams propose theories of this type.[2] This category defines sexual harassment not purely on the basis of sex subordination or gender segregation, but by the process of enforced gender conformity, consciously incorporating the harm of enforced sexuality (meaning sex-specified sexual preferences) within the definition of enforcing gender. Sexual harassment preserves male control through the creation of the workplace as a site of gender hierarchy where "masculine norms structure the working environment."[3] This theory, more than the others, accounts for the domination of males by males by explaining intra-sex inequalities based on gender hierarchies. Under this theory, equality jurisprudence must relax its understanding of sex from a strictly biological definition to a behavioral one. Sexual harassment perpetuates male and masculine control by gender regulation. Therefore, gender regulation in the workplace should be targeted and eliminated, although sexual expressiveness need not be.

Despite the language of hierarchy and implicit suggestion that the domination of one sex by another is the real harm, what is ultimately at stake, under these theories, is an individual's human agency. Title VII should protect against gender regulation by "vigilante" co-workers, but it should protect against this type of hostile action because of its capacity to deny humans their inherent right to structure their selves in the ways that they see fit. This theory frames the issue as one of a denial of an individual liberty interest: gender regulation denies human agency and an individual's power to define him or herself.

Although an individual's ability to determine his or her gender identity freely is extraordinarily important, it is not necessarily infringement upon this liberty that invokes Title VII's prohibitions. Title VII is a bulwark against infringements upon principles of equality, not liberty. Not only have the courts always interpreted Title VII from principles of equality, but the "restriction upon human agency" rationale does not provide a limiting principle. That is, what would happen if an employee felt that it was an expression of his or her sexual agency to walk around the workplace naked? Would it be discrimination for an employer to ask this person to cover up?

IV. Preventing Masculine Supremacy

The theory articulated in this Note builds from the third category of theories of Title VII protection. This Note proposes that Title VII should combat masculine supremacy—an institutionalized system discussed below. It argues, in contrast to scholars like Franke and Abrams, that the problem is primarily one of gender inequality, not restrictions on gender liberty or sex inequality. This harm is accomplished by both inter-sex and intra-sex gender regulation and, as such, should be considered sexual harassment. This theory fits comfortably within the plain language of Title VII, not because the systemic hierarchy is between the sexes, but because gender regulation cannot exist but for an individual's sex. Gender regulation forces a person of one sex to adopt his or her sex-specified gender ideal. One can only identify a person's sex-specified gender ideal when one knows the individual's sex. Although retaining the sex/gender distinction may make it more difficult to reconcile this theory with Title VII's plain language, there are practical concerns for doing so. However, sex and gender should not be conflated because of the inevitable biological restrictions that collapsing the two categories would impose upon the communal imagination when re-imagining new gender ideals for the future. Part VI proposes a new conception of gender (focused on masculinity), multiple masculinities, and an accompanying methodology of causation, which is designed to deconstruct masculine supremacy in the workplace using Title VII.

A. Understanding Masculine Supremacy

American society pushes its citizens to accept the existence of two mutually exclusive gender ideals—one for each sex. This is the "gender dichotomy." Gender regulation is the illicit means of preserving the gender dichotomy. This Note argues that the gender dichotomy, and the gender inequality it invariably produces, are the primary harms that Title VII should combat. Thus, this understanding of Title VII is grounded in principles of equality, not liberty, but abandons presumptions about sexual preferences in the process of understanding how to dismantle hierarchical structures of masculine supremacy.

Gender ideals are characterized by two aspects. The first aspect consists of traits that society believes are unique to its paired sex. For example, people once thought that "maternal" instincts were a trait possessed only by women. The second aspect of a gender ideal involves traits that both genders possess, but that must be "acted out" differently by men and women. It is primarily this second aspect of the gender ideal that produces masculine supremacy—in the workplace and society in general—in part because modern American society has narrowed substantially its belief in the existence of "sexed" traits, and in part because the second aspect is unquestionably socially produced and has become the primary tool with which the gender dichotomy is currently constructed.

Although people of the two sexes no longer exclusively perform traditional occupational sex roles, social understandings of gender have stagnated. The simultaneous retention of gender ideals and abandonment of sex roles leads to a situation in which members of each sex are assigned genders, but those genders are not necessarily the gender ideal for his or her sex. For example, although men increasingly take on caregiver roles in families, a man who takes on the primary caregiver role is viewed as having adopted the feminine gender (he is the "mommy" in the family). As a result, despite the fluidity of the roles that men and women undertake, our conceptions of gender have remained largely unchanged. The activities that women once performed take on feminine genders and the people who perform them are often viewed as effeminate. Not only are personal attributes labeled by gender (self-denigrating or overly deferential behavior may be viewed as effeminate in a man), but certain jobs and career paths may be classified in gender terms as well.

The polarization of the two gender ideals, in combination with the contemporary construction of their relationship, produces a system of masculine supremacy that infects every dimension of social discourse, of which the workplace is one part. First, the mere fact that society has only two ideals produces a cognitive effect called in-group/out-group discrimination. When two groups, such as masculine and feminine, are set in opposition to one another, human cognition leads people to distance themselves sharply from the other, and encourages them to view one group more positively than the other based in part on the reward value of group membership. Second, society requires men to be masculine and women to be feminine, where masculinity and femininity are sets of behaviors that only function effectively within a social structure that contains subordinate feminine persons and dominant masculine persons.

When the gender dichotomy becomes entrenched—especially a hierarchical dichotomy—society is precluded from deliberating about and recalibrating its gender ideals or the underlying structures that are necessary for them to function. The production of alternative ideals, especially multiple ideals, could propel us toward a more free and equal society by forcing reconsideration of the current gender ideals and their relationship to each other. More importantly, the pluralization of gender ideals would substantially decrease the likelihood of entrenching a new form of gender supremacy; that is, the existence of multiple genders for each sex substantially lessens the likelihood of future gender domination.

B. Gender Regulation: Protecting and Preserving the Gender Dichotomy

Same-sex, and often opposite-sex, harassment can be a form of gender regulation motivated by the harasser's desire to preserve the gender dichotomy. Because masculinity is so revered by American culture, men deeply internalize the masculine image; to relinquish the image would seem like a failure. Unfortunately, part of the masculine ideal's normative goodness is related to the fact that it is not feminine; without femininity, masculinity could not claim gender superiority. But why can't we conceive of multiple nonfeminine masculine ideals? Masculinity as a construct resists plurality because gender plurality jeopardizes the gender dichotomy that is a necessary prerequisite to masculine supremacy.

Nonconformist males pose a much greater threat to masculinity, and the gender dichotomy, than any woman can. Men who do not conform to masculinity are punished more severely than women who invade "masculine" space (or threaten the boundaries of masculinity). Gender-nonconforming men pose an intensified threat, in part, because there are ultimately no meaningful physical differences that the threatened man can use to distinguish himself from the nonconformist. In addition, there is no way for a gender-conforming man to explain why a nonconforming man would choose to relinquish his claim to privilege and supremacy without diminishing the conformist's own status. The conformist is left with an uncomfortable quandary that is usually resolved through denigration, physical violence, or likening the nonconformist to a woman.

By resolving the conflict posed by the gender-nonconformist through emotional or physical violence, or gender regulation, the gender conformist not only extinguishes the threat, but reinforces his own gender ideal of masculinity. This dialectical process allows the harasser continually to reaffirm his conformity with the gender ideal while defining masculine norms in opposition to those who refuse to conform, those who support redefining the gender roles, and those who are feminine (contributing to the constant reintroduction of the gender dichotomy).

A person's desire to conform to gender ideals will depend upon some combination of the following: the manner in which gender ideals are presented to the individual during the process of gender assignment, the extent to which deviant gender ideals are presented as normatively positive, the individual's predisposition and/or cognitive readiness to conform to social teachings, the extent to which the individual comes into contact with gender nonconformists, and the extent to which the individual considers social sanction a meaningful threat.

Physical restraints or limitations (such as height and weight), as well as certain developmental difficulties (mental retardation and learning disabilities), may render an individual unable to comply with certain gender ideals. Some individuals who cannot physically comply with gender ideals consider themselves defective, but continue striving for the gender ideal—compensating for their physical limitation where possible. Others, especially those who are unable to compensate for their deviations, will reject the dominant gender ideal (or the aspect that negatively affects them) to retain their sense of self-esteem.

V. The Inadequacy of Sexual Harassment Jurisprudence

If one accepts the argument that Title VII must prevent gender regulation because such regulation enables structures of masculine supremacy to thrive, then [the Supreme Court's methodology in *Oncale*[4] of] sex flipping is inadequate. . . . Sex flipping does not discover gender regulation in all cases, and it reinforces the gender dichotomy as a system of thought.

Sex flipping cannot capture many forms of gender regulation in a society of multiple and varied gender identities. Sex flipping is an effective methodology in a world in which two sexes conform unilaterally to one of two gender ideals. If all men and women are either "masculine" or "feminine," sex flipping will prove whether discrimination was based on sex. (This schema can account for the feminine man or the masculine woman.) Sex flipping would be appropriate because either a person has paired the "wrong" gender identity with his or her sex, and by sex flipping one can see that the "correct" pairing would eliminate discrimination, or the pairing is "right," in which case any difference in treatment is not sex discrimination. However, sex flipping is inadequate because individuals do not conform solely to either the masculine or the feminine ideal; men and women who do not conform to their sex-specified ideal do not simply de facto conform to the other sex's gender ideal. For each sex, any of a number of gender identities can attach, and they are not all equally socially accepted. Certain gender identities are of markedly less social value than others are, but sex flipping does not detect inequality within the sexes when that inequality is based on differentially valued genders.

What if a man is perceived not to be masculine, but also not to be feminine? Is such a thing possible? If it is, then what good does it do to ask whether the harasser would similarly discriminate against a woman in his position? When same-sex harassment occurs between males, this method might detect the ability of "masculine" men to violently dominate "feminine" men; but it is not concerned with whether ideally masculine men are allowed to dominate nontraditionally masculine men violently. Understanding sex discrimination as a problem solely between the two sexes (or between the two genders) without simultaneously seeing it as part of a struggle for gender-group coherence within each sex-group skews the real focus.

Not only is sex flipping under-inclusive in a world of plural gender identities, but it is also affirmatively harmful for social and intellectual progress. Sex flipping preserves the bipolar gender dichotomy. For example, Justice Scalia's opinion in *Oncale* assumes that sexual harassment can be identified and measured, almost scientifically, if one compares the employer's treatment of members of one sex with its treatment of members of another sex. This presumption—that one sex can provide a control group for the other—implies that Title VII must be understood within the theoretical framework of two genders in which one is dominant. Because sex flipping is only an effective methodology for detecting sex discrimination if we conceive of gender in terms of the gender dichotomy, using sex flipping as the sole method of proof of sex discrimination reinforces the belief in two genders. Requiring sex flipping as a methodology contributes to society's inability to develop conceptions of plural gender categories for the sexes. The methodology eliminates the possibility that masculine genders other than the prevailing masculine gender ideal might exist (i.e., masculine genders that are not the functional equivalent of the feminine gender ideal).

There are also several secondary reasons why sex flipping is an inadequate method of testing for same-sex harassment. Both men and women may be harassed because of their genders. It is absurd to assume that if both sexes are harassed, Title VII is negated and no claim exists for either. Moreover, sex flipping poses significant problems of proof when dealing with single-sex work environments.

VI. "Multiple Masculinities": An Answer for Sexual Harassment Law

A. The Theory of Multiple Masculinities

The theory of multiple masculinities is premised on the notion that society must not only tolerate gender nonconformity, but foster alternative visions of masculinity. Individual men should be free to deviate from the masculine gender ideal, and be assisted in pluralizing multiple masculine ideals through social acceptance.

Many theorists argue for society to accept gender nonconformity. Implicit in their arguments, however, is the assumption that we should not think in terms of categories. Instead, men and women should be free to adopt portions of the two gender ideals as they choose. This framework embraces the premise that the two polar genders exist, and anyone who does not fit comfortably within their "assigned" gender must be some combination of masculine and feminine. Kathryn Abrams argues that this freedom, "the capacity to put together the disparate elements of self—biological being, gendered subject, worker, sexual actor," is essential to a sense of personal agency.[5]

Society must enable men to deviate from the masculine gender ideal; however, the conceptual framework of gender in which the poles of a "gender continuum" are "masculine" and "feminine" should be rejected. This conceptual framework requires one to assume that when a person moves away from one pole, he or she is moving closer to the other. Although this continuum framework superficially promotes gender plurality, it does so in a way that re-entrenches the gender dichotomy. Moreover, it does not force people to exercise their imaginations in re-conceiving masculinity: it merely allows men to incorporate more aspects of femininity into their gender identities.

In order for society truly to engage in the process of developing new visions of masculinity, it must reconstruct gender as a multitude of categorical variables in which "masculine" and "feminine" are categories with subcategories. These subcategories (masculinities and femininities) may overlap but are not identical. The theory of "multiple masculinities" calls for society to conceptualize gender ideals pluralistically and accept the ability of multiple femininities and multiple masculinities to coexist as ideals in the same community (however defined). Freeing ourselves from the gender dichotomy frees us to envision what other "masculinities" might look like, and allows us to embrace and affirm those alternative visions as not only acceptable, but ideal.

. . .

2. Images of Masculinity and Gender Plurality

Society has yet to embark seriously upon the pluralizing of masculinity the way that it has with femininity. The work that is being, and has been, done by feminists to deconstruct the essence of femininity needs to be done in a more aggressive way with masculinity. When a man does not conform to what we know to be masculinity, too large a portion of our society is willing to use social and physical pressure to make him conform. A man might be viewed as gender-nonconforming either because he exhibits traits that have been traditionally identified with the feminine, or because he does not exhibit certain traits that comprise traditional masculinity. An example of the first kind of gender nonconformity is a man who exhibits a particularly nurturing or sharing disposition or who is particularly emotionally expressive. An example of the latter kind of nonconformity is a single man who is not (hetero)sexually active.

. . .

Society needs to be able to conceive of a man who does not have to relinquish a position of respect and stature within a community merely because he exhibits traits not currently conceived of as "masculine," such as empathy, passivity, open-mindedness, or nurturing. These are not feminine skills; they are often taught only to women, but are very important to being a man.

3. Sexuality

Because heterosexuality is so central to the masculine gender ideal, a man is usually viewed as gender-nonconforming if he is anything other than heterosexual. Therefore, sexual expressiveness plays a key role for males; males have a vested interest in ensuring that others know of their heterosexual sexual preferences so that they may be viewed as conforming to the masculine gender ideal. In fact, other males may view silence suspiciously unless they receive circumstantial evidence of heterosexuality, such as being married or dating women. A man whose sexual expression is ambiguous or nonheterosexual is a strong candidate for gender regulatory sexual harassment.

For women, homosexuality is also viewed as gender-nonconforming to the dominant feminine idea, but it is not as anathema to femininity as it is to masculinity. Instead, women risk harassment if they are sexually expressive at all. That is, either a woman is heterosexually expressive, in which case the woman is "inviting" harassment, or she is homosexually expressive, in which case she provokes harassment by "advertising" her gender nonconformity. Women are thus best able to avoid sexual harassment by refraining from sexual expression entirely.

4. Multiple Masculinities

The theory of multiple masculinities is not intended to canonize a new universal masculinity; it is intended to teach men that they have many options for expressing their manhood and to delegitimize the penalties imposed by society when men act in nontraditional ways. It is about creating composites of masculinity that positively reinforce and respect nonconformity with the currently dominating gender ideal(s). Most importantly, it is designed to allow society to realize that such men are not less worthy as men if they act in nontraditionally masculine ways. In fact, new masculinities might be construed as sexually attractive, reinforcing gender plurality through sexuality.

. . .

B. Multiple Masculinities and Title VII Jurisprudence

Armed with the theory of multiple masculinities, we can revisit the question of which method is appropriate for deducing when same-sex harassment is because of sex. Instead of sex flipping, a judge should focus on the assailant's treatment of subsets of gender within a given sex group. Courts should employ a counterfactual assumption that requires them to imagine, in place of the victim, a person of the same sex who, unlike the victim, exhibits the gender ideal assigned to that sex. It is the victim's failure to conform his gender identity to this assigned gender ideal that elicits the harassment. This harassment is "because of sex" since sex is integrally paired with gender identity. In other words, but for the victim's sex, his gender identity could not be deemed proper or improper, and so would not have led to discrimination.

A court should compare the way that an employer (or co-worker) treats men or women who exhibit nontraditional masculinities or femininities to the way that he or she treats men or women who epitomize their respective gender ideals. Comparing different masculinities and femininities is the only way to prove the cause of the assault (the pairing of a nontraditional gender with the victim's sex). This examination does not entail an exclusive focus on gender, but rather a careful examination of the motivation behind the harassment, the pairing of sex and gender within individuals. Where harassment is motivated by the particular ways in which an employee manifests his or her sex (through gender), a court must find that the employee was discriminated against because of his or her sex.

. . .

NOTES

1. Vicki Shultz, *Reconceptualizing Sexual Harassment*, 107 Yale Law Journal 1683, 1690 (1998).

2. Kathryn Abrams, *The New Jurisprudence of Sexual Harassment*, 83 Cornell Law Review 1169, 1215 (1998).

3. *Id.* at 1219.

4. *Oncale v. Sundowner Offshore Servs., Inc.*, 118 S. Ct. 998 (1998).

5. Abrams, supra note 2, at 1220.

37

"It's like Living in a Black Hole": Women of Color and Solitary Confinement in the Prison Industrial Complex

Cassandra Shaylor

Angela Tucker awoke at six a.m. cowering in the corner of her cell, shaking uncontrollably, unable to breathe. A fifty-four year old African-American woman, Tucker suffers from hypertension, diabetes, and asthma. Though she was confined alone in this cold, dark cell for six months, she finally had reached her limit. She repeatedly called for guards to help her, but they refused to respond. A few hours later, she was subjected to a strip-search and taken out of her cell to the shower. When she returned from the shower, she refused to re-enter the cell. She begged to be placed in a larger space, to be put in a cell with another prisoner. She explained that she was claustrophobic, and that since she had been placed in solitary confinement both her blood pressure and her blood sugar had risen to dangerous levels. Her pleas were ignored. Instead she was confronted by a cadre of fourteen guards who threatened to use physical force against her, including shooting her with rubber bullets, if she refused to enter her cell. She chose to comply, but insisted that she be placed on the medical doctor's visiting list. A couple of days later a psychiatric doctor came to her cell and prescribed a combination of Prozac and Buspar, two psychotropic medications, to cure her "anxiety problems." She remains in solitary confinement and has received no medical attention for her serious medical conditions. As someone who has been in and out of the prison systems for fifteen years, she says, "I thought I had seen most of what they can dish out. But this here is the worst. I never seen anything like it. Living in here is like nothin' you could ever begin to imagine. It's like living in a black hole."[1]

I. Introduction

Angela Tucker's experience in solitary confinement in a women's prison is not unique. It reflects the increasing brutality in prisons, particularly in prisons for women. . . .

II. Control Units

Control units represent the penultimate synthesis of technology and space in the service of social control and dehumanization within the prison. For women at VSPW [Valley State Prison for Women], this punishment regime consists of twenty-three hours a day of isolation in cramped, cold, dark cells, sometimes involving total sensory deprivation. These cells are approximately eight feet by six feet, the size of an average bathroom. Women in the SHU are allowed nine hours outside a week. This is the only opportunity they have to interact with other women. Although the cells originally were designed with small windows, the institution recently blacked out these windows, removing any sense of a world outside.

Control units are also referred to as security housing units (SHUs), violence control units (VCUs), or maxi-maxi facilities. There is a frightening trend in prison construction toward building separate "supermax" prisons, that is, entire institutions modeled on the control unit. Forty states, the federal system, and the District of Columbia all have at least one control unit. Women have generally been confined in control units within already existing women's prisons, but the increasing brutality in those institutions indicates that female supermax facilities are likely in the not-so-distant future. Whether free-standing units within an existing institution, or prisons built specifically for housing prisoners in solitary confinement, conditions in these spaces and the effects on the individuals housed within them are strikingly similar. The expanding use of control units reflects the increasingly repressive character of prisons. It is important to note that isolation and sensory deprivation are now used to some degree in most penal institutions, including many county jails. Control units are specifically designed for these purposes, but many prisons do not require a separate unit to employ these tactics.
. . .

III. Women in Control Units

Prisoners and advocates for prisoners see the increasing use of control units as instruments of gender domination and torture. . . . Women do resist: they speak up; fight back; or participate in individual and class action lawsuits, which represent individual and collective challenges to the conditions of their confinement. Such challenges, however, are viewed harshly and often result in confinement in the SHU, the sole objective of which seems to be to break women. Little else explains such oppressive structures within women's prisons.

According to the women interviewed by this author at VSPW, women in the SHU are under constant surveillance and denied any privacy. The cell doors are designed to allow guards to see in at all times. This makes the women extremely vulnerable to sexual harassment and abuse. Male guards watch women in the showers, often turning off the water if the women complain. The toilets are located in the cells, within view of the guards, who often harass women while they are on the toilet. When guards conduct pat searches they are supposed to act in a professional manner and avoid embarrassing inmates; however, women prisoners report that male guards regularly grope them with the palms of their hands.

Though male guards are not permitted to conduct strip-searches, they are often present when such searches occur. The presence of this level of sexual harassment creates an environment which inevitably leads to even more serious sexual assault and abuse. A story was recently reported to this author by three women in the institution about a woman who is housed in the SHU, who was allegedly raped by a guard while living in general population. The rape resulted in pregnancy and because she refuses to have an abortion, she has been sent to the SHU. Due to their relative lack of power, women prisoners are vulnerable to such attacks by guards. This is especially true when they are isolated from other women. The sense of entitlement male guards feel as a result of their status in a masculinist institution within a patriarchal culture, coupled with the subordinated status of female prisoners as women and as "property of the state," promotes such abuse. The cult of silence preserved by the masculinist guard culture protects guards from anything but the lightest disciplinary sanctions.

. . .

The use of [cell] extraction teams is a routine practice in supermax facilities; women are not exempt from it. For women, however, this treatment is uniquely traumatic because male guards usually perform the extraction. The incidents are highly sexualized: women are rendered immobile, placed in a position of extreme vulnerability, stripped of all of their clothing, and then subjected to a full body search. Because about 60 percent of women in prison are survivors of some form of physical or sexual abuse, cell extractions for many of them are not only traumatic in the moment, but result in a re-experiencing of past trauma. Claudia Johnson said, "It is about humiliation and total loss of dignity, and I don't care what they call it. I call it rape."[2]

. . .

Control units are built without any concern for the detrimental effects they have on the women within them. Solitary confinement has a particularly devastating effect on mentally ill women, many of whom are sent to the SHU because they "act out" in general population as a result of their mental illness. Many women are prescribed psychotropic medications, but most receive no meaningful psychiatric treatment. Within penal institutions, the medicalization model is widely used against women. This author has interviewed women who can barely speak because they are so heavily drugged and has been told about others who rarely move from their bunks because the medication virtually immobilizes them. Some women talk to themselves or yell incessantly at their cell doors, while others experience paranoid delusions and hallucinations. Many cover themselves in urine and feces. These behaviors represent stages of psychological breakdown that have been observed in prisoners of war. For these women, their own bodies become their primary sites of resistance. Unfortunately, this behavior perpetuates the guards' perceptions of them as violent and legitimizes longer sentences in the SHU.

. . .

IV. Control Units for Women as Racialized Spaces

The prison is a site for social control of all women, but solitary confinement is a space reserved for particular women. Of the fifty-two women in the SHU at VSPW, 61.4 percent of them are women of color. Over 40 percent of the women are "Black," 21 percent are "Hispanic/Mexican," and 5.9 percent are categorized as other. Though the dehumanization processes in the SHU replicate that which happens in the larger prison, the purpose of which is to produce docile bodies, these processes are more extreme and have more detrimental effects on women housed in the SHU.

In general, discipline for women in prison is extremely harsh, especially in comparison to discipline for men. Women are far more likely than men to be sentenced to the SHU for minor infractions. While men are confined to control units for allegedly attacking guards, participating in gangs, or selling drugs in the institution, women are placed in the SHU for spitting at guards, for fighting with other women, or for attempting suicide. A central function of prisons in general is to punish women who fail to subscribe to a model of femininity that historically has been (re)produced in discourse as white, pure, passive, heterosexual, and located in motherhood. When women operate outside of this model, even slightly, they are disciplined harshly for doing so.

Women of color in prison face a double bind in this regard. As Kimberlé Crenshaw points out, Black women have never been perceived to fit this description of patriarchal notions about femininity, because racism denies them access to these norms.[3] Black women are prefigured as aggressive and recalcitrant; guards, therefore, are predisposed to view them this way and discipline them accordingly. This analysis can be extended to Latinas and Native American women in prison. Latinas are perceived to be loud and belligerent, sexually aggressive, or immigrants who are unable to speak English. Native American women are perceived as backward, savage and/or primitive, especially when they seek to preserve religious rights while imprisoned. These views of women of color rely on stereotypes of white femininity as a model against which to judge "other" women.

Beyond the racist politics of the SHU, as represented by the disproportionate confinement of women of color there, the dehumanization practices that take place within it in can also be read as racialized. Women are degraded, sexually humiliated, and denied minimal medical care and any meaningful human contact. Women are often denied basic necessities, such as food and hygiene supplies. They are made to beg for sanitary napkins and toilet paper and are often told during the last week of the month that the prison has "run out." Such practices resonate with larger histories of racism that dehumanize people of color.

. . .

V. Purposes of the Control Unit

One purpose offered by the state for control units is the reduction of violence within the prison. . . . Research indicates that women are more prone to violent behavior as a result of confinement in solitary units, but violence against themselves. Many women in solitary confinement release their frustration and anger by engaging in self-harming behavior, including suicide attempts and self-mutilation. . . . Confinement in the SHU has devastating psychological effects on most women housed there. Extended periods of idleness and social isolation result in vicious mood swings, crying spells, and intense feelings of paranoia. . . .

A second professed reason for control units is to reduce expenses—isolation means fewer people allowed access to vocational and educational programs and to rehabilitative, religious, and recreational services. Diminished access to these programs in control units is linked to the trend of dismantling programs in the prison system in general. This move away from rehabilitation and toward punishment is now the prevailing trend in prison administration. Control units are one part of this move toward repression and brutality. The reality is that expenses are not reduced as a result of the introduction of control units. It is actually much more expensive to maintain control units than those units that house the general population, because of the level of security involved and the increase in health-related expenses. . . .

A 1989 Prison Discipline Study found that the most common disciplining strategy used against jailhouse lawyers was solitary confinement.[4] This study found that jailhouse lawyers were found to be by far the largest number of those in control units. Other categories of prisoners who were found to be placed in solitary confinement in disproportionate numbers were: Blacks, mentally disabled individuals, gang members, political prisoners, Latinos, gays and lesbians, and people with AIDS.

. . .

VI. The History of the SHU

. . .

The first control unit prison emerged in 1983 at USP Marion, a federal prison for men in Illinois. USP Marion became the model for the current wave of control units and solitary confinement strategies throughout the country. Ostensibly in response to a violent incident, the entire prison was locked down. That lockdown has never been lifted, effectively transforming the entire prison into a control unit. The tactics developed at Marion have been applied at prisons all over the country. These tactics were instrumental in the design of the high tech federal control unit at Florence, Colorado, which houses 550 people in permanently locked down cells.

The only control unit specifically designed for women political prisoners was opened at Lexington Federal Prison in Kentucky in 1986. The unit employed multiple tactics to destroy the women's senses of self and to break down their political convictions through sensory deprivation and small-group isolation. The unit housed three political prisoners: Alejandrina Torres, Puerto Rican independentista; Susan Rosenberg, North American anti-imperialist; and Silvia Baraldini, Italian national and anti-imperialist. The structure was built underground and the interior was entirely white, which resulted in reports from the women of hallucinations of black spots and strings on the walls and floors. The women were made to wear large, shapeless clothing and were forbidden to hang anything on the white walls. What little contact they had with their jailers was often in the form of disembodied voices addressing them through loud speakers. They had only occasional contact with the outside, mostly with their lawyers. After an intense campaign waged by a broad coalition of concerned people, the unit was shut down in 1988. The legal decision was based on the political nature of the placements—the court determined that the women were housed there as a result of their political beliefs and that such placement was unconstitutional. Although the courts came close to admitting that there are political prisoners in the United States, the decision did not declare that such treatment rises to the level of cruel and unusual punishment. The decision was undermined when the U.S. Court of Appeals ruled that prisons are free to use political associations and beliefs to justify different and harsher treatment. Since Lexington closed, other units, modeled on Lexington, have opened in other parts of the country. Women in the federal prison at Marianna, Florida, for example, and other prisons across the country, are reporting increasingly brutal, similar conditions. Where once such units housed mostly political prisoners, now all prisoners are potentially subject to this level of social control.

VII. *Current Trends in Prison Construction*

. . .

Prisoners are often used as human trials for new technologies prior to adequate testing. New "beanbag" bullets were recently introduced in California prisons. Maria Hernandez, a woman imprisoned at VSPW, was the test case for these bullets. In direct violation of protocols concerning the use of these weapons, a guard fired directly into her back. The bullets exploded on impact, bore into and burned her skin, leaving large and permanent scars on her back. In the first week that these bullets were used at VSPW, five women were shot with them.

. . .

VIII. *The Emerging Prison Industrial Complex*

. . .

Corrections officials and guards now take a wholly combative stance toward prisoners, rather than a rehabilitative or even a custodial one. They receive training in military combat techniques and the use of high tech weapons. One recent example of this growing militarism is the videotape of the "training" in a private prison in Texas which showed guards brutalizing prisoners. Every aspect of guard culture is modeled on the military. Guards dress in fatigues and combat boots and subscribe to a military hierarchy. At VSPW, guards force women to march in single file lines around the prison. In the administration building at VSPW, a trophy case in the lobby contains memorabilia of the Special Emergency Response Unit (SERT), a cadre of guards who are trained in special military techniques to be used in crisis situations at VSPW. A photograph of this unit shows twelve men in camouflage fatigues and grey berets. In place of the patch that usually reads "Army," is a patch which says "VSPW." The trophy case also contains a plaque, with a bullet casing attached to it, inscribed with the name of the "Top Gun," the most skilled "sharpshooter" in the unit.

The growing militarism in prison does not result from an actual need for such excessive punishment—after all, . . . 80 percent of women are in prison for non-violent offenses and a vast majority of them are never violent within the prison. Prisons on the whole do not reduce violence. Despite the imprisonment binge, the rate of violent crime has in fact remained steady. Prisons do perpetuate violence, however, in the form of destruction of families, and in the wholesale destruction of economic and political power in the communities in which those families live. Prisons also provide economic opportunities for corporate and government systems, which thrive on the violence they perpetuate against those communities.

A central example of corporate involvement in the prison industrial complex is the Corrections Corporation of America. It is currently the most profitable company in the privately run prison industry. American Express and General Electric have contributed to private prison construction. Financial powerhouses, such as Merrill Lynch & Co., Inc., Smith Barney Shearson, Inc., and Goldman Sachs & Co. are currently underwriting prison construction through the sale of private, tax-free bonds which require no voter approval. Furthermore, the construction industry is not the only private interest profiting from prisons. Everything from Dial Soap to AT&T is marketed to corrections officials. Health care companies and food service providers compete for lucrative prison contracts.

. . .

Perhaps most disturbing about this political economy is the growing exploitation of prison labor. As growing numbers of women are arrested and imprisoned, they increasingly become a part of this exploited class of laborers. Prisoners work to produce shrink wrap packages for Microsoft and handle reservations for TWA. California voters passed Proposition 139, the Inmate Labor Initiative of 1990,[5] which paved the way for inmates to be leased out to private industry, reinstating slavery through the explicit repeal of the principle that prison work would be voluntary. The initiative states in part: "The people of the State of California find and declare that inmates who are confined in state prison or county jails should work as hard as taxpayers for their upkeep, and that those inmates may be required to perform work and services."[6]

In California, a semi-autonomous state agency called the Prison Industry Authority (PIA) was created to make industries within the prison self-sustaining and profitable. The PIA mission statement no longer refers to rehabilitation or training; it focuses only on maximizing profits. Ultimately, prisoners find that they do not learn marketable skills in prison and are rarely able to find jobs similar to the ones they performed inside (or any job at all, for that matter). A gendered division of labor exists within prison industries; women have generally worked in laundry, upholstery, fabric production, and data entry, while men have worked in metal and wood production, automotive shops, dairies, and slaughterhouses. At VSPW, women prisoners produce eyeglasses for LensCrafters through PIA-Optical. These women are paid less than one dollar an hour, are forced to work overtime or risk losing their jobs, and are prevented from organizing against dangerous and exploitative work conditions.

. . .

IX. Race, Gender, and the Prison Boom

The material reality of this "booming industry" is the proliferation of prisons. In the last ten years, twenty prisons have been built in California. Three were prisons for women. This expansion is part of a national historical trend. Though only two or three women's prisons were built per decade between 1930 and 1950, there were seven built in the 1960s, seventeen in the 1970s, and thirty-four in the 1980s. Scholars and activists who address issues of imprisonment seldom acknowledge the expanding population of women prisoners and the proliferation of women's prisons. This expansion is not insignificant: while the number of men in prison has doubled in the last decade, the number of women has more than tripled. Thus, women play an ever-growing role in the increasingly profitable punishment industry, an industry in which the financial stakes are incredibly high.

The United States now incarcerates approximately 2 million people, a number equivalent to the population of a large city and more than any other industrialized country in the world. Though women comprise only about 7.37 percent of those incarcerated, or about 113,000 people, they are the fastest growing population in prison. Prisons today constitute elaborate warehousing systems into which members of the expendable classes, such as the poor, unemployed, homeless, mentally ill, and drug-dependent, are dumped.

. . .

Prevailing political investments in "tough on crime" measures result in longer, harsher sentences that discriminately affect communities of color. As a result, the prison itself is increasingly a racialized space, thus affecting women in unique ways. Approximately 35 percent of women in prison are African-American and 24 percent Latina, numbers significantly larger than their respective representation in national demographics. About 80 percent of these women have at least two children. Thus, there is also a largely unexamined impact on communities of color, especially children in those communities, who are also affected by the "imprisonment binge."

. . .

XI. Conclusion

Angela Tucker's analogy to the black hole with which this article began is an apt description of the control unit and, as such, serves as a structuring metaphor for my discussion of women of color in solitary confinement. In scientific discourse, a black hole is defined as:

> a region of space, created by the total gravitational collapse of matter, whose attractive gravitational force is so intense that no matter, light, or communication of any kind can escape. [It is] difficult to observe for two reasons. First, [it is] "black"—no light from inside can escape to make it visible. Second, [it is] a very small object. Thus, it can be "observed" only by deducing its presence from the effects that its gravitational field has on matter lying outside the black hole. . . . Time and space are warped; time is slowed down and space stretched out near a black hole. . . . [The pressure in a black hole is so great that] a person [encountering it] would be ripped to shreds. . . . Black holes are predicted to occur at the endpoint of the evolution of sufficiently massive stars.[7]

In terms of the SHU, this analogy to the black hole is multi-layered: the "blackness" of the SHU is reflected in both its racialized nature and the darkness of the cells themselves; the degree of force within the SHU is experienced by the women through physical brutality and sexual violence; the space of the SHU is oppressively small; mental stability is warped; the experience of passage of time is transformed; and communication flowing both into and out of the SHU is severely restricted. There is also a connection between the massive expansion of the prison industrial complex and the SHU. The prison industrial complex is now so comprehensive and far-reaching that it distorts everything around it. It creates a political system which thrives on the implementation of "tough on crime" measures and an economic system which relies on demonizing and terrorizing entire communities of people. As a result, our society is increasingly a "carceral" one; a high level of surveillance is present in all of our lives. The "endpoint of the evolution of a sufficiently massive" project such as the prison industrial complex is the imprisonment of entire communities and the isolation and dehumanization practices of the SHU.

. . .

NOTES

1. Interview with Angela Tucker, Valley State Prison for Women, in Chowchilla, Cal. (Feb. 6, 1998).
2. Interview with Claudia Johnson, Valley State Prison for Women, in Chowchilla, Cal. (Oct. 30, 1997).
3. See generally Kimberlé Crenshaw, *Demarginalizing the Intersection of Race and Sex: A Black Feminist Critique of Antidiscrimination Doctrine, Feminist Theory and Antiracist Politics*, in 1 Feminist Legal Theory 443 (Frances E. Olsen, ed., 1995).

4. See *The Prison Discipline Study: Exposing the Myth of Humane Imprisonment in the United States*, in Criminal Injustice: Confronting the Prison Crisis 92, 92–97 (Elihu Rosenblatt, ed., 1996).

5. See Julie Browne, *The Labor of Doing Time*, in Criminal Injustice: Confronting the Prison Crisis 61, 68 (Elihu Rosenblatt, ed., 1996).

6. *Id.*

7. 4 The Encyclopedia Americana International Edition 33–34 (1992); 4 Collier's Encyclopedia 238–39 (1997).

38

The Shame of It: Gender-Based Terrorism in the Former Yugoslavia and the Failure of International Human Rights Law to Comprehend the Injuries

Amy E. Ray

. . .

Introduction

The deliberate use of rape as a weapon of war was a central strategy in the Serbian effort to seize and maintain territorial control in the former Yugoslavia. Although the Serbian policy of "ethnic cleansing" included the use of concentration camps, torture, the burning of entire villages, and mass executions, it was the use of rape as a weapon of war that captured the media's eye and the world's attention. The mainstream media have focused on rape, but many other gender-based crimes also have occurred, including forced pregnancy, forced motherhood, prostitution, and spousal and familial abuse. As a result of these crimes, the victims have been ostracized socially, further prostituted, and some have attempted or committed suicide. In the process of voyeuristically sensationalizing the rape of thousands of women, many media have failed to contextualize these crimes within the lives and within the culture of the survivors. The women interviewed have become objectified as "rape victims," rather than portrayed as the complete and multi-faceted women that they are—women suffering many kinds of injuries, only one of which is rape, and surviving. They have indeed become "a nameless, faceless group, victims with neither name nor identity."[1]

At the same time, however, the fact that we learned of the systematic rape of women in this war almost simultaneously with its occurrence is significant. For the first time, the use of rape as a military strategy at least has been reported, even if reported incompletely. Warring states always have used the sexual terrorism of women to win wars, either by setting up brothels in order to boost the morale of soldiers; by using the systematic rape of the "enemy's women" as a direct weapon calculated to subjugate an entire community or group of people; or by raping to impregnate and, therefore, "taint" the bloodline of the enemy. In the past, however, these abuses were considered an inevitable part of war. Indeed, despite the thousands of women raped and prostituted during World War II, Vietnam, and the Bangladesh-Pakistan War, no one ever had been tried for rape as a war crime until this conflict.

The public nature of the terrorism of women in the former Yugoslavia, then, is unique, affording us the opportunity to examine its dimensions and its consequences.

. . .

I. *The Terrorism of Women in Bosnia-Herzegovina*

. . .

[O]ur first task is to describe the injuries suffered by the women in the former Yugoslavia and, in particular, the ways in which these injuries are gender specific. By elucidating the gender-specific nature of many of the crimes committed against women, we then will be able to examine the law's failure to comprehend these injuries.

. . .

A. Rape as a Strategy of War

"This is ethnic rape as an official policy of war . . . . It is rape under orders: not out of control, under control."[2]

The victimization of the women in the former Yugoslavia begins with rape: not isolated incidents of soldiers gone astray, but rather a carefully conceived and effective war strategy of the systematic rape of thousands of women. Current estimates are that tens of thousands of women were raped as part of the Serbian war effort. The victims' ages ranged from six to eighty-one, and the rapes were condoned by, ordered by, and committed by commanding officers. When entering a village to be seized, one of the first actions typically taken by the Serb aggressors was to rape publicly several women thereby forcing the Croatian or Bosnian population to flee.

. . .

The rapes were committed in front of as many as two hundred witnesses, including children. As a result, the raped women became constant reminders to the entire community, their families, and themselves of Serbian suppression and domination.

In addition, the rapes often were committed by men familiar to the women. . . . Thus, in addition to the injury of sexual violation, the women of the former Yugoslavia experienced the additional trauma and overwhelming sense of betrayal associated with sexual violation by persons previously trusted.

Once the town was secured, women and men were separated. The women and children then were taken to a detention facility, and the rapes continued. A mission sent by the European Community to investigate the treatment of Muslim women in the former Yugoslavia concluded that rape was not incidental to the main purpose of the aggression; rather, it was perpetrated as a strategic purpose in and of itself.

Rape was used as part of a carefully conceived plan to terrorize entire communities, driving them from their homes and demonstrating the power of the invading forces.

In order to understand fully both the purpose and the effect of these rapes, however, we must appreciate the significance of rape within the cultures of the former Yugoslavia. Within these cultures "honor" is paramount and shame results from a loss of honor. Although both men and women are bound to be honorable, women are the objects through which men's honor is determined. Any time a woman has sex outside marriage, the men related to that particular woman temporarily lose their honor. The woman, on the other hand, permanently loses her honor. The men affected by the loss may be the woman's husband, her father, or her brother. Thus, dishonor brought about by a woman's sexual activity reflects upon the entire family.

. . .

For Bosnian women, the consequences of these rapes have been severe. There have been several reports of women being abused violently by their spouses after revealing that they had been raped. Similarly, women who have come forward and testified publicly about being raped have been ostracized from the refugee camp where they had been living. The other residents reportedly did not want their refugee camp to be seen as a "rape victims" camp. Maria Olujie reports that husbands have killed or abandoned their wives, young unmarried women have been disowned by their families, women of all ages are kept from suicide only by sedatives, and others have been driven crazy by their experiences and the pressure to maintain silence about those experiences[.]

. . .

Survivors of rape in all cultures experience an overwhelming sense of shame and self-blame. The sense of shame, however, is particularly acute for survivors of rape in the former Yugoslavia, where culture attaches a particular stigma to rape. For example, after journalists visited a group of thirty-eight women in a refugee center and recorded their stories, seven of the women who had survived the worst aggression and violence committed suicide. Many other women are kept from suicide only by sedatives. As a result of family and community pressure to keep silent, accounts of rape have come predominantly from women who were isolated from these pressures. Almost all of the stories have come from divorced women, widows, or unmarried women who do not have to contend with outraged husbands or other family members.

The Serbian forces who committed these mass rapes were well aware of the cultural significance of the rape of women in these cultures. They knew when they began their campaign that the systematic rape of Bosnian and Croatian women would be a particularly effective weapon in their effort to dominate, humiliate, and completely subjugate the women, their families, and their communities. It is because of the significance of rape that its use was so successful in inflicting a reign of terror on an entire ethnic group and thereby consolidating the territorial gains made by the Serbian soldiers. In addition, because the rapes were condoned and even ordered by superiors, soldiers had unfettered access to sex, maintaining and furthering their feelings of superiority and domination. As a result of the Serbs' use of systematic rape, in particular, and ethnic cleansing, in general, nearly two-thirds of Bosnia was put under Serbian control.

B. Concentration Camps as Brothels

In addition to the rapes committed by soldiers in front of relatives and community members, Serb forces interned many of the raped women in concentration camps where the sexual brutalization continued. Although it is not clear how many women were interned in these camps, it is clear that the purpose of these camps was the same purpose served by all brothels near military personnel during times of war: guaranteed access to native women. Women imprisoned in these camps were raped, and raped, and raped again. Many also were raped and then murdered.
. . .

C. Forced Pregnancy and Forced Motherhood

Forced impregnation and motherhood is yet another facet of the sexual terrorism of the war in the former Yugoslavia. Although pregnancy can be expected to result from the massive rapes, the Serbian aggressors purposely attempted to impregnate women and to hold them as prisoners until it was too late to abort the fetus. Although it is impossible to know the precise statistics (especially given the veil of silence forced upon survivors), recent estimates are that approximately 1,000 women were impregnated as a result of rape. Numerous survivors report that they were told by the aggressors, "[Y]ou are going to have a chetniky [Serbian extremist] baby, and we will wipe out the Muslim blood"[3] or "Now you'll have a Serb baby."[4]

To appreciate the significance of these abuses, we must again consider the cultures of the Balkan region. Because "soil" and "blood" are metaphors for male honor and because occupying a woman's uterus is synonymous with occupying physical territory, forcible impregnation "pollutes" the Bosnian or Croatian bloodline with Serbian blood. The goal of making Muslim women bear "Serbian babies" reveals the patriarchal nature of these cultures in which the sperm determines ethnicity. Although the gender-specific nature of these crimes in particular cannot be denied, as only women are capable of conceiving and bearing children, the fact that the sperm is believed to be the sole determinant of ethnic identity further illustrates the crimes' gendered nature.

Although connected, the injuries caused by forcible impregnation and forced maternity are distinct:

> The expressed intent to make women pregnant is an additional form of psychological torture [to the rape itself]; the goal of impregnation leads to imprisoning women and raping them until they are pregnant; the fact of pregnancy, whether aborted or not, continues the initial torture in a most intimate and invasive form; and the fact of bearing the child in rape, whether placed for adoption or not, has a potentially lifelong impact on the woman, on her liberty, and on her place in the community.[5]

Even under the best of circumstances pregnancy is invasive in terms of its effects on the mother's body. The experience of invasion is multiplied, however, when the pregnancy is the result of rape because the fetus represents the continued violation of the mother.

Similarly, after birth, the presence of a child who is the product of rape serves as a constant reminder to the woman, her family, and her community of the sexual torture endured by the mother and the domination perpetrated by the Serbs. Not surprisingly, many of the women impregnated as a result of rape experience feelings of disgust and revulsion toward their pregnancies and the children they bear, frequently leading to the rejection of these children following their birth. Those who do not reject their children must raise and care for a child they were forced to bear. As those who raped the women often expressed their intent to force the women to have a Serb baby, mothers of such children are forced to raise the intended symbol of their domination. Regardless of whether these women keep their children or not, however, they are dishonored forever by the public manifestation of their sexual impurity, a shame neither they nor their families can ignore.

D. Prostitution

Although prostitution already has occurred in the Serbian concentration camps, further prostitution of many of the victims of the sexual terrorism in the Balkans is inevitable. Although women become involved in prostitution under objective circumstances that differ, there are several conditions that are common to victims of prostitution. Where these conditions exist, prostitution will result, if not for all of those subject to the conditions, then certainly for some and probably for most.

The first of these objective conditions is social isolation. When women are isolated socially from their community and especially from their family, they are far more likely to be induced into prostitution than if they have maintained familial and community connections. At its international meeting of experts on prostitution in 1986, the United Nations Educational, Scientific, and Cultural Organization (UNESCO) recognized that the displacement of refugee persons often results in prostitution.

The second objective risk factor is a history of incest or rape. . . .

The third objective risk factor is economic deprivation. Although women as a group are poorer than men in every society, women at the lower end of the socioeconomic scale within a society are particularly at risk for being induced into prostitution. . . .

Finally, we know that prostitution will result from the use of women for sex during a military conflict because it always has. "The women that men no longer need after a war are often recycled from the military market to major cities where businessmen congregate and sailors dock."[6] At its 1986 international meeting of experts on prostitution, UNESCO recognized military brothels as "the oldest form of sexual manipulation on a massive scale"[7] and cited war as one precursor for prostitution. . . .

From a brief analysis of the applicability of these objective factors to the life circumstances of the women in the former Yugoslavia, it appears that some, and probably many, of them will be prostituted now that the war officially has ended.
. . .

E. Persecution Based on Nationality, Ethnicity, and Gender

Although not usually considered separate identifiable injuries, persecution of the women in the former Yugoslavia because of their nationality, their ethnicity, and their gender also was part of the overall sexual terrorism waged by the aggressors. Although these bases for persecution are linked inextricably from the victim's perspective (after all, she lives in Bosnia-Herzegovina, is Bosnian-Muslim, and is a woman all at the same time), they nonetheless constitute distinct injuries in terms of their cumulative effect. For it is one injury to be targeted because of your nationality; it is another injury to be targeted because you are of the "wrong" ethnicity; and, it is yet a third injury to be targeted because you are a woman. The female victims of Serbian ethnic cleansing were targeted for each of these reasons. Given this combination of who they are, the crimes committed against them were tailored to have the most devastating effect. Although these three sources of oppression cannot be separated in terms of their effect on their victims, the international community must recognize that each injury constitutes a distinct part of the sexual terrorism perpetrated by the aggressors of this war.

II. *International Law and Sexual Terrorism in the Former Yugoslavia*

. . .

Accountability is the first step toward restoring the moral and political order of the survivors' society. Participating directly in that process helps restore survivors' sense of control over their own destinies, while lifting their sense of shame and powerlessness. So, while silence may be necessary during the initial period of some survivors' trauma recovery, participation in rebuilding the moral foundation of their societies by establishing accountability for war-related atrocities may be critical to their longer-term recovery.

Any peace, then, must address human rights abuses, particularly the gender-based crimes, and allow the survivors of those crimes to participate directly in the process of bringing the perpetrators to justice.
. . .

A. Grave Breaches of the 1949 Geneva Conventions

Under the 1949 Geneva Conventions, "only grave breaches are subject to universal jurisdiction . . . triggering the obligation of every nation to bring the perpetrators to justice and justifying the trial of some crimes before an international tribunal."[8]
. . .

Article 2 of the Statute of the International Tribunal explicitly gives the Tribunal the power to prosecute persons "committing or ordering to be committed" certain grave breaches, including: "(a) wilful killing; (b) torture or inhuman treatment, including biological experiments; and (c) wilfully causing great suffering or serious injury to body or health."[9] In addition, Article 2 replaces the notion of "protected persons" with a specific designation of "civilians." As a result, civilians are protected from the commission of "grave breaches of the laws of war," even if the conflict is interpreted legally to be an internal, as opposed to an international, war.[10]

Significantly, the Statute's definition of "grave breaches" does not explicitly include rape or any of the other gender-based crimes perpetrated by the Serbs. . . .

Despite the absence of an explicit reference to rape or any other gender-based crime, the International Committee of the Red Cross has declared that the grave breach of "wilfully causing great suffering or serious injury to body or health"[11] includes rape. For those women interned in concentration camps, it seems clear that their abuse will rise to the level not only of "wilfully causing great suffering or serious injury to body or health," but also of "torture or inhuman treatment."[12] Serbs who have murdered the women they have raped and tortured also are clearly guilty of the grave breach of "wilful killing." In addition, forced pregnancy and forced motherhood should constitute violations of "causing great suffering or serious injury to body or health."[13] To the extent that the internment of women in concentration camps is recognized to have been for the purpose of sexually abusing them, those abuses, too, should be redressable under these provisions.

The beatings and killings by family members following the release of these women, however, may not be considered "grave breaches" because the Tribunal may determine that the Serb perpetrators did not willfully cause these crimes. Thus, despite the fact that the Serbs purposely used sexual terrorism as a weapon of war because they knew its effect in the Bosnian and Croatian cultures, it is unlikely that they will be held accountable for crimes that occur following the release of the victims. Furthermore, it is likely that Serb aggressors will not be held accountable for the prostitution that will result now that the victims have been released.

B. Violations of the Laws or Customs of War

The 1907 Hague Convention (IV) Respecting the Laws and Customs of War on Land and annexed regulations prohibit belligerent parties and their armed forces from certain forms of conduct during war. This prohibited conduct includes: "(a) employment of poisonous weapons or other weapons calculated to cause unnecessary suffering; (b) wanton destruction of cities, towns or villages, or devastation not justified by military necessity; and (c) attack, bombardment, by whatever means, of undefended towns, villages, dwellings, or buildings . . . ."[14] Although these rules of land warfare prohibit certain methods of waging war, they focus primarily on property. Bosnian and Croatian women could argue that the rapes constitute a "weapon calculated to cause unnecessary suffering" under subsection (a).

Subsections (b) and (c) also seem to prohibit using civilians as military targets by proscribing the wanton destruction or attack of cities and towns where civilians are most likely to live. However, the language of subsections (b) and (c) speaks of towns, villages, and other physical locations, rather than specific impermissible methods of waging war on persons because they represent the acquisition of territory. Within the cultures of the former Yugoslavia, occupying a woman's uterus is synonymous with occupying territory, and "soil" and "blood" are metaphors for men's honor. When sexually dominating women is equated in the mind of the aggressor with conquering territory and subjugating the enemy, the distinctions between civilian and soldier, and women and territory effectively collapse. Because the Hague Regulations target crimes experienced primarily by men, however, they are not drafted in a way that comprehends the unique victimization of women in this war. Therefore, it is unlikely that the perpetrators of gender-based crimes can be prosecuted under subsection (b) or (c), or perhaps under any provisions of the Hague Convention.

C. Genocide

Article 4 of the Statute for the International Tribunal states that the Tribunal will prosecute persons accused of genocide. . . .

The crimes perpetrated against Bosnian and Croatian women include murder, causing serious bodily and mental harm, and imposing conditions of life calculated to bring about their physical destruction. The question, then, is whether Bosnian and Croatian women constitute a national, ethnical, racial, or religious group. As discussed earlier, the Serbs have targeted these particular women because they are Bosnian nationals, because they are Bosnian-Muslim, and because they are women.
. . .

By definition, genocide recognizes intersectional harms in that it recognizes the unique harm of being targeted for physical harm or extinction on the basis of group identity. Yet, because gender is not a group identity sufficient to invoke the laws against genocide, at least one facet of the intersectional harms suffered by the women survivors is not acknowledged under the law of genocide. . . .

The statute, however, recognizes only persecution on the basis of nationality, ethnicity, race, and religion as sufficient to constitute genocide. Because the law of genocide does not identify gender as one of the bases for persecution that can give rise to a charge of genocide, part of the victims' experience goes unrecognized and, therefore, unredressed.

D. Crimes against Humanity

Under Article 5 of the Statute for the International Tribunal, the Tribunal has jurisdiction to prosecute specific crimes against humanity. Crimes against humanity are considered to be the most serious war crimes and constitute those human rights crimes (1) perpetrated in a pervasive, systematic manner; and (2) that result from premeditated, systematic, governmental policies. Isolated offenses are not considered crimes against humanity, no matter how heinous. Under the Statute of the International Tribunal, the following categories of crimes will be treated as crimes against humanity by the Tribunal: "(a) murder; (b) extermination; (c) enslavement; (d) deportation; (e) imprisonment; (f) torture; (g) rape; (h) persecution on political, racial or religious grounds; and (i) other inhumane acts."[15]

Rape is included explicitly in the list of offenses that will be treated as crimes against humanity. As recognized by many observers, rape certainly was perpetrated on a systematic scale during this war. In addition, the internment of Bosnian and Croatian women in concentration camps can be prosecuted as "imprisonment" under subsection (e). To the extent that women were subjected to severe physical or mental pain or suffering with the purpose of humiliating them or of inflicting illegal, cruel, inhuman, or degrading punishment on them on a systematic scale, the perpetrators also should be subject to prosecution for torture under subsection (f). Finally, as we probably can characterize the women's internment in concentration camps as "sexual bondage," the perpetrators may be prosecuted for the crime of "enslavement" under subsection (c).

As with other human rights provisions defining prohibited bases of persecution, subsection (h) reveals its patriarchal roots in its omission of "sex" from its list of prohibited grounds for persecution. The exclusion of sex from subsection (h) means that even if the physical injuries inflicted on the women of the former Yugoslavia are considered crimes against humanity, the additional injury of being targeted because they are women will not be considered a crime against humanity. Presumably then, persecution on the basis of gender is not considered a crime against humanity. Yet, rape is defined as a crime against humanity, and sexual persecution is the essence of what Bosnian and Croatian women have endured. Surely the combination of repeated rapes, prostitution, forced pregnancy, forced maternity, physical torture, and sexual slavery—all ways in which women in this war were persecuted because of their gender—rise to the level of the "acute revulsion" necessary for a practice to be designated a crime against humanity. Once again, the Statute of the International Tribunal seems to refuse to recognize and, therefore, to redress a central characteristic of the crimes endured by the women of the former Yugoslavia.

III. Redefining International Human Rights in Light of the Sexual Terrorism of the Balkans

. . .

[I]n addition to rape, the definitions of "grave breaches" and crimes against humanity must include explicitly prostitution, forced pregnancy, and forced maternity. The use of sexual terrorism as a method of war must be recognized as a violation of the laws and customs of war prohibited by the Hague Regulations. In addition, because the Serb aggressors knew that physical beatings, social ostracism, prostitution, and even murder would result from their sexual terrorism of Bosnian and Croatian women, they should be held responsible for these violations, despite the fact that these manifestations of the terrorism did not occur until after the women were released from Serbian control. Finally, the definitions of genocide and crimes against humanity must include persecution on the basis of gender. To include ethnicity, race, religion, and nationality as prohibited grounds for persecution, yet to exclude gender, is to acknowledge that victims are targeted because of their ethnicity, race, religion, and nationality, while denying that they are targeted because they are women. The Serbian method of waging this war should have eradicated any doubts that women are targeted for persecution because they are women. If the Serbs are to be held fully responsible for the crimes they have committed, gender-based human rights violations must be acknowledged explicitly and must be redressed independently of other violations.

In addition, to fail to explicitly include gender-based human rights violations among war crimes provisions is to deny the full humanity of the principal victims of this war. Human rights law acknowledges the part of women that is like men but not the part of them that is uniquely woman:

> Women's absence shapes human rights in substance and in form, effectively defining what a human and [what] a right are. . . . [W]hat violates the dignity of others is dignity for [women]; what violates the integrity of others is integrity for [women]; what violates the security of others is as much security as [women] are going to get. . . . Half of humanity is thus effectively defined as nonhuman. . . .[16]

. . .

[T]he exclusion of gender-based crimes from the jurisdiction of the Tribunal clearly illustrates that despite the many international agreements addressing discrimination against women, when women's human rights are violated in war, their abuses will be investigated and prosecuted only to the extent they resemble abuses men also experience (such as rape, torture, imprisonment, and murder). That they are raped, prostituted, impregnated, tortured, and murdered because they are women is ignored. This limitation of the Tribunal's jurisdiction is particularly important because war crimes tribunals are one of the few vehicles for individual accountability under international human rights laws. The vast majority of human rights agreements can be enforced only by other states, meaning that individuals rarely can have their specific injuries redressed. A war crimes tribunal, however, provides the unique opportunity to examine how much progress we have made in our ability to name and prosecute crimes against individuals. As illustrated by the jurisdiction of the Tribunal created to address war crimes in the former Yugoslavia, the international community has made little progress in naming and prosecuting gender-based crimes.

. . .

What is needed, therefore, is not only the inclusion of gender-based crimes into international war crimes tribunal jurisdiction, but also a redefinition of when such a tribunal may act and against whom.

B. The Public/Private Dichotomy and the War in the Former Yugoslavia

. . .

C. A New Response

. . .

Because we are socialized to think of times of "war" as limited to groups of men fighting over physical territory or land, we do not immediately consider the possibility of "war" outside this narrow definition except in a metaphorical sense, such as in the expression "the war against poverty." However, the physical violence and sex discrimination perpetrated against women because we are women is hardly metaphorical. Despite the fact that its prevalence makes the violence seem natural or inevitable, it is profoundly political in both its purpose and its effect. Further, its exclusion from international human rights law is no accident, but rather part of a system politically constructed to exclude and silence women.

The appropriation of women's sexuality and women's bodies as representative of men's ownership over women has been central to this "politically constructed reality." Women's bodies have become the objects through which dominance and even ownership are communicated, as well as the objects through which men's honor is attained or taken away in many cultures. Thus, when a man wants to communicate that he is more powerful than a woman, he may beat her. When a man wants to communicate that a woman is his to use as he pleases, he may rape her or prostitute her. The objectification of women is so universal that when one country ruled by men (Serbia) wants to communicate to another country ruled by men (Bosnia-Herzegovina or Croatia) that it is superior and more powerful, it rapes, tortures, and prostitutes the "inferior" country's women. The use of the possessive is intentional, for communication among men through the abuse of women is effective only to the extent that the group of men to whom the message is sent believes they have some right of possession over the bodies of the women used. Unless they have some claim of right to what is taken, no injury is experienced. Of course, regardless of whether a group of men sexually terrorizing a group of women is trying to communicate a message to another group of men, the universal sexual victimization of women clearly communicates to all women a message of dominance and ownership over women. As Charlotte Bunch explains, "The physical territory of [the] political struggle [over female subordination] is women's bodies."[17]

Given the emphasis on invasion of physical territory as the impetus of war between nations or groups of people within one nation, we may be able to reconceive the notion of "war" in order to make human rights laws applicable to women "in the by-ways of daily life."[18] We could eradicate the traditional public/private dichotomy and define oppression of women in terms traditionally recognized by human rights laws by arguing that women's bodies are the physical territory at issue in a war perpetrated by men against women. Under this broader definition of "war," any time one group of people systematically uses physical coercion and violence to subordinate another group, that group would be perpetrating a war and could be prosecuted for human rights violations under war crimes statutes. Such an

understanding would enable women to seek the prosecution of any male perpetrator of violence against women, regardless of whether that violence occurred inside a bedroom, on the streets of the city, or in a concentration camp in a foreign country.
. . .

The problem with this re-conceptualization of the definition of war (and it is a big problem) is that it accepts and legally effectuates the notion that women are property—that our bodies are the physical territory in a war of subordination. Although the purpose would not be to accept this notion, but rather to subvert the male-defined notion of war in a way that turns it on its head and benefits women, women would have to acknowledge legally that our bodies can be analogized to property. Because such an analogy returns us to the root of the problem, we should be reluctant to make it. Nevertheless, this analysis, at the least, illustrates why the politically constructed reality of international human rights law cannot simultaneously (1) comprehend the reality of sexual terrorism and its effect on women's human rights; and (2) do so in a way that acknowledges the full humanity of women. In order to fit within an understanding of "war" that even approximates our historical understanding of what "war" is, women must deny that we are complex human beings and instead become property once again.

Conclusion

The sexual terrorism perpetrated by the Serbian army against the women of Bosnia and Croatia was used as an effective and devastating weapon of war. The terrorism extended far beyond the massive rapes reported by the media and included most of the manifestations of sexual violence seen in the past. Although an international tribunal has been established to address human rights violations occurring during this war, its jurisdiction does not recognize the gender-specific nature of the crimes and, therefore, excludes a central component of the sexual terrorism perpetrated by the Serbs. In addition to including explicitly gender-based crimes, we must acknowledge that what came before and what will come after the specific incidents of war is more sexual terrorism against the survivors. Indeed, it is because of the sexual subordination of women in the cultures of the Balkans that the Serb strategy was so effective. In order to address the sexual terrorism that occurs every day in the lives of women in the Balkans and in the lives of women all over the world, human rights and what constitutes war and peace must be reconceptualized. Only by acknowledging that women are sexually terrorized daily in every country in the world and by holding the individual perpetrators, as well as the states, responsible, will the term "human rights" include women's experiences.

NOTES

1. Maria B. Olujie, *Coming Home: The Croatian War Experience* 22 (1993) (unpublished draft) (on file with the American University Law Review).

2. Catharine A. MacKinnon, *Crimes of War, Crimes of Peace*, 4 UCLA Women's Law Journal 59, 65–66 (1993).

3. Olujie, supra note 1, at 26.

4. International Human Rights Law Group, *No Justice, No Peace: Accountability for Rape and Gender-Based Violence in the Former Yugoslavia*, 5 Hastings Women's Law Journal 91, 95 (1994).

5. Rhonda Copelon, *Gendered War Crimes: Reconceptualizing Rape in Time of War*, in Women's Rights, Human Rights: International Feminist Perspectives 202 (Julie Peters and Andrea Wolper, eds., 1995).

6. Kathleen Barry, Female Sexual Slavery 76 (1979).

7. UN Educational, Scientific, and Cultural Organization, International Meeting of Experts on the Social and Cultural Causes of Prostitution and Strategies for the Struggle against Procuring and Sexual Exploitation of Women 6 (March 1986).

8. Copelon, supra note 5, at 201.

9. The Statute of the International Tribunal is also annexed to the Report of the Secretary-General Pursuant to Paragraph 2 of Security Council Resolution 808, UN Doc. S/25704, annex (1993), reprinted in 32 I.L.M. 1192 (1993) [hereinafter Report of Secretary-General].

10. Christopher C. Joyner, *Strengthening Enforcement of Humanitarian Law: Reflections on the International Criminal Tribunal for the Former Yugoslavia*, 6 Duke Journal of Comparative and International Law 79, 83 (1995).

11. Report of Secretary-General, supra note 9, at 37–38, 32 I.L.M. at 1192.

12. *Id.*

13. International Law Anthology 230 (Anthony D'Amato, ed., 1994).

14. Report of Secretary-General, supra note 9, at 35, 32 I.L.M. at 1192.

15. *Id.*

16. Catharine A. MacKinnon, *Crimes of War, Crimes of Peace*, 4 UCLA Women's Law Journal 59, 60–61 (1993).

17. Charlotte Bunch, *Transforming Human Rights from a Feminist Perspective*, in Women's Rights, Human Rights: International Feminist Perspectives 15 (Julie Peters and Andrea Wolper, eds., 1995).

18. Copelon, supra note 5, at 208.

39

Commercial Sex:
Beyond Decriminalization

Sylvia A. Law

. . .

IV. Effective Legal Remedies to Protect Commercial Sex Workers from Violence, Coercion, and Abuse

Commercial sex workers are vulnerable to violence, rape, and murder, and often the police do not take their complaints seriously. Further, the law of statutory rape makes it a crime to engage in sex with a person under the age of consent. Since the 1980s there have been dramatic changes in the legal and social understanding of violence against women in the United States. These new understandings, laws, practices, and services have not been extended to commercial sex workers. . . . The 1994 federal Violence Against Women Act provides additional remedies. Nonetheless, the protection of existing criminal laws has been systematically denied to women who sell sex for money, including teen girls. Applying existing laws to protect women who sell sex for money requires focused attention and rethinking of basic assumptions.

. . .

F. Commercial Sex Workers and Protection against Violence: The Politics of Change

Commercial sex workers have not shared in the protections created by the transformation in the legal, public, prosecutorial, and police understanding of rape and domestic violence, or in the social services created to meet crisis needs. Commercial sex workers are often victims of rape and other forms of domestic violence. The police systematically ignore their complaints. As a matter of formal legal rule, these women are not excluded from the protection of the law, unlike married women thirty years ago who could not, legally, be raped by their husbands. As a general matter, people who violate some criminal laws are not thereby barred from claiming protection of the law. People convicted of speeding or tax fraud are still entitled to protection if they are mugged. Nothing in the formal substantive definitions of the crimes of statutory rape, rape, assault, or domestic violence excludes commercial sex workers. Nonetheless, reforms to protect rape victims and battered women from abuse have not been extended to women who work in commercial sex. Indeed domestic abusers commonly defend themselves by asserting that the abused woman is a prostitute or a slut.

Experience in relation to the prosecution of rape and domestic violence suggests that crimes of violence against commercial sex workers will be taken seriously and prosecuted effectively by police and prosecutors only if these people are trained and sensitized to the special problems presented by violence against women in commercial sex. Effective enforcement also requires that victims of violence must be given a reliable sense that authorities will listen to their complaints. The literature of reform in relation to rape and domestic violence reveals almost no concern with the situation of commercial sex workers.

Domestic violence shelters often explicitly exclude commercial sex workers. According to [Margaret] Baldwin:

> Domestic violence shelters remain in effect inaccessible to women and girls in prostitution, for reasons as precise as express policies excluding drug and alcohol dependent women from admission to shelters, as well as denying access to women who engage in illegal activities of any kind. . . . [O]nce women are admitted to shelters, they often feel constrained to lie about their circumstances, reducing the possible benefits of proffered support to a painful farce.[1]

Space is limited. Women in the shelter may feel more comfortable if the excluded groups are kept out. Funders sometimes impose restrictions. The only groups that offer shelter to sex workers threatened by violence are a number of small organizations that offer "rescue" services. BREAKING FREE, a non-profit organization founded in Minnesota in 1996, provides counseling, advocacy, job training, and referral services for women wanting to leave commercial sex work. While the service seems laudable, women who do not wish to leave commercial sex work also have a legitimate claim to protection against criminal violence.

It is disturbing that commercial sex workers are denied protection against violence. Commercial sex workers may be in greatest need of police, prosecutorial, and social services to enable them to resist violence. The plight of teen sex workers is particularly compelling. As suggested earlier, enforcement of statutory rape laws against men who purchase sex from underage girls seems feasible, justifiable, and likely to discourage commercial sex with teenagers. But such an enforcement effort will not happen without a focused police and prosecutorial effort. Further, criminal law enforcement does not address the underlying situations that lead girls to commercial sex.

. . .

Removing criminal sanctions against commercial sex would make it easier to protect sex workers from violence and rape, because women could complain without fearing prosecution. But, even if the criminal sanctions against commercial sex remain, much more could be done to apply general criminal law to protect these women from violence. Essex County, New Jersey offers one model of more effective police protection for commercial sex workers. When Patricia A. Hurt became the county's first Black woman chief prosecutor, she announced that her top priority was to address a series of unsolved murders of sex workers in Newark, New Jersey. She created a task force of fourteen detectives who worked to develop trusting relations with the women who work on the street. Task force members arrested several people for crimes against prostitutes ranging from murder to sexual assault. The task force confronted a challenge in building cases for a jury that rested on the testimony of commercial sex workers. But, as one member of the task force observes, "Just because you've prostituted yourself, doesn't mean that you weren't beaten and raped."[2] When sex workers come to understand that the officers know this, they are willing to trust them and provide information. The officers encouraged street workers to jot down license plate numbers and remember names and identifying features. The fact that commercial sex is illegal makes the job of those seeking to protect them from violence more difficult, but not impossible.

Just as rape was not effectively prosecuted until special units were created to provide support to the victims and to prosecute with skill and vigor, so too, it seems unlikely that violence against sex workers will be addressed effectively without focused programs. Further, opposition to programs like that in Newark can be anticipated. Why should a society in which crime is rampant and police resources generally insufficient to the task devote special attention to protecting commercial sex workers against violence and coercion? The objection has some force. Patricia A. Hurt's answer is that because commercial sex workers are particularly vulnerable, they deserve special help from the law enforcement community.[3] Other officers involved in the program offer a different, instrumentalist, justification for the program. Because the sex workers spend a good deal of time on the street, they are valuable sources of information about a range of criminal activity that threatens a poor community.

Similarly, the San Francisco Task Force on Prostitution recommended that local prosecutors adopt a policy declining to prosecute those who engage in commercial sex. The Task Force "concluded that prosecution of prostitution has exacerbated problems in the industry including violence and chemical dependency, while enforcement further marginalizes prostitutes."[4] It found that "prostitutes are afraid to call the police when they are crime victims, for fear of being arrested themselves."[5] The group urged that the resources saved by ending the prosecution of commercial sex workers be redirected toward more vigorous enforcement of laws against noise, trespassing, and littering that fuel neighborhood concerns. Further, they called for "training to improve the ability of the District Attorney's office to successfully prosecute cases of rape and other assault in which prostitutes and other sex workers are the victims."[6]

From a political perspective, one attractive feature of the programs adopted in Newark and proposed in San Francisco is that they can be adopted at the local level. While local officials cannot repeal state criminal laws, local authorities have large discretion to determine whether and how laws will be enforced. In the short term, it seems unlikely that any state legislature would adopt the reforms advocated in this article. But a local mayor or district attorney might do so. Feminists, commercial sex workers, social workers, clergy, and others concerned about violence against commercial sex workers, and the exploitation of children, could seek reforms from local officials. Local experiments, along the lines attempted in Essex County and proposed in San Francisco, would allow other localities and states to evaluate whether these changes are wise. The disadvantage of local reform instituted as a matter of discretionary law enforcement policy is that it is fragile. In Newark, Patricia Hurt was removed from office, for reasons unrelated to her initiative on commercial sex. The recommendations of the San Francisco Task Force were rejected, and prosecution of commercial sex workers stepped up when a more conservative administration came to power.

NOTES

1. Margaret A. Baldwin, *Split at the Root: Prostitution and Feminist Discourses of Law Reform*, 5 Yale Journal of Law and Feminism 46, 79–80 (1992).

2. Alan Feuer, *Guardians on the Streets of Despair*, New York Times, July 28, 1998, at B1.

3. *Id.*

4. Carol Leigh, *A First Hand Look at the San Francisco Task Force Report on Prostitution*, 10 Hastings Women's Law Journal 68 (1999).

5. *Id.*

6. *Id.* at 72.

40

Converging Stereotypes in
Racialized Sexual Harassment:
Where the Model Minority Meets Suzie Wong

Sumi K. Cho

. . .

II. Converging Stereotypes and the Power Complex

. . .

B. Racialized Gender Stereotypes

. . . [T]he process of objectification that women in general experience takes on a particular virulence with the overlay of race upon gender stereotypes. Generally, objectification diminishes the contributions of all women, reducing their worth to male perceptions of female sexuality. In the workplace, objectification comes to mean that the value of women's contributions will be based not on their professional accomplishments or work performance, but on male perceptions of their vulnerability to harassment. Asian Pacific women suffer greater harassment exposure due to racialized ascriptions (for example, they are exotic, hyper-eroticized, masochistic, desirous of sexual domination, etc.) that set them up as ideal gratifiers of western neocolonial libidinal formations. In a 1990 Gentleman's Quarterly article entitled "Oriental Girls," Tony Rivers rehearsed the racialized particulars of the "great western male fantasy":

> Her face—round like a child's, . . . eyes almond-shaped for mystery, black for suffering, wide-spaced for innocence, high cheekbones swelling like bruises, cherry lips. . . . When you get home from another hard day on the planet, she comes into existence, removes your clothes, bathes you and walks naked on your back to relax you. . . . She's fun you see, and so uncomplicated. She doesn't go to assertiveness-training classes, insist on being treated like a person, fret about career moves, wield her orgasm as a non-negotiable demand. . . . She's there when you need shore leave from those angry feminist seas. She's a handy victim of love or a symbol of the rape of third world nations, a real trouper.[1]

As the passage demonstrates, Asian Pacific women are particularly valued in a sexist society because they provide the antidote to visions of liberated career women

344 SUMI K. CHO

who challenge the objectification of women. In this sense, this gender stereotype also assumes a "model minority" function, for it deploys this idea of Asian Pacific women to "discipline" white women, just as Asian Pacific Americans in general are frequently used in negative comparisons with their "non-model" counterparts, African Americans.

The passage is also a telling illustration of how colonial and military domination are interwoven with sexual domination to create the "great western male fantasy." Military involvement in Asia, colonial and neocolonial history, and the derivative Asian Pacific sex tourism industry have established power relations between Asia and the West that in turn have shaped stereotypes of Asian Pacific women. Through mass media and popular culture, these stereotypes are internationally transferred so that they apply to women both in and outside of Asia. As his article continues, Rivers suggests that the celluloid prototype of the "Hong Kong hooker with a heart of gold" (from the 1960 film, The World of Suzie Wong) may be available in one's own hometown: "Suzie Wong was the originator of the modern fantasy. . . . Perhaps even now, . . . on the edge of a small town, Suzie awaits a call."[2] These internationalized stereotypes, combined with the inability of U.S. Americans to distinguish between Asian Pacific foreigners and Asian Pacific Americans, result in a globalized dimension to the social construction of APA women.

. . .

III. How Stereotype Convergence Shapes the Primary Injury Examining the Harassers' Actions

A. The Jean Jew Case: Hostile Environment

Dr. Jean Jew came to the University of Iowa in 1973 from Tulane University. She was hired at the same time that another physician, who was also her mentor, was appointed chair of the anatomy department in the College of Medicine. Almost immediately, rumors began to circulate about an alleged sexual relationship between the two. These rumors would persist for the next thirteen years. Despite the increasing number of incidents of harassment and vilification Dr. Jew was experiencing after joining the anatomy department, she was recommended for tenure by the department in December 1978. Her promotion, however, did not quiet her detractors. In a drunken outburst in 1979, for example, a senior member of the anatomy department referred to Dr. Jew as a "stupid slut," a "dumb bitch," and a "whore." Dr. Jew and three other professors complained separately to the Dean about the slurs.

. . . Jean Jew was the only woman tenured in the College of Medicine's basic science departments, and one of a few APA women among the University of Iowa faculty. In this homogenous setting, stereotypes flourished to such an extent the faculty did not even recognize the difference between jokes and racial slurs. One faculty member who referred to Dr. Jew as a "chink" contended that he was merely "using the word in a very frivolous situation"[3] and repeating a joke. . . . Gender stereotypes with racial overtones painted Dr. Jew as an undeserving Asian Pacific American woman who traded on her sexuality to get to the top. To Dr. Jew, this stereotyping and her refusal to accede to it played a large role in the "no-win" configuration of departmental power relations:

> If we act like the [passive] Singapore Girl, in the case of some professors, then they feel "she is unequal to me." If we don't act like the Singapore Girl, then our accomplishments must have derived from "a relationship with the chair." There were quite a few people that felt that way to begin with. They thought because I was working with the chair, I was his handmaiden. Many faculty testified that in inter-collaborative work, I was doing the work that led to publication but that he was the intellectual, with Jean Jew as his lackey. The term used was that I was the collaborative force, but not independent.[4]

. . .

Other colleagues also denigrated Dr. Jew. After he was denied tenure in 1991, one doctor filed a grievance with the university stating that his qualifications were better than those of Jew, who had been tenured. To support his case, the doctor submitted an anonymous letter to the dean, which claimed that Jew's promotion was due to her sexual relationship with the chair. The letter stated, in fortune-cookie style, "Basic science chairman cannot use state money to . . . pay for Chinese pussy."[5] . . . On the very day that the senior departmental faculty were to evaluate Jew for promotion to full professor, the following limerick appeared on the wall of the faculty men's restroom:

> There was a professor of anatomy
> Whose colleagues all thought he had a lobotomy
> Apartments he had to rent
> And his semen was all spent
> On a colleague who did his microtomy.[6]

The faculty voted three in favor, five against Jean Jew's promotion, and she was denied full professorship.

B. The Rosalie Tung Case: Quid Pro Quo

Rosalie Tung joined the University of Pennsylvania Wharton School of Business (hereinafter Business School) in 1981 as an associate professor of management. In her early years at the Business School, she earned praise for her performance. In the summer of 1983 a change in leadership brought a new dean and new department chair to the school. According to Tung, "Shortly after taking office, the chairman of the management department began to make sexual advances toward me."[7] In June 1984, the chair awarded Professor Tung a 20 percent increase in salary and praised her highly for her achievements in the areas of research, teaching, and community service.

However, when Tung came up for tenure review in the fall of 1984, the chair's evaluation of her performance changed dramatically. "After I made it clear to the chairman that I wanted our relationship kept on a professional basis," she stated, "he embarked on a ferocious campaign to destroy and defame me. He solicited more than 30 letters of recommendation from external and internal reviewers when the usual practice was for five or six letters."[8] Although a majority of the department faculty recommended tenure, the personnel committee denied Professor Tung's promotion. Contrary to the rules, the department chair deliberately withheld news of the decision for one week so that he could deliver it to Tung on Chinese New Year's day. He offered no reason for her tenure denial. Tung later learned through a respected and well-placed member of the faculty that the justification given by the decisionmakers was that "the Wharton School is not interested in China-related research."[9] Tung understood this to mean that the Business School did "not want a Chinese-American, Oriental" on their faculty.[10] Of over sixty faculty in the management department, there were no tenured professors of color or tenured women. At the entire Business School, which had over three hundred faculty, there were only two tenured people of color, both male.

Tung filed a complaint with the Equal Employment Opportunity Commission in Philadelphia alleging race, sex, and national origin discrimination. She also filed a complaint with the university grievance commission. Tung's file and those of thirteen faculty who were granted tenure within the previous five-year period were turned over to the grievance commission. During this process, the peer review files revealed that out of multiple batches of mailings, the department chair had arranged specifically to solicit negative letters—only three such letters were in her file—two of which were from the chair himself! One of the chair's negative letters was written only six months after his rave review in June 1984. Professor Tung's file constituted an impressive list of achievements with over thirty letters consistently praising her as one of the best and brightest young scholars in her field, including one from a Nobel Prize laureate. Her contributions had been acknowledged by her peers through election to the board of governors of the Academy of Management, a professional association of over 7,000 management faculty. Tung was the first person of color ever elected to the board.

IV. How the Convergence Shapes the Secondary Injury: The University Response

A. The Jew Case

Following the denial of her application for full professorship in 1983, Dr. Jew registered a complaint of sexual harassment with the university affirmative action office, the Anatomy Review and Search Committee, and the university's academic affairs vice-president. No action was taken on her complaint. In January of 1984, her attorney, Carolyn Chalmers, submitted a formal written complaint alleging sexual harassment to the vice-president. In response to this complaint, a panel was appointed to investigate Dr. Jew's charges. On November 27, 1984, the panel made four findings: (1) a pattern and practice of harassment existed; (2) defamatory statements were made by two members of the anatomy faculty; (3) there was inaction by the administration; and (4) there were resulting destructive effects on Dr. Jew's professional and personal reputation both locally and nationally. The panel recommended that the administration take immediate action to inform the department of their findings and that a "public statement be made on behalf of the University of Iowa."[11] The university took no meaningful action. In utter frustration at the university's unwillingness to correct the hostile work environment, Jew and Chalmers took the case to court.

Jean Jew's first suit in federal district court alleged that the University of Iowa failed to correct the hostile work environment from which she suffered. After fourteen days of testimony, Judge Vietor issued a ruling, finding inter alia that the University of Iowa had failed to respond to Jew's complaints. The judge also found that sexual bias played a significant role in her denial of promotion to full professor in 1983. He found that four of the five professors who voted negatively on her promotion had displayed sexual bias. He ordered the university to promote Jew to full professor and awarded over $50,000 in back pay and benefits dating back to 1984, a rare set of remedies, given the federal courts' historic deference to university academic personnel decisions.

Jew also filed a defamation suit in state court in October 1985. The suit alleged that she was the victim of sexually based slander perpetrated by another member of her department. The six-woman, one-man jury unanimously found for Jew and awarded $5,000 in actual damages, and $30,000 in punitive damages. Jew had won both her legal battles, but her adversarial relationship with the University of Iowa was not over.

One of the most disturbing aspects of the university's behavior in the *Jew* case was its attempt to use the defense of academic freedom as a shield for slanderous faculty comments and university inaction. The university attempted to dismiss Jew's complaint, arguing that the statements later found to amount to sex discrimination and sexual harassment were merely legitimate criticism and "speech protected from regulation by the First Amendment."[12] Thus, the university argued that it was under no obligation to regulate speech privileged by the First Amendment's implied recognition of academic freedom.

Judge Vietor rejected out of hand the university's academic freedom argument. Despite the unsuccessful attempt to sanitize the harmful speech as academic freedom, the university stated that it would appeal the judge's decision on First Amendment grounds in October 1990. . . .

Only when considerable community criticism surfaced did the university decide to cut its losses and accept the validity of the verdict. In an editorial criticizing the university's tactics, Professor Peter Shane of the University of Iowa College of Law wrote:

No proper concept of academic freedom . . . could immunize the public denigration of Dr. Jew as a "Slut," a "Chink," a "Bitch" and a "Whore"—all this by people actually permitted to vote on her qualifications for promotion! Neither should academic privilege protect the circulation of unfounded rumors about any person. . . . The only

connection between academic freedom and Dr. Jew's experience is that university officials essentially ostracized her for insisting that promotions be evaluated in a way that
does not disadvantage women. That ostracism and the consequent chill on her sympa-
thizers' expression surely did compromise academic freedom.[13]

. . .

The university's unwillingness to accept responsibility for the racialized sexual
harassment of Jean Jew extends beyond the attempt to appeal the decision. The
depth of complicity between the university and the adjudged harasser is revealed in
the fact that the University of Iowa paid the legal expenses for the offending professor's defense in the defamation suit for over five years, as well as the $35,000
judgment entered against him by the court. Clearly, the administration sided with
the wrongdoer, even though its own internal investigative panel supported Dr.
Jew's claims, and even after a verdict was returned against him. The university's
adversarial treatment of Jew, its inaction following the internal committee's findings, its futile appeal attempt, and its shouldering of the harasser's individual civil
liability reflect a disturbing pattern whereby academic institutions circle the wagons to protect the harasser against the harassed.

. . .

B. The Tung Case

Following forty hours of hearings, the university grievance commission found that
the university had discriminated against Tung. Despite a university administrative
decision in her favor, the provost overseeing the matter chose to do nothing. Professor Tung suspects that race and gender stereotypes played a role in shaping the
provost's inaction:

> [T]he provost, along with others in the university administration, felt that I being an
> Asian, would be less likely to challenge the establishment, because Asians have tradi-
> tionally not fought back. In other words, it was okay to discriminate against Asians,
> because they are passive; they take things quietly, and they will not fight back.[14]

. . .

Despite the university's non-response to its own internal committee's findings,
Rosalie Tung pursued her EEOC claim. In its investigation, the EEOC subpoenaed
her personnel file along with those of five male faculty members who had been
granted tenure around the same time her tenure application had been denied. The
University of Pennsylvania refused to turn over the files; and the case, known as
University of Pennsylvania v. EEOC, eventually reached the Supreme Court.[15]
Among its claims, the university asserted a First Amendment privilege of "academic freedom" as a defense to the subpoena. It argued that one of the essential
First Amendment freedoms that a university enjoys is the right to "determine for itself on academic grounds who may teach."[16] Insofar as the tenure system determines "who may teach," university attorneys argued that disclosing the personnel
files and peer review evaluations would create a "chilling effect on candid evalua-

tions" and result in "the impairment of the free interchange of ideas that is a hall-mark of academic freedom."[17]

Rejecting the university's claims, the Court gave little weight to the university's assertion that compliance with the subpoena would violate its First Amendment rights.

. . .

The unanimous decision in favor of Tung and the EEOC, by a conservative Rehnquist Court, set an important precedent in establishing baseline procedures for Title VII claims in academic employment. *University of Pennsylvania v. EEOC* represents the Court's willingness to alter (at least somewhat) its long-standing tradition of absolute deference to higher education's decision-making processes in the face of allegations of egregious discrimination and harassment. The *Tung* case exposed and finally rejected the "academic freedom trumps harassment and discrimination" rationale that had served to hide the evidence of wrongdoing in tenure denials.[18]

V. Conclusion: Toward a Theory of Racialized Sexual Harassment

In light of the prevalent converging racial and gender stereotypes of Asian Pacific American women as politically passive, and sexually exotic and compliant, serious attention must be given to the problem of racialized sexual harassment as illustrated by the two cases discussed.[19] On a theoretical level, new frameworks that integrate race and gender should be developed to account for the multi-dimensional character of harassment that occurs and is challenged across races, social classes, and borders. The law's current dichotomous categorization of racial discrimination and sexual harassment (to name only two) as separate spheres of injury is inadequate to respond to racialized sexual harassment.

Both the *Jew* and *Tung* cases can be described in terms that would place them within the parameters of "usual" sexual harassment jurisprudence. . . .

However, both cases also contain elements of a unique form of injury that is not as readily captured in conventional harassment terms. The specifically racialized feature of the injuries to Tung and Jew inheres in the harassers' and the institutions' processing of their victims as not only women, but APA women. In both cases, there is clear evidence of racialized references being hostilely deployed against the women. . . .

Moreover, the injuries suffered by the women uniquely result from the synergy of race and gender. To understand the uniqueness of this type of injury, more nuanced conceptions of the victims' and the harassers' subjecthoods are necessary. APA women and women of different racial backgrounds possess subjectivities that are not coterminous with an essentialized Western female subjectivity. The injuries suffered by Tung and Jew materialized not only according to the set of abstract employment rights the law observes, but also along the lines of their subjecthood as APA women. In both cases, the primary injury harassers formulated their harassing plans of action in full light of their subject positions as white males vis-à-vis the APA women they targeted. The nature of their culpable behavior is therefore best described in terms of their self-understandings as occupants of racially dominant subject positions. In order to deter such harassment, the law should acknowledge the particular white male supremacist logic at work in such subject formations.

In a similar fashion, the law must incorporate a fuller conception of workplace power relations, so that the synergistic effects of race and gender are given the consideration they warrant. The decisions of the wrongdoers in these two cases at the primary and secondary levels were informed by a particular set of perceptions and preconceptions of the APA women involved. Both the isolation of the victims as APAs and assumptions about their passivity led the wrongdoers to create a "steamroller" dynamic that was designed to further disadvantage and disempower their victims. Also, the overt deployment of racial stereotypes in the Jew case became a prime mode through which her position was destabilized. These particularized forms of power imbalance and power deployment against women of color (here, APAs) require a legal discourse that understands and addresses the unique subjecthoods of the actors it seeks to regulate and protect.

. . .

NOTES

1. Tony Rivers, *Oriental Girls*, Gentleman's Quarterly (British ed.), Oct. 1990, at 158, 161, 163.

2. *Id.* at 163.

3. *Jew v. University of Iowa*, 749 F. Supp. 946, 949 (S.D. Iowa 1990).

4. Interview with Dr. Jean Jew, in Berkeley, California (Oct. 15, 1991), cited in Sumi Kae Cho, *The Struggle for Asian American Civil Rights*, at 71 (1992) (unpublished dissertation, University of California, Berkeley) (on file with author) (citation omitted).

5. Plaintiff's Memorandum in Opposition to Defendants' Motion for Summary Judgment at 19, 5 of Timeline addendum, *Jew v. University of Iowa*, 749 F. Supp. 946 (S.D. Iowa 1990) (No. 86-169-D-2).

6. *Id.* at 6 of Timeline addendum.

7. Rosalie Tung, *Asian Americans Fighting Back*, Speech at University of California, Berkeley, California (Apr. 1990), in Rosalie Tung, *Tung Case Pries Open Secret Tenure Review*, Berkeley Graduate, Apr. 1991, at 12 (copy and videotape of speech on file with author).

8. *Id.*

9. *University of Pa. v. EEOC*, 493 U.S. 182, 185 (1990).

10. *Id.*

11. Plaintiff's Memorandum in Opposition to Defendants' Motion for Summary Judgment at 7 of Timeline addendum, Jew (No. 86-169-D-2).

12. *Jew*, 749 F. Supp. at 946.

13. Peter Shane, *Harassment Is Not Privileged Speech*, Daily Iowan, Sept. 28, 1990, at 8A.

14. Tung, supra note 7, at 31.

15. *University of Pa.*, 493 U.S. at 186.

16. *Id.* at 196.
17. *Id.* at 197.
18. *Id.*
19. While I choose to focus here on the theoretical challenge posed by the problem of racialized sexual harassment, there are other challenges APA feminists should undertake.

On a doctrinal level, critical race feminists should be particularly concerned about the way in which "academic freedom" as a First Amendment defense is selectively deployed by universities and faculty organizations as a legal strategy to sanitize discriminatory acts and the circulation of stereotypes. A critique of the use of "free speech" and the First Amendment to sanction discrimination has been initiated by critical scholars analyzing law. See generally The Price We Pay (Laura Lederer and Richard Delgado, eds., 1995); Mari Matsuda et al., Words That Wound (1993); Linda S. Greene, *Sexual Harassment Law and the First Amendment*, 71 Chicago-Kent Law Review 729 (1995).

On an advocacy level, women's and Asian Pacific American organizations should affirmatively address racialized sexual harassment. The organizations should seek ways to counter the compounded vulnerability that Asian Pacific and Asian Pacific American women face in confronting both primary and secondary injuries. For a related argument, see Kimberlé Crenshaw, *Race, Gender and Sexual Harassment*, Southern California Law Review 1467, 1468 (1992) (referring to the dynamics of racism and sexism in the workplace as the "dual vulnerability" confronting women of color).

Finally, the problem of racialized sexual harassment of Asian Pacific American women, even in elite employment sectors such as institutions of higher education, derives in part from internationalized stereotypes. At an international level, these stereotypes feed upon unequal power relations, military history, and uneven economic development between Asia (especially in the Philippines and Thailand) and the U.S. Thus, critical race feminists who are committed to eradicating the sources of racialized sexual harassment must not limit their efforts to the U.S., but also must look to the lives of sister counterparts overseas.

41

The Violence Against Women Act and the Construction of Multiple Consciousness in the Civil Rights and Feminist Movements

Jenny Rivera

. . .

Introduction

The enactment of the Violence Against Women Act (VAWA) in 1994 was, ostensibly, a success of historic proportions on various political and social fronts. It has significantly furthered efforts to legitimize a feminist anti-violence agenda within the political mainstream by providing federal criminal and civil legal remedies for female survivors of violence. Indeed, significant portions of the VAWA were originally viewed as highly controversial, in part because of their feminist origin. These provisions, and consequently the VAWA in toto, were politicized in a derogatory manner prior to the VAWA's passage. When the VAWA was finally signed into legislation, it marked the end of a protracted political and educational campaign conducted in Congress and across the country on gender-motivated violence.

While the enactment of the VAWA is undeniably a victory for feminism, and as such served as a vehicle for a sophisticated national discourse on violence between intimate partners, the passage of the VAWA is also a civil rights victory. This Article argues that, at a time when the hard-won gains of civil rights and feminist struggles are being challenged and dismantled, both movements must work together cooperatively. In order for cooperation to be successful, cooperation cannot be based or forged solely on the mutual need for a solid constituency. Rather, cooperation must be the acknowledged result of the application of civil rights and feminist doctrines to the issues and problems faced by women and people of color in society. The VAWA represents an important opportunity for civil rights activists and feminists to identify common goals and philosophies of their respective social and legal reform movements, and an opportunity to convert their doctrines into practice through joint action.

The recognition that the civil rights movement can be gender-conscious and gender-responsive, and that the feminist movement can speak to issues of race and ethnic discrimination—that both movements can be constructed in such a way as to account for and respond to the particular issues and concerns of women of all races and ethnic backgrounds—allows for collaboration between the proponents of these two movements. As a consequence, both movements will benefit and can fully pursue their mutual goals of equity and justice. The concept of a multiple consciousness which governs and informs these movements can be realized.

. . .

II. The Violence Against Women Act

A. When Civil Rights Anti-Discrimination Doctrine and Feminist Theory Meet

Not surprisingly, introduction into mainstream society of the theoretical ideologies and particular experiences underlying civil rights and feminist movements has been challenging. Only after much advocacy, education, lobbying, and politicking within various communities, and at the federal and local government levels, have women succeeded in promoting and implementing an anti-violence agenda. The legislative history of the VAWA is revealing in this respect because it is characterized by more than the usual hesitance and resistance to new legislation. An examination of the initial opposition to the VAWA lays bare gendered notions at that opposition's core. Moreover, this legislative history signals potential danger areas in the enforcement of the VAWA of particular concern to women of color.

For example, while the VAWA provisions permitting enhanced sentencing for sex crimes were well received, there was less enthusiasm for, and at times direct opposition to, the section creating a new civil rights cause of action and the interstate enforcement of domestic violence provision. While objections to these provisions were clothed in the language of legal discourse and concerns about the analytical framework of the legislation and its constitutionality, they also reflected resistance to the break from traditional notions of women's status.

The VAWA's recognition and provisions for enhanced sanctions on sex crimes was perhaps more easily acceptable because it mirrors traditional responses to rape that seek to protect the sexual purity of women by punishing transgressors of that protected female sexual image. In contrast, the civil rights remedy and the interstate enforcement provision strike at the very heart of traditional conceptions of female power and subjugation because they remove acts of violence against women by intimate partners from the protected space of the private home, and subject them to public scrutiny and potential civil liability.

Criminal sanctions for domestic violence are the result of efforts by feminists to eradicate the "public-private distinction" that until recently protected abusers and their actions from public scrutiny. Civil sanctions for violence against women, such as civil protective orders, tort claims, and now the VAWA civil rights provision, have roots in both civil rights and feminist struggles. The civil rights movement brought about public scrutiny of and civil remedies for discriminatory behavior through passage and implementation of the Civil Rights Act of 1964, Civil Rights Act of 1991, and the Bilingual Education Act. Feminists recognized both stranger or "public," as well as intimate or "private" violence against women as stemming from sexism. The VAWA combines the contributions of both civil rights activists and feminists. Subjecting intimate partners to federal penalties and liabilities, similar to those imposed on a stranger who commits an act of violence against a woman, is a practical consequence of the contributions and collaboration of feminism and civil rights activism, signaling the potential for the continued collaboration of these movements in ensuring that the VAWA is effective in redressing, and ultimately ending, violence against women.

B. The VAWA as Gender Conscious–Gender Responsive Civil Rights Legislation

. . .

When considering those provisions of the VAWA which truly incorporate a gender responsive civil rights approach to violence against women, it is those sections which speak directly to the issues of women of color which reflect multiple consciousness. Moreover, it is not solely particular VAWA provisions working in isolation which make the legislation unique and uniquely applicable to women of color. Rather, it is the various sections of the VAWA working in tandem which make the VAWA a gender conscious–gender responsive civil rights law; one which provides legal recourse to all women survivors of domestic violence, regardless of race, ethnicity, culture, and/or language.

One of the primary aspects of the legislation is its ambitious attempt to respond to the particular ways women experience violence. First, it recognizes the prevalence of violence between intimate partners, and, because it applies to former intimate partners, it also recognizes that violence does not necessarily terminate when the relationship ends. Second, the VAWA avoids making the all too common mistake of judging women who stay in violent relationships by adversely characterizing them as "failing" to take aggressive steps to curtail the batterer's conduct, or otherwise blaming women for their abusers' conduct. Rather, the VAWA provides for the establishment of programs and law enforcement strategies that will, at least in theory, create an environment in which women can feel they have real options to negotiate the violence. If these programs and strategies are effectively established and enforced, women will have more resources, such as shelters and support services, and police will be better able to respond appropriately to domestic violence with education and enhanced resources.

Another way in which the VAWA incorporates the experiential and doctrinal foundations of civil rights and feminist anti-discrimination theory and activism is by providing for the installation and integration of programs and services responsive to the different situations faced by women of color. This ensures the applicability of particular VAWA projects to a diverse population of women, and also enhances the VAWA's overall vitality. For example, in several sections the VAWA mandates the inclusion of representatives from various communities, including communities of color, in the development and strategic planning of VAWA mandated or facilitated enforcement, education, and research projects.

. . .

The VAWA recognizes that within communities of color there are different issues and discrete culturally based concerns. For example, law enforcement and prosecution federal grants are available for, inter alia, purposes of "developing or improving delivery of victim services to racial, cultural, ethnic, and language minorities. . . ."[1] Further, states must set forth in their grant applications the demographics of the service population, including information on "race, ethnicity and language background . . ."[2] in order to qualify for a grant.

. . .

Several sections of the VAWA are most likely to provide assistance to Latinas and other non-English speaking or immigrant groups of women in particular, despite the general lack of specific data on these domestic violence survivors. First, Subtitle G amends the Immigration and Nationality Act, and authorizes immigrant women and children who are survivors of domestic violence to petition for legal status on their own. As a result, Latina immigrant survivors and other immigrant women survivors of domestic violence may apply for legal status without relying on an abusive spouse or parent. In effect, Subtitle G removes leverage the abuser may have against a woman previously available to him because of the abuser's legal petitioning standing.

. . .

An additional section of the VAWA which is of particular use to Latinas and other non-English speaking or immigrant women is the provision which establishes the national domestic violence hotline, with its attendant bilingual services. The hotline serves as a federal resource to women in a private anonymous setting. The very existence of such a federally funded service communicates an important message to society that the federal government is committed to efforts to end violence against women. By recognizing the need for bilingual services, the government has also sent the message that culturally and linguistically sensitive legislation is efficacious and necessary.

The VAWA also establishes a fund for community projects on domestic violence. Under the "Demonstration Grants for Community Initiatives" section, the VAWA authorizes grants to nonprofit organizations to "establish projects in local communities involving many sectors of each community to coordinate intervention and prevention of domestic violence."[3] Community leaders must be involved in the program planning and development process.

. . .

C. The VAWA's Limitations: When Gender Collides
with Anti-Discrimination Doctrine

. . .

1. Civil Rights Remedy—Subtitle C
Civil rights advocates and feminists generally recognize the historical benefits of civil litigation and the role civil rights and women's rights cases have played in improving the status of women and people of color. The VAWA civil rights remedy, however, contains certain difficulties related to its usefulness.

First, access to the legal system, including the courts, continues to be a major obstacle for women of color. There are too few Latino, African American, and Asian officials in the legal system, serving as judges, lawyers, clerks, court officers, and other court personnel. People of color, and women of color in particular, are isolated and have little faith in our legal system. . . .

Second, the legal system has not always served as a positive vehicle for reform with respect to the struggles of women of color. Often, cases have furthered oppression or justified acts of injustice. . . .

Third, and perhaps the determinative factor in the equation, is the likelihood of obtaining satisfactory relief through this civil process. Since the scope of the civil rights provision is as yet untested, the extent of the relief courts will grant is unknown, and the possibility of securing financial compensation from the litigation is uncertain. [Editors' note: Indeed, in *United States v. Morrison*, 529 U.S. 598 (2000), the Supreme Court struck down the provision of VAWA that authorized a civil remedy concluding that Congress lacked constitutional power to enact such legislation.]

. . .

Fourth, there are too few attorneys interested in these cases and competent to develop the litigation required to succeed. . . . In essence, the fact is that the survivor of domestic violence must be aware of the possible legal remedies in order to engage the system, and the survivor must have counsel available and ready to develop litigation in untested waters. Currently, the likelihood that women of color can be full participants in this litigation process is minimal.

. . .

2. Self-Petitioning Provision—Subtitle G
While in theory the section of the VAWA authorizing immigrant women domestic violence survivors to self-petition for legally recognized status has the potential to dramatically alter, for the better, the status of undocumented immigrant women who are survivors of domestic violence, in practice Subtitle G has its limits. There is the obvious problem of informing and educating immigrant women about their rights under the VAWA and the INA. This is no easy task considering the history of distrust of the INS, as well as the difficulty in reaching a population which survives, in part, as a result of its underground nature and anonymity. The difficulty of reaching immigrant women survivors of domestic violence is compounded by the fact that many are often isolated and cut off from information venues by the

abusers, or as a direct consequence of their limited English proficiency. Immigrant women are thus even more isolated than other domestic violence survivors because they cannot, or perceive that they cannot, pursue the existing avenues for assistance without fear of deportation or removal from the United States. Moreover, within their own immigrant communities, family and community members often cannot be relied on for assistance because of those members' resistance to recognizing domestic violence within their families' lives.

The other practical hurdle to the full utilization of Subtitle G is the lack of sufficient numbers of advocates and lawyers to assist immigrant women through the petition process. Not only do immigrant women survivors require assistance with the petition process, but like other survivors of domestic violence, they are generally in need of protection from the abuser. They are just as likely as other women survivors to need shelter, police protection, and, if available to them, orders of protection.

3. State Intervention—Mandatory Arrest Provisions

Although the VAWA authorizes federal jurisdiction and invokes federal authority over particular anti-violence initiatives and claims, there are VAWA sections which seek to influence state-based initiatives by applying federal policies directly to the state VAWA appropriations grantees. The VAWA provision which requires the adoption and implementation of mandatory arrest procedures reflects current feminist preference for and utilization of this strategy.

In order for states and local governments to be eligible for VAWA grants under Subtitle B, Chapter 3, they must

(1) certify that their laws or official policies—
(A) encourage or mandate arrests of domestic violence offenders based on probable cause that an offense has been committed; and
(B) encourage or mandate arrest of domestic violence offenders who violate the terms of a valid and outstanding protection order.[4]

State and local governments must also certify that they prohibit dual arrest—the practice by police officers of arresting both the abuser and the woman—and mutual restraining orders—the practice of issuing orders of protection against both parties.

Support [of] and opposition to mandatory arrest policies and laws are contentious and the issues surrounding the implementation of mandatory arrest policies remain unresolved. Nevertheless, since the VAWA adopts the implementation of local mandatory arrest policies and laws as a federal goal, the impact of such policies at the local level on women of color must be considered.

The task of analyzing and critiquing the utility and effect of mandatory arrest policies on women of color is difficult because of the lack of research and evaluation of the subject. However, I have previously articulated my deep concern with the utility and implementational effects of mandatory arrest as applied to Latinas.[5] These concerns are founded on two aspects of mandatory arrest.

First, because it is a law enforcement model which is only effective to the extent that the woman has no control over the actions taken by police officers, it is philosophically in opposition to feminist and civil rights doctrines which have been founded on notions of individual and community empowerment and community-based control. While some supporters have argued that mandatory arrest is itself an empowering mechanism, the lack of information on the experiences of women of color with mandatory arrest policies, belies reliance on prior evaluations of mandatory arrest practices and procedures. Even without such information we can, nevertheless, consider theoretical and historical observations and arguments concerning communities of color and women within those communities.

A second troubling aspect of mandatory arrest is that it adopts and furthers an invasive state law model. Dependence on initiatives which are strategies for authorizing state involvement in individual relationships has proved debilitating for communities of color and women. To the extent that the VAWA's provision encourages the increasing utilization of mandatory arrest at the local level, these concerns take on even greater urgency. Uncertainty as to the application of mandatory arrest to communities of color, and the general failure to contextualize law enforcement strategies in such a way as to reflect the history of abuse by police and the state is a significant problem with the VAWA.

4. The VAWA Appropriations—Funding for Battered Women's Shelters and Social Services

. . .

While the shelter system has provided many services to women of color, the future availability and adequacy of these services are uncertain, despite the additional VAWA appropriations, because the appropriations merely grant additional money for an existing system; a system with serious institutional problems. Those problems have resulted in the failure to provide sufficient, culturally appropriate services for women of color, especially women who do not speak English.

Under the Violence Prevention and Services Act, state grantees must:

> give special emphasis to the support of community-based projects of demonstrated effectiveness carried out by nonprofit organizations, the primary purpose of which is to operate shelters for victims of family violence and their dependents, and those which provide counseling, advocacy, and self-help services to victims and their children.[6]

To the extent that funding of shelters and services is prioritized in such a way as to benefit organizations and entities with a history of this work, programs developed by women of color which are community-based may proceed in the funding process at a disadvantage because of their inexperience and insufficient history with the contract bidding process. There may be an adverse impact on Latino community-based programs which do not have a history of working on domestic violence issues.

. . .

Conclusion

Recommendations for the increased utilization of all sections of the VAWA by women of color must promote the integration of women of color into the political system and into civil rights and feminist movements. The collaborative agenda that can be developed together by participants in the civil rights movement and the feminist movement is possible so long as women of color have an equal voice in the political dialogue. Any and all programs financed and promoted under the auspices of the VAWA must be designed and implemented with the assistance and under the direction of women representing diverse communities. Representational programs have long been integrated into various federal initiatives. A fortiori women of color and programs run by women of color must receive their fair share of VAWA allocations and decision-making power. Legislation that purports to address gender-based violence must also address the concerns and issues of women of color specifically. This requires addressing discrimination based on race, national origin, culture, and language. The passage of the VAWA brings us part of the way towards addressing these issues. Through the cooperative efforts of civil rights activists and feminists, the VAWA can fulfill its obligation to all women, and can become part of a more fully collaborative activism that is the culmination of the struggles of women and people of color against violence as systemic oppression.

NOTE

1. 42 U.S.C. § 3796gg (1994).
2. 42 U.S.C. § 3796gg-1.
3. 42 U.S.C. § 10418(a).
4. 42 U.S.C. § 3796hh(c)(1).
5. Jenny Rivera, *Domestic Violence against Latinas by Latino Males: An Analysis of Race, National Origin, and Gender Differentials*, 14 Boston College Third World Law Journal 231, 243–49 (1994) (discussing law enforcement strategies in domestic violence cases as applied to Latinas).
6. 42 U.S.C. § 10402(a)(2)(B)(ii).

42

Cultural Evidence and Male Violence:
Are Feminist and Multiculturalist Reformers on a Collision Course in Criminal Courts?

Holly Maguigan

. . .

Introduction

The American criminal justice system faces an important question: Can the courts permit defendants to introduce evidence of cultural background without condoning violence by men against women and children? In those trials in which cultural evidence is received, is the information entitled to such unquestioning deference that its receipt signals the recognition of a "cultural defense" to male violence?
. . .

I. The Misplaced Focus on a Separate Cultural Defense as the Cause of Tension between Feminist and Multiculturalist Reform Goals

Advocates of a new, separately defined defense argue that its recognition is necessary to overcome the injustice of holding defendants from different cultures to the monolithic standards of the dominant one. Some opponents of the creation of a separate defense argue that recognition of pluralism, at the expense of the presumption that all know the law's requirements, would lead to relativism and chaos. Others, including some feminist scholars, argue that such a defense has already been recognized, but should be rejected because it condones violence against women.

Discussion of these issues is not, in fact, joined in any other than a purely theoretical fashion. There is not and will not be a separate cultural defense because as a practical matter such a defense can be neither defined nor implemented. In short, debate over a new cultural defense is misguided because the use of cultural information is not new, a workable legal definition of culture is impossible to develop, and the information is not being offered in court to create a separate defense. The current separate-defense debate obscures the real, practical problems of accomplishing reform goals that appear to be in competition with each other.

The multiculturalist reform goal is a system that takes a more pluralistic approach to the assessment of blame and the imposition of punishment. The operation of the current criminal justice system results in higher conviction rates and longer sentences for outsider defendants than for defendants who are part of the dominant culture. Scholars have suggested that at least part of the explanation for those disparities is that the present system does not reflect the shared values of a multicultural society but instead reinforces the white, traditionally male-identified values of the dominant culture.

. . .

The question of a separate defense is often addressed in legal, anthropological, and popular literature primarily in terms of three large categories of defendants rather than in the context of a doctrinal analysis. The first of these major categories consists of people born and enculturated outside the United States. . . .

A second category of defendants involves people born and enculturated in an indigenous culture within the United States which has some recognized claim to its own system of laws. . . .

The third major category includes defendants born and enculturated within a "subculture" of the United States without an entitlement (recognized by the dominant culture) to its own system of laws.

. . .

In the context of American criminal practice, if a culture is defined at least in part in terms of its differences from the dominant one, the resulting categorizations can obscure the absence of an accurate, monolithic definition of the "other" culture. In addition to the multiplicity of claims theoretically available as the different springboards of a separate cultural defense, there are problems for separate-defense theorists in choosing the characteristics of a culture that would justify, usually in moral terms, excusing ignorance of or inability to conform behavior to the law. Assuming those characteristics are identified, the practical implementation of a separate defense suggests the necessity of a pretrial examination of an individual defendant's degree of participation in the culture of origin. Some authors perceive an additional problem: the unfairness in affording members of minority cultures a defense that is unavailable to members of the dominant one. This argument ignores the work of scholars who explain that the standards of the dominant culture operate now as a cultural defense by supporting traditional defenses.

. . .

In cases involving violence against women and children, there is the additional question whether formal recognition of a cultural defense would contravene international human rights norms. Most criminal court judges will not see the trials before them as appropriate fora for resolving the question of whether this country adheres to the Convention on the Elimination of All Forms of Discrimination Against Women and, if so, whether such adherence trumps a defendant's right to raise a cultural defense.

. . .

Many observers, both advocates and opponents of a formal "cultural defense," share the belief that increasing numbers of people accused of crime in this country are asserting such a defense. They view the phenomenon as a by-product of a recent "influx" of immigrants, mainly Asians, to this country. Some observers incorrectly posit a situation in which defendants use "cultural defenses" primarily in family violence cases. In fact, the use of cultural information is not a new phenomenon. It is not limited to immigrants. It does not occur primarily in cases involving violence against women or children. Finally, most culturally different defendants who try to introduce background evidence do not assert a freestanding cultural defense.

. . .

For many years, cultural background evidence has been proffered to challenge the sufficiency of prosecution evidence regarding a defendant's state of mind. In guilty pleas, the information has been used to convince prosecutors and courts that, because they lacked the mens rea necessary for a conviction on the top count charged, defendants should be permitted to plead to lesser offenses or should receive lighter sentences than would seem warranted in the absence of cultural information. In trials, the information—often in the form of both lay and expert testimony—has been offered for a similar purpose: to demonstrate that the defendant's mens rea differed from that required for conviction. The information has been proffered in connection with both excuse and justification defenses.

. . .

It is when "social framework" evidence, in the form of cultural information, is offered by men accused of family or anti-woman violence that there appears to be competition between feminist and multiculturalist values. The theoretical debate about recognition of a formal cultural defense misses that point. A separate cultural defense is not the cause of a conflict between multiculturalism and women's rights in criminal trials. Nor is it the answer to the current problems defendants face when trying to use cultural information. The real issue facing the courts is the adequacy of the current mechanisms to receive cultural information and to do so without endorsing family violence.

II. Cultural Evidence in the Criminal Justice System: Existing Mechanisms

. . . Even in the absence of formal recognition of a freestanding cultural defense, the apparent conflict between multicultural and feminist reform goals arises when the receipt of evidence of defendants' cultural backgrounds threatens to reverse recent progress in recognizing the gravity of family and anti-woman violence. The risk is that, even without formalized abandonment or weakening of proscriptions against family violence, permitting evidence of the refusal of the defendant's culture to enact or enforce proscriptions against such violence will have the effect of condoning it in this country.

. . .

The discussion of the legal system's response to cultural evidence in family violence prosecutions is organized according to the procedural postures in which the issue arises. A focus on discrete procedural stages permits the development of a picture of how, in the course of actual criminal proceedings, cultural evidence is proffered by defendants, received or excluded by judges, and—when received—challenged by prosecution cross-examination and rebuttal evidence. The procedural stages are addressed in the order of the relative frequency with which they seem to occur: guilty pleas, trial claims based on impaired mental states, and finally trial claims based on the reasonableness of defendants' mental states.

A. Use of Cultural Background Information in Plea Bargaining and Sentencing Proceedings

. . .

Much recent discussion in legal scholarship and in the popular press has focused on three California prosecutions in which immigrant defendants used cultural information to reach non-trial dispositions: *People v. Kong Moua*,[1] *People v. Tou Moua*,[2] and *People v. Kimura*.[3] These cases exemplify two common strategies employed by defense counsel in urging the exercise of discretion. The first strategy utilizes a mens rea analysis to argue that the defendant lacked criminal intent at the level at which the act was charged because of the action's endorsement by the norms of the defendant's culture of origin. The second strategy involves advancing a mitigation argument that not only incorporates the role of the defendant's cultural norms in undermining the requisite intent, but also presents a specific claim that those norms operated to render the defendant "insane" in the legal terms of the dominant culture.

Defense counsel for Kong Moua pursued the first strategy. The defendant was charged originally with felony rape and kidnapping. He offered information during plea negotiations and later at sentencing that he believed that his advances to the victim, whom he understood to be his intended bride, were a welcomed part of the Hmong customary marriage ritual, zij poj niam. He described her resistance to his subsequent rape of her as necessary to consummate their betrothal and as a culturally appropriate response from a virtuous, willing woman. A criminal complaint was filed after the woman reported the rape to police and prosecutors. Information about the Hmong practice of marriage-by-capture was used first to convince the prosecutor to agree to a plea to the misdemeanor of false imprisonment and subsequently to convince the judge of the appropriateness of leniency at sentencing. Fresno County Superior Court Judge Gene M. Gomes said that the sentence, ninety days' imprisonment and one thousand dollars' restitution, was imposed after he became educated on the practice of zij poj niam and following consultation with the elders of the victim's and the defendant's families.

Kong Moua's case has been incorrectly characterized as one involving a "cultural defense." Rather, it was a case in which cultural information influenced the plea negotiations and the judge's sentence. . . .

Kong Moua's misdemeanor sentence generated media attention, criticism from feminists, and discussion among scholars. Stated simply, the disposition in Kong Moua may be seen as a retreat, under the guise of cultural pluralism, to the dominant culture's view that crimes of violence against women are not serious and that the price of anti-woman violence is not high. Such a view has long been represented in American criminal courts' treatment of rape cases.

In the second case, Tou Moua's lawyer made similar use of cultural background evidence to show the basis of the defendant's belief that his criminal responsibility for violence against a woman was less than that charged. . . .

In *People v. Kimura*, the cultural evidence that inclined the prosecutor to agree to a manslaughter plea similarly involved information about a culture in which men's decisions controlled women's fates. [Fumiko] Kimura, charged with first-degree murder, reached a negotiated non-trial disposition after presenting information that the drowning of her children and her own attempted suicide were intended to purge the shame of her husband's infidelity.

There are two distinctions between Kimura's use of cultural information and its use by Tou Moua and Kong Moua. The first relates to the content of the information. In *Kimura*, the defendant's crimes against her children were described as those of a person who was herself a victim—acted upon by the imperatives of patriarchal culture—rather than as an actor. Tou Moua and Kong Moua had both claimed entitlement to exercise power. The second difference is that in *Kimura*, defense counsel cast his appeal to the prosecutor during plea negotiations in terms of temporary insanity. The court accepted Kimura's manslaughter plea and sentenced her to one year of incarceration, time which she had served already in pre-trial custody, and five years' probation with a recommendation of psychiatric counseling. Criticized by some scholars, the disposition provides a useful illustration of the difficulty of reconciling a description of behavior which is normal in one culture with the legal implications of deviance from the norms of another. Kimura's act in response to the shame and consequent devaluation of herself and her children by her husband's infidelity would have been involuntary manslaughter in Japan, her country of origin. If Kimura had not reached a plea agreement and had been required to stand trial in the adversarial criminal justice system in her new country, however, she risked that her culpability would be reduced only if the fact-finder found that her motivation fell within American definitions of psychiatric defenses.

. . .

B. Use of Cultural Evidence in Support of Traditional Defenses at Trial

. . .

1. *Claims That a Defendant Is Not Guilty by Reason of Excuse or Is Guilty of a Lesser Offense*

. . .

With excuses, cultural evidence is often introduced or proffered to demonstrate that a defendant's mental status was impaired to an extent inconsistent with a finding of criminal responsibility. Currently defined excuses, including the defense of insanity, do not always comfortably accommodate claims based wholly or in part on defendants' differences from the dominant culture. Tensions often surface when a defendant attempts to translate a culturally different background into the conclusory medical terms customarily used to define mental status excuses. A core common issue, both in recent cases involving immigrants and in older ones involving African American defendants, is the identification of evidence that is actually helpful in assessing responsibility. For example, many experts are unable to diagnose the mental state of a defendant from a different culture.

. . .

Another difficulty facing culturally different defendants who argue existing excuses is that judges may misinterpret the proffered evidence as the assertion of a claim of a separate cultural defense. That problem arose in the case of Helen Wu, a Chinese national who was convicted in California of second-degree murder in the 1989 killing of her son. There the experts were not impeded by cultural bias in their assessment of the defendant. Their testimony was admitted as relevant to the defense's claim of unconsciousness. The prosecution, however, successfully objected to a requested jury instruction on the relevance of cultural information to her not-responsible defense.

The defendant and lay witnesses had testified at trial about her relationship with the boy's father and about the forces that impelled her to a belief that she should die and that the child should not be left behind to the care of his father. The defense had also offered experts who explained the relationship between Wu's enculturation and her unconsciousness of the act of killing her son. The defense had requested the following instruction to the jury:

> You have received evidence of defendant's cultural background and the relationship of her culture to her mental state. You may, but are not required to, consider [that] evidence in determining the presence or absence of the essential mental states of the crimes defined in these instructions, or in determining any other issue in this case.[4]

The trial court refused to give the instruction, apparently confusing it with one that would have defined a separate defense. The judge commented that he did not want to put the "stamp of approval on [defendant's] actions in the United States which would have been acceptable in China."[5] Defense counsel preserved the trial record by explaining the integration of cultural and psychiatric testimony with the excuse of unconsciousness. On the basis of that record, Wu's conviction was reversed on appeal, and the appellate court directed that the requested instruction be given at the retrial.

The trial judge in *Wu* was not alone in confusing the offer of cultural testimony with the assertion of a new substantive defense. Observers often make the same mistake when they assess the outcomes of other family violence cases. They interpret reduced verdicts as reflecting approval of the defendants' beliefs rather than as outcomes in which the defense evidence raised doubts about the level of guilt.

. . .

In the second of defendants' beliefs, the manner in which outsider men excuse their actions may well be seen as a retreat to the still-recent time in which dominant culture men offered similar explanations for killing women: the actions stem from adherence to the social norm of male domination of family. The ease of accommodation between traditional definitions of excuse or mitigation and the norms of an outsider culture poses a major problem from the standpoint of victims' advocates and feminist observers. In some cases the mitigating excuse claim is expressed as the stress of assimilation or "culture shock" rather than as an attempt to validate the norms of the culture of origin. In others, however, a defendant's adherence to patriarchal norms is specifically described as information relevant to excusing or mitigating culpability. These are the cases, more than the ones involving witchcraft or culture shock, which seem to send a message that is dangerous for women.

The argument that the defendant's culpability for killing his wife was decreased by his cultural belief in male dominance was successful in the Brooklyn trial of Dong Lu Chen. Kings County Supreme Court Justice Edward Pincus, sitting without a jury, explained his verdict of manslaughter in the second degree (rather than murder or first-degree manslaughter) on the basis of the defendant's formative experiences within the culture of mainland China:

> Were this crime [bludgeoning his wife to death with a claw hammer because of her infidelity] committed by the defendant as someone who was born and raised in America, or born elsewhere but primarily raised in America, even in the Chinese American community, the Court would have been constrained to find the defendant guilty of manslaughter in the first degree. . . . [B]ut based on cultural aspects, the effect of the wife's behavior on someone who is essentially born in China, raised in China, and took all his Chinese culture with him except the community which would moderate his behavior, the Court . . . based on the peculiar facts and circumstances of this case . . . and the expert testimony . . . find[s] the defendant guilty of manslaughter in the second degree.[6]

The defendant was sentenced to five years' probation. This disposition and the judge's rationale have been interpreted as the result of an uncritical acceptance of expert testimony on cultural difference without consideration of the apparent endorsement of a belief in men's entitlement to dominate women.

. . .

2. Claims of Not Guilty by Reason of Justification or Mistake of Fact

In both justification and mistake of fact defenses, the argument is that the defendant was reasonable in perceiving a situation and that, if the perception had been correct, the defendant's action would not have been criminal. The risk demonstrated in such cases is that where the issue is the reasonableness of a defendant's mental state, judges and juries are liable to impose the dominant culture's standards of reasonableness as if they were universally applicable. A defendant's challenge to the prosecution's case will often fail when a court excludes evidence that would make information, which is available to a minority-culture defendant, also accessible to the finder of fact.

Yvonne Wanrow, charged with killing a man, offered cultural evidence at trial in support of her self-defense claim. The defense theory was that the jury should consider cultural factors in determining the reasonableness of her perception of the danger she faced and of her belief that it was necessary to use deadly defensive force. Her ultimate appellate victory is usually discussed as a "woman's self-defense case," but little attention is paid to her effort to introduce cultural evidence. Wanrow was accused of homicide of a stranger whom she had heard was a sexual molester of children and who appeared suddenly in the home where she was staying. She testified that she thought he posed an imminent danger to her and her young son. The trial judge excluded cultural evidence intended to contextualize the defendant's resort to violence to protect her family.

The proffered expert, whom the intermediate appellate court described only as "an expert witness on Indian culture," would have explained the cultural importance of family. His testimony would have allowed the jury to understand the tension in Wanrow's circumstance between the cultural value of respect for elders and the culture's abhorrence of "unnatural sex acts" and the resulting impact of those competing factors on the defendant's state of mind in a confrontation with an older man whom she believed to have molested other children. She was convicted.

Although her conviction was overturned on appeal, Wanrow failed to persuade either the intermediate appellate court or the Supreme Court of Washington that the trial court erred when it excluded the testimony regarding the impact of culture on her state of mind. The refusal of both courts to find error in the exclusion of cultural evidence stands in stark contrast to the state supreme court's holding that it was reversible error to fail to instruct the jury in a way that required them to consider the impact of her gender.

At Wanrow's trial, multiculturalist and feminist interests did not compete. Rather, they intersected and informed both her fear and her perception as a Native American woman of the need to use a weapon against a man who was armed only with his hands. The case presents an example of the failure of trial and appellate judges to understand such an intersection: Their willingness to permit contextual analysis from one standpoint, but not another—as if the perspective of the defendant's gender could be isolated from the perspective of her culture—is fundamentally problematic. *Wanrow* illustrates the flaws in the assumption made by some commentators that existing defenses do, as a matter of current practice, accommodate cultural information. These scholars fail to analyze the discretionary role of judges in rulings concerning the admission of evidence.

Fifteen years after Wanrow's trial, a trial court judge in Kodiak, Alaska exercised discretion in evidentiary rulings to permit the jury to hear the full experience of an Aleut woman on trial for homicide. Kathryn Charliaga, charged with killing her husband, said that she acted in self-defense and that the act occurred after a long history of abuse at his hands.

The defense offered, in addition to lay testimony about the violence she had experienced in the past, testimony of two experts. The first described the operation of Battered Woman Syndrome and its impact on the defendant's perceptions at the time of the killing and on her inability to escape the past violence. The second expert testified specifically about women's subservient roles in Aleut villages and described the Aleut culture as one that not only tolerated wife-battering, but also offered no support for a woman's attempts to leave the relationship. Charliaga was acquitted.

The cases of *Wanrow* and *Charliaga* illustrate the uselessness of positing a simple dualistic choice between criminal justice reform aimed at decreasing pluralistic ignorance and reform aimed at incorporating the standpoints of women. In both cases, the impacts of gender and culture on the defendants' actions were inextricably linked. Their different trial outcomes illustrate the necessity of admitting cultural evidence at trials in order to avoid silencing or distorting women's voices. A feminist argument in favor of excluding all cultural information risks silencing the voices of women defendants and ignores the constraints that various cultures place on women.

. . .

III. An Approach to Cultural Evidence That Combats Pluralistic Ignorance without Trivializing Family Violence

. . .

Observers who believe that cultural information is being received too readily by courts with the effect of condoning anti-woman violence often focus on cases involving male defendants accused of crimes against family members. Their call for the exclusion of cultural information ignores the impact such a rule would have on the cases of women accused of crime. They ignore, too, the fact that many advocates for women victims oppose a blanket exclusion of cultural evidence, even one aimed at demonstrating the legitimacy of patriarchal values. Finally, the call for total exclusion implicitly concedes that defense cultural information cannot be challenged effectively in court.

. . .

The starting point for achieving a balanced approach is the courts' application of existing precedents for the admissibility of cultural evidence, not to support a separate defense, but as part of a challenge to the sufficiency of the prosecution's proof of mens rea. As a general rule, applicable in all criminal prosecutions, cultural information should be received when it is proffered for the purpose of explaining the social framework of a defendant's state of mind. A ruling that the evidence is admissible is only the first step. As with any other defense evidence, an admissibility determination is not tantamount either to an endorsement of the content of the evidence or to the result that the information will go unchallenged by the prosecution.

Judges' threshold rulings in this area will be made on the same evidentiary basis as are other decisions to admit lay and expert evidence. Like those decisions, they are traditionally matters left to a trial court's discretion. Discretionary evidentiary rulings are rarely reversed on appeal. There is in these cases always a risk that judges will not exercise discretion in a content-neutral way.

In an analogous context, the Supreme Court made clear that a judge's threshold determinations on the admissibility of expert testimony are not to be based on the message contained in the testimony: "The focus, of course, must be solely on principles and methodology [of proffered expert testimony], not on the conclusions they generate."[7]

. . .

It is important to recognize the significance of the prosecution's obligation to confront defense evidence on culture. The social costs of permitting consideration of cultural evidence can be high in any prosecution, and are demonstrably high in this country when the issue is family violence. An acquittal may be interpreted as a judgment that a "reasonable man" is permitted to be violent against his wife (or his children, or a woman he wants to make his wife, or even another man who interferes with his control of his wife). Convictions on lesser counts in such cases are seen as sending a message that the behavior, even when criminal, is not serious.

This is a message that many women respond to with fear. After the announcement of the probationary sentence in the *Chen* case, the president of the New York Chapter of the National Organization for Women (NOW) said that the sentence had created "an open season on women," and the executive director of Asian Americans for Equality said that Chen "set back the women's fight for equality in Chinese culture."[8] The New York Asian Women's Center received calls and visits from frightened battered women, one of whom reported her husband's response: "If this is the kind of sentence you get for killing your wife, I could do anything to you. I have the money for a good attorney."[9] Despite the judge's repeated comments that the verdict and sentence were based on the "peculiar" facts before him, the case has been interpreted as sending a general message minimizing the significance of wife-killing.

The *Chen* case demonstrates the need for effective refutation of invalid cultural evidence and makes clear that the very pluralistic ignorance that cultural information seeks to address can be reinforced by unchallenged testimony. The expert testimony of anthropologists, psychologists, and sociologists can serve to support racist, anti-immigrant, and sexist stereotypes and can invite both acquittals and prejudice against other members of a culture based on those stereotypes.

. . .

Not all women's advocates believe that a general rule preventing defendants from offering evidence to explain the social framework in which they acted is the appropriate solution to the problem of verdicts that appear to sanction anti-woman violence. After the *Chen* verdict, NOW filed a complaint against the trial judge criticizing specifically his receipt of cultural information. Asian groups, including women's groups, originally endorsed NOW's action, but they withdrew their original support of the complaint because it called for a blanket prohibition against the receipt of cultural evidence. The refusal to join that call has been portrayed unsympathetically, perhaps because of a failure to understand its basis in a distrust of the ability of dominant-culture judges to adjudicate fairly the claims of minority-culture defendants without the aid of social framework evidence.

Conclusion

Accommodation of the voices of overlapping groups of outsiders does not require hearing one group while silencing another. The cases of defendants such as Fumiko

Kimura, Kathryn Charliaga, Yvonne Wanrow, and Helen Wu demonstrate the intersectionality of the interests of the two groups. That intersection is demonstrated also in the aftermath of the *Chen* sentence. Awareness of the intersection is too often missing from the analyses of both courts and scholars.

Change resulting from reliance on prosecutors to convince judges and juries that crimes of family violence are not simply customary behaviors will be accomplished only through extended practice and experience. Trial and guilty-plea results will not always be satisfactory; there inevitably will be cases in which prosecutors' presentation of accurate information will not overcome stereotypes offered by the defense. Yet no quick-fix alternative exists that does not undermine both feminist and multicultural concerns or rely on conclusion-driven evidentiary rulings by judges.

An unacceptable quick fix is a rule permitting the exercise of discretion to exclude consideration of evidence regarding a defendant's state of mind on the basis of its content, because the defendant had a state of mind that was unacceptable or incomprehensible to dominant-culture trial judges. This conclusion is informed in part by an awareness that, although most defendants (including those accused of family violence) are men, some are women. Women from all cultures are routinely perceived as having states of mind unacceptable to the dominant culture.

This conclusion is informed also by the certainty that, among the people incarcerated in this country, the massive overrepresentation of people of color is the result, at least in part, of the inability or unwillingness of judges and juries from the dominant culture to understand, without information aimed at overcoming their ignorance, the perceptions or actions of people from minority cultures. Permitting judges to exercise discretion in a way that allows a conclusion-based exclusion or limitation of cultural information at trials risks endorsing the notion that traditional, white-male values in fact represent a universal that defines not only the identity of this country but also the norm against which all accused individuals are measured.

NOTES

1. No. 315972-0 (Fresno County Super. Ct. Feb. 7, 1985).

2. No. 328106-0 (Fresno County Super. Ct. Nov. 28, 1985).

3. No. A-091133 (Santa Monica Super. Ct. Nov. 21, 1985).

4. *People v. Wu*, No. E007993, 1991 Cal. App., 35 Lexis 1229 (Cal. Ct. App. Oct. 24, 1991).

5. *Id.* at 37.

6. Chen, No. 87-7774, Proceedings, Dec. 21, 1988, at 301–03 (on file with author).

7. *Daubert v. Merrell Dow Pharmaceuticals, Inc.*, 113 S. Ct. 2786 (1993).

8. Leslie Gevirtz, *Immigrant Receives Probation in Slaying of Wife*, UPI, Mar. 31, 1989, available in Lexis, Nexis Library, UPI File.

9. Alexis Jetter, *Fear Is Legacy of Wife Killing in Chinatown; Battered Asians Shocked by Husband's Probation*, New York Newsday, Nov. 26, 1989, at 4.

43

Ignoring the Sexualization of Race: Heteronormativity, Critical Race Theory, and Anti-Racist Politics

Darren Lenard Hutchinson

. . .

The problem of violence against oppressed social groups provides an excellent setting for exploring the multidimensionality of subordination and for developing a challenge to anti-racist essentialism. . . . [P]ublished accounts and available statistical data regarding oppressive violence targeting gay, lesbian, bisexual, and transgendered people of color indicate that much of this violence involves the use of sexual subordination to perpetuate racial harms. Despite the deployment of sexualized violence against gays, lesbians, bisexuals, and the transgendered of color to further racial oppression, anti-racist theorists have not constructed a substantial critique of heterosexism in their work, nor has the issue of sexual justice for gay, lesbian, bisexual, and transgendered people been incorporated into the agendas of most anti-racist political organizations. In fact, several anti-racist theorists have questioned the importance of including sexual identity as a protected category within existing civil rights law.

. . .

[T]he very history of gay and lesbian politics, through which people of color have recognized and resisted multidimensional oppression [has centered around violence]. For example, New York City's "Stonewall Riots of 1969," which many scholars point to as a catalyst for the modern "gay rights movement," began when a group of Puerto Rican, Black, and poor gay, lesbian, transgendered, and gender non-conforming individuals resisted the repeated physical and other forms of harassment they endured from local police.

On the particular evening of the riots, police, as they had often done on prior occasions, "raided" the Stonewall Inn (a gay bar) to harass patrons and to arrest individuals, charging them with "lewdness" or "solicitation." People of color, women, the poor, and the transgendered were often targeted for arrest and harassment. The oppression that these individuals faced was undeniably multidimensional in nature—resulting from interwoven gender, race, sexuality, and class hierarchies. The subordination of people of color by the New York police was a manifestation of sexualized racism: racial and sexual hierarchies rendered them vulnerable to police abuse and constructed their sexual identity as particularly offensive and improper. Although gay, lesbian, bisexual, and transgender statuses were generally deemed transgressive and intolerable by the officers, subordinate racial status separated people of color from white gays, lesbians, and bisexual and transgendered individuals. The disparate treatment of gays, lesbians, bisexuals, and the transgendered of color suggests that the transgressive sexual practices of people of color might be perceived as particularly deviant and threatening to heterosexual normalcy, a result that is consistent with the legacy of negative stereotypification of the sexuality of people of color. Thus, the Stonewall rioters, these early radicals from gay and lesbian communities and communities of color, responded to a multidimensional system of sexualized racial violence and harassment directed toward them by the "protective" arm of the state. A "racial" reading of the Stonewall Riots provides a historical context for the problem of violence against gay, lesbian, bisexual, and transgendered persons of color[.]

. . .

Existing statistical studies of such violence also suggest that oppressive violence involves a complex fusion of homophobia, racism, patriarchy, and class domination. . . . [T]here are only a limited number of empirical analyses of homophobic violence, despite the politicization of this violence in gay and lesbian communities and the efforts of several anti-violence organizations to collect such data. An even smaller number provide information regarding the race of the victims and assailants, due in part to the failure of gay and lesbian politics to address issues of racial subordination and of anti-racist organizations to confront homophobia. Furthermore, when researchers investigate homophobic violence, their data may not provide a representative sample of the gay, lesbian, bisexual, and transgendered community because many victims are "closeted" and, therefore, fail to report their victimization. The general invisibility of people of color means that their experiences are even more unrepresented in these data. Many gays and lesbians, moreover, distrust law enforcement due to a history of victimization and harassment by police officers and, thus, often do not report such violence to law enforcement officials. As a consequence, statistics compiled by police departments may distort the magnitude of homophobic brutality.

Conscious of these methodological difficulties, . . . [the] data suggest that race might increase the vulnerability of gays, lesbians, bisexuals, and the transgendered of color to homophobic violence and subject them to additional harassment and further abuse by police officers when they report their victimization.

One of the most comprehensive studies of homophobic violence was conducted by Gary David Comstock. The Comstock Survey compiles the results of a survey of 291 gays and lesbians of different class and racial backgrounds.[1] Participants in the survey responded to a series of questions regarding their experiences with homophobic violence. The survey also compiles the results of thirty-four other studies of homophobic violence. The Comstock Survey presents its results in two broad categories: "general" and "specific" violence. The general violence category gathers information based on participants' responses to a single question generalizing all incidents of violence (e.g., "Have you been assaulted because you are lesbian or gay?"), or by collapsing together and summarizing answers to a series of questions regarding particular kinds of assaults (e.g., "Have you ever been raped, robbed, or beaten because of your sexual orientation?"). The "specific violence" category presents data detailing the percentage of individuals who have experienced certain subcategories of violence and harassment, such as assaults, rape, and vandalism; in the specific category (unlike the general category) the data for the subcategories of violence remain disaggregated.

Both the general and specific violence categories demonstrate racial patterns. Under the general violence category, for example, the Comstock Survey finds that 58 percent of lesbians of color compared with 41 percent of white lesbians reported victimization; among men, 70 percent of men of color and 59 percent of white men reported victimization. Thus, when asked whether they have experienced homophobic violence generally, a higher percentage of persons of color responded affirmatively. The subcategories or specific categories contain shifting results. In some categories, a higher percentage of people of color experienced such violence; in other categories, the rate of victimization was greater among whites. Still in other subcategories, the rate of victimization was equal. Overall, lesbians of color and white gay men reported higher rates of victimization in the various subcategories. These data may mean that lesbians of color and white gay men report a greater breadth of assaults. Comstock, however, fails to account for the differences between the general and specific categories. In particular, Comstock does not state whether white male participants (who, overall, reported a lower level of victimization) had higher rates of violence within the subcategories because certain individuals suffered multiple attacks or because the attacks they experienced involved combinations of offenses in the various subcategories.

Other studies support Comstock's finding that people of color experience homophobic violence in rates exceeding those of whites. While these studies tentatively support a finding that race subjects people of color to higher rates of anti-gay/lesbian violence, more research is needed due to the methodological difficulties associated with gay and lesbian surveys and because the number of studies that have provided racial data remains too small to draw any final conclusions. Nevertheless, even if statistical data ultimately prove that race does not subject people of color to greater victimization rates, racial hostility will still likely play a role in precipitating individual acts of sexualized violence.

The Comstock Survey also details and documents the tense relationship between law enforcement and gay, lesbian, bisexual, and transgendered communities. Police officers and the courts have historically been indifferent to or even active participants in the marginalization of gays and lesbians through oppressive violence. Comstock confirms this history of hostility with statistical data. Specifically, the Comstock Survey finds that 73 percent of the victims of all forms of homophobic violence declined to report the incidents to police, while 58 percent of victims of more graphic attacks declined to report the incidents. Other surveys confirm these results.

The alarming implications of these data increase when the findings are controlled for racial backgrounds. In particular, 82 percent of victims of color, as opposed to 72 percent of white victims, did not report their victimization to police.

The Comstock Survey also examines police responses to reports of homophobic violence, categorizing the victims' descriptions of police reactions as "helpful, courteous," "indifferent," "hostile," "physically abusive," and "competent." These data suggest that a higher percentage of gays and lesbians of color than whites experience harassment and abuse from police when they report incidents of homophobic violence. Specifically, 42 percent of people of color, compared with 16 percent of whites, described police responses as "hostile"; 8 percent of people of color, compared with 3 percent of whites, described police responses as "physically abusive"; and 17 percent of people of color, compared with 65 percent of whites, described police responses as "helpful, courteous." The racial patterns in these data confirm a history of particularized hostility between gays, lesbians, bisexuals, and the transgendered of color [and] law enforcement (a history evidenced by the Stonewall Riots) and affirm the general tension between communities of color and the police. These findings also demonstrate the importance of implementing anti-heterosexist agendas within critical race theory and other forms of anti-racist discourse and placing anti-racist politics within gay and lesbian liberation discourse. For example, if anti-racism and gay politics seek to challenge police insensitivity and hostility directed toward all members of their respective communities, then they must recognize and confront the ways in which race and sexual oppression interact to shape oppressive police conduct.

. . .

[A] history of sexualized (and gendered) racial oppression has played a central role in the social, economic, political, and legal oppression of people of color. Consistent with the inherent goals of any authentic anti-racist agenda, race theorists and activists have aggressively challenged this legacy of sexualized racial oppression. Anti-racists, however, have confined their responses almost exclusively to those forms of sexualized racial oppression that appear heterosexual in nature (or which anti-racist activists have construed as heterosexual victimization). . . .

The disparate anti-racist responses to homophobic and heterosexual forms of racism perpetuate patterns of social subordination, a result that is patently inconsistent with the goals of any liberationist movement. Heteronormativity in anti-racist discourse creates a discriminatory model of racial justice in which heterosexual status serves as a prerequisite for obtaining the advocacy and creative analysis of anti-racist theorists and activists. Heterosexuals are thus privileged in racial discourse, while gay, lesbian, bisexual, and transgendered persons are subordinate. Heteronormativity in anti-racist discourse, therefore, compounds the marginalization of gay, lesbian, bisexual, and transgendered people of color, who already face racial, class, gender, and heterosexist oppression from the greater society. The perpetuation of social subordination and privilege by a "liberatory" movement is clearly contradictory.

The exclusion of anti-heterosexist politics from anti-racism becomes even more troubling when one considers that "heterosexuality" is typically a privileged status.

While heterosexual identity is a source of social power (for persons of any race), it has also served as a source of subordination for people of color. If heterosexual status can become stigmatized and an instrument of racial oppression, then it is logical and, indeed, likely that gay, lesbian, bisexual, and transgender identities (which are generally marginalized social categories) can also serve as sources of racial oppression and disadvantage.

. . . In addition to rendering anti-racism internally inconsistent and discriminatory, anti-racist heteronormativity causes a host of other problems and inadequacies. First, the failure of anti-racists to challenge heterosexism conflicts with the inherent purpose of anti-racism—responding to the many, often subtle, ways in which people of color are oppressed in a white supremacist society. By ignoring how the sexualization of race subordinates gay, lesbian, bisexual, and transgendered people of color, anti-racist activists and theorists permit an entire category of racial oppression—homophobic racial subordination—to escape their needed analysis and critique. Thus, contrary to the inherent goals of anti-racism, a species of racial oppression remains unchecked (perhaps endorsed) by anti-racist theorists and activists.

Heteronormativity also harms anti-racist politics and the larger body of progressive political action. On the one hand, anti-racist heteronormativity divides communities of color and hinders the formation of coalitions within communities of color to combat racial oppression. Heteronormativity may also place anti-racist activists in collusion with, and provide legitimacy for, conservative political organizations—organizations that might endorse agendas contrary to the needs of communities of color. In addition, essentialism—in all social movements—prevents collective political action across the terrain of socially oppressed groups. By deploying essentialist politics that deny the importance of combating all forms of inequality, progressive social movements often deteriorate into a futile battle of oppression-ranking, which paralyzes the coalitional potential.

NOTE

1. Gary David Comstock, Violence against Lesbians and Gay Men 32 (1991).

44

Requiring Battered Women Die:
Murder Liability for Mothers under Failure
to Protect Statutes

Michelle S. Jacobs

. . .

This article explores the legal dilemma of a growing number of women who find themselves . . . at the intersection of domestic violence and child abuse: women who are accused of murdering their children when spouses or significant others have actually killed the children in a household where violence rules. These women may have either a justification or an excuse defense available to them but are effectively precluded from taking advantage of such defenses either through the ignorance of their lawyers or by gender bias in the application of criminal law.

Progress has been made in educating the public, law enforcement, and the actors within the judicial system about the realities of violence against women and against children within the home. However, the critical interconnections between violence against the mother and violence against her children have not been fully understood by our courts. No consistent theory has been developed for the defense of mothers that is based on the connection between the abuse that a mother is receiving at the hands of the violent partner and her ability to prevent harm to her children. In fact, though public awareness of child abuse increased at the same time as awareness of domestic violence increased, the two seem to work at odds with each other. As awareness of the abuse increases, so does the likelihood of prosecution for the mother—despite the fact that both mother and child are abused by the same person. Courts have been reluctant to excuse the mother's failure to save the child from abuse on the grounds that she herself has been abused. In fact, the mother's encounter with violence in a sense heightens her dilemma. The courts reason that since she is aware of the violence that occurs in the home, she should do more to ensure that her children are shielded from that violence.

Nor have advances in post-conviction relief benefited the women whose children have been killed by a violent intimate. Many states have developed post-conviction remedies for women who can establish that they were battered by spouses whom they killed. However, when a woman is convicted of the murder of her child, she will not qualify for a clemency petition, despite the fact that the death of the child was actually caused by the same abuser the woman would have been justified in killing. This article suggests that the mother should be able to assert that she is justified in not protecting the child because of the risk of death or serious bodily injury to herself.

Criminal liability for these mothers is increasingly based on a "failure to protect" or omissions theory. Ordinarily, a person accused of a crime is required to commit a voluntary act (actus reus) with a required state of mind (mens rea) before society will attach criminal significance or liability to the person's behavior. There are crimes, however, which are either specifically defined in terms of failure to perform some specified act or failure to act when there is a legal duty to do so. A parent's common law duty to her child falls into this category. Both parents have a duty to clothe and feed their children and maintain basic necessities. The parental duty to the child is, at least theoretically, not without limit. A duty to act is limited initially by the actor's ability to perform the expected act. The primary issues for the parents are the extent and nature of the acts they must perform to satisfy this duty. While a parent is expected to expose herself to a greater degree of risk to save her child than would a stranger, the parent is not required to risk death or serious bodily injury. Parents are expected to take every step reasonably possible to prevent harm to their children.

Though the law holds both parents to the same duty, society particularly expects that the mother will be the child's protector. The mother is expected to suppress any individual identity or needs of her own in order to serve and protect the needs of her child. She is expected to use more than reasonable efforts to protect her child, to do more than the law requires. She is expected to use every effort. When a child dies through abuse at the hands of someone other than the mother, and the state determines that the mother failed to take reasonable steps to save her child, the mother can be prosecuted for "failure to protect." There appears to be no discussion in the cases of what constitutes "every reasonable" step possible to satisfy the duty to act. The unspoken assumption may be that the mother can end the abuse by simply picking up the phone and calling the police. Such assumptions ignore the realities of violence by the significant other. By making such assumptions, the courts are in fact requiring that mothers risk serious bodily injury or death before their duty to act is satisfied.

. . .

I. Society's Views of Motherhood and Child Abuse

. . .

B. Society's View of Child Abuse

. . .

Child abuse policies have been formulated by workers who have an inherent bias against mothers. The total fixation on the child's interests alone causes the workers to make determinations about the child's best interest without reference to contextual reality. These actions can lead the workers and the child's legal representatives to argue that the child should be removed from the mother, despite the fact that the mother and the child have a real emotional attachment and despite the fact that the state may be unable to provide an adequate alternative placement for the child. The child victims in these situations are frequently described as innocent—indicating however subtly that the mother is not. Although we can forgive or maybe excuse the mother for remaining in a violent relationship, on some level we may still view her as an implicit agent in her own abuse. We cannot forgive or excuse her for failing to prevent the abuse or death of her child. If forced to compete for the sympathies and interest of the public, a totally innocent child trumps a battered woman any day. We find this sentiment expressed, though not in those terms, in the works of Alice Miller, a Swiss psychologist. As Miller points out, "The situation of an adult woman confronted by a brutal man is not the same as that of a small child."[1] Miller's work has been quoted by some feminists as well, who seek to explain why it is appropriate to hold the mothers criminally responsible for failure to protect. For example, Professor Mary Becker advocates that:

> Adults in a household should be responsible for injury to the child if they knew or should have known about the abuse and could have taken steps to prevent the abuse by leaving with the children or reporting the abuse to the authorities. The assumption should be that the adult who was not literally a hostage—not literally coerced at every available second—could have acted to end abuse. Although the adult might have found herself or himself in circumstances such that protection of the child seemed impossible, the child is still a child. No matter how weak the mother, she is in a much better position than the child to prevent abuse and owes a duty of care to her children.[2]

Professor Becker's language echoes the language of some court opinions holding abused mothers liable for failing to protect their children. By focusing exclusively on what is happening to the child—without considering the full context of how the abuser's violence affects every member of the household—agencies perpetuate the continuance of violence within intimate space. Blaming the mother avoids the necessity of examining the ways in which the courts', police, and public unwillingness to address the issue of violence within the home contributes to the ongoing empowerment of the abuser. The image presented of the mother of abused children is that she does not care about or take seriously her personal circumstances and how they affect her children. Therefore, it is easy to reach the conclusion that she is somehow deviant or unfit because she keeps her children in a household where there is violence. The service provider's inquiry may go no further. The agency, psychologist, or lawyer is not required to ask whether the mother had an alternative to remaining in a violent household. The fact that no alternatives exist is irrelevant. In fact, legal, social service practice, and psychological theory all hold women responsible for child abuse even when a male assailant is clearly identified and is also battering the mother.

At the other end of the spectrum, some feminist scholars are reluctant to attribute any blame to the mother for a child's injury or death at the hands of a violent intimate. The reluctance to do so is bound up in the unwillingness to allow children (their existence and relationship to women) to define women's actions, status, or conditions of existence. They seek to free women from permanent attachment to the status of mother, thereby eliminating what can be viewed as a major component of the oppression of women.

Both approaches are acontextual. To deny that harm has been done to the children by the mother forces the mother's advocate to represent her as the "good" mother to gain the court's and the public's sympathy, understanding, and trust. This position is troublesome. A "good" mother would never find herself in a situation where she was being abused, and even if she did, she would never "allow" her children to be abused. As more becomes known about the plight of children living within violent homes, the feminist legal community has been conflicted in its theoretical examination of the ties between mothers who have either actively abused their children or who have failed to protect children from known abusers. This conflict and the silence which it generates are quite apparent when viewed in contrast to the activity of feminists in the development of laws and theories to help women who have been raped or who have themselves been battered in the home. It has been suggested that the silence may be partially attributable to the absence of a compelling female adult victim in the failure to protect cases. The cultural orientation and pressure to place total responsibility on the mother seems overwhelming. When faced with two individuals who might compete for the title of victim, even some feminists will pick the child as being the "truly" innocent person and therefore deserving the title. We are backed into this choice because of the insistence of relying on the dichotomy of victim versus independent agent. What is the feminist theoretical view of women who are both victims and agents, who want to be seen as reasonable, but at the same time commit acts which even women find difficult to understand?

. . .

II. Development and Expansion of Failure to Protect Laws

. . .

C. Criminal Liability

. . .

While the failure to protect laws are written in gender neutral terms, their application and broad effect are gendered. Women are overwhelmingly prosecuted under these statutes because they are deemed to have primary caretaking responsibilities for the children and because they are within reach of the law. Men may not be within reach, either because of flight or because no legal parental ties to the biological father have been established. Most importantly, because men are increasingly more likely to be the actual perpetuators of the violence, women are left to prevent the violence.

The imposition of an affirmative duty to protect a child from an abuser's violence creates a problem when the protecting parent fears retaliation from the abuser. Protecting the child in this situation can prove dangerous to the intervener and to the child. Only three states—Iowa, Minnesota, and Oklahoma—have expressly created an affirmative defense for a parent who finds herself at risk of death or serious bodily injury if she acts to protect the child. In order to exercise the defense, the defendant must have reasonably believed that to interfere would result in additional injuries to the child or to the defendant. The reality of the child's injury or death makes it difficult to view the mother's situation from her perspective at the time of the incident. Sympathies for the child's suffering can obscure the fact-finder's ability to properly evaluate the mother's choices.

Finally, it is difficult to locate many of the women who face the quandary of being both battered and non-abusing mothers in the criminal justice system. Because of the threat of life imprisonment, without the possibility of parole, or even the possibility of having death imposed, many mothers plead to second degree murder or involuntary manslaughter. Often we only become aware of them if they are referred to in the appeals of their spouses or significant others.

. . .

IV. Battering and Determinations of Reasonableness

I pray that everyone who ever knew and will know me will forgive me for not being a strong person.[3]

Mothers who are battered confront the same thorny issue as battered women who kill: can their behavior be seen as reasonable? The issue of reasonableness of the battered mother's behavior is one for the jury. The fact-finder's wide latitude in these cases highlights the need and importance of fashioning an appropriate defense which will accurately portray the mother's circumstances for the jury. However, what the jury hears is shaped by the trial judge through procedural and evidentiary rulings, as well as by his instructions to the jury. The trial court is guided, as are jurors, by the cultural and stereotypical view of mother as the selfless protector of the child. Adherence to stereotypical views can impede the court's ability to evaluate probative evidence on the issue of reasonableness.

In a review of the cases of women charged with failure to protect, no women were excused from liability. None of these cases explain what behavior by the mothers might constitute "every step reasonably possible." Can society envision and accept a situation in which the mother does not offer her own life to save that of her child? Case law indicates it is difficult for the court to reach that conclusion. Legal scholars must begin to describe and explain the reactions of the mothers as being reasoned actions. Though that may go against the grain of the "child savers," the approach is consistent with a sound criminal law theory. Consider the following narrative:

> I'm here because my husband wanted to kill me, and since he couldn't, he killed my baby instead. He knows that I'd rather be dead than have my child dead, so this worked out better for him. I have lost all of my children now, and it will be a slow

death for as long as I live knowing that he took the one thing I've ever had as my own. It started one afternoon when I was sleeping in a very deep sleep because he kept me up for two days in a row. I hadn't been out of his sight for almost three years. Can you imagine that? He locked me in when he went out, and mostly we stayed home. The beatings were a regular part of our life, so when he called me, I was trained to jump up and run to him. This day he told me that our son had fallen and hit his head on the edge of the table. I took one look at him and knew that he hit him with something, and that my son was in serious trouble. He died waiting in the same emergency room that I had been in two nights before after my husband tried to kill me. He wouldn't even let me hold my son as he died. I don't remember what happened after that except that I was screaming that my husband killed my son and that the hospital let him die. My husband was arrested there, and four days later at my son's funeral, I was arrested and brought to Riker's Island. He told the detectives that I hit my son on the head with a hammer that the police found in the trash-can in our kitchen. They said both our fingerprints were on it. Maybe they were, but I did not kill my son! Now he has taken everything from me. I've spent my life running from one hit to another. I've been beaten up since I've been here too. . . . Everyone hates a woman who sleeps while her child is being killed. The only reason I don't hate myself is because I don't even exist anymore after twelve years of being abused.[4]

. . .

The plight of these women and their children is almost too painful to read. Yet, the narratives illustrate several points: (1) violence towards the child may be unexpected and reflect an escalation in violence previously directed only at the mother—this raises a question of whether the mother knew or should have known that her child was at risk; (2) the mothers are not necessarily passive observers of their children's death—in some cases they may be physically unable to help; and (3) above all else, given the abuser's propensity to violence, the mother's behavior was reasonable. By reasonable, I mean that the mother, based on the information available to her at the time, can form a reasonable belief that further intervention would create the risk of death or serious bodily injury to herself or increase the risk of harm to her child. If her determination is correct, then she should not be held liable for the death of the child. Her action or inaction should be seen as justifiable. A reading of the narrative . . . requires neither an argument for diminished capacity nor one of coercion or duress, but can and should fit squarely within the accepted standards of reasonable behavior in a jurisdiction that uses a subjective or hybrid standard of reasonableness. In a state with a purely objective standard of reasonableness, battered mothers, like other battered women, may find it difficult to raise issues of abuse in their own defense.

Courts have characterized the behavior of battered mothers as being unreasonable because allegedly the mothers "did nothing" when their children were killed. However, there are at least three ways—besides actually doing nothing—in which a mother can be viewed as "doing nothing." . . . [F]irst . . . the mother "did nothing" because she was not present during the abuse and had no prior notice of it. . . . [S]econd . . . [the] mother . . . "did nothing" because she knew of the abuse but appeared unable to do anything about it. The third potential category of mothers who "do nothing" are those who have attempted to do something to protect their children but were unsuccessful. The courts remain unable to distinguish between a mother who truthfully does nothing because she does not care and the three types of mothers identified here. Rarely is there an effort to distinguish among them. On those occasions where a court does recognize that the mother made an effort, it frequently trivializes the measures undertaken by the mother. Therefore, for the mother there can be no set of facts upon which she can successfully argue that further action placed her at risk of death or serious bodily injury.

. . . When we require the mother in an abusive relationship to rescue the child at any cost, we deprive her of the right to make a reasonableness assessment, a right given to any other defendant faced with potentially life threatening choices.

Any effort to portray the battered mother's inability to save the life of her child as reasonable will meet stiff resistance from the public. The resistance was and continues to be demonstrated in the public's unwillingness to view as reasonable the defensive behavior of women trapped in violent relationships. . . .

NOTES

1. Alice Miller, Banished Knowledge: Facing Childhood Injuries 77 (Leila Vennewitz, trans., Doubleday, 1st ed. 1990).

2. Mary E. Becker, *Double Binds Facing Mothers in Abusive Families: Social Support Systems, Custody Outcomes and Liability for Acts of Others*, 2 University of Chicago Law School Roundtable 13, 21 (1995).

3. Mike Folks, *Rubin Outlines Mom's Defense: Control by Spouse Who Beat Daughter*, Florida Sun-Sentinel, Nov. 4, 1994, at 1B (statement by Pauline Zile contained in a letter disclosed by her counsel).

4. Beth E. Richie, Compelled to Crime: Gender Entrapment of Battered Black Women 108 (1996) (the narrative of "Carolyn," who was arrested for first degree murder in the death of her child).

45

Between Vengeance and Forgiveness: Feminist Responses to Violent Injustice

Martha Minow

. . .

II. *Punishment Versus Reconciliation*

In the world of international human rights, the development of a litigation framework marks for many the proud accomplishment of the past and the aspiration for the future. Thus, the Nuremberg and Tokyo war crimes trials following World War II stand as the important human rights innovations. The current efforts to prosecute individuals for crimes committed in the former Yugoslavia and in Rwanda revitalize and extend the earlier experiment in ways that move the world ahead on the course toward articulate and enforceable human rights. Domestic trials brought against former Nazis, such as Klaus Barbie and Adolf Eichmann, further implement the vision of human rights, enforced by law. Similar triumphs are trials against those who authored and implemented the Dirty War in Argentina, the tyrannies of Eastern Europe, and torturers around the world.

What these trials do is apply to atrocities the crucial elements of a rule of law. Accountability for wrongdoing, public fact-finding in a setting marked by fairness and restraint, and certain and unbending punishment exacted by the state after full process, translate the desires for vengeance and redress into lawful, official action. Public trials can also provide occasions to educate, to set the record straight, to prevent social amnesia or denial about what happened, and, ideally, to deter future atrocities.

A contrasting vision calls for restorative justice. It is less familiar and less institutionalized than the retributive approach. Its advocates view the adversarial trial as failing to focus adequately on victims and the task of repairing harms. Restorative justice emphasizes the humanity of both offender and victim, and repair of social connections and peace as more important than retribution. . . . Under restorative justice, repairing relationships between offenders and victims and within the community takes precedence over law enforcement. Forgiveness and reconciliation are central aspirations. Also elevated are the goals of healing individuals, human relationships, and even entire societies.

One reason to pursue these aspirations is pragmatic and psychological. Retributive approaches may reinforce anger and a sense of victimhood; reparative approaches instead can help victims move beyond anger and beyond a sense of powerlessness. Reparative or restorative justice can secure public acknowledgment and condemnation of the wrong, although through mechanisms that differ from prosecution, conviction, and punishment of wrongdoers. Restorative justice can also afford victims the position of relative power represented by the capacity to forgive—whether or not the individual victims proceed then to forgive particular perpetrators. Where victims do forgive, it is as much for their own healing and embrace of a future without rage as it is for the benefit of the offender.

. . .

Seeking re-acceptance of the wrongdoers in society, restorative justice tries to build on the offenders' capacities for accountability, understanding, and prevention of future offenses. Finally, reparative justice efforts seek to break the cycles of violence that in some ways are perpetuated when the state itself authorizes violent responses to violence, as in the death penalty.

. . .

Efforts for reparations and apologies for atrocities similarly focus on healing and restoration. In the United States, restorative justice discussions have largely focused on juvenile crime and mediation of disputes, including mediation of criminal offenses, and on specific governmental grants of reparations or apology. Campaigns for reparations for the 60,000 Japanese-Americans interned in United States camps during World War II similarly, in 1988, successfully secured governmental apology and symbolic monetary payments as efforts to repair individual and social damage. The state of Florida authorized reparations in 1994 for the survivors and descendants of the town of Rosewood, Florida, an African-American town destroyed in 1923 in a racially motivated incident with the knowledge of government officials. The legislative effort, news coverage, and documentary movies surrounding the event helped to restore the memory of the incident and the individuals affected by it after decades of silence and suppression.

. . .

III. Feminists on Both Sides

There is no general feminist theory for responding to violence; indeed, there apparently is no general feminist response to criminal justice, international law, or even domestic violence issues. Many feminists resist the very idea of "general" or "grand theories" as inevitably partial, while risking the pretense of universality. Instead, many feminists stress the importance of attentiveness to particularity and context, even while highlighting a larger pattern of unequal power and respect on the basis of traits such as gender, race, and class.

There is a troubling pattern in the "particulars" that guide feminist approaches to violence and, especially, to criminal justice. To put it bluntly, feminists have pushed for greater retribution, including criminal prosecutions, for violence done to women, and more caring, empathic responses to women who risk criminal charges for their own conduct. This pattern smacks not only of inconsistency, but also of unreflective desires simply to advance what is good for women. Even if that were the only criterion, more general reflections would be required because of the basic feminist insight into the variety of women's positions and interests. Some women are the mothers, daughters, or sisters of men facing retributive justice, even as some women are the victims of male violence; some women are the victims of other women's violence. A feminist approach to atrocities requires some effort to think across circumstances, even while specifying the kinds of particularities that could or should matter in a sensitive set of responses. There are in fact germs of more general ideas in feminist work, and these ideas support both the prosecutorial, punishment response to violence and the restorative, reparations approach. Drawing them out more explicitly may make conflicts between the two approaches more stark, but this is a first step in a process of broader reflection on a useful set of ideas on the subject of responses to atrocity.

. . .

Similarly, human rights groups have identified sexual violence during the Rwanda Genocide and its aftermath as a crucial target for human rights initiatives. They document deliberate propaganda efforts used to exploit and inflame ethnic tensions. One particular technique portrayed Tutsi women as both attractive and dangerous. Testimony by survivors of the genocide suggest that the assaulting Hutus perpetrated rapes and sexual abuse of Tutsi women and girls in systematic ways. Rather than the behavior of individual soldiers who lost control, the rapes and sexual slavery should be viewed as war crimes or violations of other legal protections.

In the United States, women's initiatives have pressed successfully for adversarial trials as the proper response to a range of harms and wrongs affecting women. Thus, more vigorous criminal prosecutions of rape and incest, criminal prosecutions of rapes committed by husbands, federal civil actions treating gender-based violence, including rape and abuse, as violations of civil rights, and employment discrimination actions for sexual harassment, all express a vision of adversarial trials as the proper framework for realizing justice.

On the restorative justice front, some feminists have supported mediation, the use of third parties to facilitate problem-solving approaches to conflicts, but usually not in the context of violence. Indeed, feminists are more likely to express concerns about mediation in the context of violence and abuse than to endorse it. Feminists have argued for de-criminalizing maternal drug abuse and developing excuses and pardons for women who commit violence against those who have abused them. The battered-women's defense and clemency drives for women who kill their batterers are specific examples. Feminists have also urged compassionate approaches to women who have been charged with child neglect and abuse, most notably when those women have themselves been victims of abuse. Yet, strikingly, feminists are not among those advocating forgiving, restorative approaches toward offenders who commit violence against women, or other kinds of violent crimes.

At the same time, some feminist theorists have argued more abstractly for an ethic of care in the practice of justice, either as a complement or a substitute for the dominant adversarial paradigm. Stressing nurturance of human relationships, this ethic of care would seem a perfect theory to undergird restorative justice. The image of peaceful political expression by the Mothers of the Plaza de Mayo protesting the "disappearance" of their children in Argentina suggests a kind of political action compatible with an ethic of care. Some observers worry, however, about the ultimate lack of political power in such protests.

. . .

[F]eminist activists tend to support adversarial trials and punishment as responses to harms to women, but restorative processes to understand and reintegrate women who commit violent harms. Some feminist work also supports inclusionary restorative processes, seeking ultimately forgiveness, as responses to terrorism and other atrocities.

Perhaps I should simply stop here, and admit that feminists simply have been interested in what is good for women. Yet, I have already suggested ways in which some feminist work moves beyond those confines. . . . I will suggest in two specific examples, potential collisions between the two perspectives are already coming to light in specific contexts of interest to feminists. Therefore, I will press for a more general theory, and explicit acknowledgment and treatment of the competing approaches.

IV. Two Examples

The first example arises in the debate over whether prosecutors should adopt a "no-drop" rule in pursuing charges of domestic violence. Cheryl Hanna, for example, has written powerfully about the dilemma.[1] The drive for a criminal justice approach to domestic violence can founder, she suggests, if the victim retains control over the decision to prosecute, because the very intimidation and injuries at stake may then halt the push for accountability and punishment. Victims of domestic violence who do not want to testify against their abusers may change their stories to protect the batterers, themselves, or children in the home. Therefore, some prosecutors have experimented with "no-drop" policies that either refuse to halt a prosecution simply because the victim refuses to testify or else provide support and advocacy for the reluctant victim to enable prosecutions to proceed. As one prosecutor explains, "[B]atterers must not be allowed to control justice."[2]

Yet, no-drop policies deprive or constrict the victim's choices and refuse deference to her own assessment of the promises and perils of proceeding with prosecution. This result troubles feminists who seek to elevate respect for women. Disrespect for women's own agency is one of the central targets of feminist law reform efforts. . . . Others argue against a no-drop policy.

The debate over no-drop policies should also be understood in light of the contrast between prosecutorial and restorative approaches to violence. Some women are reluctant to prosecute because they want to maintain loving ties and rebuild the relationship with the offender. Although for some women, at some times, this desire may reflect economic and emotional dependencies, for some women, at some times, it reflects an empathic, inclusionary response to violence. Even the offender is a victim; even the offender deserves help and forgiveness.

The problem for feminists is how to assess whether a particular survivor of violence wants to forgo prosecution out of strength or out of weakness. . . .

[A] restorative approach may reflect as healthy a form of self-respect held by the victim as would a retributive approach. . . . [A] full expression of the ideas behind forgiveness would lead many people away from prosecution, and that is why the no-drop debate includes a collision between the punishment and restorative approaches. This dimension of the no-drop debate deserves as much attention from feminists as the more general issues of respecting women's autonomy and self-determination.

The second example of a collision between the punishment and restorative responses to violence arises in assessments of reparations for women who have suffered horrific violence. Prime Minister Ryutara Hashimoto of Japan offered a letter of apology and monetary reparations to some 500 survivors of the 200,000 "comfort women" or sexual slaves imprisoned by the Imperial Army during World War II.[3] Only six of the women accepted the offer. Most others rejected it largely because the fund came from private sources rather than from the government itself. . . . Some argued that only prosecutions by the Japanese government would adequately express governmental contrition and redress the abuse. Others have supported discussion of the comfort women in textbooks as a kind of reparation through memory.

The debate exists; it occurs directly in a terrain of concern to feminists. It represents a collision between prosecutorial and restorative approaches. Is there a correct or admirable position in this debate? Is there one that can be informed by feminist ideas?

V. Toward Answers

My own understanding of feminist ideas suggests that a single answer will not and should not be forthcoming. Attention to context and particular settings and interests will be crucial. . . .

In that spirit, then, I suggest three initial ideas to guide the choice between prosecutorial and reparative approaches to atrocities. First, priority should be given to restoring respect and self-respect to victims, regardless of the response that is chosen. In general, this creates a presumption against no response. Yet, the entire range of potential responses should be included in this norm. A failure to prosecute OR to seek reparations OR apology OR some other public response to an act of violence is presumptively disrespectful of the victim, even if the perpetrator is unavailable or unwilling to participate. This means that a range of responses, sponsored by the government or other collectivities, must be developed even when prosecution of the offender or apology by the perpetrator is impossible.

Second, attention to the victim's own desires matters, but the victim may need psychological and material support to be able to develop and express a desire free from fear or self-degradation. Hence, practically speaking, victim-witness programs should be strengthened and made available even to victims who do not want to participate in prosecutions. Social welfare supports should also be available to survivors of violence in the immediate aftermath to enable relatively autonomous choices about prosecution, forgiveness, and the range of potential responses to the violence.

Third, governments should explore and establish alternatives to prosecution and retribution to permit institutional settings for those who prefer reparative, restorative responses to violence. Perhaps formats such as truth commissions could be created following episodes of serious violence, even when they fall short of massacres and mass atrocities. Legislative hearings to debate reparations and executive considerations of clemency and apologies should be institutionalized so that more people can expect to participate in the discussions, and pursue those avenues along side or instead of prosecutions.

. . .

NOTES

1. See generally Cheryl Hanna, *No Right to Choose: Mandated Victim Participation in Domestic Violence Prosecutions*, 109 Harvard Law Review 1849 (1996).

2. Donna Wills, *Domestic Violence: The Case for Aggressive Prosecution*, 7 UCLA Women's Law Journal 173, 179 (1997).

3. Seth Mydans, *WWII Rape Victim Accepts Japanese Reparation*, Dallas Morning News, Dec. 13, 1996, at 61A.

46

Enhancing Autonomy for Battered Women: Lessons from Navajo Peacemaking

Donna Coker

Introduction and Overview: Battering and Antisubordination

Navajo Peacemaking is a form of what is sometimes called "informal adjudication." As part of the effort to revitalize Navajo common law and traditional Navajo adjudicatory processes, Peacemaking's importance within the Navajo Nation has grown in recent years. Peacemaking has also been the focus of international and national attention as a form of alternative dispute resolution and, more recently, as a form of restorative justice. This article builds on original empirical research to investigate the use of Navajo Peacemaking in cases involving domestic violence. . . .

Navajo Peacemaking is a process in which a Naat'aanii (peacemaker), familiar with Navajo common law and traditional Navajo stories, guides disputing parties to develop a resolution. A Peacemaking session includes members of the extended families of the disputants and may also include community members with relevant expertise (e.g., alcohol treatment counselors and social workers). Peacemakers understand Peacemaking as a spiritual process in which the primary purpose is the restoration of hozho, roughly (but inadequately) translated as "harmony."

A significant body of scholarship, much of it written by members of the Navajo judiciary and the solicitor general for the Navajo Nation, describes Peacemaking's use in domestic violence cases. In general, this literature argues that non-Native adjudication would be improved by the application of Navajo concepts of justice and the Navajo process of Peacemaking. Peacemaking proponents argue that Peacemaking, unlike Anglo adjudication, allows parties to reach the underlying problems, diminishes the ability of the offender to deny and minimize his abuse or his responsibility for the abuse, and provides support for the victim.

Many feminist anti–domestic violence scholars and activists have been understandably skeptical of the use of informal processes such as Peacemaking in domestic violence cases. The concerns are that informal methods of adjudication may ignore domestic power hierarchies and thus facilitate the batterer's ongoing violence against the victim, resulting in unfair and coerced "agreements." Informal processes may create an occasion for the batterer, his family, and perhaps even the victim's family, to blame the victim for the batterer's anger, violence, or both. Further, a focus on the particular needs of individual victims and batterers may fail to represent society's substantial interest in preventing domestic violence.

The debate between advocates of formal and informal methods of intervention in domestic violence cases fails to address some of the concerns that are of greatest importance to many battered women. These concerns illuminate Peacemaking's potential benefits for some battered women. The most important of these concerns is the ability of domestic violence intervention strategies to realize change in the material and social conditions that foster battering. Material conditions are implicated both in women's vulnerability to battering and in understanding why some men batter women they purport to love.

. . .

While battering is a phenomenon of gender subordination, it may also be a function of racism, poverty, and conquest. If feminist anti–domestic violence work is to be liberatory, it must recognize the importance of these intersections in women's lives. Ignoring the importance of these oppressive structures in the lives of battered women results in interventions that ultimately fail the women whose lives are most affected by those structures: poor women and women of color.

It is also important to recognize the relationship of battering to poverty, racism, and conquest in the lives of some men who batter. Feminist scholarship must explore this connection for several reasons. Interventions that recognize oppressive structures in the lives of battering men may discourage some men from battering. Further, both men and women experience racist and economic oppression. To ignore racist and economic oppression in the lives of men who batter is to ignore their importance in the lives of battered women. Finally, recognition of oppressive structures in the lives of batterers is important because many battered women seek that recognition.

. . .

I. Domestic Violence Cases in Peacemaking

A. Women, Gender, Conquest, and Domestic Violence in the Navajo Nation

The material, psychological, and spiritual circumstances of Navajo people—circumstances that are a direct result of colonization—are related to both the occurrence of domestic violence and women's responses to such violence. Colonization has diminished Navajo women's social and economic status. This diminishment in status combined with material deprivation and the subordination of Navajo cultural and political life creates social conditions that foster domestic violence.

U.S. policy has diminished the status of Navajo women through both direct and indirect means. Direct attacks on women's status include governing policies that privilege male tribal members over female members and federal aid to religious institutions that promote male authority. Indirect attacks on women's status include land management policies that diminish the economic importance of women's work, education policies that result in the devaluation of clan and kin relationships, and policies that burden or outlaw Native religious practices in which women often play significant leadership roles. The result is greater reliance on federal assistance, frequently unavailable or underpaid wage labor, and a disruption in the family and clan relationships that define obligations and often serve to protect women.

Traditional Navajo culture is a "partnership society" in which "complementary [gender] roles arise from the deepest traditional beliefs tribal people hold about how they were created and should function in the universe."[1] The political and social manifestation of this belief in gender complementariness, as evidenced by the relatively important status of women and children, was particularly troubling to early European colonizers, who frequently set out to instill male-female and parent-child hierarchies. The emphasis on male authority remained central to U.S. policy. While the process of colonization and the concomitant disempowerment of Navajo women is ongoing, three events in the history of U.S.-Navajo relations bear particular attention: the capture, forced march, and internment of Navajo people in Fort Sumner in 1864; the imposed livestock reduction of the 1930s; and the mandatory schooling of Navajo children in boarding schools. These three events serve as cultural markers for many Navajo—moments in which their injuries are concrete and quantifiable. Each marks a significant downward shift in the status of Navajo women. Together these events and their aftermath illustrate the effects of U.S. colonization and the subsequent material and spiritual harms to Navajo people.

. . .

Navajo parents who grew up in boarding schools were often subjected to cruel models for raising children. These models were not only abusive but were abusive in ways that were intentionally destructive of Indian identity and self-esteem. As explained by the director of a program for Navajo men who batter:

> [We teach battering men the difference between] [d]iscipline [and] punishment [of children.] A lot of times . . . we just never really made a distinction. And a lot of us [are] coming from boarding school: our parents and us and all of our children. . . . You know, the belts, the paddles, the standing in the corner, [the] punishment[s], . . . [the] reading the Bible. They know all these things. That was all built in, very military kinds of control that they had . . . in the name of Christianity, . . . that really became [a] very overt means to control, and . . . people still really deal with some of those issues.[2]

I spoke with many Navajo who believe that the effects of the boarding school experience live on in the parenting practices of adult survivors. They believe that the current younger generation is particularly confused because older generations were alienated from tribal life by boarding school experiences and were thus unable to teach Navajo history and culture to their children. This effect is compounded by the number of parents who were taught abusive patterns for family and intimate relationships. The result is "a whole generation of [people growing up in] boarding schools where the parents did not learn any parenting skills at all and . . . the wounds . . . are intergenerational."[3]

Thus, the combination of several factors undermined the political and economic status of Navajo women: the move to a wage economy, the disruption and overt intervention in Navajo legal practices that protected women in their relationships with husbands, and the imposition and influence of European patriarchal cultures. The effects of colonization, including internalized racism, boarding school childhood abuse driven by a particularly virulent racist ideology, the use of alcohol as "wages" and the development of alcoholism as a major health issue, and unemployment, are "wounds to the soul" that may intersect Anglo-European notions of gender dominance in the lives of some Indian men and endanger the women and children closest to them. Not surprisingly, many of the Navajo battered women's advocates I spoke with discuss domestic violence in terms that combine insights regarding the effects of ongoing colonization with the more gender-focused understandings of the broader U.S. battered women's movement.

Research and anecdotal evidence suggest that domestic violence is a significant problem for Navajo people. Yet there are very few shelters for battered women and their children. There are few programs that provide legal assistance directed specifically to battered women, and the criminal justice system is seriously understaffed.

In addition, battered women in the Navajo Nation must contend with the problems that face many poor women in rural areas, including lack of transportation and the near impossibility of hiding. Many rural Navajo homes do not have telephones. One battered women's counselor described the experience of a woman who only had access to a phone several miles away at a chapter house. She had to flee her husband, walk to the chapter house, call the program's emergency number, and wait—alone, at night—for someone from the program to pick her up. . . .

B. Peacemaking: Theory and Practice

. . .

Traditional Navajo thinking does not separate religious and secular life; rather, all of life is sacred and imbued with spiritual meaning. The concept of k'e, fundamental to Navajo common law, expresses an interdependence and respect for relationships between humans, the natural world, individuals and family, and individuals and clan members. This interdependence operates to define Navajo common law, which derives from relational frameworks in which "responsibilities to clan members are part of a sophisticated system that defines rights, duties, and mutual obligations."[4] "The individual and the community are part of the kinship that exists among all life forms and the environmental elements. Harmony is the desired result of the relationship with all life forms, including humans, animals, and plants."[5] Relational justice does not necessitate the subordination of the individual, however. Traditional Navajo thought and law are radically egalitarian and eschew coercion. Individuals do not speak for others, not even for members of their own family.

These concepts of relational justice provide the foundation for the practice of Peacemaking. In Peacemaking, parties meet with a peacemaker and others who have either a special relationship to the parties (e.g., family and friends) or relevant expertise (e.g., alcohol treatment counselors and hospital social workers). Each participant is given a chance to describe the problem that the petitioner has identified as the reason for the session. The peacemaker then leads the group in developing recommendations and agreements designed to ameliorate or solve the problem.

Peacemaking is structured around procedural steps. It begins with an opening prayer in both Navajo and English. After the peacemaker has explained the rules, the petitioner is allowed to explain his or her complaint. The respondent is then asked to respond to the petitioner's complaint. Next, the peacemaker provides a "[b]rief overview of the problem as presented by the disputants."[6] Family members and other participants, including traditional teachers, may then join the discussion, providing their description or explanation of the problem(s).

The peacemaker, usually chosen by his or her chapter, is a respected person with a demonstrated knowledge of traditional Navajo stories. He or she must be someone who possesses the power of persuasion, because peacemakers do not judge or decide cases. Their power lies in their words and their influence. Peacemakers "show a lot of love, they use encouraging words, [when you] use [Navajo] teaching to lift [participants] up you can accomplish a lot, [if you] are very patient."[7]

Peacemaking may be hard for outside observers to understand, because it seems to combine so many different things: mediation, restorative justice, therapeutic intervention, family counseling, and Navajo teaching. Understanding is also made more difficult because of the significant differences in the practice of various peacemakers and the different approaches used for different kinds of problems. Peacemaking practice is fluid, flexible, and thoroughly practical, fitting the process to the situation. . . .

The Peacemaker Court Manual also stresses the need for flexibility:

> It cannot be stressed, repeated or urged enough that the Peacemaker Court . . . is not frozen in its present form forever. As an experiment which has been carefully built upon Navajo custom and tradition, we will have to see whether it meets the needs of the Navajo People . . . and we will have to see what changes need to be made.[8]

Peacemaking is a formal part of the Navajo legal system, developed and overseen by the Navajo Nation judiciary. There are two primary routes by which cases reach Peacemaking: court referral and self-referral. Criminal cases may be referred by the court as the result of diversion or as a condition of probation. The Domestic Abuse Protection Act creates special rules for domestic violence protection order cases: A referral to Peacemaking must be approved by the petitioner, and the peacemaker must have received special domestic violence training. In all other civil cases, the rules allow courts to refer cases to Peacemaking over a party's objection, but in practice judges seldom refer civil cases involving allegations of domestic violence unless both parties agree to the referral. In addition to court referral, Peacemaking may be initiated by a petitioner on a claim that he or she has been "injured, hurt or aggrieved by the actions of another."[9] Self-referred cases make up the majority of Peacemaking cases. In a self-referred case, the peacemaker liaison seeks authorization from the district court to subpoena the respondent and all other necessary parties identified by the petitioner.

C. Peacemaking's Potential in Domestic Violence Cases:
Systemic and Individual Responsibility and Transforming Context

. . .

While larger social forces create the social landscape that makes battering possible, the batterer's personal supports for controlling behavior may be critical in his decision to batter. The most important of such supports may be his experience in his family of origin and his relationships with friends. Lee Bowker's research found that abusive husbands who saw their friends daily committed more severe and more frequent acts of wife abuse, were more likely to assault children, and were more likely to assault their partner while pregnant than were men who saw their friends less frequently.[10] Bowker suggests that "[t]hese correlations point to the possibility of a male peer subculture of violence that justifies wife beating, and strongly suggests that the better integrated the battering husband is into this peer subculture, the more severely he is likely to beat his wife."[11]

Also significant are the number of abusers who experienced or witnessed violence in their homes of origin, with the strongest correlation being for those men who witnessed their father abusing their mother. Thus, some number of abusers may have family members who tacitly approve of wife-beating or who are long practiced in denying its existence.

Peacemaking may address societal and familial support for battering in two ways: through confronting family and batterer denial of battering's existence and its harm and through gaining material assistance for the victim. Peacemaking may confront the denial of the abuser—denial that he committed the violence, that it was harmful, and that it was a moral choice not compelled either by the victim's "provocation" or by life's circumstances. Peacemaking proponents argue that the ability of the victim, her family, and the abuser's family to confront the abuser directly about his violence makes it harder for him to deny his wrongdoing.

In a case involving family violence, a young man related his excuses, exhibiting denial, minimilization, and externalization. One of the people who listened was the young man's sister. She listened to his story and confronted him by saying, "[Y]ou know very well you have a drinking problem. She then related the times she had seen him drunk and abusive. . . . [S]he told her brother she loved him very much and was willing to help him if only he would admit his problems. He did."[12]

Bluehouse described this confrontational aspect of Peacemaking:

> [T]here may be issues of domestic violence where there's some denial, the victimizer may be intellectualizing which becomes very obvious in Peacemaking, because family members will know. [They will say,] "this doesn't sound like you." . . . [Family members may say,] "Uncle, I can't understand why you are talking to your family like this [in Peacemaking]; is this another side of you? We like this side of you, we'd like to see more of this side of you. We've seen you . . . deal with your wife in a cruel and inhumane [manner], so why all of a sudden in a Peacemaking room with a person from the outside [do you behave this way]?"[13]

Families cannot always be counted on to confront an abusive family member, however. Family members may deny, minimize, and blame the victim for the batterer's violence. Peacemakers note that parents in particular are prone to cover for their son and blame his partner. Thus, peacemakers must confront familial or parental denial in order to confront the batterer's denial. "[I]f there is a lot of denial you have to confront the person with respect and love, but you have to cut through [the denial], and you have to confront them."[14]

Denial and familial solidarity are not the only impediments to families confronting batterers. Family members—his or hers—may be too afraid of the batterer to confront him or too focused on hiding the past or current violence in their own households. In such cases, if the batterer is confronted, it must be by the peacemaker.

Peacemaking also provides a forum for the victim's family to intervene on her behalf. For example, in one case an uncle was a copetitioner with his niece. The uncle expressed concern that his niece's daughters took her husband's side in arguments and that both the father and the daughters verbally and physically abused the mother.

In addition to encouraging family participation, Peacemaking may also provide a mechanism for transferring material resources to the victim, thus lessening her economic and social vulnerability. This could occur in three ways. First, the abuser or his family or both may agree to provide nalyeeh (reparations) in the form of money, goods, or personal services for the victim. Nalyeeh is a concrete recognition that the harm of battering is real and that responsibility for it extends beyond the individual batterer. In addition, both abuser and victim are likely to be referred to social service providers and to traditional healing ceremonies. The assistance given by agencies and by traditional healers often results in increased community and governmental material support. Finally, the victim's family may overcome past estrangement from the victim and agree to provide her with assistance.

. . .

Peacemaking may also provide material assistance through referrals to social service agencies and traditional healing ceremonies. Peacemaking agreements often include an agreement from the batterer to engage in affirmative steps toward changed behavior, such as alcohol treatment and traditional healing ceremonies. For example, in my file review of domestic violence cases, four of the fourteen that reached agreements included the batterer's attendance in alcohol treatment and the woman's attendance in Al-Anon meetings.

. . .

The ideal model for intervention proposed by battered women's advocates has been a "coordinated community response." In a coordinated response, criminal sanctions are accompanied by strong supports for battered women. Prosecutors craft their strategies so as to maximize victim safety; police provide victims with information about rights as well as referrals to services including shelters; courts routinely order victim compensation; and detectives and prosecutors follow up with victims to monitor threats or intimidation tactics of the batterer. In addition, the

justice system works closely with service providers to assist women in safety planning and advocacy with other systems, such as public assistance, child protective
services, and employers, and also to encourage support from victims' family and
friends. The reality in many jurisdictions, however, is very different. Without these
supports, legal intervention may not create the kind of change in either the victim's
or the batterer's milieu necessary to provide real safety or to enhance the victim's
autonomy. The emphasis on legal intervention has served to develop prosecution
and civil protection order proceedings without commensurate development of services and resources for women. The compensation formally available through protection order statutes and criminal codes is seldom ordered by the court.
. . .

Attention to the context of the abuser's life threatens to devolve into victim
blaming: He has a hard life, and she should be more supportive and understanding.
This is a serious danger because the batterer is often quite adept at "explaining"
why he beats her: Life beats him, he was drunk, or his father was cruel. In addition, stories that describe the abuser's violence as pathological and an illness fail to
account for his choice of victims and for the peculiar vulnerability of wives, girlfriends, ex-wives, and ex-girlfriends. For Native women who are all too aware of
the impact of racism and colonialism in the lives of Native men, the mix of patriarchal rhetoric that "real" men are in control may intersect the reality of racist and
colonial subordination to create a gendered and cultural double-bind. This may be
compounded by batterers' propensity to blame the victims for their violence.
. . .

Traditional Navajo thinking generally takes the pragmatic approach, assuming
that certain qualities of human nature are "givens"; thus the question is, given
human nature, how does one construct a world that best enables harmonious behavior? Peacemaking proponents write that Native justice systems focus on restoring harmony of relationships rather than on guilt-based adjudication. However,
contrary to the notion that this means that the offender is "let off easy," relation-
ship-oriented justice may mean that the offender is held to a higher level of responsibility than is true under adversarial adjudication. To understand why this may be
so, it is useful to examine the Navajo concept of nayee', or "monsters" as it is commonly translated in English. According to anthropologist John Farella, a monster is
"anything that gets in the way of a person living his life."[15] Nayee' include depression, obsession, and jealousy. The benefit of naming something a nayee' is that the
source of one's "illness"—one's unhappiness or dysfunctionality—once named may
be cured.

> [T]he vague and subjective is transformed into something very concrete . . . merely by
> labeling the experience. . . . This is what ritual is about, making the intangible exquis-
> itely real and then manipulating it. The second thing that must happen is that society
> must be altered. People must expect the patient to be transformed, and they must par-
> ticipate in that transformation.[16]

Healing ceremonies are designed to rid a person of nayee', whether the monster's
presence is reflected in physical or emotional ill health. Healing requires that the

person be actively involved in the curing. A healing ceremony is a costly endeavor for a family not only because it is expensive and involves time-consuming labor, but also because it threatens to expose the family to public scrutiny. The family must commit to whatever ongoing healing requirements are imposed by the healer. Thus, the very process of organizing a ceremony may shift familial understandings of the patient's illness and may (re)focus material and emotional resources on the patient's well-being. "The sheer work involved in organizing a ceremony functions to heal the social problems that are always associated with illness. . . . And the symbolism and re-enactment of the ritual makes an illness that was previously vague and unmanageable into something that is real and tangible enough to be manipulated."[17]

A healing ceremony, therefore, remakes the patient by attempting, in part, to remake his world: his story of himself, his family's story of him, and the material resources available to promote his well-being. Peacemaking, at its best, is a healing ceremony; it seeks to remake the world—the batterer's world, creating the possibility of a different life and a different point of view, and the battered woman's world, marshaling resources and supporting her struggle for greater autonomy.

. . .

II. *Peacemaking and the Problems of Informal Adjudication*

. . .

A. The Coercion Problem

The coercion problem has two different and equally important aspects: coercion in the process and coercion through forcing victim participation. Coercion in the process results from the ability of the batterer to intimidate the woman or to wrest control of the mediation. The batterer's use of methods of intimidation, subtle or not, may continue his controlling behavior through the mediation process and result in an unfair agreement. This concern is underscored by the recognition that battering is not a one-time incident but rather a controlling system of behaviors that constrains the victim's autonomy. Behaviors become symbols for past incidents of abuse and serve to intimidate the woman: the way he rubs his forehead when he is really angry or the flinty look in his eyes. Battered women in mediation may find themselves negotiating for their safety. Battering relationships are frequently marked by a history of such negotiations, prompted by the victim blaming rules of the batterer: "I won't hit you if you'll have dinner ready on time; I won't hit you if you're always sexually available; I won't hit you if you keep the children from making a mess."[18]

. . .

The second type of coercion problem arises when battered women are forced to participate in informal adjudication. This is frequently an issue in mediation related to family law issues, particularly child custody. Mediation gives the batterer access to the victim, which may allow for an additional site for intimidation and physical abuse. The batterer may attack the woman in the parking lot after the session, follow her home and learn where she lives, or use the session to verbally abuse and blame her. . . .

The lack of screening for safety and the inability of respondents to decline appearance for good cause—including fear of the petitioner—are surely among Peacemaking's greatest weaknesses. Without safeguards, a session may provide the abuser an opportunity to physically assault, threaten, and intimidate his partner or ex-partner. This allows batterers to initiate Peacemaking to flush a woman out of hiding. A petitioner may be prompted by his partner's separation, his desire to see his children who are in hiding with their mother, or in response to a partner's domestic violence protection order. . . .

Because Peacemaking is a "traditional" activity, some women may also feel a more subtle form of coercion to attend out of respect for their elders and for Navajo tradition.

. . .

For the most part, problems of coercion could be remedied with procedural changes. In general, the coercion problems underscore the importance of (a) allowing battered women to choose whether to participate; (b) giving battered women information about Peacemaking's process as well as alternatives to Peacemaking, about its strengths and limitations, and about available services that will allow an informed choice; (c) taking measures to ensure the woman's safety through lethality assessments of the batterer, through safety planning with the woman, and through declining to have a session when it is too dangerous; and (d) the importance of a strong antisubordination, antisexist normative Peacemaking process. . . .

B. The Cheap-Justice Problem

Restorative justice processes such as family group conferencing or victim-offender mediation may place too much emphasis on the importance of offender apology. This creates two kinds of cheap-justice problems: First, an overemphasis on offender rehabilitation at the expense of expressions of moral solidarity with the victim may ignore the victim's needs and coerce the victim to forgive the offender; second, a sincere apology or reconciliation between the offender and the victim may fail to address the victim's primary needs.

Restorative justice programs are sometimes captured by a focus on offender rehabilitation, which pressures victims to cooperate with offender-centered measures and assumes that offender rehabilitation will meet the victim's needs. The victim becomes merely a means to the end of "healing" the offender. In the most egregious cases, mediators may pressure victims to offer offenders forgiveness. If the victim is made to feel responsible for forgiving or aiding the offender, the justice aspect of the process—the recognition of the harm as unilateral rather than mutual and the recognition of the immorality of the offender's behavior and its harm to the victim—is in jeopardy. . . .

A second concern arises when apologies are overvalued: Words are cheap. Even when the focus is to make the victim whole, rather than to reform the batterer, facilitators may value apologies at the expense of more material changes. Giving a privileged place to the apology of the abuser is particularly problematic in battering relationships. It is wrong to think that apologies are necessarily hard for abusers to make; abusive men often have a history of making apologies for their behavior. Some batterers are particularly adept at using apologies to manipulate their partners and others. Further, the batterer need not be insincere at the time of the apology for the apology to be ineffective. Without changes in his belief system, in his social networks, and often in his corollary behaviors such as drinking and drug use, he is likely to resort to battering again when faced with the inability to get his wife to comply with his demands.

. . .

In Peacemaking, the use of nalyeeh, the ability to encourage concrete commitments to personal change (alcohol treatment and batterer's treatment programs, and traditional healing ceremonies), coupled with a focus on familial responsibility, may go a long way in ensuring that apologies are accompanied by concrete changes in behavior.

C. The Normative Problem

The normative problem that exists in mediation stems from the ideology of mediator neutrality coupled with the hidden or informal rules that disadvantage women, enact gendered understandings of appropriate mediating behavior, and largely ignore claims of past injustice between parties. In family court mediation, the ideal mediator is supposed to be neutral, with the sole purpose of effectuating the desires of the parties. . . . The insistence on a purportedly neutral mediator fails to identify the immorality of the batterer's (past, present, ongoing) behavior and limits the support a mediator can give a battered woman.

. . .

Peacemakers do not pretend to be neutral with regard to the application of behavioral norms. Though the parties are never asked to agree explicitly to the use of traditional Navajo norms and values, it is likely that all participants have some generally accurate expectation regarding those norms and expect them to be applied in Peacemaking. The role of the peacemaker (or naat'aanii) is to guide the parties to a decision rather than to tell them what to do, but the "naat'aanii's opinion about the right way of doing things is important to the parties. The 'lecture' or opinion [of the naat'aanii] is also important for the process of naat'aah or planning."[19] The peacemaker is an interested person who instructs participants in appropriate Navajo behavior. She may use Navajo creation stories and journey narratives to teach a moral lesson.

While Peacemaking does not subscribe to the ideal of a neutral mediator, there may be other normative problems in practice. Peacemaking's fluidity and focus on restoring relationships creates the possibility of bias and informal rule application. . . . Common biases in the Navajo context may be an overemphasis on the importance of alcohol in explaining domestic violence and a promarriage (or antidivorce) bias.

. . .

D. The Communitarian/Social-Change Problem

. . .

Implicating the community serves to draw the connections between women's economic and social conditions and battering. This analysis then points to a wider view of remedies and a wider pool of resources to support those remedies. In addition, recognizing community responsibility provides a more complete description of the "gender entrapment" to which women are often subject and thus assists the woman in naming the sometimes invisible bonds that make freedom so hard to find. Domestic violence cases require a more expanded and clear notion of community responsibility and the use of an antimisogyny norm. The failure to give the term "community responsibility" real content fails to account for structural disparities in power—disparities that frame and provide context for the interactions between participants in restorative justice processes.

Peacemaking differs from group conferencing, in part, because its normative community may be more clear. First, it identifies traditional Navajo processes as best for Navajo problems. Community is thus defined as Navajo. However, the understanding of both "traditional" as well as "Navajo" may be contested. For example, battered women's advocates worry that Peacemaking's reliance on clan and familial relationships is misplaced. These advocates worry that the value of traditional stories and the importance of clan and familial relationships are seriously undermined in a setting in which many younger Navajo have little or no understanding of or respect for those stories or values.

> [The] Navajo value system has been so confused, has been so adulterated by the dominant society. . . . [My aunt's] grown daughter was getting beaten by her husband and the aunt . . . didn't understand why the daughter wasn't satisfied [with her marriage.] After all[, her husband] didn't drink and he was a good provider. So people's experiences make them put one thing as more important than anything else. So maybe if you grew up in an alcoholic household, then you think that if the husband doesn't drink, then that is the most important thing.[20]

This general breakdown in clan relations is exacerbated by the intergenerational effects of abusive boarding school experiences and by the advent of a wage economy that gave Navajo men more economic power than Navajo women. As one battered women's advocate told me, "They don't even respect their parents[;] how can [peacemakers] expect them to . . . [respect] their spouse . . . ?"[21] Similarly, some battered women's advocates point to the fact that significant numbers of Navajo are not fluent in the Navajo language, and thus stories and teachings in Navajo do not carry either the literal meaning or the cultural resonance that peacemakers presume. Battered women's advocates also worry that clan relationships that would ensure compliance with Peacemaking agreements are seriously compromised. Criticisms of Peacemaking's reliance on fragile or nonexistent clan relationships may fail to account for the diversity of Peacemaking practice and the pragmatic practice of many peacemakers. Many spoke of the alienation of people and saw their role as trying to help people understand the relevance of traditional teaching. Peacemakers see their practice both as (re)creating traditional concepts of clan and family responsibility and as utilizing these relationships to reform behavior. This creates certain contradictions. Many peacemakers agree with concerns regarding the loss of traditional values but do not appear to share a uniform or fixed understanding of traditionalism or a belief that only those who are traditionalists will be moved by Peacemaking. Some peacemakers seem to assume that parties must have some basic understanding of traditional Navajo thinking, however tenuous or inchoate. Others seem to see Peacemaking as a vehicle for restoring Navajo values, even for the completely ignorant, and particularly among the young. In addition, some peacemakers are not at all hesitant to use the coercion of Anglo adjudication or the threat of police action when necessary to encourage cooperation.

. . .

Conclusion: Lessons from Navajo Peacemaking

. . .

The Navajo Peacemaking experience underscores the necessity of an antimisogyny norm. Peacemakers who equate battering with a conflict or disagreement may domesticate the abuse. When peacemakers are clear that the abuse is an important object of intervention and that it is harmful and the responsibility of the abuser, it provides the possibility for real change in the batterer's thinking. It can reframe the battering. It may force the batterer to listen to "his family tell of the ordeal and . . . what they went through during this time of terror."[22]

Despite these potential benefits, Peacemaking is no more ideal at meeting the goal of promoting women's autonomy than are other imperfect interventions. Indeed, as described in this Article in some detail, Peacemaking's current practice creates real dangers for some women, primarily because it coerces participation in self-referred cases. Additionally, safety is compromised because Peacemaking does not routinely provide battered women with the information they need to make an informed decision about whether to enter Peacemaking. Some peacemakers appear biased against divorce, thus sandwiching women between the separation focus of formal adjudication and a stay-married focus in Peacemaking. But this is not always the case. Some peacemakers routinely assist women in obtaining a divorce, some women come to Peacemaking expressly to use the process to gain a divorce, and a significant number of women take their case to family court when they are unhappy with Peacemaking's results (or with their partners' failure to change).

What are the lessons of Navajo Peacemaking for designing informal domestic violence intervention strategies? First, such a process must have safeguards to limit the abuser's ability to use the process to locate and continue to abuse the woman. Cases should be screened to identify battering. Respondent victims should be able to opt out. They should be given full information regarding the pros and cons of the process (as compared with others), and should be assisted with safety planning. Such a process would borrow from Navajo Peacemaking the understanding that fairness need not mean neutrality. This is particularly true with regard to the facilitator's understanding of violence and controlling behavior. The facilitator should use not only an antiviolence norm but also an antimisogyny norm. Peacemaking demonstrates the power of stories used in the furtherance of such a norm. In pluralistic American culture, stories compete. The facilitator in the informal process I imagine would, much as the most common batterer's treatment programs now do, support a story that values women's autonomy.

Like Peacemaking, this process should allow for a description of the oppressive structures that operate in the life of the batterer without reinforcing his sense of "victimhood" or entitlement. This underscores the process's link to social justice, spirituality, and the capacity for individual change. It allows women to affirm cultural and political identity—their solidarity with men in antiracist, anticolonialist work—without sacrificing their right to be free of gender-related violence. Such a process should value connection and relationships but should equally value choice—enlarging women's ability to choose by increasing women's resources.

. . .

The Navajo "art and science of dealing with crime" provides some valuable lessons for thinking about the future of anti–domestic violence work. Intervention strategies that broaden women's choices, that address their material and context-specific needs, are the strategies that will be most effective. Peacemaking is not perfect—no domestic violence intervention is perfect—but Peacemaking offers possibilities for women that are largely unavailable in other intervention strategies.

NOTES

1. Gloria Valencia-Weber and Christine P. Zuni, *Domestic Violence and Tribal Protection of Indigenous Women in the United States*, 69 St. John's Law Review 69, 93 (1995).

2. Interview with Cheryl Neskahi-Coan, Director of the Family Harmony Project, and Helen Muskett, counselor with the Family Harmony Project, in Shiprock, Navajo Nation, N.M. (Apr. 16, 1997) (notes on file with author).

3. Interview with Anonymous Battered Women's Advocate, in Navajo Nation (n.d.) (notes on file with author).

4. Raymond D. Austin, *Freedom, Responsibility, and Duty: ADR and the Navajo Peacemaker Court*, 8 Judges' Journal, Spring 1993.

5. Valencia-Weber and Zuni, supra note 1, at 87.

6. Philmer Bluehouse, *Training Materials for Community Education* (Apr. 20, 1999) (unpublished manuscript, on file with author).

7. Interview with Crownpoint Peacemakers, in Crownpoint, Navajo Nation, N.M. (Apr. 15, 1997) (notes on file with author).

8. James W. Zion and Nelson J. McCabe, Navajo Peacemaker Court Manual 157 (1982).

9. Peacemaker Ct. R. 3.2(a), in Zion and McCabe, supra note 8, at 102.

10. Lee H. Bowker, Beating Wife-Beating 54–55 (1983).

11. *Id.* at 54.

12. Robert Yazzie and James W. Zion, *Navajo Restorative Justice: The Law of Equality and Justice*, in Restorative Justice: International Perspectives 165 (Burt Galaway and Joe Hudson, eds., 1996).

13. Interview with Philmer Bluehouse, Coordinator of the Peacemaker Division of the Judiciary Branch of the Navajo Nation, in Window Rock, Navajo Nation, Ariz. (Apr. 20, 1997) (notes on file with author).

14. Interview with Crownpoint Peacemakers, supra note 7.

15. John R. Farella, The Main Stalk: A Synthesis of Navajo Philosophy 51 (1984).

16. John Farella, The Wind in a Jar 132 (1993).

17. *Id.* at 131.

18. Karla Fischer et al., *The Culture of Battering and the Role of Mediation in Domestic Violence Cases*, 46 Southern Methodist University Law Review 2117, 2159 (1993).

19. James W. Zion and Robert Yazzie, *Indigenous Law in North America in the Wake of Conquest*, 20 Boston College International and Comparative Law Review 55, 78 (1997).

20. Interview with Anonymous Battered Women's Advocate, in Navajo Nation (n.d.) (notes on file with author).

21. *Id.*

22. Donna Coker, Notes from Window Rock File Review (Apr. 23–24, 1997) (on file with author).

Permissions

Grateful acknowledgment is made to the following for giving us permission to quote from copyrighted material. In a number of articles, we made minor modifications or omissions.

American Indian Law Review
Lorie M. Graham, *"The Past Never Vanishes": A Contextual Critique of the Existing Indian Family Doctrine.* © 1998 by the American Indian Law Review. Published at 23 American Indian Law Review 1 and reprinted with permission of the American Indian Law Review and the author, Lorie M. Graham.

American Journal of International Law
Hilary Charlesworth, *Feminist Methods in International Law.* © 1999 by The American Society of International Law. Published at 93 American Journal of International Law 379 and reprinted with permission of the American Society of International Law.

American University Journal of Gender, Social Policy and the Law
Martha Albertson Fineman, *Cracking the Foundational Myths: Independence, Autonomy, and Self-Sufficiency.* © 2000 by American University Journal of Gender, Social Policy and the Law. Published at 8 American University Journal of Gender, Social Policy and the Law 13 and reprinted with permission of the American University Journal of Gender, Social Policy and the Law.

American University Law Review
Amy E. Ray, *The Shame of It: Gender-Based Terrorism in the Former Yugoslavia and the Failure of International Human Rights Law to Comprehend the Injuries.* © 1997 Washington College of Law of the American University. Published at 46 American University Law Review 793 and reprinted with permission of the American University Law Review.

Buffalo Law Review
Darren Lenard Hutchinson, *Ignoring the Sexualization of Race: Heteronormativity, Critical Race Theory and Anti-Racist Politics.* © 1999 by the Buffalo Law Review. Published at 47 Buffalo Law Review 1 and reprinted with permission of the Buffalo Law Review and the author, Darren Lenard Hutchinson.

Case Western Reserve Law Review
L. Amede Obiora, *Bridges and Barricades: Rethinking Polemics and Intransigence in the Campaign against Female Circumcision.* © 1997 by the Case Western Reserve Law Re-

view. Published at 47 Case Western Reserve Law Review 275 and reprinted with permission of the Case Western Reserve Law Review and the author, Leslye Amede Obiora.

Feminist Studies, Inc.
Maxine Baca Zinn and Bonnie Thorton Dill, *Theorizing Difference from Multiracial Feminism.* © 1996 by Feminist Studies, Inc. Reprinted with permission of the authors and the Feminist Studies, Inc.

Harvard BlackLetter Law Journal
Joan Williams, *Implementing Antiessentialism: How Gender Wars Turn into Race and Class Conflict.* © 1999 by the President and Fellows of Harvard College and The Harvard BlackLetter Law Journal. Published at 15 Harvard BlackLetter Law Journal 41 and reprinted with permission of the Harvard BlackLetter Law Journal and the author, Joan Williams.

Harvard Civil Rights–Civil Liberties Law Review
Laura Ho, Catherine Powell, and Leti Volpp, *(Dis)Assembling Rights of Women Workers along the Global Assembly Line: Human Rights and the Garment Industry.* © 1996 by the President and Fellows of Harvard University. Published at 31 Harvard Civil Rights–Civil Liberties Law Review 383 and reprinted with permission of the Harvard Civil Rights–Civil Liberties Law Review.

Rachel L. Toker, *Multiple Masculinities: A New Vision for Same-Sex Harassment Law.* © 1999 President and Fellows of Harvard University. Published at 34 Harvard Civil Rights–Civil Liberties Law Review 577 and reprinted with permission of the Harvard Civil Rights–Civil Liberties Law Review.

Harvard International Law Journal
Celestine I. Nyamu, *How Should Human Rights and Development Respond to Cultural Legitimization of Gender Hierarchy in Developing Countries?* © 2000 by the President and Fellows of Harvard College. Published at 41 Harvard International Law Journal 381 and reprinted with permission of the Harvard International Law Journal.

Houston Law Review
Karen H. Rothenberg, *Gender Matters: Implications for Clinical Research and Women's Health Care.* © 1996 by the Houston Law Review. Published at 32 Houston Law Review 1201 and reprinted with permission of the Houston Law Review and the author, Karen H. Rothenberg.

Journal of Contemporary Legal Issues
Patricia Smith, *Autonomy, Aspiration and Accomplishment: Some Steps and Barriers to Equality for Women.* © 1998 University of San Diego School of Law. Published at 9 Journal of Contemporary Legal Issues 257 and reprinted with permission of the Journal of Contemporary Legal Issues.

Journal of Criminal Law and Criminology
Michelle S. Jacobs, *Requiring Battered Women Die: Murder Liability for Mothers under Failure to Protect Statutes.* © 1998 by Northwestern University School of Law. Pub-

New England Law Review

Martha Minow, *Between Vengeance and Forgiveness: Feminist Responses to Violent Injustice.* © 1998 New England School of Law New England Law Review. Published at 32 New England Law Review 967 and reprinted with permission of the New England Law Review and the author, Martha Minow.

New York University Law Review

Holly Maguigan, *Cultural Evidence and Male Violence: Are Feminist and Multiculturalist Reformers on a Collision Course in Criminal Courts?* © 1995 by New York University Law Review. Published at 70 New York University Law Review 36 and reprinted with permission of the New York University Law Review and the author, Holly Maguigan.

New York University Press

Nancy E. Dowd, *In Defense of Single-Parent Families.* © 1995 by the New York University Press and reprinted with permission of New York University Press and the author, Nancy E. Dowd.

Sage Publications, Inc.

Esther Ngan-Ling Chow, *The Development of Feminist Consciousness among Asian American Women* in Social Construction of Gender © by Sage Publications, Inc. Reprinted with permission of Sage Publications, Inc. and Esther Ngan-Ling Chow.

Maxine Baca Zinn, *Family, Feminism and Race in America* in Social Construction, Inc. © by Sage Publications, Inc. and reprinted with permission of Sage Publications, Inc.

Southern California Law Review

Sylvia A. Law, *Commercial Sex: Beyond Decriminalization.* © 2000 by the University of Southern California. Published at 73 Southern California Law Review 523 and reprinted with permission of the Southern California Law Review and the author, Sylvia A. Law.

Southern California Review of Law and Women's Studies

Mary Eaton, *At the Intersection of Gender and Sexual Orientation: Toward Lesbian Jurisprudence.* © 1994 by University of Southern California. Published at 3 Southern California Review of Law and Women's Studies 183 and reprinted with permission of the Southern California Review of Law and Women's Studies.

St. John's Journal of Legal Commentary

Barbara Bennett Woodhouse, *Children's Rights.* © 2000 by St. John's University St. John's Journal of Legal Commentary. Published at 14 St. John's Journal of Legal Commentary 331 and reprinted with permission of St. John's Journal of Legal Commentary and the author, Barbara Bennett Woodhouse.

Stanford Law and Policy Review

Matthew Diller, *Working without a Job: The Social Messages of the New Workfare.* © 1998 by the Board of Trustees of the Leland Stanford Junior University. Published at 9 Stanford Law and Policy Review 19 and reprinted with permission of the Stanford Law and Policy Review and the author, Matthew Diller.

Stanford Law Review

Angela P. Harris, *Gender Violence, Race, and Criminal Justice.* © 2000 by The Board of Trustees of Leland Stanford Junior Stanford Law Review. Published at 52 Stanford Law Review 777 and reprinted with permission of the Stanford Law Review.

Mari J. Matsuda, *Beside My Sister, Facing the Enemy: Legal Theory Out of Coalition.* © 1993 by Mari J. Matsuda. Published at 43 Stanford Law Review 1183 and reprinted with permission of the Stanford Law Review.

UCLA Law Review

Donna Coker, *Enhancing Autonomy for Battered Women: Lessons from Navajo Peacemaking.* © 1999 by The Regents of the University of California UCLA Law Review. Published at 47 UCLA Law Review 1 and reprinted with permission of the UCLA Law Review and the author, Donna Coker.

UCLA Women's Law Journal

Edward J. McCaffery, *Equality of the Right Sort.* © 1996 by the Regents of the University of California. Published at 6 UCLA Women's Law Journal 289 and reprinted with permission of the UCLA Women's Law Journal and the author, Edward J. McCaffery.

University of Cincinnati Law Review

Patricia Hill Collins, *African-American Women and Economic Justice: A Preliminary Analysis of Wealth, Family, and African-American Social Class.* © 1997 by University of Cincinnati. Published at 65 University of Cincinnati Law Review 865 and reprinted with permission of the University of Cincinnati Law Review.

Lisa C. Ikemoto, *The Fuzzy Logic of Race and Gender in the Mismeasure of Asian Women's Health Needs.* © 1997 by the University of Cincinnati Law Review, University of Cincinnati. Published at 65 University of Cincinnati Law Review 799 and reprinted with permission of the University of Cincinnati Law Review and the author, Lisa C. Ikemoto.

Utah Law Review

Brenda Cossman, *Turning the Gaze Back on Itself: Comparative Law, Feminist Legal Studies, and the Postcolonial Project.* © 1997 by the Utah Law Review Society. Published at 1997 Utah Law Review 525 and reprinted with permission of the Utah Law Review and the author, Brenda Cossman.

Villanova Law Review

Tonya L. Brito, *From Madonna to Proletariat: Constructing a New Ideology of Motherhood in a Welfare Discourse.* © 1999 Villanova University. Published at 44 Villanova Law Review 415 and reprinted with permission of the Villanova Law Review and the author, Tonya L. Brito.

Virginia Law Review

Nancy D. Polikoff, *We Will Get What We Ask For: Why Legalizing Gay and Lesbian Marriage Will Not "Dismantle the Legal Structure of Gender in Every Marriage."* © 1993 by the Virginia Law Review Association. Published at 79 Virginia Law Review 1535 and reprinted with permission of the Virginia Law Review.

About the Contributors

Anita Allen-Castellitto is Professor of Law and Philosophy at the University of Pennsylvania Law School. She is coeditor of *Debating Democracy's Discontent: Essays on American Politics, Law, and Public Philosophy.*

Taunya Lovell Banks is Jacob A. France Professor of Equality Jurisprudence at the University of Maryland School of Law.

Tonya L. Brito is Associate Professor of Law at the University of Wisconsin Law School.

Patricia A. Cain is Professor of Law at the University of Iowa College of Law and author of *Rainbow Rights: The Role of Lawyers and Courts in the Lesbian and Gay Civil Rights Movement.*

Hilary Charlesworth is Professor and Director of the Centre for International and Public Law at Australian National University and author of *Writing in Rights: Australia and the Protection of Human Rights.*

Sumi K. Cho is Professor at the De Paul University College of Law.

Esther Ngan-Ling Chow is Professor of Sociology at American University. Her publications include *Women, the Family, and Policy: A Global Perspective; Race, Class, and Gender: Common Bonds, Different Voices;* and *Transforming Gender and Development in East Asia.*

Donna Coker is a Professor at the University of Miami School of Law.

Patricia Hill Collins is Charles Phelps Taft Professor of Sociology and Chair of the Department of African-American Studies at the University of Cincinnati. She is the author of *Black Feminist Thought: Knowledge, Consciousness, and the Politics of Empowerment* and *Fighting Words: Black Women and the Search for Justice* and coeditor of *Race, Class, and Gender: An Anthology.*

Brenda Cossman is Professor of Law at the University of Toronto in Canada. Her publications include *Bad Attitudes on Trial: Pornography, Feminism and the Butler Decision, Subversive Sites: Feminist Engagements with Law in India,* and *Secularism's Last Sigh?*

Bonnie Thornton Dill is Professor of Women's Studies at the University of Maryland and Director of the Consortium on Race, Gender and Ethnicity. She is coeditor of *Women of Color in U.S. Society* with Maxine Baca Zinn.

Matthew Diller is a Professor at the Fordham University School of Law, Coordinator of the William and Burton Cooper Chair on Urban Legal Issues, and Associate Director of the Louis Stein Center for Law and Ethics.

Nancy E. Dowd is Chesterfield Smith Professor of Law and Associate Director of the Center on Children and the Law at the University of Florida Levin College of Law. She is the author of *In Defense of Single-Parent Families* and *Redefining Fatherhood,* both available from New York University Press.

Mary Eaton is Associate-in-Law at Columbia Law School and a J.S.D. candidate at Columbia University.

Martha Albertson Fineman is Dorothea S. Clarke Professor of Feminist Jurisprudence at Cornell Law School. She is the author of *The Neutered Mother, the Sexual Family and Other Twentieth Century Tragedies* and *The Illusion of Equality: The Rhetoric and Reality of Divorce Reform* and editor or coeditor of numerous collections in feminist theory, including *Mothers in Law: Feminist Theory and the Legal Regulation of Motherhood.*

Lorie M. Graham is Assistant Professor of Law at Suffolk University Law School.

Angela P. Harris is Professor at the University of California at Berkeley School of Law. Her publications include *Gender and Law: Theory, Doctrine, Commentary* (with Katherine Bartlett) and *Race and Races: Cases and Resources for a Diverse America* (with Juan Perea, Richard Delgado, and Stephanie Wildman).

Berta Esperanza Hernández-Truyol is Levin, Mabie & Levin Professor at the University of Florida Levin College of Law.

Laura Ho is an attorney at Saperstein, Goldstein, Demchak and Baller in Oakland, California.

Darren Lenard Hutchinson is an Assistant Professor at Southern Methodist University Dedman School of Law.

Lisa C. Ikemoto is Professor at Loyola Law School in Los Angeles.

Michelle S. Jacobs is Professor at the University of Florida Levin College of Law.

Sylvia A. Law is Elizabeth K. Dollard Professor of Law, Medicine and Psychiatry and Codirector of the Arthur Garfield Hays Civil Liberties Program at New York University. Her publications include *Pain and Profit: The Politics of Malpractice* and *Blue Cross: What Went Wrong?*

Holly Maguigan is Professor at the New York University School of Law.

Mari J. Matsuda is Professor at the Georgetown University Law Center. Her books include *Where Is Your Body? and Other Essays on Race, Gender and the Law*; *Words That Wound: Critical Race Theory, Assaultive Speech, and the First Amendment*; and *We Won't Go Back: Making the Case for Affirmative Action.*

Edward J. McCaffery is Maurice Jones, Jr. Professor at the University of Southern California Law School. He is the author of *Fair Not Flat: How to Make the Tax System Simpler and Better*, *A New Understanding of Property*, and *Taxing Women.*

Peggy McIntosh is Professor and Associate Director at the Wellesley College Center for Research on Women. She is the founder and Codirector of the National S.E.E.D. (Seeking Educational Equity and Diversity) Project on Inclusive Curriculum.

Martha Minow is Professor at the Harvard University Law School. She is the author of *Making All the Difference: Inclusion, Exclusion, and American Law* and *Not Only for Myself: Identity, Politics and Law*; editor of *Family Matters: Readings on Family Lives and the Law*; and coeditor, with Gary Bellow, of *Law Stories.*

Celestine I. Nyamu is Institute of Development Studies Fellow at the University of Sussex, Brighton, United Kingdom.

L. Amede Obiora is Associate Professor at the University of Arizona James E. Rogers College of Law.

Twila L. Perry is Professor and Judge Alexander Waugh, Sr. Scholar at Rutgers University Center for Law and Justice.

Nancy D. Polikoff is Professor at The American University Washington College of Law.

Catherine Powell is Associate Clinical Professor and Executive Director of the Human Rights Institute at the Columbia University School of Law.

john a. powell is Marvin J. Sonosky Professor of Law and Public Policy and Director of the Institute on Race and Poverty at University of Minnesota Law School.

Amy E. Ray is staff attorney at Pisgah Legal Services in Asheville, North Carolina.

Jenny Rivera is Associate Professor at the City University of New York School of Law at Queens College.

Dorothy E. Roberts is Professor of Law at Northwestern University and a Faculty Fellow at the Institute for Policy Research. Her books include *Killing the Black Body: Race, Reproduction, and the Meaning of Liberty* and *Shattered Bonds: The Color of Child Welfare.*

Karen H. Rothenberg is Dean and Majorie Cook Professor at the University of Maryland School of Law. She is coeditor of *Women and Prenatal Testing: Facing the Challenges of Genetic Technology.*

Cassandra Shaylor is the Codirector of Justice Now in Oakland, California.

Patricia Smith is Professor of Philosophy at Baruch Center and the CUNY Graduate Center and the editor of *Feminist Jurisprudence.*

Rachel L. Toker is an attorney with Arnold & Porter.

Leti Volpp is Associate Professor at The American University Washington College of Law.

Joan Williams is Professor at the American University Washington College of Law and the Director of the Program on Gender, Work and Family. She is the author of *Unbending Gender: Why Family and Work Conflict and What to Do about It.*

Barbara Bennett Woodhouse is David H. Levin Chair of Family Law and Director of the Center on Children and the Law at the University of Florida Levin College of Law.

Maxine Baca Zinn is Professor of Sociology at Michigan State University and senior researcher at the Julian Samora Research Institute. She is the coeditor, with Bonnie Thornton Dill, of *Women of Color in U.S. Society,* among other books.

Index